Praise for *The Divorced Dad's*

"A valuable source of information for all fathers ... breakup of a relationship. Knox provides relief f... hope (of raising their children) and who mig... bitterness."

— **Jeffery M. Leving,** President, National Institute for Fathers and Families, Inc., Chicago, Illinois; Author, *Fathers' Rights*

"*The Divorced Dad's Survival Book* is long overdue! This book gives divorced fathers the information they need to help deal with the problems they face."

— **Judye Foy,** International Vice President, Community Relations, Parents without Partners, Inc., Chicago, Illinois

"Provides excellent insights into the 'human side of divorce' from the father's perspective. Knox speaks personally to the divorced or divorcing father, and warns against forsaking the children."

— **Ken Lewis, Ph.D.,** Director, Child Custody Evaluation Services of Philadelphia, Inc., Philadelphia, Pennsylvania

"Knox's chapter on gay fathers will help ease the process of 'coming out,' and work toward eliminating much misunderstanding and stereotypical impressions about gay fathers."

— **Jerry J. Bigner, Ph.D.,** Professor, Department of Human Development and Family Studies, Colorado State University, Fort Collins, Colorado; Author, *Parent–Child Relations*

"It is hard to imagine a relationship between divorcing spouses and their children that wouldn't be improved by this book."

— **James Walters, Ph.D.,** Professor Emeritus, Department of Child and Family Development, University of Georgia, Athens, Georgia; Past President, National Council on Family Relations

"A roadmap for survival in the jungle of divorce! This is a must read for every divorced father whether the divorce has been amicable or one from hell."

— **Robert Sammons, M.D., Ph.D.,** Private Practice, Grand Junction, Colorado

"The biggest recipients of the teachings of this book will be the children. Any divorced dad reading Knox will undoubtedly become a better father."

— **Blair Carr,** Attorney; Daughter of a Divorced Dad

THE DIVORCED DAD'S SURVIVAL BOOK

How to Stay Connected with Your Kids

David Knox, Ph.D.

with

Kermit Leggett

A MERLOYD LAWRENCE BOOK

PERSEUS BOOKS

Reading, Massachusetts

A CIP record for this book is available from the Library of Congress.
ISBN: 0–7382–0317-3

Perseus Publishing is a member of the Perseus Books Group

1 2 3 4 5 6 7 8 9 10—03 02 01 00
First paperback printing, June 2000

Perseus Publishing books are available at special discounts for bulk purchases in the U.S. by corporations, institutions, and other organizations. For more information, please contact the Special Markets Department at HarperCollins Publishers, 10 East 53rd Street, New York, NY 10022, or call 1–212–207–7528.

Find us on the World Wide Web at http://www.perseuspublishing.com

To Bob Sammons, M.D., Ph.D.
for his kind insistence that this book be written

Contents

Foreword

In this long-awaited book, Dr. David Knox has given us handwoven knowledge, genuinely shared with single fathers at any stage of the divorce process. Smoothly held together with choice references to many different personal histories, Dr. Knox has put together the definitive guide for all men (and, if they care, women, too). He chronicles tales from the home front, clearly demonstrating different methods of behavior and positive reinforcements to everyone involved in the divorce proceedings. It is his willingness to share with us the methods to alleviate the confusion for both parents and children that makes this book so valuable. Although Dr. Knox shows men how to develop procedures that will help them win well-deserved time with their children, he also illustrates that "winning" might not be in everyone's best interest and that the benefits of mediation can be great. He presents hands-on "get you through it" plans that can help fathers remain positive, involved parents. In a straightforward and approachable manner, Dr. Knox has clearly illustrated how men can develop their fathering skills, stay involved with their children, and evaluate their own capabilities as fathers and ex-spouses. From the Chapter 1 self-assessment on "Your Survival Potential as a Divorced Dad," to the final page of "Resources and Websites," this informative, engaging, and educational book can serve to guide even the most volatile of custody cases to a successful conclusion. Dr. Knox has given us all the material and the encouragement to use it. No matter what your circumstances or the role you play in the divorce—the father, concerned friend, ex-spouse, or attorney—this book has information for you. David Knox has given us a road out of the conflict. I encourage you to take it.

Maralyn Facey
Former West Coast editor, *Divorce Magazine*
Founder and editor, "Solo: A Guide for the Single Parent"
(Hall/Sloane Publishing)

Preface to the paperback edition

As a dad going through divorce, this book is for you. Nothing will be more important to your children and to you than that you stay connected with your children before, during, and after the divorce. If you are like many divorcing dads, you will confront various legal, economic, and emotional barriers to your staying connected with your children. Be relentless with the gusto of a hounddog and let nothing interfere with the relationship with your children. Dads are not replaceable. Read this book and let me and other divorcing dads going through divorce know if we can help. Check out the Message Board in The Divorce Room at www.heartchoice.com or e-mail me directly at divorce@heartchoice.com.

This book is not about ex-wife bashing. My former spouse had and has many wonderful qualities, including her devotion to our children, her nurturing skills, and her ability to take care of the business of parenting. The children have flourished under her care and enjoy good relationships with her as well.

Although these guidelines are what worked for me, each divorced father will need to adapt them to his own particular circumstances, selecting those that feel right for him. There is no single course of action for all of us. Nevertheless, the message of this book is that noncustodial divorced fathers can take control of their situation (if only by the way they perceive their situation) and make choices that will help to ensure their continued involvement in their children's lives.

I would like to acknowledge several people who contributed to this book. Dr. Ken Lewis read and provided detailed feedback and suggestions for revising the manuscript. His expertise in helping fathers to stay connected with their children is reflected in the following pages. Others who contributed both content and work on this project include John Beckert, Karen Crowell, John Daniels, Maralyn Facey, Stacie Hatfield,

Jennifer Huckle, Stewart LaNeave, LaShonda Mabon, Sandy MacKay, Wendy Nieves, Bob Sammons, Jack Turner, James Walters, Bill Walz, Jack Wright, Jr., and Marty Zusman. To them I am indebted. Finally, I would like to thank Marnie Cochran of Perseus Publishing for her support for this paperback edition.

No divorced dad has a corner on how to survive the experience and stay connected with his children. I am no exception and invite your feedback and insights about your own divorce. Please e-mail me at divorce@heartchoice.com.

David Knox, Ph.D.
Greenville, North Carolina

Introduction and Overview

> Fathers can and do redefine themselves in ways that allow them to stay engaged and feel good about fathering even in the face of what may seem to be overwhelming obstacles brought about by marital transitions.[1]
>
> Kay Pasley and Carmelle Minton

Douglas MacKay is a divorced father of three children in Stonington, Connecticut, who shared his experience in the following poetic lines:

> I hear them briefly through thin wire.
> Their smell is gone from the pillowcases.
> A visit this weekend will provide another snapshot, a touch
> Will we ever share the same ground?
> When will I ever be allowed to tell them stories over campfires of past warriors?
> O great spirit, give me strength to keep trying, for I love them so.[2]

Fatherless families are on the rise. According to the U.S. Census Bureau, 16.5 million children under the age of 18 live apart from their dads.[3] While there are other reasons (never having married the father, estrangement from the father, or widowhood) than divorce for why these children live primarily with their mothers, divorce continues to be a major culprit. Currently there are an estimated five million divorced dads in America.[4] Six hundred thousand new divorced dads join their ranks each year. Sociologist David Popenoe of Rutgers University predicts an ominous trend:

> [T]he percentage of American children living apart from their biological fathers will reach 50 percent in the next century. Think about it. Half of all children without fathers to say good night to them. Many, when asked who their father is, will answer, "I don't have one."[5]

Divorce usually means that dad becomes the "noncustodial parent"—in other words, his children live with their mother but "visit" him. His

1

availability to his children drops from 100% when he is married to about 25% after the divorce. The context is usually short weekend visits that are over too soon when the children return to their mother for another 2 weeks.

Divorced dads are often too trusting that their former wives and the legal system will act to encourage their relationships with their children. Before the dad knows it, he may be cut out of regular access to his children and relegated to a monthly child support check. Professor Maureen Pirog-Good (and her colleague Lydia Amerson), codirector of the Institute for Family and Social Responsibility at Indiana University in Bloomington, Indiana, detailed in their 1997 article "The Long Arm of Justice: The Potential for Seizing the Assets of Child Support Obligors" how each state "will now be able to reach across state lines to seize property, garnish wages, and secure money directly from a delinquent parent's checking account located in another state."[6] The researchers are talking about dads who don't live with their children. There is no mention by the authors of the right or need for these fathers to spend time with their children, and this attitude is all too common in the literature.

Our society quite often characterizes divorced fathers as "deadbeat dads." Their private experiences have been hidden from public view and they are understandably distressed. Professor Terry Arendell, chair of the Department of Sociology and Anthropology at Colby College in Waterville, Maine, interviewed 75 divorced fathers and reported that:

> More than three-fourths of the participants insisted that divorce had meant their victimization: "Men are discriminated against in divorce, plain and simple." Further, no one, not even men who managed to avoid being mistreated during the dissolution process, was immune from future victimization. "As long as children are minors," many insisted in various ways, "fathers risk disenfranchisement as parents" and can be reduced to being "only faceless money machines" for former wives. Lost in divorce, they claimed, were their rights to fatherhood, discretionary control of their earnings, exercise of familial authority, and autonomy to plan and handle their futures.[7]

This plight of divorced fathers is unprecedented in history. Sociologist Ralph LaRossa at Georgia State University researched the social and political history of fatherhood and found that, prior to the industrial revolution, "men almost always had been awarded custody of their children after divorce."[8] Men were the primary socializers of their children (particularly in matters of religion) and were legally responsible for their conduct. When the children left home, they most often wrote to their fathers as heads of the household. Those days are gone.

The culture of motherhood and the "tender years" doctrine (young children need mothers more than fathers) dominate divorce hearings on who the children will live with when their parents divorce. Bernard Goldberg, a CBS News correspondent, came face to face with the courts over custody of his son. He wrote that, for fathers whose marriages end, "the American judicial system is an Orwellian nightmare intent on proving that 'mother knows best' and that being a father doesn't necessarily mean having children."[9] In this era of shifting gender roles, the very definition of "parent" has become nearly identical to that of "mother."

So much for the bad news. The good news is that a growing number of divorced dads are reuniting to restore their roles as fathers in their children's lives. The American Coalition for Fathers and Children is planning a march on the mall in Washington, D.C., in the year 2000 to emphasize the importance of shared parenting following divorce. Other organizations, such as Fathers' and Children's Equality and the National Fatherhood Initiative, provide a way for divorced fathers to connect with others who are denied regular access to their children.

Divorce need not be war. But it sometimes is. When a petition for the custody of one's children is filed with the court, when a subpoena for one's financial records is issued, and when one's joint safe deposit box is emptied, the gloves are off. At stake is the father's emotional and financial survival; but more importantly his relationship with his children is seriously threatened.

As any military strategist knows, sizing up one's opposition, deflecting vollies, and launching an offensive help to accomplish one's goal. This book is intended to be a manual for the noncustodial divorced dad having a single objective—staying connected with his children. It is not a legal manual but rather a map of the battlefield and a plan of action. State law governs custody and there are enormous differences between the states and their laws. As a divorced father, it is important that you educate yourself on the laws in your state (both statutory and case law). Go to the library, photocopy the laws, read them, and then take them to your attorney.

The children of divorced dads are going through their own traumas. Family life as they knew it is shattered, dad is never there, and alternate weekends become suitcases and visits to a new and strange apartment. Feelings of insecurity, self-blame ("Did I cause the divorce?"), and abandonment may overcome your children. They may be suspicious of your attempts to soothe them; after all, you don't live at home anymore.

Showing your children where you live, giving them a calendar marked with the dates you will be with them, and showing up on those dates will help reduce their anxiety about the divorce. Some children may even like the extra time and attention you give to being with them. The idea that children are *necessarily* scarred by divorce is a myth. Specific things you should *never* do when you are with your children include trashing their mother, using them as messengers, or asking them to take sides. The conflict between parents is what traumatizes children, not the divorce itself. Putting them in the middle is the worst thing you can do.

When your children are with their mother (which they will be most of the time), it is important to use the time to do something you enjoy, avoid feeling sorry for yourself, and be careful of the potential for alcohol abuse. Divorced dads who come home each evening to an empty apartment may be vulnerable to substance abuse to relieve the pain of separation from their children and feelings of failure over the divorce. Exercise and a sensible diet are better for your health and sanity.

Some ex-wives encourage healthy relationships between the children and their dads, others are ambivalent, and still others may set out to destroy those relationships. This can take the form of talking negatively to your children about you, making sure they are not available when you call, and taking them out of town when they are scheduled to be with you. Although there is nothing you can do about her badmouthing you, your attorney can get her back into court for depriving you of your visitation. This process is expensive and time-consuming, but perhaps the only consequence that will effectively change her behavior. A divorced friend of mine had to go back to court four times before the judge told his ex-wife that if she interfered with his visitation again, he would give the father full custody; she stopped interfering, and has been cooperative ever since.

The whole litigation scene should be avoided if at all possible. A great alternative is mediation, which involves you and the child's mother negotiating the issues (within state guidelines) of custody, child support, visitation, and spouse maintenance with a neutral mediator. If you and your ex-wife can talk about such issues as how you will share the parenting of your children, the money they will need and who will pay it, when each of you will be with the children, and what money (if any) one spouse may need from the other, you will save thousands of dollars in legal fees and years of frustration. Having a custody evaluation conducted by a custody evaluator to guide the mediator and parents in their deliberations is usually beneficial to a positive outcome with which all parties can be satisfied.

Not all spouses can or should try to mediate their divorces—those who want to hide financial records, punish the partner, or keep the children away from the former spouse are examples.

Some ex-spouses end up fighting in court. It is both expensive ($12,000 is average) and time-consuming (3 years) compared with mediation, which costs about $1000 and takes about 3 months. If you must go to court, go prepared—do your homework on custody law in your state, hire the most experienced domestic attorney you can afford, make sure the attorney will commit to your case as a priority, and strike first. If you wait until you have heard from your wife's attorney, you may be at a disadvantage already. Remember to try mediation first; it that fails, promptly set your attorney in motion.

Your attorney will advise you to get your name off all credit cards held jointly with your ex-wife, move half the money in any joint/checking accounts, and so on. He or she will also advise you about your personal life—to keep spending low, avoid any visibility with a new partner, and *under no circumstances* should you abscond with your children.

Going for joint legal and physical custody will protect your access to your children both now and in the future. I made a mistake by agreeing to give my ex-wife custody, as it never occurred to me that she would ever make any attempt to interfere in the relationship with my children. I was wrong.

Reversing a court order at a later time through a custody modification order is time-consuming and expensive. Although staying connected with your children following divorce depends on the good will and cooperation of your ex-wife (or your hiring a very aggressive attorney in the absence of such), another hurdle is getting your children to accept a new partner in your life. Most divorced men end up in new relationships. Some children welcome a new partner in dad's life, but others are slow to accept such a partner. Still others are downright hostile. Divorced dads can ease their acceptance by continuing to spend time alone with their children, exposing them to the new partner now and then for short periods of time, and not *requiring* the children to accept the new partner immediately or at all. Insisting that they accept—let alone love—the new partner will not work. In time, they will develop the relationships that are comfortable for them.

Chapter 10 was written for new partners of divorced dads by the author's new partner. It will alert the new partner to the drawbacks—and there are several—of becoming involved with a divorced dad: His kids will often come first, his money will, in large part, go for child support or spouse maintenance payments, and he may be chronically depressed over being denied access to his children. Divorced dads also come with pluses: The new partner can see what kind of parent he is (something that can't be observed in a person who has never had a child), he is probably accepting of his new partner already having children, and he is usually willing to have a child in the new relationship.

Make no mistake. The role of dad's girlfriend is difficult. Coping with his kids' rejection is the hardest part. Family life as they knew it has been destroyed and they may blame her for their loss. Never mind that their parents' marriage ended for a variety of reasons. She may end up with the blame until they are old enough to judge the situation for themselves.

Because most of the 5 million divorced dads are heterosexual, this book emphasizes the heterosexual perspective. It is estimated that 1 million divorced dads are gay, with almost 1 million children involved. Our heterosexist, homophobic society discriminates against gay men in general, but gay dads get an even larger dose of prejudice. Most heterosexuals, being welded to traditional gender roles, don't like gay men; acceptance by gays may also be difficult to achieve, as being a father is inconsistent with the free lifestyle touted as the ideal. Judges are quite often merciless towad gay dads and rarely give them full or joint custody out of fear that they will molest their children or promote them into the gay lifestyle. Although research suggests that neither of these events is likely to happen, cultural fear is sufficient to deny gay dads a rightful place in their children's lives. Chapter 11 looks at some of these issues.

Three-fourths of divorced dads remarry, most within 3 years. Remarriage symbolizes for children the final end of the family they once knew. Adjustment is easier when dad waits a few years between marriages and gives the children plenty of notice that he is considering such a move. But aside from the children, divorced dads are often vulnerable to rebound romances and should wait at least 18 months to heal from the divorce before making a commitment to marry again. Love may be sweeter the second time around, but it is also riskier. Spouses in second marriages (at least in the first few years) are more likely to divorce than spouses in first marriages. This may reflect the fact that remarried spouses are less willing to stay committed to unhappy relationships than spouses in first marriages.

Important issues for divorced dads to discuss before a second marriage include whether or not additional children are desired, whether or not the new dad will adopt his new wife's children, and the respective economic contributions to the relationship and to the partner's children.

Sorting all of these issues out does not guarantee smooth stepfamily living. Most spouses in new stepfamilies go through several stages of adjustment, including illusions of problem-free stepfamily living, coping with the reality of rejection, fighting back, and, finally, getting relaxed. Children have rights too, including the right to gradually accept stepfamily living or reject it completely as they get older.

The book ends with the same message it began with: Dads are important to the development of their children and, short of abducting their children, should do whatever is necessary to stay involved and connected with them.

Although there are cultural attitudes to the contrary, being divorced need not mean losing one's children and having divorced parents need not mean losing one's father. Although it has been necessary to face a few unpleasant truths about adult relationships (such as the often adversarial attitudes of divorcing spouses) in this book, its main concern is never to deprecate ex-wives or to trivialize a mother's value to her children. Rather, *The Divorced Dad's Survival Book* is an effort to encourage fathers to *continue being fathers* and to emphasize that this goal is always worth pursuing, no matter what personal or legal obstacles alienation from their spouses may bring. This book is for noncustodial divorced fathers, but it is written out of concern for the millions of children in modern society who face fatherlessness as a result of decisions beyond a child's control. These ideas depend not on the superiority, but rather the *equality*, of a father's importance in the parenting task. Activizing divorced dads is the first step to breaking down the legal and social barriers that separate men from their sons and daughters when parents go their separate ways.

Society is changing, with over 1 million divorces occurring annually. Traditional divorce has resulted in a radical change in family structure—with children and dads taking the hit. The time has come to redesign and restructure the way children continue to be nurtured by their parents who no longer live together. Children benefit from the attention, nurturing, and resources of both parents. Keeping children connected to their dads results in a clear win for children, their dads, ex-wives, and society.

Act Now

> The presenting complaint for many fathers who come for treatment in the midst of a divorce crisis seems to be the threat of losing their relationship with their children.[1]
>
> John Jacobs, M.D.

Robert Bly, an important figure in the fathers' rights movement, describes the experience of a 35-year-old man whose parents had divorced years earlier:

> [H]e began to wonder who his father really was. He hadn't seen his father in about ten years. He flew out to Seattle, where his father was living, knocked on the door, and when his father opened the door, said, "I want you to understand one thing. I don't accept my mother's view of you any longer." The father broke into tears, and said, "Now I can die." Fathers wait. What else can they do?[2]

Whether you left your wife or she left you, divorce may have negative emotional consequences for everyone involved. Even those men who are truly happier living without their ex-wives can expect to feel displaced and lonely because of their changed role in the family. Women get primary physical custody in the majority of divorce cases. A typical visitation schedule allows the noncustodial father to be with his children every other weekend, holidays on alternate years, and 4 weeks in the summer, which amounts to less than one quarter of the year. You may fear becoming a "visitor" in your children's lives. However, it is important to keep in mind that your children cease having a father only when you give up *being* their father. If you want to maintain your role as parent, you must persevere. This chapter will look at the kinds of feelings divorced fathers can expect to have, some of the problems to be experienced, and why it is important to stay the course, whatever the obstacles. It will also consider some of the things you can do now to protect your relationship with your children.

Because children whose parents divorce are most vulnerable to having the relationship with their dads disrupted up to age 15, my focus will be on children in these early developmental years.

REAL MEN HAVE FEELINGS, TOO

As a divorced father, you may get the sense that you have lost your place in the family. Although you are still your children's father, you no longer live with them and may feel "split off" and displaced. But you must remain clear in your own mind, and also make it clear to your children, that your family continues even though you no longer live with them. Your kids now have two homes instead of one, but you are still their father! Although the new conditions will require a period of adjustment, your love and sense of responsibility toward them will not change. Your determination to maintain a parental relationship with your children is perhaps the most important step to take to overcome your sense of displacement.

Any sense of belonging that can be salvaged from your divorce will help you deal with other emotional difficulties. Nearly all divorced men feel some degree of loneliness and depression, and for divorced fathers, these feelings can be particularly intense. Psychologist E. Mavis Heatherington at the University of Virginia in Charlottesville (and her colleagues Martha Cox and Roger Cox) conducted interviews with divorced fathers at different intervals (2 months, 1 year, 2 years) after the divorce and compared their findings with fathers who were still married. Compared with the fathers in intact marriages, the researchers observed that the divorced fathers spent more hours at work and less time at home. "For many fathers this seemed to involve an active avoidance of solitude and inactivity. Several fathers spoke of doing anything to avoid returning to an empty home."[3] When they weren't working, they were more likely to be in bars or with friends. One of the loneliest times for divorced dads is driving away after returning their children to their mom's after spending a weekend with them. One father I talked with who saw his kids every other weekend said, "You feel like there's a basketball in your throat cause you know you won't see them again for two weeks and you fear they will forget you." See Chapter 5 ("What to Do and Not Do when Your Children Are with Their Mother") for suggestions in coping during these important times.

Along with loneliness and depression, many divorced fathers feel a sense of guilt. The sources of these feelings are as varied as the actual people who experience them. Fathers who voluntarily leave their marriages

```
┌──────────┤ SELF-ASSESSMENT ├──────────┐
```

YOUR SURVIVAL POTENTIAL AS A DIVORCED DAD

This chapter's self-assessment is intended to give you some idea of how you will fare in the days ahead as you experience the divorce process and its effect on you and your relationship with your children. Read each sentence below and circle the appropriate number according to the following key:

1 = Definitely Not   4 = Mostly Yes
2 = Mostly Not   5 = Definitely Yes
3 = Sometimes

	DN	MN	S	MY	DY
1. I would rather be divorced than married to my children's mother	1	2	3	4	5
2. My relationship with my children has remained the same or gotten better since I separated from their mother.	1	2	3	4	5
3. My economic situation has remained the same or gotten better since the divorce.	1	2	3	4	5
4. I feel my children's mother and I can work out our differences without lawyers.	1	2	3	4	5
5. My children's mother encourages me to spend time with my children.	1	2	3	4	5
6. My children's mother and I agree on the amount of child support.	1	2	3	4	5
7. My children's mother feels that I am a good father for our children.	1	2	3	4	5
8. My children will continue to live close to me so that I can continue to see them regularly.	1	2	3	4	5
9. I have no fear of being replaced by a new stepfather.	1	2	3	4	5
10. I am happier being divorced from than married to my children's mother.	1	2	3	4	5

Add the numbers you have circled. The lowest possible score is 10, which means that you have a rough road ahead. The highest possible score is 50, which means that your future as a divorced father looks bright. An intermediate score is 30. The higher your score, the better you will survive as a divorced father.

may feel guilty for hurting their children. On the other hand, fathers whose wives leave them may blame themselves for not trying harder to keep the family together. The culture is no help. Divorced fathers are referred to as "deadbeat dads," disappearing fathers, and Disneyland daddies. These are negative images of uninterested and disengaged fathers.

A divorced father is also prone to feeling as though he has lost control of his family life. A judge (man or woman) may control when he is allowed to see his children. His former wife can try to keep his children away from him (and in the short run she can get away with it). If his ex remarries while the kids are young, he may face the ultimate fear of being replaced by another man in their lives. These fears, however, are mostly unfounded. As long as you are intent on maintaining your relationship with your children, your chances of staying connected are increased.

THE ROAD AHEAD: STAGES OF A DIVORCED FATHER'S LIFE

Looking back over the 10 years since my divorce and talking with other divorced dads, there are various stages that divorced dads go through.

Stage 1: Ambivalence over the Divorce

The immediate changes in your life may lead you to ask whether you have done the right thing. Going to sleep and waking up without your children in the house and having no contact with them for weeks at a time can cause deep anxiety, even in those cases where a father is otherwise happier for having escaped an unhappy marriage. All decisions in life entail trade-offs, and this is nowhere better illustrated than in the case of the father who makes the decision to divorce. Sixty percent of the divorced fathers studied by Professor Heatherington and colleagues said that their divorce might have been a mistake, that they should have tried harder to resolve the conflicts, and that their current single lifestyle was unsatisfying. According to the researchers, "divorced men complained of feeling shut out, rootless and at loose ends, and of a need to engage in social activities even if they were not pleasurable."[4]

The first years of the divorce are very hard. Psychiatrist John Jacobs of the Montefiore Hospital and Medical Center, Bronx, New York, reported that admissions to psychiatric hospitals are nine times higher for divorced men than for married men. Moreover, car accidents, successful suicides, and deaths caused by heart attack and other illnesses are also higher around the time of separation.[5] This situation suggests that, perhaps for the first time, these men (who formerly focused most of their attention on their careers) are discovering the importance of relationships. Not only are their relationships with their ex-wives no longer sources of emotional intimacy, but their children, whom they have taken for granted, are no longer immediately and constantly present in their lives. Although one's work can provide a distraction, it does not replace the longing for being connected to others. Divorced men who have strained emotional ties with both their ex-wives and children do not cope well.

A small percentage of dads find that coping with the emotional pain is very difficult and attempt to reduce the pain and ambivalence by returning to the marriage. If you consider going back, you and your spouse should see a marriage therapist to work on the problems that led to the separation. Appendix V will assist the reader in finding a credentialed marriage and family therapist.

Even though reconciling the relationship with your ex is an option to keep open, it is unrealistic to be hopeful that you will reunite and live happily ever after. Most couples have let their relationship deteriorate too much and getting it back on track happens for only a small percentage. One couple whom I counseled had been separated for 2 months and had tried to reconcile for their three children. But it didn't work. The husband said:

> I know it would have been easier for the kids for us to go back. But I no longer loved my wife and I just couldn't seem to get the feelings back. I just didn't want to wake up for the rest of my life wishing I were someplace else.

However, some couples are able to get back together. And they are successful in staying together. Professor Howard Wineberg at Portland State University found that couples who have a strong religious background and who attend church regularly are among those separated couples who are more likely to reunite and make a go of it.[6] Having a strong common value (religion) and being able to forgive one's partner both contributed to getting back together. A husband whom I saw explained how he and his wife got back together:

> Even after we separated we still continued to go to church . . . but we sat far apart from each other. One night when the congregation was singing, I felt

> drawn to her so I just walked to the pew where she was standing alone and handed her the hymnal. We started singing . . . and that was the beginning of our getting back together. We're still together after 7 years.

Although reconciliations such as this one do occur, couples who take their differences so seriously that they are willing to face the trauma of separation are more likely to go their separate ways—permanently.

Stage 2: Hope that the Divorce Will Go Smoothly

Because most fathers will be unable to reconcile with the children's mother, they hope that the separation and divorce will go through without a hitch. At least they will be able to agree on how to divide things up, share parenting of the kids, and work out a way to minimize the impact of the divorce on the kids. Dream on. People who were once lovers and intimates can become enemies whose focus on what is best for their children takes a back seat to punishment and revenge. Love has become war and both the parents and their children become casualties.

Stage 3: What Really Happens

According to the U.S. Census Bureau, of the almost 12 million single parent homes, 82% are headed by women.[7] This means that 82% of fathers are noncustodial. In effect, the almost 17 million children in these homes live with their mothers and "visit" their fathers (if their fathers are available to them). One father said of his discovery of this new role:

> It's like I'm some Uncle Henry they visit on weekends . . . they live with their mom but they visit me . . . like they visit somebody in the hospital . . . for Christ sake . . . I'm their dad.

Another change is that the children's mother, with whom you have been embroiled in a legal battle over property, child support, and custody, can now take steps to come between you and your children. Rather than have the children ready when you get there, she may make sure they aren't even in the house or are "sick" and "can't come out." Then, when they finally do emerge, they may act as though they are going to prison (and you are the warden!). The mom who so carefully orchestrated the children's participation in dad's birthday and Father's Day may now let these occasions pass unnoticed. You must clearly separate your negative feelings for your ex from the love you have for your children. If you allow yourself to believe that they don't care about you and stop the visits, then that will only confirm for your children that you don't care about them. One father told me that he just couldn't stand the rejection. His children had moved out of state and when he called them, they were quiet and nonresponsive and made it clear they did not want to talk with him. "I just quit calling," he said. This may be exactly what the children's mother hoped for.

Stage 4: Trial-and-Error Responses

Because the role of the divorced father is new, we learn to fill it only through trial and error. For example, when the kids are not happy to see you, should you ignore their indifference or scold them? When they forget Father's Day, should you forget it or call them on it? And when they tell you they would rather go back early this Sunday, should you remind them that this is your time or offer to take them back even earlier? When your former spouse calls to say that she needs to take the children to see her sick father on your weekend, is it better to acknowledge the importance of your ex-father-in-law in your children's lives, or should you remind your ex-wife that the court order allows for no such exception to your visitation? Issues like these will arise time and again. Unless you are careful, you may react out of anger and make matters worse.

A major theme of this book is that a divorced father must take the high ground and think first and foremost of his long-term relationship with his children. (I have not always done so, and regretted this mistake later.) When your former spouse calls and says the children need to see their sick grandfather on your weekend, respond with complete agreement. But also make it clear that the next weekend when the children are scheduled to be with her would be a good "makeup" weekend. If she won't trade weekends, no deal. Alternatively, the divorced dad might take his children to see his ex-wife's father.

When your former spouse calls and says that the children are sick and that she will take care of them (on your weekend), tell her that you will call their doctor, see what needs to be done, and do it. You will pick them up at the regular time. Whenever you are faced with a difficult situation such as this, remember to stay focused on your children's welfare and you will make the right decision. But remember also that *spending less time with you is usually not in their best interest.*

Stage 5: Things Settle Down

Although you may need to call the sheriff if your wife won't let the kids come out of the house on your visitation schedule or take her to court if she leaves town with them, the time will come when the attempts to thwart your access stop. Both your ex-wife and children will come to know how important your time with the children is and accept that "dad's time" is something that will occur. This promotes stability in your children's lives because they know the schedule when they will be with you. It also gives them a clear message that they are important to you. No matter what anyone else says, they see that you care about them.

Stage 6: A Special Bond with Your Children

As events work themselves out, you will gradually build a new relationship with your kids. It will be different from the relationship you had with them before the divorce, but, in some ways, it can be better. Strong father–child relationships that emerge from divorce require fathers who are determined to maintain a strong bond with their children and children who are resilient enough to weather the changes. But there is a specialness in knowing that both father and children can come through a difficult time and keep a close relationship. One father told me, "Your kids never say anything to you, but both of you know that you have been separated by circumstance. And they know that you never abandoned them and that they have always been important to you. That's the message that sticks with them."

Stage 7: Continued Changes

As years pass, your relationship with your children will continue to change: Your time with them will decrease as they graduate from high school, attend college, and/or enter the working world and move away. Your relationship with your former spouse will also continue to affect your children. Most divorced couples mellow with age, and they may even become friends. But others remain at war. When they do so, the children, even as adults, continue to suffer as innocent bystanders. Quite often the children of divorced parents go off to college and avoid returning home, as that would only renew their feelings of being caught in the middle of an ongoing parental conflict. One young adult said of the divorce of his parents:

I purposely moved as far away from home I as could—I moved to Europe. I never wanted to be in the same town with my parents again and be subjected to the disapproval I felt from each parent when I wanted to see the other. I've moved so far away that neither expects me to visit them but they both know I'm glad for them to visit me. And they do—individually—so I get to see my folks with never any of the tension and conflict that I felt when I lived in the same town.

Even though this particular case turned out OK in the long run, its message is that, for years, this young man's relationship with his father has suffered as a result of his parents' inability to take control of their feelings for their son's sake.

In closing this section, it is important to keep in mind that the stages don't always follow this sequence. For example, the ambivalence you may feel over the divorce in the beginning can occur several stages later. "You're never sure how things would have turned out had you stayed married, " said one father. "And while you turn the page and adapt to your life as a divorced father, you're not immune to thinking about what might have been."

ROADBLOCKS TO THE DIVORCED FATHER'S RELATIONSHIP WITH HIS CHILDREN

Perhaps the greatest roadblock to your continued relationship with your children is the ill will of their mother toward you. Although you once loved each other and shared a life together with your children, everything has changed and she can now become your worst enemy. She has the children more than 75% of the time throughout the year and can use this time to her advantage. If the children are young, they are very sensitive to her perceptions and influence. Girls may be even more vulnerable than boys, as they may identify with their mothers and feel that their fathers have rejected them as well. However, boys who are very closely bonded with their mothers may also identify with their mothers' feelings toward the father and adopt a similar attitude toward him.

Because the mother may physically prevent them from seeing you and teach them to hate you, it may become very difficult to control your anger. Some divorced fathers stop seeing their kids because they cannot stand any contact with their ex-wives. Although you may reduce your anger by not going to pick up your children, the result of avoidance is self-blame for not staying connected with your children. One father I spoke with lamented his retreating from his kids:

> I was torn up every time I had to deal with my ex. It was clear she was turning the kids against me. So I just up and left and got away from the whole thing. It's years later, and I look back, and know that I made a mistake. I should have put up with whatever I had to to stay connected to my kids. We are virtual strangers now and I'm sure they blame me . . . and I blame myself.

This man's story should stand as an example of missed opportunities and the regret they often cause, even if the opportunities are few and far between.

Many divorced fathers have good relationships with their former wives. They are fortunate. One divorced father told me that his ex always cooperated in every way for him to be with their son. In retrospect, he said, she was a better ex than a Mrs.

> She calls me weeks in advance and asks what "we" are going to do for his birthday. She then says that she'd like to have me over for dinner and that we celebrate his birthday with a cake that she'll bake. She also calls me and tells me that he's been talking about me and missing me and wonders if it would be OK if she were to bring him over. She's not dumping him on me to go shopping—she genuinely wants him to have a very close relationship with me. My divorced buddies with kids think I'm kidding when I tell them about my ex.

A theme that I will return to over and over in this book is that it is important to maintain as positive a relationship with your ex as possible. To the degree you can do so, everyone wins—your children, you, and your former spouse. But in too many cases, the struggle over marital property, custody, child support, and so on can embitter former spouses for years, giving rise to displaced aggressions that may lead either parent to use the children to hurt the other. It is imperative that you refrain from venting such frustrations on your children, even if that is exactly what she does when they are with her. Children will remember, when they are old enough to understand, which of you placed them most in the middle. Once again, the high road is the only way around this pitfall. But it is not an easy road by any means.

Sometimes hiring lawyers poisons the relationship between the soon-to-be former spouses. Using divorce mediators not only costs less and takes less time, but also encourages cooperation rather than hostility between divorcing parents. That cooperative atmosphere is much better for your children all around. Because mediation is such an important alternative to traditional, lawyer-engineered divorce proceedings, I discuss it in detail in Chapter 7.

A major difficulty for some divorced fathers is living a great distance from their kids. Some former wives who have custody are legally allowed to move to another state, making it very difficult for the father to see his children. Maintaining a relationship with your relocated children in this case is a special challenge. How to go about doing this is discussed in Chapter 4.

Teenagers prefer the company of their peers. As your children mature, you may find that even on "dad's weekend," they would rather be eating a burger with their friends from school than going to Disney World with dad. Supporting these relationships is an important skill for divorced fathers to develop. In fact, many of these peers will also have divorced dads, which gives your teenager a new perspective on your position at this crucial time. Imagine your child talking to a peer whose father never calls or shows up for visits. If you have set a standard of always showing up and being there for your kids, their friends might actually tell them how lucky they are. Time with peers is important for kids, but you must also consider that your adolescent children still need their father as a source of moral development, career decision making, and sex role identification. They can only get these things from you if they are with you, so don't give up your kids completely to their friends.

Some divorced fathers have both cooperative spouses and mediated divorces, yet still have little contact with their children. These fathers blame neither their spouses nor their lawyers, but rather themselves. Alcohol/ substance abuse, ill health, and a demanding job are typical explanations. Overcoming these obstacles is no less difficult than any of the others we have discussed, but in this case, the focus of blame is clearly on the father rather than his ex or attorneys.

Other fathers feel totally inadequate in the role of father. One divorced man told me that he picked up his son on the first weekend after the separation and took him to a ball field to play catch. He discovered that he had absolutely no skills in relating to his son, felt totally inadequate as a father, and never saw the boy again after that weekend.

PERSEVERANCE WILL PAY OFF

It is clear that persevering to be with your children after separation/divorce is not easy. Although I never considered giving up, I can sometimes understand fathers who do. The pain of separation, rejection, and harassment from your ex can be avoided by walking away, thus sparing the children from being torn between two conflicting parents. I know fathers who have left their relationships with their children behind and never looked back. They reasoned that their children had new stepfathers and were better off when they (the divorced fathers) dropped out of the picture; or they planned to surface later, when the children were older. Nevertheless, staying involved in your children's lives *now* is worth the effort.

First, it is important to keep in mind that your children will not live with their mother forever. A child who is 5 typically has 13 years before he or she leaves home. A child of 10 has 8 years, a child of 14 has 4 years, and so on. You can see the end of the time when your children will live with their mother, but you do not have to wait until your kids are 18 to know that your relationship with them is good. At age 15 (and sometimes earlier), many children who live with the least supportive mothers begin to see the game for themselves and choose to live with their fathers. But whether at 14, 15, or 16, the clock is always ticking in your favor as your children grow toward adulthood and greater independence each day.

Your former spouse may, for the moment, control the environment your children live in, the information they are exposed to, and the interpretation of that information. One divorced father told me that shortly after he left the marital home, his ex did not pay the electric bill (even though she had the resources to do so) and allowed the electricity to be turned off. This was in August, when the summer heat was intense. He guessed that his ex had blamed the heat on him, to make it seem he didn't care what happened to his children. What better way to convince young children that they have been abandoned than to heat them up in August and blame it on the departed dad?

This example illustrates the power of control custodial mothers have over their children, but it also contains a hint of the consequences for the mother–child relationship when she abuses that power. If this same former spouse were to heat up the house again this summer, the children (much older now) would quickly announce that they are going over to dad's, where it's cool. A mother attempting to deceive preteens can succeed; a mother playing the same games with young adults only makes herself look foolish.

Bill Walz is a psychologist in Asheville, North Carolina. He regularly counsels divorced fathers who are struggling with the pain of being separated from their children by an embittered former spouse. Walz has made a startling observation over the years. He found that the plan some ex-wives have to erase the father from the children's minds backfires:

> Not only do the kids find out that their mothers lied to them, but they often come to resent their mothers for depriving them of a childhood that included regular contact with their fathers. Hence, the custodial mother cannot hood-wink her children forever but must eventually relate to them as adults. Meanwhile, the relationship the father has with his children as adults will not carry this baggage of resentment.[8]

The message to you as a father is clear: Your former spouse is risking her relationship with the children while yours has no such liability. Stay the course.

In the meantime, use the limited time you may have with your children to build a stable relationship. As a divorced father, you are free to spend your time with your children as you wish. Some fathers take their children alone for extended vacations in the summer, which is something married fathers can rarely do. Divorced fathers are free to negotiate solely with their children about how they will spend their time together—a major advantage for divorced fathering.

ACTION YOU SHOULD TAKE NOW

As already noted, not all divorced fathers have uncooperative spouses. Indeed, many divorced couples have reasonably civil relationships and some are even friends. But even an amicable divorce is a difficult experience for a father. One of the most important steps you can take to help yourself and your children through the process is to contact other divorced fathers in your community. When you discuss your experiences with them, you quickly discover that you are not alone, that other fathers have dealt with the same issues that you are now dealing with. I will forever be indebted to my divorced father friends who taught me the importance of perseverance. Seeing that another man has maintained a close relationship with his children despite a very difficult divorce will inspire you. When you ask other divorced fathers to tell you about their experiences, you will often discover an immediate empathy and willingness to share the details of their despairs and triumphs with you. Divorced fathers are the best teachers. They have been there. In addition to personal contacts, there are several organizations committed to helping divorced dads to stay connected with their children. Parents Without Partners is an excellent example (see Appendix V).

After getting emotional support from divorced dads who have been through the experience and contacting organizations relevant to your interests, begin to educate yourself in preparation for the potential legal confrontation ahead. If you and your ex-wife disagree about custody, you will probably need to go to court. Because few attorneys know the details of statutory and case law regarding custody in their state, you must go to the library and look up the custody laws passed by the state legislature as well as the custody decisions (case law) that have been made by judges in your state. Photocopy and begin to read this material. I will discuss how to use it in Chapter 8.

Doing your homework on custody laws in your state may be difficult as you may be frustrated in your attempts to stay connected with your children. Because a major source of frustration may be your ex-wife's interference in your relationship with your children, you may become obsessed with your anger for her. Don't. Dr. James Walters, past president of the National Council on Family Relations, notes that "anger does more to the container in which it is held than the one for whom it is intended."[9] If you nurture your anger, your blood pressure will shoot up, your heart rate will increase, and you will have trouble sleeping. Rather than destroy yourself from the inside, redirect your energies toward how you will spend your time with your kids and focus on their well-being.

Another proven way to reduce stress is to engage in at least 30 minutes of strenuous exercise every other day, assuming your doctor doesn't advise against it. Not only will you feel better, but you may be able to respond more rationally when interacting with your former spouse, attorneys, and children who won't eat your cooking.

Just as exercise is something you should do, excessive drinking or other drug abuse is something you must avoid. Divorced fathers are particularly vulnerable here because the emotional suffering can be intense. Alcohol and other drugs may make the pain go away, but this is a short-term remedy that can have catastrophic consequences for you and your children.

Substance abuse not only jeopardizes health and safety, job security, and relationships, but can also threaten your access to your kids. The national organization Mothers Against Drunk Driving (MADD) is encouraging family court judges to consider parental substance abuse issues when determining custody and visitation rights.

Coping with divorce can be overwhelming. If you become so frustrated that you find yourself no longer capable of controlling your alcohol or drug use or if you begin to think seriously of suicide, it is time to check in with a psychologist or psychiatrist. Some of these professionals are divorced fathers and know what you are going through. If you feel you are on the edge, don't hesitate to talk to one.

There is another benefit to seeing a therapist. In addition to getting help for yourself, you provide an excellent model for your children. Because they may also benefit from therapy to help them through the divorce (I discuss this possibility at more length in Chapter 2), it is helpful for them to know that dad is not too proud to ask for help.

Finally, you must make a special effort to understand what your kids are going through. Whatever difficulties you may have, you are an adult and have some control over how you respond to your situation and what you do about it. Your children are much more vulnerable and feel helpless as they see their parents at war with each other. Becoming aware of the divorce through their eyes makes us much more empathic with our children. Their perspective is the topic of the next chapter.

Understand Your Children's Perspective

The yearning for the reunion of one's parents might be attributed to the child's fantasy life for a reunion of happy parents he or she never knew.[1]

Henry J. Friedman, M.D.

Children are always unpredictable. One man related to me his daughter's reaction to the news that her parents were separating:

My wife and I assembled the children in the living room, and I began to explain that mom and I were not getting along and had decided to get a divorce. As soon as I mentioned the word "divorce," my 9-year-old daughter fell to the floor, put her hands over her eyes, and began to writhe in anguish. I fell to the floor, too, and told her that I was her daddy and would always love her. I also told her that I was moving to a new apartment that had a pool. At that moment, she took her hands from her eyes, looked at me, and said, "Does the pool have a diving board?"

For all of the trauma divorcing parents assume children experience, they can never be sure what their children are thinking. Just as parents experience divorce differently, so do kids. But these experiences vary depending on gender, personality, and temperamental wiring. Two siblings may react very differently to their parents' divorce. Some of your children may be very responsive to your attempts to keep sanity and balance in their lives despite a sea of turmoil, while others may panic no matter what you do. According to the Census Bureau, about 1 million children experience the divorce of their parents every year.[2] Although divorce is typically regarded as an emotional disaster for everyone, it does not *have* to be, particularly for children.

A few months ago, I went sailing with a friend and his 7-year-old. We had sailed farther from shore than we realized when a strong wind and rain began to blow. At first, the boy was frightened, but then his father, knowing his son loved thrill rides, assured him that we were lucky because the boat would become a roller coaster when the wind kicked up. The rain would just wash the deck so we wouldn't have to do it when we got back to the dock. What the boy had initially perceived as frightening had become an adventure. True, divorce isn't thrilling for anyone, but it is how it is viewed that is important.

Although children learn from their culture that divorce is a devastating ordeal, they will look to their parents for signs of how badly the winds will blow. If they are taught that there will be changes, that changes occur throughout life, and that adapting to the change is what is important, they will have a very different reaction than if they are told that divorce means the end of the world and that they will be damaged forever. The best place to start smoothing the way for children's adjustment is when they first find out about the separation.

BREAKING THE NEWS

Parents dread telling their children about the separation and divorce. The adults are often so caught up in their own emotional whirlwind that there never seems to be a good time to tell the kids, as parents also dread the reaction of their children and the pain they fear it will cause them. The result is that divorce is a surprise to most children. Very few find out about the separation until it is actually happening. Some wake up to discover that their father has moved out. Whenever children find out, it is a crisis event that sets in motion what parents fear—children feeling rejected, abandoned, and guilty. Sometimes these feelings set in motion a barrage of negative behavioral changes in the children, including disobedience, aggressiveness, and emotional withdrawal from parents.

Ideally, parents should agree to tell their children together that they are getting divorced. The explanation should be simple. The details of who did what and why the parents are divorcing should not be a part of the explanation (don't make trial "evidence" a part of your explanation). Some possible words dad may say are:

You know that your mom and I haven't been getting along. It has been this way for a long time and we have tried to make it better. But we haven't been able to. After thinking and talking about our relationship for months, we have decided it will be best to separate. I will be moving to a new apartment that I will show you before I move out. But even after I move I will continue to see you regularly. The divorce is our decision and is because of our relationship. You are not the cause of our divorce. We both love you and we always will.

These words convey several important messages to the children, namely, the divorce is a joint decision and neither partner blames the other, the divorce is not the fault of the children, the parents will continue to love the children, and the children will know where dad will be living and that he will continue to see them regularly.

Unfortunately, not all divorcing spouses feel amicable enough to tell their children about the divorce without blaming each other. Rather, each may say that the other parent wants a divorce. In effect, they try to capture the child's allegiance. Big mistake. How parents label the divorce and the amount and duration of conflict between them have more to do with the way children adjust to divorce than any other factor. Starting the divorce with volleys against the other predicts a long war with no winners and anxious children.

One way to help children understand divorce is to explain it in terms they can relate to. Acknowledging a friendship of theirs that went sour is one way to go about this:

Remember when you and your friend got upset with each other and stopped seeing each other? The same has happened to mom and dad. We have just become frustrated with each other and want to go our separate ways. It does not mean that we are leaving you, only each other. You will continue to live in the same house, go to the same school, and be able to play with your friends. We're both still your parents and we love you.

Comments like these will help your children ride out the storm of emotions that will beset them as you and your wife go about the business of ending your marriage. It will be helpful if you can anticipate some of these emotional responses. In many cases, your children's feelings will be similar to your own at the beginning of the divorce.

FEELINGS CHILDREN TYPICALLY HAVE ABOUT THEIR PARENTS' DIVORCE

Franklin D. Roosevelt knew the power of fear when he said, "We have nothing to fear but fear itself." Fear of the unknown feeds on itself, and the less children know, the more they may worry. The greatest fear children face is that they will be abandoned. Seeing the father leave the house and noticing his absence at the dinner table alters the child's sense of security. "If mom left dad, will she leave me next?" is a frightening question children may ask themselves. They quickly conclude that she won't, but are nevertheless thrown off balance by the anxiety of even thinking such a question.

Fear of abandonment is accompanied by fears about the future. With the mother and father still sorting out the conditions of their separation and divorce, the children may have a lot of unanswered questions about the future. Where will we live? Where is dad going to live and will we see him? Will mom remarry and does this mean a new dad and his kids will be moving in with us? What will happen to our summer vacations at the beach? What will happen to Christmas and my birthday? These questions come in rapid succession with no answers. Life, predictable and settled when mom and dad lived together, is now uncertain.

Children also experience a profound sense of rejection when their parents divorce. Some view their father's absence as evidence of personal rejection. "If he really loved and cared about me," the child thinks, "he would not have left me." Some children do not think in terms of husbands leaving wives (their mothers) but rather in terms of the fathers leaving them. In addition, the remaining parent may be so incapacitated by the divorce as to be unable to function as a nurturing parent. What the child experiences is double rejection—a parent who leaves and one who remains but can't function.

A third wave of rejection is experienced when children see both parents romantically involved with new partners. The children may jump to the conclusion that they are of no value because parents leave them to seek other companions. Rejection impacts the child's self-concept, which translates into "I am not important and neither parent loves me." These are dysfunctional scenarios children spin for themselves and affect adjustment to their parent's divorce.

Some children feel guilty and responsible for the divorce. One teenager told me that if she had been more pleasant to be around, her father would never have left:

I was always a problem . . . out drinking late with my boyfriend, making bad grades, and taking over the house with my friends. My dad moved into a place where he doesn't have to deal with me and he's got his whole apartment to himself. I knew he and my mom weren't getting along so I know he wouldn't stay for her. And since I had drifted away from him, he just didn't have a reason to stay around.

Younger kids sometimes still feel that the world revolves around them, which means that if one of their parents left, it must be because of some wrong done by the child. Whether sins of omission or commission, some children are haunted by the idea that if they had just done X or not done Y, things would be different. Now that the separation has occurred, these children feel helpless to correct a situation—and guilty.

Sociologist R. Neugebauer, who taught at York University in Ontario, interviewed 40 children between the ages of 7 and 18 whose parents had divorced when the children were from 2 to 11 years old. Although the children experienced a range of feelings including anger, sadness, anxiety, and depression, they unanimously described the separation of their parents as a relief, "that is, the solution to their unhappy home life."[3] Cyril, age 11, said:

Um . . . well, it was a relief. There was no more fighting. I was still unhappy because my dad was gone . . . my mom seemed happier. Well, at least it was much calmer. The knots in my stomach were beginning to clear, so things were much better.[4]

(Although there will be negative emotional consequences, there can also be positive outcomes in many divorce situations.)

Just as spouses may grieve that their marriage is over, children grieve that family life as they knew it is dead. A profound feeling of sadness and depression may engulf them. This grief may include denial ("This isn't really happening"), hope ("My parents are going through a bad time but will get back together"), and anger ("Why are they destroying my life and family?").

When parents are at war, children are in a no-win situation. If they talk about or show a preference for either parent, the other parent is likely to disapprove and sometimes punish the child. One child of divorced parents said, "My father told me that if I loved him I would visit him. But my mom told me that if I loved her, I wouldn't visit my dad." The most positive evaluations of divorce tend to come from children whose visitation arrangements meet their needs. Conversely, the least positive evaluations come from those who feel deprived of contact with the noncustodial parent.[5]

SELF-ASSESSMENT

How Difficult Will the Divorce Be for Your Children?

To gauge how your children will adjust to the divorce between you and their mother, read each sentence below and circle the appropriate number. The higher the number circled, the easier it will be for them to adjust to divorce.

1 = Definitely Not	4 = Mostly Yes
2 = Mostly Not	5 = Definitely Yes
3 = Sometimes	

	DN	MN	S	MY	DY
1. Prior to the separation/divorce, my children had a very good relationship with their mother	1	2	3	4	5
2. Prior to the separation/divorce, my children had a very good relationship with me.	1	2	3	4	5
3. Even though we are separated/divorced, my former wife and I remain friends.	1	2	3	4	5
4. My former wife is supportive of my relationship with our our children.	1	2	3	4	5
5. I am supportive of the relationship my children have with their mother.	1	2	3	4	5
6. My former spouse and I have made it clear to our children that we, not they, are the cause of our divorce.	1	2	3	4	5
7. My former spouse and I cooperate about visitation to ensure there is no conflict between us on this issue.	1	2	3	4	5
8. My former spouse and I agree on the amount of child support.	1	2	3	4	5
9. My spouse and I will not be going to court over the divorce.	1	2	3	4	5
10. The children and I will continue to live close to each other so that I can see them regularly.	1	2	3	4	5

Add the numbers you have circled. The lowest possible score is 10, which means that your children will have a very difficult time adjusting to the divorce. The highest possible score is 50, which means that your children will have a relatively easy time adjusting to the divorce. An intermediate score is 30.

Children may feel resentment when they learn that they were not consulted about decisions that affect them. Specifically, they learn that they will see their dad twice a month and a month in the summer. Or worse, that they will be moving or that their mother or father will be moving to a distant city. Their status as children who are accorded little power and who have no control over what happens to them is pressed into their awareness again and again. They don't enjoy it any more than you do when a judge dictates their access to someone they had always thought of as a permanent member of their household. Neugebauer's study showed that "children unanimously express a very strong preference for flexible and unrestricted contact with the non-custodial parent."[6]

Until now, your kids probably thought of divorced parents as some other kid's parents. But now, this divorced label is applied to them. Because divorce still carries a social stigma, children don't like being stigmatized as "from a broken home" and fear reactions from other kids and teachers. With time, they discover that both their teachers and peers are quite familiar with divorce and don't look down on them. Talking with other children (Parents Without Partners) whose parents are divorced can help normalize their family situation.

Children quite often hold out the hope that their parents will get back together. Children derive a sense of security when their parents live in the same house—at least the children know what to expect (even though the parents may fight). The knowledge that their parents are divorcing and will live apart exchanges the security of what children feel for the uncertainty of what may follow. Some literally dream that their parents will make up and get back together. Others may decide that if they are "really good," mom and dad will get back together. Some maintain this fantasy for up to a year, but many have given it up by then. This chapter's Self-Assessment is designed to give you some picture of how hard it will be for kids to adjust to the finality of divorce.

THINGS YOU CAN'T CHANGE

Some children notice an immediate change in their standard of living at the time of separation and don't like it: The cable television may be cut, the summer beach trip canceled, and the family may move to more cramped living quarters. Dad may also have moved into a dump with no TV. Other children may experience an improved standard of living. Although child support payments usually aren't enough to account for this, the mother may have wealthy parents or her own resources. She may also remarry. Because the mother has custody of the children in most cases, her remarriage tends to increase her standard of living and that of her children. Sociologist Frank Furstenberg at the University of Pennsylvania and his colleagues studied a nationally representative sample of children aged 11 through 16 and found that almost 60 percent of the white divorced mothers and 12 percent of the black divorced mothers had remarried within 5 years.[7] But such a remarriage does not necessarily stabilize the child's home life. Indeed, they also found that 37 percent of children whose parents remarry reexperience the disruption of the new stepfamily by another divorce.[8] One 14-year-old who had been through two of her parents' divorces said:

> You learn not to count on anything. At first I liked both of my new parents and their kids and we were all getting along great. Next thing I know, my mom announces that she and her new husband are splitting up and that we are moving to Florida. So I tell her I want to live with my dad and his new wife and my mom lets me. Then my dad gets divorced from his wife and he tells me he can't take care of me because he's on the road all the time . . . so I end up in Florida with my mom. It's not a very secure feeling to know your whole life can change when your parents start a squabble in the back room.

After years of relative stability (although from your perspective, likely a very unhappy stability) before the divorce, kids may get frustrated about the flurry of changes they are asked to accept for the sake of a parent's happiness.

Another big change felt by children is that, during and after a divorce, they end up spending less time with parents. Mothers may become preoccupied with new jobs. Dads are no longer there on a day-to-day basis. Indeed, the access children have to their noncustodial dad drops from 100% to less than 25%. Even when they are with him, he may be stressed from work or the costs associated with the divorce. This results in less supervision of children—younger ones have more accidents ("latchkey kids") and older children become more vulnerable to drug use, out-of-wedlock pregnancy, and brushes with the law. School performance may also drop, the parent now being "too busy" to help with homework/projects or look at the child's papers on a daily basis. Although most single parents will try to continue to be vigilant, the fact that the father is no longer in the home usually means that he now has less involvement with the decisions that affect his children.

The absence of the father from the home also usually means that decisions such as where his children attend school, the courses they take, and whether/when they go to religious services are issues over which he may have little control. Children might benefit from his influence in each of these areas.

Another important factor in how a child adjusts to divorce is his or her age at the time of the separation. Preschool children (from 3 to 6) seem to have an easier time adjusting to divorce than older children (from 9 to 14 or so). Preschoolers are less aware of what is going on and may have an easier time coping, but they still need consistent and frequent contacts with both parents at this age. On the other hand, children under 3 can have a pronounced fear of abandonment sometimes called "separation anxiety." Such children may not have grasped the idea that people and objects still exist even when they can't be seen, and the absence of a parent can be very distressing for them. Very young children may have a hard time parting with their mother even for 8 hours of day care, so a 3-day visit with you may be quite distressing for them at first. Only patience and attention will teach the child that he or she is just as safe with dad.

Only by age 7 or 8 do children develop a sense of independence. Still, sometimes older children are frightened by divorce as they are more impacted by the negative cultural images about divorce, have more questions about their threatened future, and can feel being drawn into the war between their parents. In addition, both mothers and fathers may be more protective of younger children and give them extra attention, which may cause jealousy or a sense of rejection for older siblings.

Over time, the effects of age on the adjustment of children seem to disappear. The adjustment of the parents to the divorce and how they treat each other are more important factors in how children ultimately experience divorce. Low levels of conflict, a strong relationship with the mother, and an active and involved father predict an easier transition. As the children grow older, their fear of the unknown is replaced by a new sense of certainty. After about 2 years, children have not only given up the fantasy that their parents will get back together, but have also usually settled most of the unknowns about where they will live, with whom, and how long they will see the other parent. If their father has maintained regular and consistent contact with them, their fear of abandonment is gone. In many cases, children will adjust more quickly to separation and divorce than their parents. By the fifth year after the separation, aside from the family having less money to live on, most issues the children are experiencing are unrelated to the fact that their parents divorced. Stress related to school performance, acceptance of one's self and a changing body, boy–girl relationships, adjustments with peers, drug use, and so on are issues common to all children whether or not their parents are divorced. Nevertheless, divorce and whether dad stays connected with his kids has a profound effect on them.

MY "DAD"

Mom & Dad are getting a divorce,
I guess time has taken its course.

The were great lovers,
And now who knows how long it will take Mom to recover.

Dad says he will still be around for us kids
     but Mom knows that won't be enough
For times ahead are going to be rough.

So she gets another job to make ends meet,
And Dad becomes a dead-beat.

No holidays, phone calls, or child support checks like he promised,
So much for being honest.

Now that we are out of his life,
He has found himself a new wife.

And a kid to call him "dad"
Why does he give her what I never had?

No one knows where my dad is now,
But I'm determined to find him somehow.

It's been seven years since I've seen his face
And now . . . not even a trace.

It is just as well, cause I've turned out just fine,
And my life is in line.

But I can't help but wonder about all those years
     . . . when I find him, I will point my finger,
Because he is the cause of so much anger.[9]

THINGS YOU CAN DO TO HELP

Although there is nothing you can do to erase the base-level anxieties children will naturally have about divorce, there are steps you can take to minimize their suffering.

Minimize Conflict with Your Former Spouse

Perhaps the most important thing you can do for your children is to make your best effort to cooperate with your former spouse. Your doing so will not only reduce the fear your children feel about their future, but will also cut down on your own level of anger. Conflict gives rise to more conflict. Once you start throwing barbs, your ex will respond in kind. And even though you may win an issue, all you have is someone waiting to get back at you.

Specific things you can do to reduce conflict with your former spouse include keeping the children out of your disagreements (argue if you must when they cannot hear) and agree in front of them on at least one topic (their discipline). Some motivated former spouses may seek a marriage therapist's help to learn how to reduce conflict and communicate effectively (see Appendix V for locating a marriage therapist). The goal of seeing a marriage therapist is not to call off the divorce and get back together, but to learn how to interact in a cooperative way. Such a skill will not only benefit you and your former spouse in making your divorce more bearable but will also improve the adjustment of your children to the divorce.

Even while you try to resolve your differences with your ex-spouse peacefully, you must avoid encouraging your children's fantasies that you and their mother will patch things up. Once you have reached the decision to divorce, make it clear to your children that, just as they were not the cause of the divorce, there is nothing they can do to change or prevent it.

Make Talking about the Divorce Acceptable

Because the children will be sad and grieving that you and their mother are divorcing, make it clear to them that it is acceptable to feel angry and sad and to talk about these feelings. Your kids may get mad at you for leaving and express this in various ways. Encourage them to discuss their feelings with you, even if these may be a little hostile at times. If you show them that you remain committed to them as a father, their hostility will pass. Keeping the channels of communication open will help your kids adjust sooner.

Maintain Strong Relationships with Your Children

Children who have a strong relationship with at least one parent adjust more easily to divorce than children who have marginal relationships with both parents. A strong relationship provides an anchor for the children during the turbulent divorce process. Otherwise, the children may feel they are adrift on a sea of uncertainty. Children who have strong relationships with both parents (and who maintain these strong bonds) are most advantaged. According to Professors Robert Hess and Kathleen Camara:

> The threat of divorce lies in the disruption of relationships with the parents. Disruption in these primary bonds interferes with the child's developmental progress and presents both cognitive and emotional problems that may persist long after adjustments have been made in routines of daily life.[10]

The message for divorced fathers here is, once again, to stay close to the kids and help them stay close to their mother.

There are other things you can do to minimize your kids' fears. For instance, in addition to taking and showing your children where you will be living, be sure to give them your phone number. After you take them back to their mom's, call them and ask them to call you so that they know how to reach you by phone.

Also, consider giving your children a large calendar and circle in red the weekends, holidays, and times in the summer they will be with you. Physically seeing where you live, talking to you on the phone, and having a calendar all help to provide your children with the security that their dad is still there.

Don't Promise More Than You Can Deliver

For reasons already mentioned, divorced fathers are sometimes tempted to promise their children more than they plan to or are capable of delivering. Remember that children whose parents have just divorced may feel abandoned and are trying to find a new sense of security in their lives. A dad who gives them a calendar showing the dates that they will be together should follow through. Or promise them nothing—"I'll try to see you whenever I can but I've been very busy with work lately." To promise and not show is to renew feelings of rejection and to cut a deep chasm of mistrust in your relationship with your children. It may be better to be a father who promises to see his kids only once a year (and who shows up) than to be a dad who promises weekly visits and phone calls and continually disappoints his children.

Know when to Consult a Professional

Some children are very sensitive and temperamental. Divorce for them is a major, almost debilitating, crisis. Symptoms suggesting that your son or daughter might benefit from seeing a professional therapist include anger. Anger encompasses several types of behavior, including rage (yelling at mother or father), defiance (refusal to follow authority; a "make me" attitude), and destructive behavior (wrecking his/her bedroom; destroying photographs or treasured possessions). Another warning sign is withdrawal, where the child goes into seclusion and shows little or no interest in activities with peers, parents, or siblings. The child may refuse to eat or sleep; he or she may lose weight and be generally sullen and sad. In addition to loss of appetite, overeating for comfort is also a pattern indicating that the child's emotional needs are not being met by parents or friends. Eating disorders are dangerous both mentally and physically, and should be treated as soon as possible. These disorders are most common in young women, but not unheard of in young men.

A steady and consistent drop in school performance also indicates that the child is distracted by unresolved family issues that interfere with his or her academic ability. This can occur for other reasons and is often temporary, but should the difficulty become acute, a therapist might save the child having to repeat a grade. Finally, you should also seek the advice of a therapist if your child makes and repeats direct statements of great guilt that cannot be reassured by parents or if he or she begins to talk about suicide.

Another warning sign that a child may need professional help is "cross-gender parenting." In these cases, a son may try to take the father's place in his mother's emotional life. Such a child fears to leave mom alone, even if that means going to a movie or some other favorite activity. This pattern is problematic because it is not only socially inappropriate, but harmful in that a child needs and deserves a child's life.

Most children will not need therapeutic intervention after their parents' divorce. However, children who are performing poorly in school, have no satisfactory social relationships, have low self-esteem, and who are always sad or angry and withdrawn, will probably benefit from seeing a psychiatrist or child psychologist. Children who are temperamentally very sensitive, whose parents are psychologically incapacitated by the divorce and unable to nurture their children, and children who feel a strong sense of rejection or abandonment are particularly vulnerable. One adolescent whose parents had divorced shot himself and left a note, "I couldn't take it any more." You must be on the lookout for warning signs, particularly in the beginning of the separation. Call your local mental health center or ask your family physician for a referral if you feel your child's symptoms warrant an appointment. In most cases, however, the most negative effects of divorce on your children will be short-lived, and their long-term adjustment may be even better than if your marriage had continued.

Some Possible Benefits of Having Divorced Parents

Some children experience the divorce of their parents as a relief from the constant conflict. One teenager I talked with said:

> I was glad my parents split up. I couldn't stand to listen to them argue and bicker every night. And when my dad drank, things got violent. So when I hear about how sad a broken home is supposed to be, they're not talking about me. It was an actual relief when I learned dad was moving out. They should have split years ago.

Some children even see the divorce as a way of escaping from a bad relationship with their dad. One man told me:

> I never felt accepted by my dad. He always wanted me to be somebody I wasn't. I wasn't interested in sports or student government or being on the debate team. We fought all the time. I'm glad my folks split so that I did not have to put up with his rejection on a daily basis.

Of course, a better scenario for this young man would have involved his father being more accepting of him as an individual, but, barring that possibility, his parents' divorce may have considerably improved his self-image.

Developing a greater commitment to marriage and to sticking it out is another positive for children who experience the divorce of their parents. Professor Judy Colich, a family life specialist, interviewed adult women whose parents had divorced and found that they had a strong commitment to making their own marriages work.[11] An older student in the Marriage and Family course I teach at East Carolina Univeristy had this to say:

> These days, when things stop being fun, people get divorced. And they end up marrying someone else till that stops being fun. My parents divorced and later remarried and said that they should have stuck it out the first time. I've had trouble in my own marriage, but my partner and I were committed to work it out and divorce was never an option. Commitment means no back doors.

Other benefits of divorce were revealed by researchers Nancy Lang and Marjorie Pett (1992), who interviewed 157 adults (115 women, 42 men) about how they experienced the divorce of their parents. Some of the positive outcomes identified by the respondents included that their parents were happier being apart, decreased tension in the house, and the opportunity to spend time alone with each parent. One adult whose parents had divorced when he was a child said:

> When my dad and mom were married, we always did things as a family and I spent very little alone time with either parent. Once they split, my mother and I spent a lot of time together during the week and my dad and I would do things together on weekends. I really think I am closer with each parent because of this alone time with each parent.[12]

Although divorce is never a fun experience, it is not the end of the world, either. People have always found ways to make the best of things, even especially painful events like the end of a marriage.

Maintain Your Emotional Stability

Parents who decompose (lose their job, abuse drugs, become depressed) during the divorce process make the adjustment to divorce more difficult for their children. Parents who are incapacitated by the divorce stop being support systems for their children, who feel that they must now console the parent. Such role reversal may be frightening to children who may feel that they are cast into a role for which they are unprepared. The technical term for this reversal is "parentification" and is a powerful force in custody cases. A "parentified" child is a child in need and the courts will seriously consider modification of custody to correct this problem. If you feel emotionally unstable, consider contacting a therapist.

CONCLUSION

Divorce is difficult for everyone involved, but it need not be destructive for your children. Take an active and sympathetic interest in how your children are responding to the pressures they feel. Although some children are not approachable and can't talk about feelings, others are and can. Whether open or not, all children have feelings about the divorce and know what they really need from their dad. The following by Jennifer Kwaitkowski, whose parents divorced, reflects her feelings about the focus of what she wanted from her dad.

WHAT HE NEVER GAVE YOU

At Christmas, he bought you the new Barbie doll to take to show and tell.

On Valentine's Day, he got you that three foot teddy bear to sleep with at night.

At Easter, he got you a bouncing bunny to play with in the backyard.

On your birthday, he bought you that special edition porcelain doll to have tea parties with.

On your first day of kindergarten, he bought you that lucky rabbit's foot so you wouldn't be scared.

On Halloween, he bought you that glowing necklace with matching earrings so you could see in the dark.

Of all the things that he bought you, he could never buy the one thing you always wanted.

The Barbie doll was not what you wanted to take to show and tell.

The teddy bear was not what you wanted to tuck you into bed at night.

The bunny was not what you wanted to play with in the backyard.

The porcelain doll was not who you wanted to have tea parties with.

The rabbit's foot was not what you wanted to calm your fears.

The glowing jewelry was not what you wanted to guide you through the dark.

It was him that you wanted to share all of these things with.

If only he would have given you a hug and said, "Everything will be okay. Daddy is here."

That's all you really wanted. [13]

Be Your Own Cognitive Therapist

The mind is its own place, and in itself
Can make a Heav'n of Hell, a Hell of Heav'n.

John Milton, *Paradise Lost*

In *Man's Search for Meaning*, Victor Frankl wrote that, while he was a prisoner in a Nazi death camp, he discovered the one thing his captors could not take from him: his capacity to view any situation positively. Frankl found the strength to survive in his ability to assign positive meaning to life despite his desperate situation. What can divorced fathers learn from Frankl? Although we don't face the untold horrors Frankl faced, we are separated from our children and our lives are in turmoil. How we view our situation (the *cognitive view* we construct) is crucial to our survival as divorced fathers.

The science of constructing a positive perspective on a negative situation is known as cognitive therapy. Drs. David Burns, Albert Ellis, and Aaron Beck are cognitive therapists who emphasize the importance of how people choose to view a situation. A familiar example demonstrating the importance of choice in viewing a situation is that in which a person looks at a half-filled glass of water and declares whether the glass is half full or half empty. Now, such choice of perception means little in regard to a glass of water, but in a divorce situation, one in which you are separated from your children, harassed by your former spouse, and humiliated by the courts, it is important to maintain your composure and balance. You can do this by making a conscious effort to see the good side of a bad situation in which you may find yourself.

Cognitive therapy assumes that the occurrence of a particular event does not *inevitably* result in your feeling a particular way. The fact that you are separated or divorced does not *automatically* result in your feeling depressed. Rather, it is the way you *perceive* the event that creates negative feelings. A divorced father who is depressed has chosen to view his divorce

41

| SELF-ASSESSMENT |

How Ready Are You to Be Your Own Cognitive Therapist?

To find out how you will fare as your own cognitive therapist, read each sentence below and circle the appropriate number. The higher the number circled, the easier it will be for you to see positives in your divorce situation.

1 = Definitely Not   4 = Mostly Yes
2 = Mostly Not   5 = Definitely Yes
3 = Sometimes

	DN	MN	S	MY	DY
1. I can usually see things from different points of view.	1	2	3	4	5
2. I am capable of seeing someone else's point of view.	1	2	3	4	5
3. It is easy for me to see the good in things.	1	2	3	4	5
4. I am more of an optimist than a pessimist.	1	2	3	4	5
5. I can see some benefits in my children having a stepfather.	1	2	3	4	5
6. I can see some benefits in being the noncustodial father.	1	2	3	4	5
7. Something good can usually result from something bad happening.	1	2	3	4	5
8. The divorce will eventually be for the best.	1	2	3	4	5
9. I can see advantages in paying child support.	1	2	3	4	5
10. My children can have a good life even though their mother and I are divorced.	1	2	3	4	5

Add the numbers you have circled. The lowest possible score is 10, which means that you will have great difficulty being your own cognitive therapist. The highest possible score is 50, which means that you are very skilled at seeing good things in difficult situations. An intermediate score is 30. The higher your score, the more skill you have in framing a situation to see benefits.

in a way that results in depression. The connection between negative perceptions and negative feelings is as follows:

Negative Cognitions Create Negative Feelings

Event	Cognition (thought)	Feeling that results
Divorce	"I am a failure"	Depression

Alternatively, the divorced father may just as well choose to view his divorce in positive terms, which will create a very different feeling. The connection between positive perceptions and positive feelings is illustrated in the following:

Positive Cognitions Create Positive Feelings

Event	Cognition (thought)	Feeling that results
Divorce	"I have escaped a bad marriage"	Optimism and courage

The reason why cognitive therapy is so important in your situation is that you cannot control your former spouse or a legal system that may be biased against you. However, you can and must control how you view these and other realities.

How you view your role as a divorced father will affect your own adjustment and that of your children. If you allow your circumstances to dictate your feelings, you may feel lonely and depressed. But, as we have seen, these feelings are directly tied to the cognitions or thoughts on which you choose to focus. A bleak financial outlook, separation from your children, an unsupportive former spouse—all are situations that you may not be able to change by direct action. But you can change the meanings you assign to them, and by doing so dramatically increase your own happiness and effectiveness in dealing with them in the long run. To get a feel for how well-suited you are to help yourself in this way, consider this chapter's Self-Assessment.

TAKING CONTROL OF YOUR PERSPECTIVE

Divorce is usually an economic disaster for men, but because they earn higher incomes than women at every age and at every education level, men are usually not economically strapped forever. Their hardest hit is the initial one of paying for a new place to stay and paying child support (and perhaps alimony). Over time, child support stops and, although the father may continue to support his children, his income usually increases with age. According to the *Statistical Abstract of the United States, 1999,* the median income of men who list themselves as "householder, wife absent" (that is, they live in a house where the wife is not present) is $32,960. Female householders with no husband present have a median income of $21,023.[1] Also, the years of an individual's peak income are between the ages of 45 and 54. Economically, the best years are ahead for dad—peak income during these years is a median of $37,624.[2]

Although keeping afloat economically is a preoccupation of the divorced father, it is important to keep in mind that this setback is temporary. All you can do now is stay on an even keel, do your job as best you can, and bear in mind that you will recover—completely. Keeping a positive outlook will help you immensely in this endeavor. Your employer will notice that you have continued to perform well despite your personal crisis, and the successes you experience at work will help bolster your self-esteem in low moments. You will also enjoy more job security, which will certainly be needed to meet the high costs associated with the divorce settlement. Drs. Alison Clarke-Stewart and Bonnie Bailey at the University of California, Irvine, studied 20 divorced custodial fathers and 25 divorced custodial mothers within 3 years of their divorces (the average length of time was 2 years) and found that men were significantly better adjusted than women. Not only were the men in the study better off financially, they had more stable and satisfying jobs, had experienced less psychological stress, and reported more psychological satisfaction in recent months. The researchers suggested that men typically place more emphasis on their careers and are therefore less traumatized when their marriages break up.

> Yet another possible explanation for the observed difference in psychological stress between men and women might be that the men in our particular sample—men who have physical custody of their children—were an exceptional group. Given their rarity, men who seek and obtain or accept child custody are quite likely to be unusual in their attitudes, confidence, and competence. It is possible therefore, that the men in our study might have been better adjusted than the women in our study even before their divorces.[3]

This evidence indicates that even your emotional struggles will eventually minimize, and your life will return to "normal" within a relatively short period of time.

No topic has been associated with the divorced father more than child support (e.g., "deadbeat dads"). According to the *Statistical Abstract of the United States, 1999*, 40 percent of the mothers awarded child support actually received the full amount. The average amount received was $3767 per year. Nevertheless, it is imperative to point that the term "deadbeat dad" is a misnomer since over 70 percent of dad's pay some or all child support.[4]

Some fathers are ordered to pay an enormous amount of child support. One divorced father told me that his ex-wife, an attorney, was able to get a judgment against him that was *more* than his total annual salary. She convinced a judge that based on her ex-husband's education and training (surgeon), he should be making X amount of dollars per year. He wasn't, but the judge ordered him to pay anyway.

Few fathers are caught in this bind, but they may feel unhappy about paying child support for other reasons. Some feel that their ex-wives squander the money or spend it on themselves, and others are embittered that their former spouses take the money but still prevent them from seeing their children. It may seem unfair that women need not account for how they spend child support money, yet fathers are legally bound to pay child support that is not tied to any assurance that they have a right to be with their children. Even though the ex-wife denies visitation to him, he is still legally responsible for paying child support. Legally, these are separate issues.

Despite these problems associated with child support, the divorced father can choose to view his payments as quality day care for his children. Of course, the vast majority of single mothers care very much about their children; at the very least, they are likely to care more about them than does a paid day-care worker. Calculate the number of hours your children are in their mother's care on a weekly basis. If she is employed, she will be responsible for your children 16 hours a day, 5 days a week (80 hours), plus 48 hours on weekends, or a total of 128 hours a week. Divide this number into the amount of money you pay weekly in child support and you will have the hourly rate you pay for the peace of mind of knowing that your kids are being cared for by a person who loves them. At $200 a week, you are paying $1.56 per hour, a great bargain! Although this may seem rather mercenary to some people, it is surely an improvement over feeling resentful about the child support payments.

Another financial burden you may bear as a divorced father is alimony (sometimes called "spouse maintenance" or "spouse support"). With the advent of no-fault divorce and more working wives, fewer spouses (15%) are being awarded alimony. Some states, such as Texas, no longer recognize alimony claims on any grounds. Still, some of us are required by the court to help support not only our children but our ex-wives as well. Once again, you need not let this expense grate your nerves and drag you down into depression or anger. Although alimony is another drain on your economic resources, an alternative way to view it is the price of a ticket to freedom. From this perspective, you may come to regard alimony as the best purchase of your lifetime. Waking up every morning into a life not burdened with tension, resentment, and unhappiness is well worth the price, even if that price is high.

A third major expense for the divorced father will be attorney fees. A positive perspective on lawyers is that they simply sell their time, just like other professionals. This accounts for your legal bill, which will document the 7-minute phone conversation you had with your lawyer 2 weeks earlier, and other charges. Rather than resent such detailed recordkeeping, be glad that he or she is spending time on your case.

Perhaps the most emotionally difficult result of divorce is loneliness. The divorced father may be surprised to learn that the cultural image of the divorced male with "unlimited" women available to him is just an old wives' tale. The women you do meet may not seem any more compatible with you than your former spouse. Life can become lonely and empty, forcing you to question whether divorce was the right decision and whether separation from your children is worth the independence you have gained.

Once again, you can concentrate on the failures of the past, or you can, by *force of will*, focus on the huge potential for success in the future. Although these successes might seem distant, try to look at the divorce as giving you the freedom to pursue an almost limitless number of choices not available if you were still married to your children's mother. Freedom to pursue a new partner, freedom to travel, and freedom to use your free time as you choose are all benefits not available to married men.

Some fathers who are happy to be divorced are often frustrated by their former spouses' continued meanness. One divorced father I met continued to receive harassing phone calls and constant interference with his attempts to talk to and visit his children, despite full and prompt payment of child support and alimony. His being upset by these events was a result of his viewing them as "things she shouldn't do," with an implied attempt to change her behavior. Of course, he wasn't able to do so, which resulted in continued frustration. He eventually realized the futility of trying to change his ex-wife and found a way to make even this work for him, rather than against him. He began to view his former spouse's "crazy behavior" as confirmation of her having qualities he did not value, which further confirmed that he had made the right decision to end the marriage.

DEALING WITH SOCIAL CONTEXTS

In addition to all of these problems, a divorced father quickly becomes aware that there is little social support for his being divorced. As a divorced male, you are suspect. Typical questions that people have about divorced fathers are: "Did he leave his wife and abandon his children for another woman?" "Why is he so selfish as to not stay married for the sake of his children?" "Does he lack the commitment and sense of responsibility to make a marriage work?" People often tend to stigmatize the divorced father as a selfish rogue.

Rather than accept these negative labels, the divorced father might view them as reflections of society's bias toward marriage. All societies depend on marriage to produce and socialize children as new members to replace the dying old. The traditional unit of husband and wife has been defined as the best possible context in which to rear children. Society quite often punishes divorced fathers, pities single mothers, and holds up the married couple as the embodiment of "family values." Never mind that many of these marriages may be social facades. Never mind that such marriages may be abusive and result in the unhappiness and wasted potential of both partners. American society wants spouses to stay married to protect the offspring and cares little for those who violate these "traditional" roles. However, divorced fathers know that they can still love, protect, and nurture their children even though they are no longer married.

Along with the cultural belief that divorce is bad comes the idea that it necessarily damages children. Psychiatrist Henry Friedman, of the Harvard University School of Medicine, has another view. He believes it is simply not true to assume that all children are damaged, either temporarily or permanently, by separation and divorce:

> It is self-evident, important, and even crucial to question the assertion that children of all ages are damaged, either temporarily or permanently, by separation and divorce. To emphasize temporary exacerbation of symptoms of loss in the short run without documenting whether or not the divorcing parents made special efforts to deal with the child's fears of significant loss is to support the contention that divorce, inevitably, is bad for children and their development.[5]

Highly conflicted, abusive marriages are *not* good for children, nor are those in which one parent is dysfunctional. Some children are better off when their parents divorce.

Sociologist Marty Zusman of Indiana University Northwest, a divorced father, emphasizes the importance of social context, which defines situations, scripts behavior, and creates outcomes. "Social context" is simply the group of people who are around your children—the most important of whom is their mother. As the custodial parent who spends a considerable amount of time around them, she is able to define situations for them. For example, she can define the children's father as one who does not care about them or as a loving father who always enjoys being with his children. Embittered former spouses are more likely to telegraph the worst definitions to their children.[6]

A child whose mother tries to turn him or her against the father may have difficulty constructing a positive image of the father. The child has his or her own image, but the mother or other relatives may be powerful in the image they project of the father. Young children living in such a social context often express these learned social scripts in terms of what they say to their father. Children who tell their father, "You are selfish," "I'm sick and can't come out of the house," and "I don't want to go with you" have, most likely, learned these scripts from their mother. The father should respond, "I'm sorry you feel that way. But if you will tell me exactly what I did to harm you, I will work on fixing it." Fathers who hear their children say such things should not be alarmed but recognize that the children are living in a social context that teaches and encourages such scripts. When they are older, they will reject such scripting by the mother. But for now, they will reflect the scripts of the context in which they live.

That social context creates outcomes means that the context in which the children live will dictate their behavior. When the context changes, so will the behavior or outcome. Hence, divorced fathers can look forward to their children becoming adults who will no longer be influenced by the controlling context of the former spouse.

FOCUS ON THE ADVANTAGES

In the meantime, it will be worthwhile to concentrate your thoughts on the positive possibilities your divorce offers you and your children. For instance, being separated from our children for days and weeks at a time may give rise to an intense desire to see and be with them. Unlike fathers who live in the house with their children and who, therefore, may regularly ignore them, we know the joy of anxiously anticipating our children and enjoying them when they are with us. Thus, the time we do have with our kids may be better for them than the time fathers spend with their children in the intact home.

We have already seen that divorced fathers can have more control over the content of the time spent with their children. If they want to hike the Appalachian trail or camp in the wilderness for a week or learn to scuba-dive with their children, they are free to do so without the permission of the children's mother. Married men must be careful that what they do with their children is "approved" by the spouse. One divorced father told me that he could never have enjoyed scuba diving with his children had he stayed married, as his spouse would have been too fearful that they would drown. "She just wouldn't have allowed it," he said. "But since the divorce we have had some of the greatest dives imaginable—with manatees, sharks, and manta rays."

Divorced dads also benefit from being able to discipline their children the way they want without interference. One divorced dad I talked with said, "My ex-wife let the kids do anything. I think rules, order, expectations, and consequences are good for kids. I'm not a drill sergeant but I do feel you can't let children do as they please."

In addition, children of divorced fathers may delight in the excitement their fathers display when they pick them up on alternate weekends, holidays, and in the summer. These children may also notice that real effort has been orchestrated on their behalf—their room is clean, there are recent photos of them on the wall, and dinner is their favorite pizza. Children who live in a two-parent home may encounter such intense attention from their fathers much less often.

Some divorced fathers had little involvement with their children during the marriage because the relationship with their former spouses was so tense that the men escaped into work or hobbies. Alternatively, the former spouse may have been so controlling and possessive that the father was peripheral to his children. Since the divorce, the father can be alone with his children and without the tension or obstruction so often present during the marriage. Hence, the divorce allows him to spend more quality time with his children even though he may not be the custodial parent. He may develop an even closer relationship with his children than would have been possible had the marriage continued.

Viewing positively the remarriage of your former wife is also possible. You may feel that your ex has replaced you as a husband, but even worse is the fear that her remarriage has replaced you as a father. Social psychologist Judith Wallerstein and her colleague Joan Kelly studied this issue in children whose parents had divorced and found that this did not happen.[7] The stepfather lacks an emotional and social history with your children and simply cannot compete with you in this arena, especially if you remain steadfastly committed to staying involved in your children's lives. You must not let jealousy defeat your purpose.

You might also learn to view your children's stepfather not as an adversary competing with you for their affection, but as a benefit to their lives. Most men have positive qualities that children can benefit from, and stepfathers are no exception. Three divorced fathers identified the positive qualities of their children's new stepfather.

> "He takes my kids fishing—something I always hated to do."
> "He's a churchgoing man—a dose of that won't hurt my kids."
> "He plays the guitar—my kids have always wanted to learn."

Of course, picking out the advantages of another man's role in your children's lives may not be your first choice of action. However, assuming that a stepfather has a genuine interest in your children, he can be a real asset to them.

In some communes, such as Twin Oaks, in Louisa, Virginia, children have numerous surrogate parents in that the adult community takes responsibility for their rearing and development. Such exposure to an array of adults broadens a child's opportunities to learn. Whenever possible, be glad that your children will have at least one other adult male in their support system. Just as you will most likely be a benefit to any stepchildren you may have, so will your children's stepfather benefit them.

LET GO OF PAST MISTAKES

Sometimes divorced fathers view the basic ideas of cognitive therapy as "fooling themselves" and believe that the "objective reality" of their situation is what affects them, not the way they view it. Shakespeare's Hamlet said, "Nothing is either good or bad but thinking makes it so." Divorced fathers who quickly adjust to the absence of their children have simply chosen to regard such absence in positive terms. This choice does not amount to fooling yourself, but simply selecting and emphasizing the positive aspects of your situation. You need not lose yourself in a dream world, refusing to face the day-to-day difficulties that happen to everyone. On the contrary, reframing your perceptions of those difficulties will make you more effective in dealing with them. Your alternative is to continue a negative view and feel miserable.

A friend of mine once visited a fortuneteller. He did it as a joke, but discovered, to his amazement, that she showed a great deal of insight into his past. Earlier in his life, he had made what he described as a terrible error in judgment, felt guilty ever since, and scolded himself almost constantly. The "psychic" observed that he was troubled about this mistake, expressed sympathy with his remorse, and quietly said, "Let it go." Perhaps the main reason this fortuneteller was able to anticipate my friend's general feeling of regret is that *everyone* has made mistakes.

All of us have made choices we regret. Decisions surrounding divorce are no exception. Perhaps we were hasty in agreeing to a property settlement we now wish we hadn't accepted. Or, we got frustrated with our children and responded inappropriately. Or, we were not as compassionate to our former spouse and her concerns as we might have been. Whatever the issues, we have all made mistakes. Nothing will help more in overcoming the consequences of those mistakes than to "let them go," and take control of the way you view your situation for the greatest benefit to yourself and your children.

CONCLUSION

Being your own cognitive therapist and taking control of your own feelings in a divorce crisis will not be easy. Even when you try your best, you will have good days and bad days, and many of us have to start slowly, taking each day as it comes. Make it your goal to resist allowing your circumstances to dictate your feelings. Rather, select how you choose to view those circumstances. Try to concentrate on the positive aspects of your experience whenever possible, and avoid crippling this effort with self-blame for mistakes you cannot undo. In time, your children will come to accept the new situation and you will gain confidence in your ability to carry on as their father despite your separation from them. In the next chapter, we will look at how you can make the time you do have with your children more rewarding.

What to Do and Not Do when Your Children Are with You

Divorced fathers measure time by memories, not by the clock.[1]

Ken Lewis

I grew up in the southern United States and my family regularly attended the Dawson Memorial Baptist Church. Around January 1 of each year, our minister would ask the congregation to mark on the church bulletin which sermon of the previous year we would most like to hear again. A favorite was "Giant Hours," in which the pastor made the point that most of life is dull and mundane except for those "giant hours" that give life meaning and purpose. Noncustodial fathers know the meaning of "giant hours" when they are with their children. Not that every hour is special, but there seem to be at least a few each weekend. This chapter is about "visitation"—the time children are with their dad.

In about 82 percent of the custodial arrangements, the woman has physical custody of the child(ren) and the father becomes the "visiting" parent. As the custodial mother-visiting father is the more typical case, the information in this chapter assumes a similar situation. Fathers who have sole or joint custody will, generally, have a much improved opportunity to maintain a positive relationship with their children. But because most dads become "visitors" in their children's lives, the father–child relationship suffers. While most mothers continue to wake up and go to sleep with their children in the house, fathers go to bed and wake up without their children present. This book is about fathers surviving divorce, but it is also about ensuring that children continue to benefit from a father in their lives. Children who grow up without fathers are more likely to drop out of school, be unemployed, abuse drugs, experience mental illness, and be a target of child sexual abuse. I will address these concerns in greater detail in Chapter 13. For now, it is important to recognize that fathers have always been important to their children. Sociologist David Popenoe at Rutgers University noted:

> In every premodern society, fathers have played the roles of protector, provider, and culture transmitter. And fathers have virtually everywhere been authority figures, although more so following the rise of civilization.[2]

Your role as father is critical to your children's development, even if conditions are less than ideal.

It's important to avoid creating an atmosphere of a "visit" when your kids come to your apartment, condo, or house. It may be difficult, particularly in the beginning, but try not to treat them like visitors. You should talk with them about changes in their lives, and in yours. However, feeling awkward in the beginning is not unusual. Everything has changed and there are no models to tell you or your children how to feel or behave. The time you are together may be court-ordered and restrictive. The place where you are together is typically your new apartment—unfamiliar, smaller, and often without many of the comforts of "home." Your behavior as a parent is also affected. For example, if you lived with your children all week, you would not hesitate to reproach your children about something like poor grades or a cluttered bedroom. But because you haven't seen them in 2 weeks, you don't want your first encounter to be negative and send your children to their rooms to brood all weekend. So you walk a thin line between being the responsible dad and not alienating your kids. Your power and authority are reduced, and both you and your children know it. This is especially true in the beginning but usually changes with time.

Because children unquestionably benefit from having a relationship with their dad, you should always try to set aside whatever problems you may have with not being the custodial parent and spend time with your children. For example, you may feel hurt that your children are not responsive when you talk with them on the phone, or feel that you have been replaced by their new stepfather, or feel that you are impoverished by child support and legal bills. In effect, the children can become a symbol of a failed marriage, of your being replaced, and of living in poverty. Nevertheless, children need their fathers, especially in the aftermath of divorce. Bonnie Barber, a professor of Human Development and Family Studies at Pennsylvania State University, compared adolescents from intact families with adolescents whose parents had divorced and found no significant adjustment differences as long as the father maintained regular and consistent contact with his children. In addition, "comparisons revealed that fathers who visited frequently, in addition to married fathers, were more involved in discussions about education, work, and family issues with their adolescents than those who never visited, or who visited infrequently."[3]

Professor Judith Seltzer at the Center for Demography and Ecology, University of Wisconsin–Madison, analyzed data from the National Survey of Families and Households to identify how often noncustodial fathers in the United States saw their children. The percentages in Table One show how often fathers who had been divorced 2 years or less visited with their children in the past year. For all we hear about deadbeat dads and other fathers who don't care about their children, these statistics indicate that recent noncustodial fathers *do* care about their children. Almost three-fourths see their children at least monthly and less than 5 percent never see their children.

Given that the mother will be the primary custodial parent with whom the children spend most of their time, divorcing fathers usually agree to or end up with one of several basic patterns of visitation. First, some former spouses agree that the father will have almost unlimited access to his children. He may pick them up after school, take them to music or karate lessons, help them with homework or take them out to dinner several times a week, and still be with them Friday and Saturday nights on alternate weekends. In such cases, the mother views the father's involvement in her children's life as valuable and encourages their time together. This arrangement benefits everyone—the children and father have regular contact with each other, and the mother has help with the work of parenting (such as homework and transportation). Unfortunately, the percentage of divorced fathers who see their children at least once a week may be low. Professors Frank Furstenberg and Christine Nord at the University of Pennsylvania

Table One. Frequency of Visitation
among Divorced Fathers[4]

Several times a week	25%
Once a week	17%
1–3 times a month	29%
Several times a year	15%
Once a year	9%
Not at all	4%

(and their colleagues) analyzed national data on children aged 11 to 16 and found that only 17 percent of divorced fathers visited their children at least weekly.[5]

In another pattern, the father is held to a strict court-ordered schedule and only allowed to see his children every other weekend from 5 PM Friday until 5 PM Sunday. This arrangement weakens the father–child bond across the 2-week period and is not in the best interest of the children or the father. Of the twice-a-month visitation with his children, one father said, "When we're together, we discuss things on a superficial level, we try to have a good time . . . but there just isn't time in a now-and-then relationship to have a normal relationship . . . it's painful." To bridge the time, some court orders allow the father to see his children for 2 hours or so on the alternate Sundays he is not with his children. This little amount is not ideal but provides a time for the father and children to check in with each other before their regular weekend.

Regardless of what the partners agree to or what the court order says, some fathers are unpredictable and erratic. The children never know whether he is coming to pick them up or not. Kids in this situation constantly wrestle with feelings of abandonment and rejection. The result is a strained father–child relationship as well as heightened bitterness between the former spouses.

Some fathers choose to have no involvement with their children. Even among those who spent time with their children while married, some walk away from the parental role and never look back. Whether it is because of feelings of inadequacy, a desire to reduce conflict, or money problems, children whose fathers disappear may wonder why they were not important enough for dad to stay in their lives. For fathers who do not want any involvement with their children, one advantage is that the children will learn to get along without their dad. One young man said of his divorced father, "He would appear and disappear every 5 years . . . I wish he had just stayed away . . . . all he did was get my hopes up." Such inconsistent behavior may be worse than just leaving your kids alone, but it is never too late to try to become involved in your children's lives if you are serious and committed.

One divorced man had not seen his children for 4 years and decided to make contact. His wife rebuffed his attempts and it took a court order for him to begin seeing his children. They also rebuffed him and made it clear that they were just fine without him. He continued to see them despite their protestations and eventually they came around. He compared his ordeal to fishing: "You have to keep the bait out and sooner or later you will get a strike."

HANDLING VISITATION

Visitation can be a difficult way of life to get used to. But there are guidelines that will help make things easier on everyone.

Be Consistent

For the first 6 months to 1 year, some divorced fathers will show up on time every available weekend the court allows. Then, whether because of career commitments, other relationships, the pain of dealing with the ex, or the rejection they may feel from their kids, some fathers begin to skip weekends. Such a pattern is devastating to children who are trying to rekindle their feelings of security regarding their parents, and particularly for dad who has moved out of the house. After you establish a regular and consistent pattern of being with your children, try to maintain it. Their feelings of self-worth are at stake.

Part of being consistent means showing up *on time*. It will be helpful to either show up at the time you have agreed to (5:00 PM Friday) or tell your kids that you will be there "sometime around 5 but no later than 6."

How late you can be also depends on the expectations of your former spouse. If you say you'll be there at 5 PM and she has made plans to be somewhere at 5:30 and you do not pick up your children until 6, she will understandably be upset. As a rule, it is important to be on time or call if you are going to be late. If you are predictably late, you should change the time when you say you will show up so that neither your children nor your former spouse will be anxious. But try to be present at the time agreed to in the court order.

Plan Your Visits

Fathers differ in terms of their amount of planning in preparation for the weekend with their children. Some fathers give no thought to what they will do with their kids and let things happen as they may. The advantage of this pattern is that it allows the kids to become part of the plan and to experience a very "normal" and laid back time with their dad. The disadvantage is that sometimes no plan means sitting around bored all weekend.

Alternatively, some fathers plan every weekend with their kids from the first meal to the time they take them back to their mom's. If this style appeals to you, you can include your kids in such planning by calling them midweek and asking what they would like to do. Some children have definite ideas about what they would like and enjoy picking and choosing. Others are indecisive and simply say, "I don't know." A typical weekend with my children included a meal cooked by dad (usually pizza that nobody liked) and watching a video. On special weekends we would do special things like go to a theme park or to the beach.

Although planning has its advantages, it is also important not to feel burdened to keep your children "happy" or "doing something" every minute they are with you. Life should be fun and exciting, but it can also be boring and dull. Letting your children experience boredom and finding creative ways to deal with it is as important as going down a water slide with them.

Some custody agreements allow larger blocks of visitation when school is out (e.g., 4 to 12 weeks), and many divorced fathers look forward to having more time with their children during the summer and some invest more planning (and maybe money) during this time. Some fathers fly their children to exotic locations, which involves getting airline tickets and hotel accommodations months in advance. Others rent beach cottages, which may also require advance reservations. If you're going to plan a big trip, you should start early.

Psychiatrist Henry Friedman at the Harvard University School of Medicine suggests that to be *only* a Disneyland dad is not in the best interest of your children. He has said:

> Any situation which revolves around the father as a visiting exclusive provider of treats and entertainments fails the essential task of post-divorce fathering. Here, the central requirement is an experience with the father which includes the time and relaxation for there to be an everyday life together.[6]

In other words, there need to be periods of time in which both father and child can be spontaneous and intimate with each other. Unlike such time afforded by a joint or sole custody arrangement, brief periods often do not provide this context. Ironically, most fathers know this but are often deprived of day-to-day contact with their children. So they are left with cramming 2 weeks or 3 months of absence into one, big, fun-filled weekend.

Still other fathers enjoy the relaxation of summer and just spend the time with their children in town. With child support and setting up a new place, it can become expensive to vacation with children. Camping is an inexpensive alternative that provides a great context for bonding. One father who takes his kids camping in the mountains every summer told me, "It's cool up there and we always have a good time." As a side note, when you do take your children out of town, give your former spouse a paper detailing where they will be and phone numbers so that she can reach them in an emergency. Should your former spouse take the children out of town, she should provide you with similar information.

Whether it is for a special weekend or not, picking up your children can be an emotionally charged time. The experience reaffirms for both dad and the children that the family no longer lives together. And, if the former spouses are conflictual, picking up the children can be a horrible experience for both parents and children. "I couldn't stand to see my parents fight," said one 10-year old. "They were just like two little kids scrapping in a sandpile." Many such conflicts might be avoided by carefully considering where and how you pick up the kids for the visit.

There is no best place to pick up your children. For amicable, cooperative parents, the home of the former spouse is a good place. It is convenient, the children are comfortable, and neither parents nor children need to depend on the schedule of a third party. For embittered spouses who can't be around each other without fighting, alternatives should be considered. These include picking up the child at school, at a sitter's, neighbor's, or friend's house.

Some parents meet at McDonald's. He drives by to see her sitting there with the kids, and as he comes in to get them, she leaves via the other door. They also meet at McDonald's for their return home. Luggage is handled by her putting their luggage in the open trunk of his car and him doing the reverse on the return. Meeting at a public place such as this is not ideal but does prevent open conflict.

When Things Don't Go as Planned

Should you have an emergency or job conflict and are not be able to pick up your children at the regular time, notify their mother immediately so that she can rearrange her schedule. You should also tell your children directly that something has come up and tell them the specific date and time you will see them next. Sometimes former spouses will "swap weekends," which keeps the father regularly plugged into his children's lives. More often, the father may have to "forfeit" seeing his children. But he can call them and make it clear that he does want to be with them.

Just as there will be times when you can't show up as promised, there may be instances where your kids aren't available when you arrive to pick them up. When you show up at your children's home to pick them up and they are not there, your emotions may be difficult to control. First, give your former spouse the benefit of the doubt. Perhaps they are late returning from a school event and got caught in traffic. Events such as this happen; when they do show up, say a cordial "hello" to your former spouse and the kids, put the stuff in your car, and be on your way.

If you discover that their not being there is intentional on the part of the former spouse, call her. If she hangs up on you, call the county sheriff and explain that you are a divorced father trying to pick up your children on a court-ordered weekend. Ask the officer to meet you at your former spouse's home where you will present the court order verifying that the children are to be with you. In most cases, the sheriff will be able to resolve the difficulty and you will see your children.

Should your former spouse not be there or contest your right to see your children (and should the sheriff not intervene on your behalf), call your attorney. He or she will most likely not be available (it is Friday afternoon) and you must wait until Monday morning to begin legal proceedings against your former spouse. In the meantime, make other plans for the weekend. Rather than brood (which is what your former spouse may want you to do), enjoy your weekend. Rest assured that you will get access to your children; your ex will not be able to defy a court order indefinitely. It may take your going to court three times, but the law is clear on this point—custodial mothers are not to deny court-ordered visitation to biological fathers.

Your Children's Adjustment

Some divorced fathers notice that their children are cold and distant when first picked up on Friday afternoon for the weekend. The children answer questions but add nothing and show no outward enthusiasm for being with dad. When children live in a context that is not supportive of the relationship with you, they learn to feel guilty about being with you and "feel" the disapproval of their mom. Only after they are with you and evaluate you for themselves do they feel differently about you.

One divorced father kept a record of how long it took his children to "thaw" after picking them up Friday afternoon: It wasn't until 2 PM Saturday that their coolness and distance began to fade. By Saturday night, the children had relaxed and were enjoying being with dad at his place. This lasted through lunch Sunday, but about 2 PM they began to "refreeze" in preparation for their return home. Such a "thaw," "enjoy," and "refreeze" pattern is functional for the child who lives in an unsupportive context. Children who show excitement and enthusiasm about going to dad's risk the disapproval of their mom. And if they return as though they have been tortured all weekend, they continue to receive mom's approval.

It is difficult for divorced fathers to cope with their children's coldness and distance. But lashing out at them or giving a cold shoulder in return will only confirm what they may have been taught all week about mean old dad. The best response is to simply ignore their sullenness and make it clear that it will not change your attitude. Not making an issue of the thawing period will help to shorten it.

Long-Distance Visitation

A final difficulty worth discussion is long-distance visitation. When fathers and children are separated by great distances, some adjustments must be made on both sides. Not only must each adapt their expectations of how often they will be together, but the father must find ways to maintain the contact despite the distance. Regular weekly phone calls at a specific time, letters, and audio cassettes in the mail help. There are also conference centers divorced men can use to see, hear, and interact with their children via television. See Appendix V for information on teleconferencing. However, such a setup not only involves a great deal of expense, but also requires the cooperation of the former spouse, as she must take the children to the video conference center.

If the former spouse is supportive of the father's relationship with his children, she can facilitate the maintenance of the relationship and ensure that the children are available for weekly phone calls, conference center get-togethers, and the like. If she is not supportive, the divorced father's worst nightmare will have begun as she can use the distance to her advantage. When he is to call, the kids will simply be "unavailable." Although he can hire lawyers and put pressure on her to comply, the expense

SELF-ASSESSMENT

How Will You Fare as a Noncustodial Father?

To find out the degree to which you are good at being a noncustodial father, read each sentence below and circle the appropriate number. The higher the number circled, the better you are in this new role.

1 = Definitely Not   4 = Mostly Yes
2 = Mostly Not   5 = Definitely Yes
3 = Sometimes

	DN	MN	S	MY	DY
1. I am OK with the amount of time I am with my children.	1	2	3	4	5
2. I see my children regularly and consistently.	1	2	3	4	5
3. My children and I enjoy the time we have together.	1	2	3	4	5
4. My ex-wife supports the relationship with my children.	1	2	3	4	5
5. I give my children time to "thaw" after I pick them up.	1	2	3	4	5
6. I respect my former wife's privacy and don't ask my children about her personal life.	1	2	3	4	5
7. I praise my children when I am with them.	1	2	3	4	5
8. I set limits on what my children can do when they are with me.	1	2	3	4	5
9. My children can bring a friend with them if they want to when they are with me.	1	2	3	4	5
10. I am careful to only say good things about my former spouse to my children.	1	2	3	4	5

Add the numbers you have circled. The lowest possible score is 10, which means that you don't like and are not good at being a noncustodial father. The highest possible score is 50, which means that you have accepted the challenges of being a noncustodial father. An intermediate score is 30. The higher your score, the better you like and are good at being in the role of the noncustodial father.

will wear him down and she can thwart his efforts. This chapter's Self-Assessment will give you some idea of how well you will be able to cope with these and other difficulties associated with visitation.

WHAT TO DO WHEN YOUR KIDS ARE WITH YOU

Once you have your children, there are several things you should be careful to do during the course of their visit with you. Because divorce can be hard on kids, especially at first, it is difficult to predict some of the situations you may experience with them. Once again, the best policy is to keep your feelings for your ex-wife separate from those for your children. You should take steps to establish a positive relationship with your former wife and avoid speaking negatively about her.

Because your children's identity is in part connected to their mother, *always make it clear that their having a good relationship with their mother is not only acceptable but desirable.* "Love your mom, enjoy her, and get along with her" are words to say frequently to your children. One of the ways to make it clear that you want your children to have a good relationship with their mother is to say positive things about her yourself: "Your mom has always loved and cared about you . . . she is a good mother" models for your children that they can feel, think, and act this way. Children may sometimes hope to win the approval of a parent by talking negatively about the other. They fear that if they display good feelings for the other parent, they will get into trouble. Make it clear to them that you want them to feel good about their mother.

It is also important to *model positive feelings about your ex-parents-in-law—your children's grandparents on their mother's side.* They are an important influence and support system for your children and encouraging contact and goodwill toward them is best for your children. How much time the kids spend with your former spouse's parents will probably be up to her, as time with them usually is shared with your former spouse rather than being taken away from your time with them. Be sure to let your kids know that you want them to feel good about grandma and grandpa.

It is also important when your kids are with you to *respect the privacy of your children's relationship with their mother.* Psychiatrist Robert Sammons of Grand Junction, Colorado, notes that "not asking about their ex is one of hardest things divorced fathers have to do . . . but it is also one of the most important."[7] Do not pry into what happens when they are at their mother's.

Do not ask questions about whom she is involved with, who came over for dinner, or the like. If they begin to tell you horror stories about what is happening at mom's, listen because there may be something you need to know about (such as an abusive situation), but disregard and discourage comments about your ex-wife's personal life.

Establishing rules when your children are with you is also important. Sometimes kids will use the guilt parents feel for divorcing to stretch the limits of what a parent will put up with in terms of staying up late, long-distance phone calls, being out of the house, and so on. Children need structure and limits and function best when they know the boundaries.

Without structure, kids may become manipulative. They may try to manipulate their parents to gain a sense of power or to get something. "But mom lets me stay up later" should be met with "that's her business. When we are together, these are the rules." Likewise, "My stepdad said he would buy it for me if you won't" should be met with "that's very nice of him. Tell him that there is a sale this week at Wal-Mart." After a few weeks of visitation, children will develop a sense of balance and a new definition of what it means to be with you. It is important to help your kids see this new relationship as positively as possible without being too indulgent or too strict.

Another important element of your kids' relationship with you is *praise*. Like everyone else, children like to be praised—often. As a parent, it is easy to focus on the messy room, the noise, and the sloppy table manners. Although it may be in their best interest to encourage neatness, respect for others, and good etiquette, it is better to look for things our children are doing right and tell them than to wait for them to do something bad and correct them. The experts call it "catch your child being good."

One way to make the most of your time with your kids is to *make time to be alone with each of them some time during the visit*. Spending time alone with each child sends the message to that child that "you are important and I enjoy being with you." When several children are involved, spending time with each is more difficult. But seize these opportunities. Perhaps one child would like to watch TV, which frees the other for a ride to the grocery store or to play tennis with you. Later, you can find an activity to enjoy with the other child.

Some divorced fathers *always have a camera ready* when their children are with them. Particularly on special weekends or summer vacations, taking photos of your children enjoying themselves helps to preserve the memory. Such photos can be placed in a photo album or displayed on a corkboard in the child's bedroom. The effect is to communicate to the child that he or she is important and helps provide a visual history of good times together. You can find a good 35mm camera for as little as a dollar at yard sales or a reasonably priced new one at K-Mart. Newer models are so easy to operate that you won't need a technical degree to get great results.

Children need their own bed in their own room. If possible, *have a separate room that becomes your children's room.* Some kids bring all of their clothes over to "visit," whereas others may keep a set of clothes at dad's. Having a separate set requires hauling less stuff each visit and gives a sense of "two" homes rather than one home and a hotel room. The children might also be encouraged to fix up their room with posters of their choosing or whatever they would like to do to the room to make it theirs. It may be difficult at first to get your youngster to understand that he or she now has two rooms—one at mom's and one at dad's—but as they spend more time there, they will be more likely to enjoy this space.

WHAT TO DO WHEN YOUR CHILD ASKS . . .

"Can I Live with You?"

Soon after the separation or during the early stages of divorce, your son or daughter may ask if he or she can live with you. This is a complicated question as it is not clear if their motive is to live with you or to hurt their mother. It is also not clear if the question may reflect mistreatment by their mother. One 9-year-old said that his mother never spent any time with him, refused to take him anywhere, and would never allow him to have friends over to his house. He also reported that he was left alone much of the time. Social Services investigated and found these accusations to be true, resulting in the father petitioning the court for reassignment of custody, which he was granted. Such cases of child neglect are not unusual. According to the U.S. Census Bureau, there are over 400,000 substantiated cases of child neglect each year.[8]

So, when your child asks if he or she can live with you, ask him or her to talk more about it. Why does he or she want to do so (a common reason is the perception that dad is more lenient)? What is it like to live at mom's? Answers to these questions will provide direction for what the divorced father should do. If the mother is an alcoholic or drug abuser and leaving your young children unattended, you should call Social Services in your community and have them investigate. Your children's safety is at stake.

"Do I Have to Go Back to Mom's House?"

This question is just another version of "can I live with you?" and once again, it may not be clear what the child is "saying" while "asking." Is the child seeking the dad's approval of the relationship with his or her mom by asking why he or she has to go back to mom's? Is the child expressing love and affection to dad for such a great weekend? Or is the child merely testing dad to see what he will say? Unless there is reason to believe the child is being mistreated at mom's and a custody change is indicated, a question about not wanting to go back to mom's should be met with compassion and firmness: "You have a great mom and we think it is best for you at this time to keep the situation [custody/visitation schedule] like it is. As you get older, your mom and I are willing to discuss changes in this arrangement. For now, let's keep it like it is. I'll see you Wednesday and then the next weekend we are together we. . . ."

"Can I Bring a Friend?"

The question (usually asked between the ages of 11 and 14) is not designed to hurt you or to minimize the value your child places on his or her relationship with you. It is, rather, a sign that friends are becoming increasingly important in your kid's life. Such friendships are important for the development of your son or daughter's social skills and should be encouraged. When your child asks, "Can I bring a friend?" the answer should be, "Of course, would you like me to take you to see a movie or what would you two like to do?" Telegraph complete support for your child bringing a friend whenever he or she wants to. Of course, you haven't seen your child in almost 2 weeks and want to spend time alone with him or her to rekindle the relationship. But this is your need, not your child's need. He or she enjoys friendships when away from you and does not want to have them interrupted by having to visit old dad. Support the friendships of your son or daughter. Doing so will only help to ensure their knowledge that you have their best interests at heart and they will continue to want to be with you.

"Can I Visit a Friend This Weekend?"

The developing importance of peer relationships in adolescence is also sometimes expressed in the request to ditch dad completely and visit with a friend on "dad's weekend." Again, do not take such a request personally but delight in the fact that your child is developing and nurturing friendships. These skills are more important than spending a weekend at dad's. So, when your child asks if he or she can skip the visit with you and be with a friend, respond, "That was nice of _____ to invite you for the weekend. What time do you want me to pick you up to take you to his (her) house? And would you like me to drive you guys anywhere?" Also, make it clear that some future weekend you would like for your child to ask his or her friend to stay overnight with him or her at dad's place on dad's weekend.

As your child reaches 14 or 15, requests to be with friends will increase. At 16, peers will become the focus of your child's free time. Again, view such peer relationships as a sign that your son or daughter is on schedule toward adulthood. If he or she did not have friends or be interested in them, you might have greater cause for worry. To ensure that some contact still exists between you and your child in middle and late adolescence, make it clear that although you are completely supportive of their friendships, you would still like to get together alone for a brief time every week. This can be as little as 30 minutes during which you get a burger or do some shopping at the mall, and will allow you to stay involved in your child's life but not interfere with their social development.

Some children will resist even 30 minutes a week to demonstrate complete independence. Try not to make a big deal of it, but make it clear that your not being together at all is unacceptable. Establish early with adolescents that although you are willing to be supportive of their time with their friends, some minimal time between the two of you is important to maintain. Solicit their agreement and cooperation regarding when the 30 minutes together will occur.

"Can I Skip the Weekend with You Because I've Got a Job?"

As with friends, be supportive of your son or daughter's job. Economic independence is essential to your child's development. Because a job can consume most of your child's free time (and after working he or she will want to be with friends), it may be more difficult to arrange any time together. But keep trying. Perhaps you could meet for a lunch break or before work? Make it clear that you want it to happen and ask for his or her help in making it happen. Thirty minutes weekly keeps you connected and confirms that you are there for and care about your child. As he or she moves to adulthood, continue to be available for brief get-togethers but be less insistent. Later, when your child is on his or her own, allow contact with you to be initiated by your child.

WHAT NOT TO DO WHEN YOUR CHILDREN ARE WITH YOU

We have talked about some things you should consider doing when your children are with you. But there are also things you should avoid doing when you are with your children.

Rule 1: Don't Ask Your Children to Take Sides

There are more subtle ways of asking your children to take sides than asking them who they would like to live with. Asking them if it is more fun at mom's or dad's, if they would rather be with you or at their mother's for New Year's, or if they like where you live rather than where mom lives all require the child to move toward one parent and away from the other. Children of divorced parents feel loyalty to both parents and become uncomfortable when asked to express an opinion that suggests a lean one way or the other. Some children resolve this dilemma by answering "I don't know," which always keeps them in the safe zone.

Rule 2: Don't Trash Your Former Spouse

Divorced fathers with former spouses who are not supportive of their relationship with their children must be careful not to criticize their former spouses in front of their children. Such criticism only serves to vent their anger and places the child in an awkward situation. Should the child defend the mother and risk the disapproval of the father? Should the child agree with dad and invite his approval—and feel guilty about betraying the mother? Psychologist Jack Turner of Huntsville, Alabama, notes that it is important that the divorced dad show respect for the role of the child's mother: "No matter how the divorced dad feels about his ex-wife, he should recognize that she is also the child's mother and show respect for her."[9]

Keep in mind that your child's self-concept is, in part, a reflection of how he or she feels about his or her mother. If you encourage your children to have a negative view of their mother, it is difficult for them to not have a very negative view of themselves, for they may be like their mother. For example, Carol's mother is moody but so is Carol. If dad says, "Your mom is crazy as hell," Carol may dislike her mother for being moody, but at times, may feel moody like her mother. Try to avoid saying, "You sound just like your mother."

Only say good things about your former spouse to your children. This is important not only because there are positive qualities about your former spouse but also because focusing your comments on these positives will allow your children to also think positively of themselves should they share some of these characteristics with their mom. There is yet another reason for focusing on your former spouse's positives, namely, by doing so, you improve your feelings for her, which makes it easier for you when your children are with her. Thoughts of their being with a caring mother are more comfortable than thoughts of their being with a vindictive and angry woman.

Rule 3: Don't Grill Your Children about Your Former Spouse

As previously noted, using your children to spy on your former spouse is something to avoid, as it puts your children in a no-win situation. If they give you information about her private life, they are disloyal to their mother; if they don't, they risk your disapproval. Other than the generic "How's mom?" avoid asking questions about her.

Rule 4: Don't Use Your Children as Messengers

Having children relay messages is inviting frustration. Not only might they forget to relay the message, but they also may inadvertently distort it. And, when the parents are at war, it places the children in the position of witnessing the parent's fury—or being the target of it, or both. One child was asked by her dad to tell her mother that he was "short on money this month and would not be sending child support." The mother yelled at the daughter that her father was an irresponsible bum. Such situations may be avoided by direct communication between the former spouses.

Rule 5: Don't Abuse Alcohol/Drugs

Divorce is a difficult time and increases one's vulnerability to relieving the pain through chemicals. The chemical most legally available is alcohol.

Studies show that divorced men, compared with married men, are more depressed, drink more alcohol, and abuse drugs more often. Taking a drink or having a beer or two can be relaxing. But settling in for an evening or weekend of drinking suggests an ill-fated course. Be alert to your alcohol (and other drug) consumption, as it can easily drift into abuse.

Rule 6: Don't Use Your Child as Your Therapist

Your children are incapable of performing in the role of therapist. A therapist is trained to empathize with your pain and make suggestions or recommendations to relieve your stress. Don't expect more of your children than they can deliver. They are, after all, only children; they have their own adjustment problems, and they cannot deal with yours as well.

Rule 7: Don't Burden Your Children with the Details of Your Divorce

Divorce is an adult matter and should be discussed with other adults. To discuss the details of your divorce with your children is to invite them to side with you, which requires that they break loyalty with their mother. Putting children in such a position is never in their best interest. Global statements such as "We are not as happy as we thought we would be and have been unable to work out our differences" blame neither partner yet tell your children that the divorce is happening. Save the details for your friends and attorney.

Rule 8: Don't Use Your Children to Meet Your Need for Companionship

Enjoying being with your children is not the same as depending on them for companionship. To do so is to burden them with "baby-sitting" dad and to interfere in their social development with peers. As a divorced father, it is important that you develop and nurture an array of adult relationships. Your children will not be with you over 75% of the time, so depending on them for companionship is unrealistic. Even if you had full custody, it is important that you have your own adult relationships. It's OK to be a friend to your child, but you must first be a responsible parent—and this may involve making decisions on their behalf that they do not like. Fathers who "need" their children for companionship lose their perspective of the father's role and thus lose their capacity to make the best decisions on behalf of their children.

Rule 9: Don't Require Your Children Initially to Share You with a New Mate Immediately

At least for the first year, try to devote the time your children are with you to them and don't require that they share this time with a new person in your life. Your children already may feel rejected and abandoned and spending the weekend with you and your new partner is most likely to be interpreted as "See! He left us for her."

If putting your girlfriend on hold is more than either of you can bear, at least balance the time. You might spend Friday night alone with your children and have lunch with them Saturday. Later in the afternoon and/or evening, you might include your new friend in something special the kids get to do (go-cart rides). Blending her in slowly and in the context of fun activities will make it easier for your children to accept her.

Rule 10: Encourage Your Children's Relationship with Both Sets of Grandparents

An often overlooked aspect of divorce is the effect it has on the relationship between the children of divorced parents and their grandparents. Divorce frequently deprives grandchildren of a continuing close relationship with their grandparents at a time when their love and support is needed the most.

The relationship between grandparents and grandchildren is generally recognized as being mutually beneficial. Freed from the responsibilities of full-time parenting, grandparents can enjoy a more relaxed and playful relationship with their grandchildren, giving them the attention that their parents might not have the time or patience to provide. Interactions between grandparents and other family members add a dimension to the grandchild's developing understanding of social roles and family relations. Grandparents are also a link to the past. By sharing their experiences, they serve as family historians and help grandchildren develop an awareness of the traditions and values that have shaped their parents' lives.

Grandchildren also indirectly benefit from the support that the grandparents frequently give to their parents. Not only may they provide financial support but also child care, advice, and being good parental role models for children. Grandparents may also provide significant emotional support for their grandchildren during the divorce.

Custody is a significant factor in determining what kind of relationship grandparents will have with their grandchildren following a divorce. In most divorces, one parent, usually the mother, is awarded primary if not sole custody. Because most custodial parents are the mothers, most custodial grandparents, then, are the maternal grandparents. Maternal grandparents are frequently called on to assist more actively in the care of their grandchildren following a divorce. Compared with grandparents in intact families, they are more likely to be living with them or seeing them almost daily, exchanging services, providing financial support, and engaging in more parentlike behavior.[10] These relationships should be encouraged.

On the other hand, noncustodial grandparents, those whose sons or daughters are not awarded custody of their children, frequently find themselves deprived of close contact with their grandchildren following a divorce. Noncustodial grandparents, usually the paternal grandparents, tend to live farther away from their grandchildren, see them less often, and provide less financial support. They stand a better chance of retaining contact with their grandchildren, though, if their own son or daughter, the noncustodial parent, also stays in close contact with the children.[11] Nevertheless, paternal grandparents are sometimes able to preserve close relations with their former daughters-in-law, even over the objections of their sons, justifying their behavior as being in the best interests of the grandchildren.[12]

Sometimes a custodial parent will purposefully try to sever the relationship in an attempt to seek revenge or vent hostility against his or her former spouse. In such cases, when grandparents are deliberately denied access to their grandchildren, grandparents sometimes have legal rights that they can pursue so as to maintain contact.

All states have passed legislation that gives grandparents the right to petition the courts for visitation privileges. Granting visitation rights is based on the determination that such continued contact is in the child's best interest. Guidelines for determining best interest are not always clearly stated, and in a few states the court presumes that visitation is in the child's best interest unless proven otherwise.[13] This is a significant change in the legal status of grandparents, who previously had no rights regarding their grandchildren without the cooperation and consent of the parents.

In the event that the bond between grandparents and grandchildren is weakened or ultimately severed, pain will inevitably be felt by both grandparents and grandchildren, who will have lost what for most of them was a very special and richly rewarding relationship.

CONCLUSION

How your children experience their time with you is an important factor in their adjustment to the divorce. By ensuring that the time is regular and consistent, you make it clear to your children that they are important to you. By doing certain things, such as praising them, setting limits, and encouraging a positive relationship with their mother and grandparents, you will increase their comfort in being around you. Your not doing certain things, such as using them to spy on your former spouse, requiring them to share you with a new partner right away, and burdening them with the details of your divorce, will also enhance their time with you.

You will also need to manage certain issues with your children. Their need to be with their peers or to work when they are scheduled to be with you and their wanting to live with you or go back to mom's early after a weekend with you are examples. Being supportive of work and peers and time with their mom will ease their fears about how you will respond to such requests.

Finally, it is important that your children experience being with you when you are not always catering to their needs. Just being in their own room or hanging out around your home is what they would be doing if you were still living with their mom. So relax, dad, and let them create their own activities some of the time. It is just as important for you to enjoy their visits as much as they do. In the next chapter, we will discuss a few things to keep in mind when your children are with their mother.

What to Do and Not Do when Your Children Are with Their Mother

It is not unusual for noncustodial fathers to be told at the last minute that they will not be able to see their children, that the children do not want to go with them, that the children are busy doing other things, or that the visit will be limited to the presence or home of their ex-spouse.[1]

Janice Roberts Wilbur and Michael Wilbur

A divorced father told me that he was woken one morning by a phone call from his 11-year-old daughter informing him that she never wanted to see him again and that she and her mom were moving six states away. The man was devastated and did not see his daughter for the next 5 years. Although these very discouraging events do happen, the more typical situation is that the divorced father is without his children except on alternate weekends, holidays, and a month in the summer. The "in-between" times are usually very difficult for most divorced fathers. There are fears that the former spouse may be "working on their heads" and turning them against him, fears that he may be forgotten or become irrelevant, or, worse, that he will become replaced by a new stepfather.

Unless the divorced dad has sole or joint custody, he will be without his children most of the time. He will wake up in the morning and go to bed at night without seeing them. Therefore, he must find a focus in his life other than his children and learn to enjoy the time he is away from them. At the same time it is important that he stay connected with his children even though he can't be with them. Managing his own life and staying connected with his children are the concerns of this chapter.

REFOCUS WHEN CHILDREN ARE AWAY

As discussed in Chapter 3, how you view a situation will affect your emotional reaction to it. There are several positive aspects of your children being with their mother that you can focus on. Just as it is important that your children spend time with you, it is equally important that they spend time with their mother. Even if you had full custody, it would be in your children's best interest for them to spend time and continue to nurture a good relationship with their mother. So, rather than focus on the fact that your children are away from you, focus on the value of them being with their mother. One divorced father said:

> I never wanted the divorce anyway. And one of the reasons I didn't was that I thought my wife was a wonderful mother. I still feel that way. So while I miss my kids, I'm glad that they are with their mother because I know she is a nurturer and will take care of them.

Not only is it best for the kids to have a good relationship with their mom, there are also advantages for you in the new custodial situation.

You should seize the time your children are with their mother as an opportunity for you to do things you can't do when they are around. Traveling with a friend will not only be less expensive without your kids but will also allow you to nurture adult relationships. In addition to traveling, you can simply relax, as there are no special meals to prepare, no listening to the kids fighting, no worrying about their needs to be entertained. Just kick back, put your feet up, and breathe. A dad who had been divorced 7 years said:

> I was devastated when the divorce happened but I've rediscovered one of my old loves—travel. I was in the service and traveled the world and never tired of it. But with a family, you aren't very mobile. Being divorced gives you a new sense of freedom. I've been to Greece twice and I'm going back.

Still another divorced dad said that he was a long-distance hiker and that hiking from Georgia to Maine is something you can't do with a family. I saw him in Virginia after he had been on the trail for 4 months. He said, "I'm like Charles Kurault, I *have* to be 'on the road.' "

The time your children are with their mother is also the best time to spend with old and new friends, without any hassles about the kids accepting your new partner (or vice versa) or your having to split your time between your kids and your partner. Relish the time you have alone with others, because you should not and cannot depend on your children to meet your needs for companionship. Just as most young adult children derive more satisfaction from being with their peers than parents, most parents derive enjoyment from being with their adult friends. It is important to do so. One divorced father said that he regularly nurtures his social garden by calling up friends and scheduling time with them. He said that with his children turning away and developing their own friendships, it was crucial for him to do likewise. According to psychologist Jack Turner, a divorced father:

> Enjoying the time you are separated from your children actually makes you a better father. If you focus on the pain of the divorce, the separation from your children, and their absence in your life, you can slip into a sullen depression. Don't do that—seize the opportunity to enrich your life and you will be a model of life enhancement for your children.[2]

On the other hand, it is also a mistake to be totally focused on your adult life when your kids are with their mother. To bridge the time you are with them, call them regularly at a set time. If you see them every other weekend, a call on the alternate Sunday night helps to keep you connected till the next weekend. Calling more often is also OK. The goal is to make it clear to your children that you are still "with them" even though you are "away" from them.

Your children being absent from you much of the time also functions to prepare you for their leaving home permanently and for their eventual independence. Custodial mothers are often jolted with sudden solitude when their children leave home for college, work, marriage, or whatever. Fathers, on the other hand, are already adapted to this reality. Both of my children have moved away from home. My adjustment to their absence was eased by the earlier noncustodial father years.

WHAT TO DO WHEN YOUR CHILDREN ARE WITH THEIR MOTHER

The most important thing you can do for your kids while they are not with you is to stay informed about their lives. This can be difficult, for noncustodial fathers often have to depend on themselves to find out what is going on in their children's lives. Some women let their former husbands know nothing about school events, hoping that if their ex does not show up he can be blamed for not being interested in his children.

Assert yourself and be aggressive in seeking information. Schools normally send only one announcement of an event, and as this normally goes to the custodial parent, it may be weeks too late when the father learns of an academic banquet or a band performance. Call your child's school and ask to be put on their mailing list. If they insist that only one announcement goes out, schedule an appointment with the principal. If he or she does not put you on the mailing list, go to the superintendent, the school board, and elsewhere. Inform all that you are the child's parent and want to be involved in your child's life. Do the same with your child's other activities—karate, dance lessons, baseball/volleyball practice—whatever your child is involved in. Call the coach and ask for a schedule of practice sessions and events. Most coaches and principals and people who work with your children appreciate your interest and are helpful. But it is your responsibility to seek the information.

If your divorce case is being litigated, you will need to have every shred of evidence that you are a father who cares about your children. Documenting what you do when you are with your children is important. But equally important is keeping a journal of what you do in reference to your children when they are not with you. Having conferences with your children's teachers, interviewing dance or piano teachers, and going to travel agencies to collect brochures are examples of significant entries in your journal.

In addition to keeping a journal for yourself, you might also consider writing letters to your children. Kids love to get mail and written messages also have a way of bridging the time the divorced father is with his children. Particularly if the father and child are separated by a great distance, writing becomes even more important. A stack of letters is a visual referent that dad is there and cares. A phone call is fleeting and cannot be "seen" when it is over.

Despite the rationale for writing, some fathers feel inadequate in this endeavor. They become anxious putting words on paper, don't know what to say, and feel that whatever they say might be misinterpreted. Anxiety over writing is particularly high in cases where the former spouse is not supportive. The divorced father may fear that she will prevent his letters from getting through or make fun of them to the children ("Your daddy can't even spell").

Demographer Judith Seltzer at the University of Wisconsin–Madison analyzed national data on nonresident fathers with regard to how often they called or wrote to their children. Table One shows the frequencies these fathers (separated 2 years or less) called or sent mail to their children in the previous year.[3] Surprisingly, 66 percent of these fathers made such contact at least once a month when they could not visit with them. These data reveal that recent noncustodial fathers *do* care about maintaining contact with their children.

In addition to phone calls and letters, fathers who are separated by great distances can interact with their children via video conferencing. Corporate executives use video conferencing for "meetings" with persons in different locations. By calling 1-800-669-1235, you will learn of the locations of video conference centers in your area. This technology enables you to see, hear, and talk with your children via television. This option is not very practical for most of us, being very expensive and requiring the cooperation of your children's mother to get them to the teleconferencing center in their area. But some dads regard it as less expensive than frequently buying plane tickets.

Many divorced fathers enjoy planning trips with their children. Reading about vacation spots, calling airlines, and arranging accommodations can be done when the children are with their mom. Of course, before making any arrangements, the father should consult with his children about their preferences. Because some children are ambivalent about where they go and what they do with dad, he can investigate activities and places he would like and ask them "how about if we go camping in the mountains when we are together this weekend?" It is sometimes easier for kids to say yes or no to something than to generate their own list. They also are unaware of the expense involved, so dad needs to identify something that

Table One. Percentages of Noncustodial
Fathers' Contact with Children
Postdivorce: Phone Calls or Letters

Several times a week	25%
Once a week	23%
1–3 times a month	18%
Several times a year	7%
Once a year	7%
Not at all	20%

will not only be interesting/enjoyable but affordable. A lot of money is not necessary to have a good time with your kids. Your *time* is the important factor. Parents without partners provides regular weekend activities you can enjoy with your children. Camping in state parks and floating down rivers on tubes can be done for little more than the cost of the gas it takes to get there.

Some parents will try to entice their children to be with them all of the time by scheduling fishing trips, beach trips, rock concerts, and the like when the children are scheduled to be with the other parent. Such a ploy places the children in a no-win situation. If they don't go on the "fun weekend," they feel they have missed something; if they do go, they incur the disapproval of the other parent.

Be respectful of the time your children are with their mother. As noted earlier, use this time to your benefit. If your former spouse does not reciprocate your respect for her time and regularly schedules special events when your children are with you, ask her directly to only do so when they will be with her, as otherwise the children cannot go. If she ignores your request and continues to schedule special events, do not relinquish the children on your weekend. Of course, you might also want to ensure that your children have a good time when with you by scheduling special events, but do be careful not to go into a competitive mode with your former spouse about who can orchestrate the more "special" weekend.

Special occasions will at times occur when your children are scheduled to be with their mother, such as your parents' 50th wedding anniversary or the children's cousins are in town. If you wish the children to be with you on these occasions, make a request in writing to your former spouse and offer for the children to be with her at a time when they are scheduled to be with you. If she is uncooperative, don't abduct the children, and allow the event to pass without the children's participation. Should your ex later request consideration for a special event, discuss the issue with the children and do what is in their best interest. Don't play "payback time" with your ex. Only your children will lose.

It will sometimes happen that your children will not be at their mom's when you phone there. Setting up a regular time to call helps to reduce the frequency of such occasions. But even then, it may not be convenient, as the children may be at a friend's house, out of town, or at the movies. Or, it may be that your ex is diverting them so that they will not be available for your call. Whatever the case, simply call back—and keep calling until you get them. Begin the conversation with your delight in getting in touch with them. Do not scold them or spend the conversation talking about why they weren't there. You can tell them the next time you see them when you will be calling but don't require that they be available. What is important is that you are able to talk with them between the times you see them. That they are available to talk at 6 PM on a Sunday is not important. But don't let actually talking to them slip by if they are not there—teach both your children and your ex that you will keep calling until you reach them.

Worse than your children not being there is their being cold and distant when you do call. Such an attitude may be related to their anger about the divorce in general but more likely will reflect the unsupportive environment there. Former wives who are angry at their ex sometimes use the children against them. One ploy is to show disapproval to any child who displays any interest in talking to or being with dad. "It's *him*," one mother says disparagingly as she tells her children that their father is on the phone. If they act excited to talk with him, she may punish them emotionally (by not talking to them), so that the children learn it is easier to be cold to dad for a brief phone call than to suffer all week at mom's.

Divorced dads should recognize that the context is controlling their children's behavior and delight in the fact that their children are bright enough to look out for themselves. They should also ignore the coldness and require virtually nothing from their children during the phone call. This translates into dad doing all of the talking about how much he misses them and enjoys being with them and is looking forward to being with them next Friday. Don't expect it to be much of a conversation. It usually isn't. A typical conversation might be as follows:

Dad: Hey!
Child: Hey.
Dad: How are you doing?
Child: Fine.
Dad: What have you been doing?
Child: Nothing.
Dad: How's school?
Child: Fine.
Dad: When we are together next weekend, I thought we might drive down to the coast and see if we can catch a fish or two. How about that?
Child: OK.
Dad: Great! I'll see you on Friday. Have a good week.

The phone call need not be long, for its function is to communicate to the children that dad is still there and is looking forward to being with them. The fact that he called (and kept trying until he reached them) is what the children will notice.

A final consideration is your financial obligation to your kids. Even though they are divorced, fathers remain important economic providers for their children. According to demographer Seltzer, two-thirds of divorced fathers who visit their children regularly and who call or write them during in-between times report that they pay child support. Only 20 percent of those who have no contact with their children pay child support.[4]

Children benefit from child support because it keeps an economic floor under them. The most impoverished of children are those with no economic support from fathers. Welfare does not make up for what fathers do not pay. Social policies are moving toward reducing welfare payments. Some criticisms against "deadbeat dads" are appropriate.

WHAT NOT TO DO WHEN YOUR CHILDREN ARE WITH THEIR MOTHER

In addition to doing certain things when you are with your children, there are certain things to avoid when they are away.

Don't Feel Sorry for Yourself and Brood

Earlier in this chapter, I emphasized enjoying the time your children are away. This requires not feeling sorry for yourself and brooding about their absence. To do so makes some fathers vulnerable to alcohol or substance abuse.

Don't Slip into Alcohol or Drug Abuse

According to Doug Mace, Alcohol and Drug Rehabilitation Counselor for 20 years at the Walter B. Jones Alcohol and Drug Treatment Center in Greenville, North Carolina, "divorced men usually escalate their alcohol and drug use. They miss their kids, feel depressed about the failed marriage, and want a little relief from the pain."[5] Professor Erma Lawson at the University of Kentucky and Aaron Thompson at the University of Missouri also noted that divorce prompts self-destructive behavioral patterns. They interviewed 30 divorced black men, one of whom said:

> I loved my ex-wife and still loved what she once was. I was very hurt every minute during the first year of the divorce and wanted it to be a nightmare 'cause I love the married life. I went wild to dull the pain, smoking pot, drinking, and engaging in self-destructive behavior.[6]

Of course, drinking when one is depressed creates a vicious cycle of feeling sad, drinking, and feeling even sadder. Instead of relying on alcohol or other drugs as a mood elevator, try exercise. It lasts longer and has no downside. In addition, divorced men need to watch their diets. Relying on Burger King for food is a quick way to increase one's cholesterol.

Don't Harass Your Former Spouse

Some divorced fathers become obsessed with revenge toward their former wives. This is particularly true of fathers who wanted the relationship to continue and whose former partners are now in new relationships. The hurt and anger are unbearable and may drive the divorced father into attempts to get back at her through harassing phone calls, letters, or other means. Resist. Focus instead on developing new relationships.

Don't Try to Control What Your Ex-Wife Does when the Children Are with Her

Give up trying to control what your former spouse does when the children are with her. Just as you have the right to take your children wherever and do whatever (within reason) you like when they are with you, your former wife has the same right. Respect each other in this regard.

Don't Get Too Serious Too Quickly in a New Relationship

As a recently separated or divorced man, you are emotionally vulnerable to a new relationship. I wrote my dissertation on Love Attitudes and found that men are more romantic than women when it comes to falling in love quickly. Women are relationship specialists and more keen at the game of love. Men often stumble into relationships, but the separated/divorced man must be particularly vigilant. This translates into holding off

```
                          ┤ SELF-ASSESSMENT ├
```

HOW WELL DO YOU COPE WITH YOUR CHILDREN BEING AT THEIR MOTHER'S?

To determine how well you get along when your children are with their mother, read each sentence below and circle the appropriate number. The higher the number circled, the easier you fare when they are with your ex.

1 = Definitely Not	4 = Mostly Yes
2 = Mostly Not	5 = Definitely Yes
3 = Sometimes	

	DN	MN	S	MY	DY
1. I am usually very busy when my children are with their mother and I don't have time to be lonely.	1	2	3	4	5
2. I feel that it is important for my children to have a good relationship with their mother.	1	2	3	4	5
3. I want my children to spend time with their mother.	1	2	3	4	5
4. I enjoy life when my children are with their mother.	1	2	3	4	5
5. I have a number of friends my own age who I enjoy when I am not with my children.	1	2	3	4	5
6. I do not abuse alcohol or other drugs.	1	2	3	4	5
7. I exercise regularly and keep in good shape.	1	2	3	4	5
8. In general, I enjoy time away from my children just as much as I enjoy the time with them.	1	2	3	4	5
9. I spend no time brooding about the divorce.	1	2	3	4	5
10. I do not harass my former wife with phone calls or letters.	1	2	3	4	5

Add the numbers you have circled. The lowest possible score is 10, which means that you are miserable when your children are with their mother. The highest possible score is 50, which means that you enjoy the time your children are with their mother. An intermediate score is 30. The higher your score, the greater is your adjustment to your children being with their mother.

any new commitments to a new partner out of a desperate need to be attached to someone (anyone?), waiting until the divorce dust clears, and finding out where you are emotionally when the sad feelings surrounding the divorce have lifted.

Don't Kidnap Your Child

Although you may be frustrated with your attorney, ex-wife, and court system over your efforts to have the access to your children that you feel is in their best interests, it is important to stay within the framework of agreements and custody orders. I discuss parental abduction in more detail in the next chapter.

CONCLUSION

The time when the children are with their mom is usually a difficult time for divorced dads. Some fear that their children may be in an environment unsupportive of the father–child relationship and feel that their children are slipping away from them. Most fathers can combat these thoughts and feelings by reframing them and using the time away from their children for enjoyment and the development of new relationships. With regular weekly contact, children will be able to see for themselves that their father cares about them and is involved in their lives. Just as divorced fathers should do a number of things including calling, paying child support, and exercising, they should also avoid feeling sorry for themselves, heavy drinking, and any harassment of the former spouse. The next chapter examines constructive ways of handling postdivorce relations with an ex-wife.

How to Interact with Your Former Spouse

Divorce . . . does not terminate psychological relationships among family members.[1]

Jean Wylder

No other relationship is as important to your child as the one you have with his or her mother. If you and your former wife have a good relationship, she will continue nurturing the relationship between you and your children. On the other hand, if you cannot be friendly with each other, she may try to turn your children against you and keep them away from you. Getting along with her is crucial to your relationship with your children.

Unfortunately, according to Constance Ahrons in her 1995 book, *The Good Divorce: Keeping Your Family Together When Your Marriage Comes Apart*, one-fourth of the 98 pairs of ex-spouses she studied had hostile, bitter, and acrimonious feelings toward each other.[2] When there are children and the ex-wife has primary physical custody, the consequences for the children and the divorced father can be devastating. Although not all bitter mothers use their children as a weapon against their ex-husband, some do. Surviving the ploys of an ex who is intent on destroying your relationship with your children is clearly a challenge.

YOUR FORMER WIFE'S REACTION TO THE DIVORCE

Former wives react to divorce differently. Some wanted the divorce and are relieved that the marriage is over. They are the ones who initiated the divorce and may already be involved in a new relationship. The former husband is history and she wants little or nothing to do with him (except

SELF-ASSESSMENT

YOUR RELATIONSHIP WITH YOUR FORMER WIFE

To get some insight into whether your relationship with your ex is good for your children, read each sentence below and circle the appropriate number. The higher the number circled, the better the relationship is for you and your children.

1 = Definitely Not   4 = Mostly Yes
2 = Mostly Not   5 = Definitely Yes
3 = Sometimes

	DN	MN	S	MY	DY
1. I feel relaxed when I talk with my former wife.	1	2	3	4	5
2. I feel forgiving when I talk with my former wife.	1	2	3	4	5
3. I feel friendly when I talk with my former wife.	1	2	3	4	5
4. I feel generous when I talk with my former wife.	1	2	3	4	5
5. My former wife supports my relationship with my children.	1	2	3	4	5
6. My former wife wants me to spend time with my children.	1	2	3	4	5
7. My former wife makes it easy for me to call my children when they are with her.	1	2	3	4	5
8. My former wife and I can discuss our children easily.	1	2	3	4	5
9. My former wife and I can negotiate a schedule change easily.	1	2	3	4	5
10. My former wife usually has the kids ready when I pick them up at her house.	1	2	3	4	5

Add the numbers you have circled. The lowest possible score is 10, which means that you have a lousy relationship with your former spouse that is bad for your children. The highest possible score is 50, which means that you have a wonderful relationship with your ex that is great for your children. An intermediate score is 30. The higher your score, the better the relationship is for you and your children.

for his money via child support and alimony). Wives who ended the marriage and feel a sense of relief may also feel guilty for breaking up the family—but not enough to try to get things back together. One wife I spoke with who had left her husband said:

> I just didn't love him anymore. He is a great person and father but I just didn't want to spend the rest of my life with him. Although I have been a lot happier since I left, I do feel bad about him and the kids not being around each other all the time. That's been the hardest part—breaking up the family.

The message here is that, even though it won't make you feel any better, your ex may well be going through similar feelings of loss and failure over the divorce.

Some wives welcome the divorced father as an active coparent. The job of the single parent is often overwhelming. Wives who feel burdened with child care, homework, and transportation often welcome the help of their former husbands and view them as coparents. They regard the active involvement of the children's father as good for their children and helpful to them as a mother. They often have joint custody of their children. But in the absence of such a formal agreement, they relate to the father as though he is a coparent. One divorced father says that his former wife seems more concerned than he is about being with his children. "She'll call me up and say I haven't been spending enough time with my son and ask if she can bring him over."

Former wives who did not want the divorce feel stigmatized by it. They are embarrassed about being a divorcée. They usually feel out of place around couples and may miss having a man in the house. These mostly very traditional wives feel the full weight of the divorce, having lost their husbands, their status as married women, and their ex-husband's income.

Psychiatrists, psychologists, and other mental health professionals identify a depressed person as one who exhibits various symptoms such as difficulty sleeping, loss of appetite, weight loss, and a generally "down" mood. The future looks bleak to them, and some are suicidal. These persons view divorce as signifying a more general failure in life and become preoccupied with its trauma. In a study of ex-spouses by Professor Gay Kitson at Case Western Reserve University, over 40 percent of the women reported that they still could not believe that the divorce was happening, and wondered if they would ever get over it. These feelings were most intense when the divorce was recent and when the husband wanted the divorce. According to Dr. Kitson, the more emotionally attached the woman was to her ex-husband, the more difficult her adjustment was. "The highly attached seem more self-absorbed with the pain of the divorce and their changed personal situation."[3]

Wives who feel they have been dismissed, who fought the divorce, and who think that their lives have been irreparably damaged may blame their former husbands and seek revenge. They may want to punish their ex-husbands by stripping them economically and keeping their children from them. In the meantime, such an ex could try to influence the children's opinions of their father so that he has a cold reception when he calls or attempts to be with them. She might view the father's attachment to his children as a source of power that she can use to punish him for his "crime" of "abandoning" her.

Disaffected ex-wives often see the divorced father as an interference. Social psychologist Judith Wallerstein and her colleague Joan Kelly found that 20 percent of the divorced wives in their study saw no value in the father's contact with his children and actively tried to prevent such contact. These women also view their ex-husbands as an interference into their new remarried family.[4] The family circle now consists of your ex-wife, your children with her, and her new husband (and maybe his children). Either way, the former husband and father (you) are excluded. If you were to move to another country, your ex would celebrate and hope that she was rid of you forever. If you try to maintain your relationship with your children, she may take it as a personal challenge. This view is the devoted father's worst nightmare.

Ex-wives might resent the relationships their children have with their fathers because they feel that fathers only play with them and do none of the work. These mothers might feel that their children enjoy being with him because he buys them things and takes them places they enjoy. She may be under intense financial pressure or may not feel comfortable taking them camping or on a cross-country trip with her. Thus, she feels burdened with their care and possesses little energy, skill, or money left over to play with them on weekends. It galls her to see her children enjoy being with their father and she labels him as the "good-time daddy." It is not a flattering label.

Other women are indifferent to their ex-husbands. They are neither accommodating to them as coparents nor concerned about blocking their access to their children. If the ex-husband wants to be the "good-time daddy," so be it. These women have, for the most part, adjusted to their new lives without the father living with them. If he wants the children for a weekend when they are scheduled to be with her, she will likely say OK. She may only ask that he make up the weekend some time when the children are scheduled to be with him.

RELATIONSHIPS WITH FORMER WIVES

Some former spouses are friends. They call each other when they need something and are always accommodating in reference to their children. Although they do not "date" or have sex, they share the value that it was their divorce, not their children's, and they have tried to make the transition to living apart as easy as possible. One such divorced couple gets together once a week for what they call "family night." They may or may not bring their new partners. This situation is unusual but it does happen. Researcher Constance Ahrons studied the relationships of 98 pairs of ex-spouses and found that about 10 percent regarded themselves as best friends or "perfect pals."[5]

A larger number (about 40 percent) of former spouses fit the mold of being cooperative partners. They are not "best friends," but they are not enemies either. They cooperate as necessary in the decision making and work of child rearing. The benefits for both children and former spouses of being cooperative are enormous. The children do not feel torn between the parents and the spouses have a greater sense of calm and well-being in their respective lives. Dr. Carol Masheter, professor of Family and Consumer Studies at the University of Utah, studied the postdivorce relationships of 265 ex-spouses and found that about 40 percent are able to be friendly and cooperate with each other for the children.[6]

Unfortunately, many ex-spouses remain angry at each other for years. Angry partners can still get the business of parenting done but they are not happy about seeing each other. They may even exchange a barb or two when they meet. But, for the most part, their conflict is controlled. The partners wish they did not have to deal with the other but recognize that, for the good of the children, they must. They do a reasonably good job of containing the conflict. About a quarter of Ahrons's couples would fit into the angry partners category.

In the worst cases, ex-spouses become and remain bitter enemies. These relationships are the most devastating to the children and to their parents.

No one wins and everyone loses. The parents are often embroiled in a continuing legal dispute over custody, visitation, or child support. No sooner is one court fight over than another court date is set on another issue. It is the worst of divorce situations. About a quarter of Ahrons's ex-spouses could be labeled as bitter enemies.

One way the former wife acts on her bitterness is to call her children when they are with their father. In one case, the divorced father told me that his former wife called their daughter who was vacationing with him to remind her of what she was missing at home. Her cousins were in town and they were going to a water slide park. She also reminded her daughter that her father had not paid child support so there would be no money for her to go to summer camp. Instead, he was using the money to take his new girlfriend on a trip to the Bahamas. Although none of what the mother related was true, by the time the conversation was over, the daughter was sufficiently stirred up so that the time she had left with her father was ruined.

How should you as a divorced father respond to such a phone call? The answer is not easy. First, your former spouse has a right to call your children when they are with you. But, if her doing so upsets your children so that they become angry with you, you may need to intervene. In response to this situation, the father told his daughter:

> When we are together and your mom calls, sometimes it upsets you and you act differently toward me. I'm going to write your mom and tell her that she is welcome to call you at any time when you are with me, but that if you are upset after the phone call I will have no choice but to refuse them after that. If you want to suggest to her not to call or to keep it pleasant when she does, that's up to you. But I want you to know what I'm going to do. Just as I don't call and upset you when you are with mom, I don't want her to ruin our time together.

Bear in mind, though, that your son or daughter bears some of the responsibility in these situations, and you must be careful not to allow him or her to use this sort of thing as a manipulation strategy. Try to help him or her learn to control how he or she responds to such events. It is a skill that will come in handy for the rest of your child's life.

More drastic than an upsetting phone call is abduction of a child by the parent. Such an abduction is defined as one parent's removal of children from contact with the other parent without legal authority. According to David Finkelhor and his colleagues at the Family Research Laboratory of the University of New Hampshire, over 350,000 abductions occur annually. One-fourth of these are by the ex-wife (the remaining 75 percent are carried out by the ex-husband). Abduction by the ex-wife usually occurs by simply not returning the child to the father per the custody order. The age of the child is usually between 2 and 3, and both boys and girls are subject to abduction. The most likely time of an abduction is during separation before the actual divorce when feelings of anger, bitterness, and revenge are high. However, some abductions occur over 2 years after a divorce. About half of the abductions have lasted between 2 and 7 days. Almost all (98%) of the children were returned or recovered.[7]

Social workers Rebecca Hegar and Geoffrey Grief of the University of Maryland at Baltimore conducted in-depth interviews of eight mothers and nine fathers who had abducted their children and found that the primary reason for the abduction was dissatisfaction with the court system in "doing what was right" about providing access to the child. Other reasons were feeling that the child was abused or neglected, wanting to rear the abducted child with his or her siblings, or responding to a request from the child.[8] One father said that his son told him flatly that he did not want to live with his mother but rather with his dad. Although abduction is an alternative to getting access to your children, I do not recommend this course. It means going against a court order and that is contempt of court. When a parent takes the child out of town, the consequences for the children may be enormous—not only is the child deprived of the other parent, but he or she is also separated from familiar surroundings such as home, toys, school, and neighborhood. Particularly upsetting to children is when they are taken to another country. Although such abductions are rare, Professors Hegar and Grief, in their study of parental abduction of children from interracial and cross-cultural marriages, noted that some parents want to reexpose their children to their own cultural roots.[9] Being uprooted to another culture can be very difficult for a child.

Should your child be abducted, be aware that the likelihood of your child being returned in a short while is very high. However, if you don't know where the child has been abducted to, and fear for the child's safety, the police are not likely to be of much help. Sociologist Peggy Plass and her colleagues studied police response to family abductions and noted:

> Although parents may call police for rational reasons, this does not mean that police do what parents expect or that parents end up feeling satisfied with how the police handled their cases. Indeed, one of the key issues surrounding po-

lice intervention in family crime in general is failure of law enforcement officers to treat these offenses like similar crimes involving nonfamily members.[10]

What you *should* do is call your attorney and get advice on how to handle the situation. In general, you will need to go back to court to get the judge to issue a court order that such abduction is not to be repeated or you get full custody.

Although your former wife is not likely to abduct your children, she will probably try to get sole custody of your children if she is angry or bitter. Part of her reason may be to punish you by keeping the children from you, but she may have other reasons.

If the husband or father has been abusive to the wife or children, she may want to protect them from further harm by getting sole custody. By cutting down on the amount of time the children are actually with their father, she feels she can reduce their exposure to abuse. Should the children be at such risk, the mother should discuss this issue with her attorney and/or social services and do what is necessary to prevent any abuse.

Other mothers want custody because it gives them the freedom to move away with the children. In 1996, the California Supreme Court said that once a custodial parent has been identified, that parent has the right to relocate and to change the residence of the child without having to prove that the move is "necessary." Rather, the noncustodial parent, usually the father, has the burden to prove to the court that the move will be detrimental to the child. If the parents have joint custody, it is much more difficult for either parent to move away and take the child. Hence, a joint custody arrangement is the father's best protection for ensuring that his ex does not move away with his children.

Still other mothers want sole custody because they feel they can keep the father at bay while they remarry and establish their new families. The less the divorced father is involved, the more easily she thinks she can get her children to bond with their new stepdad and new patterns of authority and loyalty can be established. In effect, she wants to cut the father out and start over.

Even in those cases where visitation is not a matter of dispute, the practical details can be difficult for many former spouses. Examining this issue, researcher Sharlene Wolchik and her colleagues studied former spouses a year after they filed for divorce. Almost half of the fathers complained that their former wives changed the planned visitation on short notice. For example, the father would show up Friday afternoon to find a note on the door stating that the mother had taken the children out of town. A similar percentage of fathers said that their children were not ready to leave on schedule and that they (the dads) had gotten used to waiting in the car. In anticipation of such delays, some even brought reading material to pass the time while their ex lingered with the children. Four of ten divorced fathers also reported that their former wives were not cooperative when the schedule needed to be changed. Indeed, about 50 percent said they argued about the visitation.[11]

One year after filing for divorce, former wives were even more critical of their ex. Some felt that their ex's were bad role models, used bad language, and exposed their children to people they did not approve of. Others felt their ex-husbands spoiled the children.

> He lets them get away with anything . . . like stay up late, and no homework, and watching whatever they want on TV. So when they come home after a weekend with Mr. Fun Fun, they act like they are in prison when I insist that they need to brush their teeth. It takes several days for them to get straightened out and about that time it's time for them to go back and get messed up again.[12]

Over 70% of the former wives said that their children were more difficult to manage on returning from visiting their father. If this is a problem between you and your ex, all you can do is try to remain consistent with the kids' discipline when they are with you. In time, the kids will realize that there are now two homes and two sets of rules. Make it clear to them that when they are at mom's, what she says goes!

TAKE THE HIGH GROUND WHEN POSSIBLE

It is easy to be polite and cooperative when your former wife is acting the same way toward you. But, when she deliberately tries to turn your children against you or to prevent you from being with them, you may tighten your jaw and seek revenge. Don't. Take the high ground. Do so because to respond in kind is to escalate the conflict. If you yell back at her when she yells that you are late returning the children, the yelling won't stop. Rather, meet her accusations with "I'm sorry," which allows her to "win" and diffuses her anger.

It is also important that you help your children honor their mother on Mother's Day and other such observances, even if you know that she will not help them honor Father's Day. Take them to buy a card and a gift for her.

Kids love to give presents, and may feel inadequate if they have nothing to give. Moreover, your participation will make it clear that you support the relationship your children have with their mother and want them to be comfortable around you when making references to her. So often children feel as though they can't even mention the name of one parent for fear that the other parent will be upset. Make it easy for your children to love their mother and to talk about her in a positive way. You win by their being comfortable around you.

As an aside, don't tolerate their being critical of their mother. Take their mother's side and defend her. For example, if your children say, "How could she be so dumb as to do that?" your response should be, "She had her reasons. Forgive your mother. She loves and cares about you." The issue is to try to ensure that your children continue to have a good relationship with one of the most important people in their lives—their mother.

Also implied in the "take the high ground" theme is that you never attack your former wife—even though you may feel that she deserves it. Let your lawyer go after her if she is violating your rights as a father. For example, if she refuses to let you talk to your children or to see them or has taken them out of town on your weekend, call your attorney and get your ex into court where the judge may hold her in contempt. The trouble with your attacking her is that she can use such attacks to further distance you from your children. For example, she can haul you into court, have her lawyer make you look like a monster, and have the judge cut your visitation time in half. Alternatively, he or she can order that you may only see your children "under supervision." If you must be aggressive with your former wife, do it through an attorney.

Along those same lines, you should be careful not to threaten your former wife, as she may use this against you. Simply view any attacks she makes on you as ploys to get you to lose your cool. You can only win by maintaining your cool. Divorce is a very bitter time for both the husband and the wife. Both usually say and do things they later regret. Rather than harbor resentment toward your ex, forgive her—and yourself. Turn the page on your experience and look ahead.

COMMUNICATING WITH YOUR FORMER WIFE

Establishing good communication with your former spouse is one of the best things you can do for yourself and your children. Good communication requires that both you and she acknowledge that your roles as spouses are over. Such roles involved talking about the details of your lives—what you did today, your thoughts, feelings, and so forth—but such sharing is no longer appropriate. These details should only be shared with other adults or new partners.

A problem arises when only one spouse wants to get back together. That spouse will normally continue such intimate talk in the hope of maintaining closeness. If your ex-wife wants to get back together and you do not, avoid such conversations. For example, if your spouse asks you questions such as "Do you think of me sometimes?" and "Have you ever thought of us getting back together?" be very direct and do not hold out hope if there is none. A response might be: "'Have I ever thought of getting back together' is not an OK topic for discussion." And "No, I have no interest in getting back together. We are better apart." Make it clear that there is no hope for a reconciliation.

The end of your role as spouses does not mean you cannot or should not talk about issues related to your children. Indeed, good communication between the divorcing spouses is one factor for joint custody. Anything that relates to them—their medical, social, emotional, educational, and religious well-being—is a potential topic for discussion. Keep the dialogue focused on the children, however. The danger comes when the content veers from the children and becomes an argument between the two of you that is focused on your relationship. Some former spouses can have a cup of coffee at a restaurant and discuss their children with ease. Other spouses bristle at the mere sight of each other. If it is the case that you and your wife have a hateful relationship, it would be best to stay away from face-to-face contact and monitor yourself very carefully when you must see each other.

Phone calls usually are little help to embittered spouses. They feel it is just as difficult to talk with each other on the phone as it is to talk face to face. Written agreements covering most issues such as visitation schedules, child support, and medical bills help reduce the number of problems the couple experiences later. Most formal separation agreements and divorce decrees spell out the responsibilities of each spouse. The more detailed such a document, the fewer times spouses have to interact with each other. Should you need to communicate with your former spouse about a change in schedule or whatever, a letter may be the best way. It should be clear, direct, and polite with no cute remarks ("Hi honey") or barbs ("I'm sure you won't agree to this"). Sign it "Sincerely."

WHEN YOUR FORMER SPOUSE ABANDONS THE CHILDREN

The publicity about deadbeat dads so permeates the culture that there is rarely a thought of mothers who abandon their children. Although rare, it does occur. Should this apply in your case, your children may feel very angry and depressed having been abandoned by their mother. Children are confused, question why their mother left them, and are often unable to find acceptable answers. They are left with feelings of rejection and take it personally in the sense of feeling that they must not be any good, for otherwise their mother would have loved and stayed with them.

The role of the divorced father is to be empathetic with the confusion and bewilderment of their children without attacking or blaming their mother. Words to the children might be: "Some mothers and fathers are this way. The important thing is for you to know that you are wonderful sons and daughters and that her leaving had nothing to do with you." Experts who study this issue note that abandonment is a problem of the parent and not a deficit in the child. It is important that your children understand this.

Some children benefit from talking, so make sure they know that it is OK to be sad and to talk about their mom. You might prompt them by asking, "Do you ever think about your mom? What do you think and how do you feel about her?" Your response to their talking about their mom should be empathetic. "You really miss your mom and feel hurt that she left" is an example of a response you might make when your children express sadness over the mom they never see any more. Don't try to explain why she left if you don't know. You might say, "I don't really know."

Although your children's mom may have abandoned them, it is unlikely that her parents no longer care for their grandkids. Grandparents usually love seeing their grandchildren and you should encourage and support that relationship by making your children available to spend time with their grandmom and granddad. To be loved and cared for by their grandparents takes some of the sting out of their feeling rejected by their mother. It is also possible that the grandparents have been abandoned by their daughter so that your children have something in common with their grandparents.

Some children cannot get beyond the obsession they have with their mother who abandoned them (and the same happens when dad abandons). They become depressed and develop very low self-concepts. Some start to think of suicide. Should your child reveal any of these symptoms, schedule an appointment with a psychiatrist or psychologist. Your child's mental health is too important to look the other way and hope that serious problems resolve by themselves.

POSTDIVORCE PREVENTION PROGRAMS FOR DIVORCED SPOUSES

Some communities offer crisis prevention programs for spouses who are going through a divorce. Professionals meet with a group of divorced spouses 2 hours a week over a 5-week period. Professor Cheryl Buehler and her colleagues in the Department of Child and Family Studies at the University of Tennessee in Knoxville asked spouses who had participated in one such program to identify those aspects that were the most helpful. Over 50 percent said that the section on "keeping the children out of the middle" was the most helpful part of the program. Specifically, alerting parents not to use their children to get personal information about the other parent, not to try to get their children to side with them or against the other parent, and not to say bad things about the other parent greatly improved their children's well-being in adjusting to the divorce.[13]

Other aspects of the postdivorce programs found to be helpful were "helping the children deal with their feelings," "dealing with one's own feelings," "identifying ways to cope," and "accepting that you and the former spouse have different values/parenting styles." It is important to accept that you cannot change your former spouse's values and that what she does with your children (within limits) is her business. Taking them to church or not, vacationing in another state, or taking them on whitewater camping trips are issues over which spouses may disagree. Take the position that, just as you do not want any interference in what you do with your children when they are with you, it is important to give that same respect to your former wife about how she chooses to spend her time with the children. In one sense, your children will benefit. If you were still married, your children would be exposed to a more or less uniform set of values and lifestyle. Now that you are separated, your children can have more varied experiences and increase their exposure to the real world of different values and lifestyles. Inevitably, both former spouses must adjust to the fact that each will make choices the other does not approve of.

CONCLUSION

The relationship with your former wife is the most important factor in determining how your children adjust to the divorce. If she wanted out and initiated the divorce, she is likely to feel guilty and will be very cooperative about your being with your children. But if you wanted the marriage to end and she did not, she may blame you for her loneliness as a single parent and seek revenge by taking your money, turning your children against you, and keeping them from you.

In dealing with your former wife, always take the high ground. Return rudeness with politeness, kindness for accusations. Avoid threatening her. If she is crossing the line legally in terms of denying you access to your children, consult with your attorney, and get her into court. A judge will stop her far more effectively with legally binding sanctions than you can with threats and bitterness.

Attempt to Mediate Your Differences with Your Former Wife

Agree, for the law is costly.
English proverb

As I emphasized in the last chapter, experts agree that the single most important factor in the adjustment of your children to divorce is the relationship you have with their mother. Ex-spouses who are able to resolve their differences amicably and who continue to interact cooperatively help protect their children from the negative consequences of divorce. Under such conditions, divorce need not be a traumatic event for children.

An important factor affecting your postdivorce relationship with your former spouse is whether you resolve your differences through mediation or litigation. Litigation will quite likely devastate what little civility remains in your relationship. Alternatively, hiring one divorce mediator who emphasizes your mutual cooperation will help keep things from getting nasty. Not only may you and your ex remain capable of discussing future parenting issues in a friendly way, your children will benefit from observing your positive interaction.

DIVORCE MEDIATION

In divorce mediation, a couple sits down with a neutral third party, or mediator, to negotiate various issues relevant to ending their marriage. Mediated negotiations center around three main concerns: (1) child custody and visitation, (2) division of property/assets, and (3) spousal support (alimony). The amount of child support one parent is to pay the other might also be discussed but must be within the guidelines determined by the state. The mediator meets with both spouses together and guides them as they discuss and settle these issues in a way that is satisfactory to both of them. Divorcing spouses who want to try to mediate their differences have two options: hire a divorce mediator or use a free divorce mediator supplied by the court or by a local nonprofit mediation center.

Mediation agreements become legal and binding once a judge signs the agreement. Most judges like mediation because it means one less couple tying up the court's time and shows that the couple can work out their differences. Judges also feel that parents are best able to make decisions about their children and are relieved that they (the judges) do not have to do so. Some states such as California require mediation for divorcing couples.

Divorce Mediation Is Not Marriage Therapy

For all the good that mediation can do toward preserving a working relationship between you and your ex-wife, it is important to keep in mind that mediation is *not* marriage therapy. The spouses do meet with the same mediator at the same time, but the agenda is on settling the issues of the divorce, not getting the spouses back together. Sometimes (about 5 percent of the time), divorcing couples decide during the first meeting with the mediator that they want to give their marriage one more try before ending it. In such cases, the mediator refers the couple to a marriage therapist, where the goal is to reunite as a couple.

It also sometimes happens that one spouse is in agony and may not want a divorce. When this happens, mediation stops and the mediator refers this spouse to a therapist to work on his or her grief surrounding the end of the marriage. When both spouses accept that the marriage will end, the mediation may resume. Mediation requires that both parties acknowledge that the marriage is over and that the task at hand is resolving the issues of custody, visitation, child support, division of property, and alimony.

Divorce Mediation Is Not Adjudication

Adjudication means that a judge listens to both sides and makes a decision for both spouses. The problem with this action is that the judge is a stranger to the spouses, their relationship, and children and may be at a disadvantage by deciding what is best after hearing evidence, testimony, and witnesses over a 3-day period. It is also likely that the judge may make a very informed decision. Nevertheless, adjudication takes the power away from the spouses, who should be making the decisions themselves—decisions that will affect them and their children. Finally, what the judge says, goes. The spouses must do what the judge says and cannot change the order without making a new agreement and filing that with the court.

Divorce Mediation Is Not Arbitration

Arbitration involves a third party (arbitrator) making a decision after listening to both sides of the issue. Arbitration is like adjudication except that the person making the decision is not a judge and the decision is not binding unless the couple wants it to be. That is, no matter what is written in the court order, the ex-spouses can do as they wish as long as they mutually agree. Arbitration is usually much quicker and less expensive than adjudication, but still not as good as mediation in terms of saving time and money and giving the couple control over the final decision. However, only division of property can be arbitrated. Custody or child support cannot be arbitrated.

Mediators have special training in helping spouses resolve conflict and in mediating their differences. Some are attorneys, others are mental health professionals, and still others are social workers. Some work alone and others work as a team so that you and your spouse might be seen by two mediators at the same time. Mediators may also specialize in what they do. Some specialize in custody and visitation and others in financial mediation. Select your mediator with regard to your specific needs as a divorcing couple.

Appendix IV lists mediators who are members of the Association of Family and Concilation Courts. They specialize in custody issues. Alternatively, to find out who does divorce mediation in your area, look under "mediation" or "divorce mediation" in the yellow pages of your phone book or call the Academy of Family Mediators (see Appendix V) and ask for a mediator in your area. You may have trouble locating a mediator but it is worth the time and trouble. The benefits of mediation are enormous.

BENEFITS OF DIVORCE MEDIATION

The more conflict that surrounds the end of your marriage, the worse it is for you and your children. Amy Koel of the Work and Family Research Unit of the University of Massachusetts–Boston and her colleagues studied

700 divorcing couples who fought it out in court. They concluded that the legal system sets up winners and losers—one parent "wins" custody of the children and the other parent "loses." The one who loses is labeled the "noncustodial" parent (usually the father). What should be happening is that the parents *agree* on how they will share child care responsibilities, but the legal system thinks in terms of winners and losers.

Mediation helps prevent the spouses from becoming bitter enemies. In court, divorce cases can become very nasty. Spouses often say things to hurt each other when they are ending their marriage. But the legal system makes it worse when "her" lawyer calls him names on the stand and insinuates he was a terrible husband and a worse father. "His" lawyer will shoot back by attacking her on the stand so that she looks bad. Neither spouse wins. Both are humiliated and hate each other even more for having participated in the legal process. Because domestic court is open to spectators in some states, anyone who wants to attend your custody battle may be able to do so. And because such hearings often become occasions to belittle the spouses, the airing of allegations of violence, drug abuse, and sexual indiscretions is likely to be exploited by both sides in this legal arena. Mediation, in contrast, happens behind closed doors and permits no public exposure.

Spouses who mediate their differences sit together with a third person to discuss and resolve the issues of whom the children will live with and how they will be taken care of. Such a discussion is not easy but it may be a better alternative than an expensive court fight. The money spent in court cannot be divided and used by the spouses and their children.

Mediation protects the future relationship of the ex-partners as parents. Spouses who end their marriage still need to continue to cooperate in parenting their children for years to come. Spouses who have mediated their differences and who remain friends have protected their relationship so that they can talk amicably the next time there is an issue related to the children. Spouses who have destroyed their relationship by becoming legal adversaries must resort to talking to each other through lawyers. Not only is this expensive, it is unsatisfactory. Mediation keeps the lines open between the parents. This is best for their children.

Mediation also helps the partners develop good communication and negotiation skills. In the absence of such skills, parents may yell and blame each other for problems with their children. Learning how to listen reflectively, staying on one issue at a time, and making a specific agreement to resolve that issue are important communication skills. Also, when the parents disagree, a spirit of compromise prevails. It is more important that the parents maintain their amicable relationship and "win" as a couple than that one parent "wins" the disagreement. Mediation maintains the focus that coming to an agreement and remaining friends are more important than winning any specific point.

Mediation gives parents the skills to stay jointly involved in their children's lives and to share the work of parenting. Ex-spouses who are at war cannot discuss anything about their children so they avoid each other. But former spouses who have mediated their divorce are usually more comfortable discussing and negotiating issues related to their children. They continue to cooperate over religious, educational, health, and other issues related to their children, and the less parental conflict your children are exposed to, the better.

Spouses who litigate their divorce are often shocked to find out how much it costs and surprised to know that an inexpensive alternative exists. According to divorce mediator D. Neumann, author of *Divorce Mediation: How to Cut the Cost and Stress of Divorce*, mediated divorces cost about $1000 versus $12,000 (or higher) if the couple have to go to court and fight over custody and dividing their property.[1] The money the parents save by mediating their differences can go toward enhancing the lifestyles of their children. They can also avoid both mediation and litigation by developing their own agreement (consistent with state guidelines) and filing the agreement with the court themselves.

Divorce mediation takes an average of 2 to 3 months, versus 2 to 3 years for a litigated divorce. But there are exceptions. One divorced father is in the seventh year of a litigated divorce at a cost of $40,000 to date.

Mediation is less time-consuming and costly in yet another way. Amy Koel and colleagues' study of 700 divorcing couples who had children and who did not use mediation showed that 40 percent returned to court to relitigate an issue—most often child support. Spouses who mediate their divorces are much less likely to need to return to court. Because mediation involves their discussing the issues and arriving at their own agreements, each partner is likely to feel comfortable with the agreements. In studies comparing spouses who mediated versus litigated their divorces, those who mediated reported greater overall satisfaction.[2] Mediators Marlow and Sauber, in *The Handbook of Divorce Mediation*, report that children adjust better to divorce when their parents have used mediation. This comes as no surprise, as mediated divorces involve much less conflict than litigated ones. An 11-year-old whose parents mediated their divorce said:

I never heard my parents talk about lawyers. . . . but they did talk about this mediator who one time had me come into a session and talk about where I would like to live and how often I would like to see the other parent. I told her I wanted to live with both of them and see them about the same. That's what eventually happened.[3]

Here we also see how divorce mediation can be beneficial to children of divorcing parents, as decisions are more likely to be made in the family than in consultation with lawyers.

Because spouses and the mediator draw up the mediated settlement agreement, the spouses can make the agreement much more flexible to meet the changing needs of their children over time. Whereas a document written by lawyers may detail very precisely every minute the children are to be with each parent (this is usually necessary when spouses are not cooperative), the spouses may have a clause in their mediated agreement that allows them to change the agreement by mutual consent. Court orders may also have a similar clause.

In addition to all of these benefits, there are specific benefits to ex-wives in a mediated settlement. Divorced mothers stand to benefit from mediation in two ways. First, there is the obvious help with child rearing. Some former wives who are alienated from their ex-husbands because of messy divorces end up having to do the work of child care, transportation, and supervision by themselves. Unless they have remarried, their bitter relationship with their ex will ensure that they remain true single parents. But former wives who mediate their differences get help with the work of rearing their children.

In addition, former wives who have mediated their divorces receive more predictable child support. The court system sometimes destroys the incentive of men to pay money to their former wives—even though it is for child support. Despite elaborate federal and state regulations designed to get "deadbeat dads" to pay child support, many divorced dads who don't want to pay child support don't. Tough penalties may ruin the father's credit or even cost him his driver's license in some states, but these sanctions in themselves do not force checks from a divorced father who doesn't want to pay.

The primary benefit of divorce mediation for fathers is that they are more likely to end up with greater access to their children. If the woman wants to punish her ex-husband and limit his access to the children, she may be more likely to do so through litigation. He must fight her in court if he wants to continue to be involved in his children's lives. Fathers should jump at the chance to mediate, as they face enormous odds if they go to court. However, both parties should be aware that a mediated settlement produces a "consent order." When the ex-spouses agree to "consent," they lose their right to appeal.

WHEN DIVORCE MEDIATION WILL NOT WORK

Despite the benefits of divorce mediation, it is not for everyone. Divorce mediation requires that both spouses be motivated to mediate rather than litigate their differences. If either the husband or the wife does not want mediation, it will not work. Mediation requires cooperation. Both spouses must be willing to negotiate, to give and take, and to keep the goal of reaching a mutually agreeable settlement above "winning" money or custody or things lawyers are hired to fight for. If the spouses don't cooperate to settle their differences, they'll end up watching their attorneys wage a nasty, time-consuming, and expensive battle reminiscent of the 1990 *War of the Roses* film. Dr. Ken Lewis, director of Child Custody Evaluation Services of Philadelphia, Inc. in Glenside, Pennsylvania, says that "most efforts at custody mediation fail."

Some men have been left by wives who are already involved with new partners. These ex-wives often want as little to do with the father of their children as possible and are in no mood to mediate anything. One mother said that she wanted to start over in her remarriage and the only way she could do that was to get rid of the child's father. Some wives accuse their ex-husbands of child abuse or sexual abuse as a means of putting the father off balance and making any request for time with his children a real struggle. Legal hardball, the subject of the next chapter, is the only alternative to the father who is accused of such charges.

Neither will divorce mediation work if one spouse wants to get back together. Such a goal gives too much power to the other spouse so that the negotiation that takes place is not on fair ground. For example, if you want to reconcile the relationship with your ex-wife, you will probably be willing to agree to most anything in hopes that your doing so will win her back. But, if she has no interest in getting back with you, she may take advantage of your generosity, take everything you have to offer, and still not come back to you. This happened to a divorced father who said, "I signed over everything to her to show that I loved her and wanted her back. She took it all and I never saw her again."

SELF-ASSESSMENT

IS YOUR SITUATION AMENABLE TO DIVORCE MEDIATION?

To determine the degree to which you and your partner are suited for divorce mediation, read each sentence below and circle the appropriate number. The higher the number circled, the more likely the two of you can mediate your differences.

1 = Definitely Not	4 = Mostly Yes
2 = Mostly Not	5 = Definitely Yes
3 = Sometimes	

	DN	MN	S	MY	DY
1. My former wife and I can talk about our differences easily.	1	2	3	4	5
2. It is more important to me that I remain friends with my ex than get everything I want in the divorce settlement.	1	2	3	4	5
3. It is more important to my former wife that she and I remain friends than she get everything she wants in the divorce settlement.	1	2	3	4	5
4. I make my own decisions and don't have to check with my parents or anyone else.	1	2	3	4	5
5. My former wife makes her own decisions and doesn't have to check with anyone else.	1	2	3	4	5
6. It is important to my former spouse that we save money by mediatng rather than litigating our divorce.	1	2	3	4	5
7. It is important to me that we save money by mediating rather than litigating our divorce.	1	2	3	4	5
8. Both my former spouse and I agree that it is important to resolve our differences as soon as possible.	1	2	3	4	5
9. I am not out for revenge in the divorce settlement.	1	2	3	4	5
10. My former wife is not out for revenge in the divorce settlement.	1	2	3	4	5

Add the numbers you have circled. The lowest possible score is 10, which means that you and your partner are not suited for divorce mediation. The highest possible score is 50, which means that you and your spouse will probably be able to mediate your differences. An intermediate score is 30. The higher the score, the more likely divorce mediation will work for the two of you.

Relationships in which the spouses have been abusive toward each other also are not appropriate for mediation. The wife who has been abused by her husband may be afraid of him and negotiate out of fear rather than what she feels is just. Hence, she is disadvantaged. Mediation is designed to serve the interests of both parties so that both are winners and neither becomes a loser.

Sometimes one spouse wants to punish the other. The typical scenario is the ex-wife who feels abandoned by her husband and wants to punish him by taking his money and keeping his children from him. An attorney will help her to achieve her goals; a mediator will not. The latter will insist that punishment and revenge are not acceptable motives for becoming involved in mediation.

Some spouses are not mad at the other, but rather are greedy and want to get all they can in a settlement. Hollywood celebrity Zsa Zsa Gabor once quipped, "I'm an excellent housekeeper. Every time I get divorced, I keep the house." Although mediation does not require that one be overly generous, it thrives best when the partners are not out to take everything. Such a motive works against mediation because the parties must be open and disclosing about all of their finances, assets, and holdings. Spouses who want to get and take everything will stop at nothing (including defrauding the mediator about money and assets). A just and fair settlement is not possible when one of the spouses is hiding information.

Finally, if one spouse is controlled by a parent or new spouse, mediation cannot proceed because the spouse is not free to make decisions. For example, one wife had never developed so as to be able to make decisions without her father's approval. Mediation would not have worked because he, not she, would have dictated the conditions of the settlement.

Despite the potential benefits to be gained by you, your former spouse, and your children, if your partner does not want to mediate the issues of custody, child support, and so forth, you have no alternative but to hire a lawyer to protect yourself. No one will win and everyone will lose but that is the way you must play the game. The self-assessment on page 108 gauges how suited your divorce situation is for mediation.

ISSUES OF DIVORCE MEDIATION

One of the most important issues for spouses who no longer want to live together is how they will continue to take care of their children. Custody typically means which parent the children will live with most of the time.

In more than 70 percent of litigated divorces, the mother gets custody of the children and the father "visits." In the past, most parents agreed that this pattern was best for their children. However, today more divorcing parents are deciding on joint custody, which allows both parents to have equal control of their children. A major advantage of joint custody for divorced fathers is that the mother cannot arbitrarily move away with his children but rather must satisfy certain legal requirements before doing so. Otherwise, she might move the children out of state and make it very difficult for him to see his children. From the point of view of the children, joint custody allows them to continue to have two active parents in their lives. The relationship between the former spouses also benefits. Professors Jessica Pearson and Nancy Thoennes, of the Center for Policy Research in Denver, Colorado, found that former spouses who have joint custody report being more cooperative than those where one has primary custody.[4]

Even though the parents may share joint custody, they may decide that the children will spend more time with the mother. An advantage of mediating a visitation schedule is that the parents fix the schedule the way they want it. Otherwise, the judge may tell the father that he can only see his children every other weekend, alternate holidays, and a month in the summer. There is no best visitation schedule. However, children tend to profit from frequent, regular, and consistent contact with their father. The terminology of custody law in most states is "frequent and continuing contact with both parents."

David Blankenhorn wrote in *Fatherless America* that "a man can be either a visitor or a father, but not both at the same time." He believes that everything possible should be done to avoid becoming the "visitor," as it robs children of sustained involvement with their father. Some fathers feel so distant from their children after being cast in the role of visitor that they stop "visiting" altogether, feeling that they have lost their authority and their place in the family. As Blankenhorn put it, "the children and the mother are in, he is out."[5] Nevertheless, visiting is all that some fathers are allowed and they must make the best of it.

Setting up a visitation schedule should also include time each parent will be with the children on holidays. A typical arrangement is to split a holiday so that each parent can see the children for some portion of the holiday. The same is done for the children's birthdays. Time with both sets of grandparents and extended family should also be discussed. The goal is for the children to have equal access to both sets of parents, grandparents, and extended family.

Some mediators will request a custody evaluation. The custody evaluator meets with the father, mother, child, teachers, and others and makes a recommendation regarding time allocations for the parents to be with the children. In making this recommendation, the evaluator will use the legal definition of "best interests of the child" operative in the state in which the child resides. See Appendix IV for locating a custody evaluator.

The former spouses must also decide how the economic needs of the children will be met. If the spouses go to court, the judge in most states will consider the income of both spouses, the division of property, and the custodial arrangement and will make a determination of the amount each is to pay. In general, because the mother ends up being the custodial parent most of the time (and usually makes less money), the father ends up paying her monthly child support. This is often a percentage of his gross income. In some states, the father of two children ends up giving about 50% of his gross income to his former wife for child support. Judges will use child support guidelines of their state to determine the amount of child support. Spouses who are mediating their own agreement must use these same guidelines.

Unless spouses have been married only a short time, they have accumulated assets they must now divide. This can be done by listing all of the property, cars, equipment (e.g., television sets), bank accounts, stocks, and so forth, assigning a monetary value (appraisers may be needed), and dividing the property. Dividing the property usually takes time. Sometimes, some fathers feel so guilty for leaving their wife and children that they want to give everything to their former spouse. In the short run, this may help to reduce their guilt. But, after a few years, when the divorced father is in a new relationship, he may regret having been so generous with his former spouse, as he now needs these assets and money for his new life. One job of the mediator is to protect both spouses and ensure that there is a fair and equitable distribution of assets so that neither feels "taken advantage of" now or later.

An old term for spousal support is alimony, an amount of money one former spouse (usually the former husband) pays the other (usually the former wife). In the past, alimony was the husband's "punishment" for leaving his wife and was designed to allow her to maintain her standard of living as if the marriage were continuing. But, with the advent of no-fault divorce, alimony is becoming less common. An alternative to "punishment" alimony is rehabilitative alimony in which the husband pays the former wife a certain amount of money that allows her to go back to school or to improve her skills so that she will be capable of earning a good income. Rehabilitative alimony recognizes situations where the wife as mother stayed home with the children while the husband was building his career and developing a high earning potential. Such alimony gives her a base income so that she can build her own earning potential. Rehabilitative alimony is usually awarded for a specific period of time.

Mediation may also involve discussing other issues. These include the special case of time with teenagers. Because of their need to be with their peers (which is good for their social development), it is important for parents to be flexible about their children. Teenagers 14 (sometimes younger) and up should be consulted about what they would like regarding spending time with their parents. At issue is a good relationship, and forcing a 14-year-old to visit dad for a month in the summer, when the dad will be at work most of the time, is nonsense. Better the teen bring a friend or stay for a shorter period of time. The point is to involve the teen in the discussion.

Parents might also discuss the transportation, health care, religious, and educational needs of their children. What each of these needs involves and how the parents will cooperate in meeting the needs should be decided. Parental understandings about each of these issues should be a part of the written agreement between the spouses.

RULES DIVORCE MEDIATORS PLAY BY

Divorce mediators have certain guidelines they follow when mediating with spouses about their divorce. Most mediators try to move the negotiations toward what is best for the child. What determines "best interests of the child" is identified in both statutory (Wisconsin has 14 such criteria) and case law. Knowledge of these laws, child development, and feelings of the child are all important in deciding how the ex-spouses will share the parenting of their children. Both the mediator and parents may want to ask a custody evaluator to make a recommendation. Although each former spouse may want sole custody of the children with the goal of cutting the other parent out, the mediator will usually make it clear that it is in the best interest of the children to have both parents in their lives. Some mediators will call off mediation if the spouses cannot reach an agreement that protects the access of the children to both parents.

It is also in the best interest of the children to see their parents interacting in a polite and cooperative way. The mediator will do whatever he or she can to encourage such a pattern of interaction. Indeed, mediation itself provides an excellent context in which ex-spouses can learn to interact positively. Some mediators involve children in mediation sessions to discuss specific issues and to observe their parents negotiate.

Finally, the mediator will encourage the parents to only talk positively about each other to their children. Such talk also allows the children to feel comfortable making positive remarks to one parent about the other parent. Otherwise, children feel they have to hide a part of themselves (the part that enjoys the other parent) from each parent.

The mediator is on the side of the child, not on the side of either parent. Unlike a lawyer who owes his or her allegiance to the paying client, the mediator is on the side of the *agreement*—one that is fair to each spouse. To protect their neutrality, most mediators only meet with the two parties simultaneously. This prevents the mediator from developing secrets with either spouse, which might occur if there were meetings with only one party. Occasionally, mediators will ask to meet alone (called "caucusing") with one partner to discuss a particular issue, especially when that spouse has taken an unreasonable position that threatens the success of the mediation.

Whereas lawyers are concerned with what they can get for their clients without regard to what is fair, mediators focus on an agreement that is fair for both parties. Such fairness can only occur if each party openly discloses all information to the other. Secret bank accounts, stock holdings, and the like are designed to cheat the other out of something. The mediator makes it clear early in the first session that openness is expected and ends the mediation if he or she discovers that one of the spouses is not providing full disclosure.

Because mediation involves a number of issues the mediator may not be skilled in, he or she may ask the parties to consult other professionals. For example, an accountant can provide answers to the tax consequences of dividing up the property in a certain way. The tax consequences of child support and alimony are clear. Child support is considered nontaxable income to the parent who receives it although the parent who pays it cannot deduct it as an expense. In contrast, alimony is taxable income to the spouse who receives it but a deductible expense to the spouse who pays it.

Attorneys also should be involved in mediation in an advisory role. Each parent needs an attorney to advise him or her about what topics to cover and to later review the agreement. As with any legally binding agreement, you shouldn't sign anything without first having your attorney check it over. To do so is to potentially lock oneself into a lifetime financial obligation. Consider the father who agreed to set up an enormous trust fund for his children's education. He later discovered that the payments were breaking him. He had signed the document because he felt guilty leaving his children and wanted to "make it up to them." He later asked his ex-wife to lower the amount he was to pay each month. She refused. He then petitioned the court to have the amount lowered. The court refused. Today, he is still paying.

Because the parents will feel most free to discuss and negotiate with each other if they know that what they say will not later be used against them, the mediator will ask the parents to sign a document. Such a document states that should mediation not be successful and the couple goes to court, they will not allow their attorneys to subpoena the mediator or any records resulting from the mediation for use in any legal action.

EXAMPLE OF AN AGREEMENT COUPLES SIGN BEFORE MEDIATION BEGINS

This is an agreement between the divorcing couple and their mediator, Caroline Schacht of Greenville, North Carolina:

As the divorcing couple, we agree to the following:

1. Each of us has decided to get a divorce and neither of us wants to try to reconcile the relationship nor to get back together.

2. The welfare of our children is our most important goal and we understand that this is the goal of our mediator.

3. Each of us will make complete and open disclosure of our income, assets, and debts to the mediator.

4. Each of us will have our own attorney advise us and review the final "memorandum of agreement" (written up by the mediator) before we sign the document.

5. Neither of us has a relationship with the mediator that we feel will bias him or her in guiding the mediation.

6. Each of us agrees not to subpoena or empower our attorneys to subpoena the mediator or any records resulting from the mediation for subsequent legal action.

7. Each of us agrees to pay half of the mediator's fee at the rate of _____ per hour.

8. Either of us or the mediator may terminate the mediation at any time.

This agreement is signed by us and our mediator.

Former spouse _____ Mediator_____

Former spouse _____ Date _____

EXAMPLE OF A MEDIATED AGREEMENT

The following is an example of a mediated agreement worked out by Caroline Schacht and the parents of an only child.

Mary Smith and John Smith were married on March 12, 1975, and have one child, Mike (age 12). Mary and John sought mediation to resolve the issues of parenting and child support, division of property, and spousal support.

Parenting Plan and Child Support

1. Physical Custody and Visitation

The couple will have joint physical custody with Mike staying at Mary's as his primary residence. John is to pick up Mike Friday at 5:30 PM and return him Sunday at 8 PM every other weekend beginning the first weekend in August. (The details of holidays, birthdays, summer, and school breaks were also spelled out in detail in this agreement. See Appendix II and Kidmate in Appendix V for how these issues may be detailed.) Mary agrees to be supportive of their time together.

2. Legal Custody

John and Mary agree that they will have joint legal custody of Mike so that they may both participate in his medical, educational, religious, etc. decisions regarding their son.

3. Tax Exemptions

John and Mary agree that John will claim Mike as a tax exemption as long as either of them may do so (usually through age 23).

4. Health Insurance

John agrees to carry Mike on his health insurance policy. Mary agrees to pay for all medical, dental, eye, and other health care needs of Mike until she has paid an amount equal to what John has had to pay to keep Mike on his health insurance. After that amount is met, now about $1500 annually, the couple will split the expenses.

5. College Education

John agrees to pay 80% of the published costs of attending any state-supported school Mike elects to attend for four years. Such expenses are related to food, housing, tuition, fees, and books. Mary agrees to pay 20%. This agreement is contingent on Mike maintaining at least a B average and working full time every summer.

6. Child Support

John agrees to pay Mary $800 per month in child support for Mike until he reaches age 18. This money will be paid by automatic draft of John's checking account to Mary's checking account on the 10th of the month.

7. Spousal Support

Since Mary worked while John went to school during the early days of their marriage, John agrees to pay Mary $200 per month every month Mary is enrolled as a full-time student pursuing a degree in nursing or social work for up to four years.

Division of Property

1. Marital Residence

John and Mary agree that Mary will remain in the marital residence until Mike leaves for college at age 18. At that time the house will be sold and the profits divided equally. Either party may buy out the other should they wish to do so.

2. Beach Cottage

The couple own a cottage at the beach conservatively valued at $120,000. They agree to sell the property and divide the profits equally after the balance of the mortgage is paid. They further agree to share equally in any expenses related to the sale of the house, including but not limited to a realtor's fee and house preparation/repairs.

3. Retirement

John and Mary agree that Mary is entitled to half of John's retirement (Mary has no retirement funds of her own). The value of John's retirement fund will be based on its value as of the date legal separation papers were signed. This amount is $180,000.

4. Life Insurance

The couple have two insurance policies valued at $68,000. They agree to cash these in and split the money equally.

5. Household Property

Since Mary will remain in the house with Mike, Mary will regard most of the household property as hers. The exception is the television in the couple's bedroom along with his clothes, hunting guns, duck decoys, and boat.

Future Mediation

Both John and Mary agree that if they have any future disputes or desire any modifications of this agreement, they will attend at least one mediation session to try to resolve the issues before initiating any legal action.

CONCLUSION

Divorcing spouses should consider consulting a mediator before they contact a lawyer. Mediation allows the parents to control the process and terms of their divorce. Otherwise, a judge with limited exposure to the couple and their children will make legally binding decisions that will affect their family forever. Couples who mediate their divorce report much greater satisfaction than couples who litigate their divorce. Not only do spouses learn how to resolve their conflicts themselves (thus saving them time and money they would pay to lawyers), their children benefit by being around parents who are amicable and cooperative.

Not all couples can mediate their differences. Couples in which one spouse still wants to be married, one spouse abuses the other, or one spouse is controlled by a parent or new spouse are not suited for mediation. For couples who can profit from mediation, the mediator will require that both parents be open and disclosing about their finances, that they agree not to subpoena the mediator or records for any subsequent court hearing, and that they be civil toward each other around their children. The goal of mediation is to arrive at a just and fair agreement about how the children will be cared for (physically and economically), whom the children will live with for how long each week, and whether, how much one parent will provide money for the other in terms of child or spousal support.

8

Settle Your Differences in Court if You Must

> Now is not the time to be cheap.
>
> *Manual*, National Congress for Fathers and Children

In John Ford's *The Quiet Man*, John Wayne plays an ex-boxer who wants to quit fighting. During the film, the Duke is pushed to his limit and eventually has to fight again. Similarly, many divorced fathers don't want to fight but feel compelled to do so to protect their relationship with their children. One divorced father asked, "Why do I have to beg my wife to see more of my child?"

Most men who leave their wives have no intention of leaving their children. They expect to be treated in a way that best serves the interests of the children—to share their children with their mother, which means to have fair and reasonable access to them. However, because some ex-wives are out to punish the father and keep the children from him, legal hardball can become his only option if his goal is to stay connected with his children. Dr. Warren Farrell, a strong advocate for father's rights, said at the 1996 National Congress for Fathers and Children that the right of men to parent their children will be the twenty-first century's equivalent of this century's rights of women in the workplace.[1] In the meantime, you may need an attorney.

LEGAL HARDBALL DOS AND DON'TS

Once you decide that the two of you are not capable of resolving your differences and that a mediator is not an option, you must change the way you see your situation and your spouse. You are no longer married in a castle by

| SELF-ASSESSMENT |

How Likely Are You to Have to Fight It Out in Court?

To gauge how likely you are to need an attorney to settle your divorce differences, read each sentence below and circle the appropriate number. The higher the number circled, the more you will need to litigate your differences.

1 = Definitely Not	4 = Mostly Yes
2 = Mostly Not	5 = Definitely Yes
3 = Sometimes	

	DN	MN	S	MY	DY
1. The relationship with my former wife is bitter and acrimonious.	1	2	3	4	5
2. My former wife and I disagree on the amount of child support I should pay.	1	2	3	4	5
3. My former wife and I disagree on the division of our property.	1	2	3	4	5
4. My former wife and I disagree on whether I should pay alimony.	1	2	3	4	5
5. One of us wants to punish the other one in court.	1	2	3	4	5
6. My former wife and I argue whenever we talk.	1	2	3	4	5
7. My former wife and I are no longer friends.	1	2	3	4	5
8. My former wife and I disagree over who should have custody of our child(ren).	1	2	3	4	5
9. My former wife and I don't feel mediation is an option for us.	1	2	3	4	5
10. Either my former wife or I think we can get a better deal in court than through mediation.	1	2	3	4	5

Add the numbers you have circled. The lowest possible score is 10, which means that you will probably be able to resolve your differences without lawyers. The highest possible score is 50, which means that you will need to play legal hardball because your former wife will use the legal system against you. An intermediate score is 30. The higher your score, the greater is your chance of needing an attorney.

the sea, but are heading into divorce court with an adversary who is out to wreck you. There are certain steps you should take to protect yourself.

Do Your Homework

Chapter 1 discussed the importance of your reading statutory and case law regarding custody in your state and building a file folder for your attorney. Do not depend on an attorney to know this material but give it to him or her to master after you have decided to hire that attorney.

Hire a Domestic Attorney

After doing your homework, hire a domestic attorney. Lawyer bashing is fashionable in our society, and some of them deserve it. But there are attorneys who are skilled in their profession, who ask a fair price for their services, and who will try to use the law to your benefit. Because divorce and custody and child support are all legal issues, in most cases, you need an attorney. Even if you mediate these issues with your former spouse, you *should* hire an attorney to read the agreement. Your lawyer can be your best friend and asset in your divorce proceeding. But choose wisely. Ideally, the domestic lawyer you want specializes in representing divorced fathers and has an established track record in winning favorable settlements for these fathers in terms of custody, division of property, spousal support, and visitation.

With few attorneys specializing in divorced fathers, you are not likely to find one. Finding one who specializes in domestic cases is more likely and you should hold out for one with this specialty. Appendix IV provides a listing of domestic attorneys by state and country who are members of the Association of Family and Conciliation Courts. You might also consult the yellow pages of your phone book under "Lawyers" for "Family Law, Board Certified" attorneys and talk with divorced-father friends for their recommendations.

Domestic law, the law that will affect you and your divorce, is specific to each state. If you have moved to another state, an attorney in your new state will not be knowledgeable about the domestic law in the state where your divorce proceedings will be held. There are enormous differences between states with regard to the laws governing custody and divorce. For example, in about 15 states (Pennsylvania is one), spouses can go to court over custody of their children even though they are not interested in getting divorced.

Called "bifurcation" because the issues of custody and divorce are kept separate, there are two separate court systems. As a divorced father you must inform yourself of the custody laws in your state and try to hire an attorney who has litigated cases in your state.

Ask prospective attorneys to identify specific training they have had that makes them specialists in family law in the state in which the divorce will be held, the names of any professional organizations they belong to, how many divorced fathers they have represented, and the outcomes of several cases that have been to court. It's your money you will be spending, and the average cost of a contested divorce is about $12,000.

Most attorneys offer an initial consultation at no cost. Interview at least two attorneys. In addition to their being a specialist in domestic law, make sure that they offer a refundable retainer. Lawyers charge between $100 and $300 an hour and many require a retainer or up-front money. A contested custody fight will require about 100 hours, and thus the total cost will be between $10,000 and $30,000. Most charge 10 to 15 percent of this as a retainer, requiring that you have between $1000 and $3000 up-front money. Because you want to get your money's worth, make sure that your attorney offers a refundable retainer in case he or she withdraws from your case or you become dissatisfied. Otherwise, you have lost your money and will have to start over. You should also expect monthly statements detailing what your attorney has done for you day by day and the cost of his or her time. It is your responsibility to keep payments current. Should you not have money to hire an attorney, contact the legal aid society in your community and identify what resources are available to you.

In the initial interview, discuss the degree to which your attorney will prioritize your case. A specialist who spends no time on your case is no attorney. An attorney who is available to talk with you on the phone (as an attorney and not as a therapist) and to work with you in preparing your case is the attorney you want. Judges are required by legislative statute to make decisions based on the evidence. But your lawyer must invest the time to present the best possible evidence on your behalf.

In the event that you don't find a specialist, or can't afford to hire an attorney, or can't find one who will prioritize your case, you may want to represent yourself (called *pro se*). Although lawyers discourage this, our legal system allows you to do so, which will save you a great deal of money. Fathers in states that bifurcate (or separate) divorce and custody issues can draw up their own custody papers and send them to the court and their spouse. This single act will save you $300 in legal fees.

Don't Use Your Former Spouse's Attorney

It may be tempting to use your spouse's attorney in an attempt to save money. *Don't*. Your spouse's attorney has her, not your, interests in focus and both interests cannot be served. It is unethical for an attorney to represent both the ex-wife and the ex-husband. At the very least, hire your own attorney to review any document your wife asks you to sign. You may be surprised at what you find.

Learn the Language

Appendix I details some legal terms your attorney will be using as you discuss your case. For the two of you to be on the same wavelength about what you want, you should become familiar with the legal terminology.

Sign Nothing Now

As a good general rule, *sign nothing now*. You are too vulnerable. "A signature is not an ornament," says one lawyer. Once you sign, you may not be able to recover from the damage she can do to you for your signature. Eventually, you will sign a court order having a judge's signature and that of the respective attorneys. This is the only document you want to sign unless your attorney (again, a specialist) advises you to do otherwise.

Strike First

If your spouse is unwilling to settle your differences by talking with you or through a mediator, start the first inning of legal hardball. Contact an attorney, tell him or her you want out, and serve your spouse with papers. Beat her to the punch. Researcher Ruth Dixon and her colleague studied husbands who filed for divorce and observed that those who did so were much more likely to be awarded custody.

Stay in the Marital Home

Do not leave the marital home until your attorney tells you to. If you leave before the time is right, it could work against you. Husbands who leave their marital home can be charged with "abandonment," which makes you look like the bad guy who now may owe your former spouse money in the form of "alimony" for leaving her. She may also charge you with abandoning your children to justify her getting custody and huge child support. Stay put until your attorney tells you to move out.

React Quickly

Do not be surprised if a sheriff shows up at your door serving you with papers that give her temporary custody of the children. Translation: You lose legal control. Other court actions against you might be throwing you out of your house or seizing or freezing your assets. Fight such orders immediately. Your attorney will know what to do.

End Your Financial Relationship with Your Spouse

Because in most states one spouse is responsible for the debts of the other, your spouse may be angry at you and go on a shopping spree. The bills will come in later and you are likely to get stuck paying them. One wife went shopping and put $1200 on the credit cards in one weekend. Because her husband had more income and was leaving the marriage, the judge made him pay off all of her debts. Once you decide that the marriage is over, call the number on the back of each credit card and cancel the card and call any stores you have charge accounts with and close those accounts.

Unless you move half of the money out of your joint checking and savings accounts and into a separate account, there will be nothing to stop your wife from taking all of the money out of the joint accounts and it will take you months to get any of it back. Only take half as that is the fair thing to do. Your wife can empty any account that has her name on it, and some wives do. If you and she own anything in common, fix it so that this is no longer the case. Otherwise, if you die, she gets it all. Your lawyer will advise you on this. You should also notify your local Credit Bureau that you and your spouse are no longer jointly responsible for any debts she may incur, and remove any business records from the marital home, preferably placing them in your lawyer's care.

Exercise Caution in Your Personal Life

Now is not the time to take vacations, buy an expensive car, or move into expensive living quarters. Evidence of any affluence can be used against you to get you to pay more child support and/or alimony. And you will need money to pay your attorney!

Although you may have already become involved in a new relationship, do not consider moving in with her. In fact, don't even be seen publicly with her. Judges view such behavior as abandoning responsibility to your wife and children and may punish you with stiff alimony and child support payments (up to 50% of your gross income). In some states, a year's separation is required before the parties can remarry and any involvement with another woman during that 12-month period will be to your disadvantage. Unless your formal separation agreement states that each of you can be with others, doing so can be used against you in court. Being free to date others during the period of separation is commonly referred to as "street legal."

Be Alert to Sex Abuse Charges

One ploy used by divorced women who want full custody of their children and no visitation by their ex-husbands is to charge them with sex abuse. Although making a false charge of child abuse is a misdemeanor offense, few ex-wives are ever prosecuted. Fathers are vulnerable to such a charge by doing anything that can be regarded as suspect by a judge or jurors. Although bathing a 6-year-old or sleeping with one's children can be innocuous parenting behaviors, they can be used against a father by an ex-wife yelling "sex abuser," especially when the child in question is your daughter. So, as a divorced father, you must be aware that your ex-wife is at war with you and that by charging you with sex abuse she may succeed in keeping you away from the children. Be careful.

Gerald Hill, a businessman in San Mateo, California, wrote in his book *Divorced Father* that he was denied joint custody because the child probation officer reported "I suspect child molestation" on the basis of the ex-wife's allegations. Although the charges were completely unfounded, she was successful in temporarily keeping him from his daughter (see Hill's book for the details of a long and bitter postdivorce relationship). Hill noted that any of the following are viewed by the court to fit the "profile" of a child molester: drug abuse, physical violence, few adult friends, rigid authoritarianism, and treating the female child as a mother/homemaker rather than as a child. It took Hill 9 months to get the court to reverse its decision.[2]

Although unfounded charges of physical and emotional neglect can be made by either spouse, the charge that gets the attention of the court is sex abuse. Hill writes:

> But as America knows from experience, intense public fear and indignation can flame into a witch hunt. When every rope looks like a snake, the distinction between innocence and guilt blurs, and all are destroyed. The witch hunt endangers everyone, the hunter and hunted alike.[3]

Of course, sexual abuse is a very serious threat to a child's health, both physically and mentally, so such charges are not to be dismissed lightly. If you suspect that your son or daughter may have been abused while in someone else's care (a stepfather, day-care center, or babysitter), contact your local Department of Child Protective Services, who will put you in touch with medical and psychological professionals who can help in substantiating (or dismissing) the charges. If your child has been abused, he or she will need your help and protection. But you must *not* view the situation as a handy excuse to create suspicion about your ex or her new partner.

Don't Abscond with Your Children

As noted earlier, don't take off with your children without letting your former spouse know where you are going. Otherwise, she can use this (child snatching) against you and a judge can order that you only see your children under supervision.

HOW MUCH LEGAL ACCESS TO YOUR CHILDREN DO YOU WANT?

As a married dad living with your children, access to them was never an issue. As a divorced father, unless the court document specifies that you have access to your children, you have no legal access. It is imperative that you determine the role you want to play in your children's life/development and how much physical access you want to them so that this can be written into a court order to protect your role and access. What role and rights do you want as a father? Some fathers want full-time sole custody, others want joint custody, and still others want their ex-wives to retain custody while they have the traditional visitation of every other weekend, alternate holidays, and so on. Very few fathers want no contact at all. What do you want?

Primary Factors

A number of factors affect the amount of time a father wants to spend with his children and how much time he asks the court to award. An important factor is your children's preferences. How do they feel and what do they want? You might simply ask them how much they would like to be with mom and dad. Most children have a preference for wanting to continue to be with both parents. But you don't want to spend thousands of dollars on an expensive court fight if your children don't want to be with you.

Another factor is dad's work schedule. Some fathers have schedules that do not permit spending much time with their children. One divorced father travels more than 300 miles a day and realizes there is no way he can be responsible for his two kids while he is on the road. Furthermore, he'd rather they remain with their mother, where he feels they'll be better cared for than by a day-care employee or babysitter. Other fathers have flexible jobs (university teachers) and prefer to use this flexibility taking care of their children. One such father has joint custody with his former wife and on the days he does not teach, he has his two daughters with him.

Some activities such as frequent or late-night partying do not lend themselves to responsible parenting. These divorced fathers usually prefer that the children stay with their mother most of the time. Other lifestyles in which the father is remarried, home every night, and enjoys the role of father offer the child a nurturing context. Assess your lifestyle and the degree to which you feel it is compatible with child care and child rearing.

Some new relationships lend themselves to including the kids, whereas others do not. One divorced father said that he wanted his kids with him all of the time, as did his new partner. She also had children and very much wanted his to be with hers so that they could begin to blend their new family. But another father said that his new wife viewed his children as an interference in their relationship. They liked to travel and the kids would put an abrupt end to that. She also had limited experience with children and did not want to play the role of mother. Although the father was in a position to get full custody of his children, he rejected the opportunity because it would have cost him the relationship with his new wife.

Many modern fathers are involved in all aspects of child care, from changing diapers to taking children to day care, whereas other fathers feel inept. Such ineptness is sometimes age related. When the children are infants and toddlers, some divorced fathers tend to prefer that the mother have custody of the children. However, Dr. Ken Lewis, a custody evaluation specialist, says that many of the divorced dads who come to him for help have infants and toddlers.

An important point for fathers to consider is that once a custody order is awarded by the court, any attempt to change it requires going back to court. Hence, it is important that you go for whatever custody arrangement you want the first time you go to court rather than assume that you can easily change it later. Doing so may be *very* difficult, sometimes impossible, and always expensive. Don't let your lawyer suggest otherwise.

How much time divorced fathers want to be with their children is often dependent on their opinion of their former wife as a mother. Those who regard their ex-wives as irresponsible, alcoholic, worthless mothers believe it is their mission to rescue their children. Under no conditions do they want their ex to have custody. Others consider their former wives to be great mothers and that their children are best served by being with them.

Regardless of the reason, mothers end up with primary custody considerably more often than fathers. Of 12 million one-parent families in 1998, 82 percent were maintained by the mother and 18 percent by the father.[4]

Fathers who can't imagine not being able to see their children on a daily basis and who are adamant about being actively involved with their children will want to go for either full or joint custody. Giving custody to the mother will simply not do, as the father will be relegated to the role of "visitor" for his children. But, as we have seen, the father must be interested and willing to make the necessary sacrifices in terms of his work, personal life, and sleep. Yes, parenting is exhausting.

Other Factors

A number of other factors influence how involved divorced fathers want to be in their children's lives. Fathers who resolved their differences with their former spouses through mediation are much more likely to want to see their children than are fathers who fought with their former wives in court. The bitter experience of litigation sometimes makes the fathers so angry that they avoid seeing their ex-wives and kids altogether. Also, in litigated custody cases, the mother is usually also angry at the father and may try to get back at him by turning the children against him. When he picks up the kids, he feels their coolness, which dampens his interest in being with them the next time.

Some mothers want their ex-husbands to be active fathers in their children's lives. Family Life Specialist Marilyn Ihinger-Tallman of Washington State University and her colleagues noted that this was particularly true of mothers who have sons. As fathers and sons often have more in common and share more interests than fathers and daughters, the researchers hypothesized that the mothers might feel inept in fulfilling certain roles (such as taking the boy fishing). According to these mothers, their ex-husbands are excellent role models for their sons and the more time they spend with their sons the better.[5]

Being remarried can affect the frequency with which a father sees his children. Some new wives like it that their husbands are responsible fathers and encourage them to be so. Others resent that their new husbands are interested in spending time with their children (and the money they pay in child support/alimony) and discourage such contact. In general, fathers who have remarried are more likely to see their children than are fathers who have not remarried. Demographer Judith Seltzer of the Center for Demography and Ecology at the University of Wisconsin–Madison analyzed national data from a survey on families and found that 40 percent of remarried fathers reported having contact with their children versus 18 percent of single fathers.[6]

Fathers who live in the same town as their children are much more likely to see them than are those separated by long distances. This is one of the reasons why it is advantageous for the father to insist that the custody order prohibit one parent from moving the children to another state. If she does so, the frequency of his seeing his children will drop precipitously.

IF YOU WANT PRIMARY PHYSICAL CUSTODY

Divorced fathers are rarely granted primary physical custody (1 chance in 10) and the newly separated father should not assume that he will be the lucky one. Unless he can demonstrate that he has been the primary nurturing parent for the children since birth, most attorneys will advise that he is wasting time and money to pursue primary custody.

In addition to being aware that your chance of being granted primary custody is low, you should keep three other factors in mind. First, if you lose your bid for primary custody, you are likely to end up in a worse situation in terms of visitation, child support, and property settlement than if you had sought joint custody or allowed your former spouse to have primary custody. This is because her lawyer will use all of the legal weight against you to crush you and back you off. If the judge decides against you, he or she could order limited visitation, high child support, alimony, and a biased property settlement.

Second, a court trial over custody is likely to end any possibility of an amicable relationship with your former spouse forever. Once you turn lawyers loose on each other, the emotional trauma stays with you forever, and you blame it on each other.

Third, your children may be brought into court to testify. This will also be a traumatizing event for them as both lawyers will try to confuse them and twist their testimony on the stand against the other parent. Your children can blame you for putting them through this ordeal so keep this in mind. Divorced father Sandy Mackay related that lawyers for his parents dragged him through 13 separate court fights over custody and visitation. He said no kid should have to go through that. Psychiatrist-psychologist Robert Sammons of Grand Junction, Colorado, however, warns that dragging a child through a retracted court fight is a trade-off:

> At the end of the day, the child needs to have access to both parents. Sometimes this is not possible if one parent wants full custody and the other wants joint custody. Although the court battle can traumatize the child, the long term effect may be negligible compared to having limited time with the other parent. But parents have to decide how much they want to put their child through and whether the outcome is worth it. It's not an easy decision.[7]

If you are determined to seek primary custody, and live in Texas or Oregon, request a trial by jury. Because the decision of where the children will live is more of a human, emotional issue than a legal one, the father stands a better chance of convincing 12 jurors than one judge.

In most states, judges hear the case. Judges are required to rule on the evidence that is consistent with statutory and case law presented by your attorney. Other factors are not important. Psychologist-mediator Bill Walz of Asheville, North Carolina, has observed the rulings of numerous judges and says: "Whether the judge is a woman or a man, young or old, black or white, divorced or married, a father or not, are all irrelevant.[8]

Finally, your attorney should be encouraged to emphasize the theme that the most important custody issue in the trial is the psychological need of the child to live with the father. The mother's need for the child is an irrelevant legal issue. Your attorney must convince the judge or jury that you are the primary psychological parent of the child and that it is in the child's best interest to live with you.

IF YOU WANT JOINT CUSTODY

Joint legal custody means that both parents have equal legal authority and control over the educational, medical, and psychological decisions that affect their children. Joint physical custody refers to where the children live and means that each parent has the children half of the time. Psychologist Dwayne Frutiger, a Child Development Specialist in Greenville, North Carolina, had this to say about joint custody:

> No matter what the court order says about custody—whether sole or joint—what is important is that the parents interact in such as way as to show respect for the other parent and to value the child being with the other parent. If this happens, the child will benefit. Otherwise, parents in conflict who have sole or joint custody will create stress in themselves and in their children and no one wins.[9]

Fathers who go for joint custody have several motives for doing so. Not all of them are good ones. In deciding whether you want joint custody, it is important to look at your motives.

Good Motives for Wanting Joint Custody

There are at least four good motives for wanting joint custody.

Love and Desire to Be with Your Children

Probably the best motive for wanting joint custody of your children is your love and desire to be with your children and your insistence that you will be an active and equal participant in your children's lives. Such an interest suggests that you have had this role throughout their lives. If you have not been in the active role of coparent and suddenly decide that you do want that, your motives are suspect.

Feeling that Your Children Will Benefit from Time with You

Other fathers seek joint custody because they regard themselves to be wonderful parents whose children benefit from being with them. They feel that the more exposure their children have to them, the better. These fathers do not seek sole custody, as they also regard their ex-wife as a good parent around whom children also benefit. In effect, they believe that their children are fortunate to have two loving parents and want them to benefit from each.

Protection from Inept Mother

Other fathers may seek joint custody believing that the less time the children live with their mother, the better. In effect, they are attempting to rescue the children from their former spouse, whom they view as a negative influence on the children. The father may also believe that he can't win sole custody so his next best option is joint custody. Such fathers usually view mothers as having any of several liabilities: They are preoccupied with their career and neglect their children, they abuse alcohol or other substances around the children, or they have very poor judgment. An example of the latter is the mother who left her 3-year-old locked in the house while she went to the grocery store.

Specific Benefit to Sons

Although fathers are important to daughters, psychologist Richard Warshak conducted a research project on custody outcomes for children and concluded that children in the custody of the same-sex parent (father custody for boys and mother custody for girls) were better adjusted than children in the custody of the opposite-sex parent. He went so far as to say that it is not divorce that makes adjustment harder for boys than girls but rather mother custody. Also, when children are asked their preferences, boys tend to prefer living with their fathers and girls with their mothers. Few children select the parent of the opposite sex.[10]

Dr. Warshak was also careful to point out that sex of the child is only one factor to consider when deciding on custody. Age of the child, the presence of a sister, and whether one or both parents had remarried are all factors. What is best in any specific case should be determined by having an impartial professional evaluate the entire situation. What is clear in all custody decisions is that if custody is given to one parent, access to the other parent should be regular and consistent.

Questionable Motives for Wanting Joint Custody

There is also a dark side to the motives of some fathers who seek joint custody.

Better Division of Property

Among the suspect motives is using the threat of joint custody to get a more favorable division of property settlement. Judges who give mothers custody of the children also tend to give them the house. Fathers who convince judges that they deserve joint custody end up getting a better division of property as the housing and standard of living of the father must also be considered.

Lower Child Support

Some fathers use joint custody to pay less child support. If their former spouse is awarded primary physical custody, the judge will require the father to pay heavy child support because the law assumes that she will bear the expense of taking care of the children. But with a joint custody arrangement, the expenses are shared and the justification for the former spouse getting a big child support award vanishes. The problem with this motive is that everyone may lose. The father really does not want to take care of his children, the mother has more limited resources to do so, and the children end up living with an irritated father and an impoverished mother.

Guilt

A less deceitful but still suspect motive for wanting joint custody is feeling guilty for ending the marriage and leaving the children in the lurch. Fathers sometimes feel that having joint custody will show the children that they still love them. The problem with this course is that if the father wins, he is often unprepared for the role of an active father. He may have been the traditional father who let his wife do most of the parenting work, which means that he has no skills in terms of how to take care of children. If he is awarded joint custody, the children may lose in living with a father who doesn't know how to take care of them and who is frustrated by their interference in his work/career.

Get Back at the Former Spouse

Finally, some fathers use joint custody to get back at their ex-wife. The father may have no real interest in having the children with him half of the time except that he is keeping them away from (and thereby hurting) his former wife. In effect, he is using joint custody to punish her.

Benefits of Joint Custody

Children want their parents to stay married because it maintains ready access to each parent. Children of married parents go to bed and wake up with their parents in the house. When divorce occurs and one parent is awarded custody, the other parent (usually the father) is no longer in the house and the children may be uncertain when they will see him again. Although joint custody still means that the child wakes up in the house with only one parent, there is *equal time* between parents. Just as soon as the children tire of being with one parent, it is time to go and stay with the other parent. Psychologically, the children remain connected to both parents. One 9-year-old whose parents had joint custody said:

> I spend 2 weeks at my dad's and 2 weeks at my mom's. Going back and forth isn't the greatest but I'd rather do that than not be able to spend time with both parents . . . my folks let me call the other or go over when I want to so I never feel I can't see the other when I'm with one of them.

The ability to see each parent as much as they choose is a big advantage for kids whose parents divorce, and perhaps the primary benefit of a joint custody arrangement.

Other positives derive from joint custody. Fathers who see their children regularly are happier about their relationships with their children and this translates into paying child support more regularly. Professor Judith Seltzer studied a national sample of divorced fathers and found that those who saw their children frequently were three times more likely to pay child support than those who did not see their children at all.[11] One divorced father told me: "When you send checks regularly for your kid you feel like you're still connected and doing your part as a father. I know some guys who send nothing, are always ducking their ex-wives, and would rather avoid child support than see their kid. That's not me."

Another positive consequence of joint custody is that fathers have more input into the decisions that affect their children. In sole-custody situations, the mother can effectively cut out the father from medical, educational, and religious decisions concerning the child. For example, as a joint-custody parent, you have the legal right to be involved in your child's educational and medical decisions. As a noncustodial father, you have no legal rights and your former spouse can schedule surgery for your children if she wants to without consulting you. One father said that his ex-wife wanted to put their son under the knife for a knee problem. The father had joint custody and insisted on another opinion. The son did not have the operation and was fine.

Joint custody gives the father not only more physical presence in his children's lives, but also more involvement in their development. For example, the mother may disregard the value of karate or scuba diving as activities that would be beneficial to the children's development. Fathers, on the other hand, may hold very strongly that the confidence-building and risk-taking aspects of the various activities are valuable and that such exposure would be important to the children. Both parents bring to the child more than either could alone. Chapter 13 stresses that the two-parent intact family provides enormous emotional, physical, social, and economic benefits for children. Coparenting after divorce (or the end of the marital relationship) continues to provide benefits to both children and society.

Noncustodial fathers often feel impotent against the power of their former wives. Because she has the children most of the time, she can twist their heads, take them out of town (on his clock) for "family reunions," and make sure they are busy when he calls. But with joint custody, the power in the relationship is equalized by the weight of the law. When the father is seen as an equal parent in the eyes of the law, judges are less apt to tolerate any ploys that reduce the father's access to the children.

Parents who have joint custody also have less to fight about. Only when one is more powerful does the less powerful have a reason to fight. When access is equal, the parents are eyeball to eyeball and both know they are in no position to tamper with the child's access to the other. Not returning to court is one example of less conflict. As each partner has equal power, there is little to go to court to fight over.

An obvious benefit of joint custody is the amount of time fathers spend with their children. I noted earlier that the typical noncustodial father spends less than 25 percent of the calendar year with his children. As a divorced father with joint custody, he doubles his access time to about 50 percent and is on equal par with his ex-wife. The children benefit.

As every parent knows, taking care of children is exhausting. Single parents with sole custody are the most exhausted of parents because they often have no relief or tag team to help them. A major benefit of joint custody to parents is the physical help they get in the care of their children. Indeed, some joint-custody parents look forward to when their children will be with the other parent. "I love being with my kids," one divorced father says, "but I'm not ashamed to say that I also love dropping them off at their mother's and getting a break from them."

Joint custody often results in parents who are better satisfied and who have less need to abduct their children, disobey court orders, or return to court. This means fewer contempt citations and less time taken up by sheriffs, judges, and legal clerks. Society wins when parents are allowed access to their children.

Judges and Legal Precedent

Even though there are numerous benefits for children, parents, and society when the parents have joint custody, a judge will not automatically give the father joint custody. Fathers sometimes feel powerless with regard to control over their children's lives. Such lack of control has not always been the case.

Historically, fathers have been very powerful. Under ancient Roman law, fathers had absolute power over their children including selling them or putting them to death if they chose to. This virtually unlimited control continued to be expressed in early America as judges routinely awarded custody solely to the father because it was thought that he could better financially provide for his children.

But at the beginning of the 1900s, economic and social changes began to influence the bias of the legal system regarding granting custody. Industrialization had begun taking fathers away from farming and the home and into factories, leaving mothers to care for the children. Mothers were given custody because they were thought to be the better parent for infants (the tender years doctrine). Infants need milk and moms have breasts, therefore mom gets custody. Also, with judges becoming accustomed to giving infants to mothers, they slowly evolved into giving children of all ages to mothers.

As gender roles became more flexible, judges in the 1960s began to decide custody on the "best interest of the child" doctrine, which focused more on the child's welfare than the mother's right. In practice, however, the law does not dictate which parent the judge must award custody to. Judges ultimately have the power to decide the custody issue, and as most of them have been reared by mothers, judges are biased in favor of giving mothers sole custody of their children.

To be awarded joint legal custody with your former spouse, you must prove that you are an important psychological parent to your child. You must document that you spend a lot of time with your children taking care of their physical and emotional needs. This implies that you have fed, bathed, and put your children to bed on a regular basis since birth and that you are aware of their medical needs, diets, and fears. As a father who wants legal control of your children, you must prove to the judge that you know your children's teachers, physicians, dentists, coaches, and so forth.

Dr. Ken Lewis, a custody evaluator in Glenside, Pennsylvania, emphasizes the importance of developing a theme to present in court. Such themes include "continuity" (e.g., the father does homework with the children every night and should continue this pattern), "extended family" (e.g., the father's side of the family provides numerous kinfolk with whom the children are close), and "fear of flight" (e.g., the ex-spouse is from another country and the threat of the child being taken out of the United States is lessened with the father having more frequent access). Any of these themes would be presented along with the psychological value of the father to the children.

Beyond the psychological importance of the parent, the judge considers other "best interests of the child" factors. These include the ability of the parent to provide nourishing and sufficient food, a safe dwelling, a moral environment (no drug abuse), adequate day care when at work, access to siblings/relatives, and access to the other parent. Some states such as Michigan and Florida spell out the factors judges must consider in deciding custody. Make sure you and your attorney know the conditions operative in your state as you prepare for trial.

Sometimes judges deny fathers joint custody if the children are under the age of 4, the feeling being that shuffling them back and forth is not in their best interest. Should this be your situation, have your attorney insist on a gradual increase in time periods you can be with your children to ensure that as they get older and are less affected by frequent transfers between the parents' homes, you in effect become a joint custodial parent who shares equal time with your ex.

Also, have your lawyer insist that *if* you are not initially given joint *physical* custody, you would like joint *legal* custody, which allows you to have equal responsibility and power in making decisions regarding the choice of your children's school, medical care, psychological care, religion, and recreational activities.

CONCLUSION

Once it becomes clear that your former spouse is not supportive of your relationship with your children, do your homework on statutory and case law regarding custody in your state and hire the most experienced domestic relations attorney you can afford. First decide what you want—sole custody, joint custody, or only visitation rights. Although it is possible that a judge would award you sole custody, it is not likely your attorney can present enough evidence consistent with state law for such an award. Joint physical custody is a reasonable expectation if you want your children to be with you 50 percent of the time. If this is not feasible or your request is denied, joint legal custody entitles you to stay involved in the decisions that affect your children. If your former spouse is granted sole physical and legal custody, make sure that you are granted specific regular visitation times as outlined in Appendix II. Unless the order signed by the judge is specific, you may find that your children are never available to you.

If possible, your attorney should work with your ex's attorney and develop a proposed joint physical custody plan that both sides can live with. A custody evaluation will be helpful to guide the negotiations of the attorneys. Although such a plan will take time and money, it will be less costly than if these issues must be argued in court. Also, the judge may come up with a plan that neither of you like, but which both of you must legally follow.

9

Give Your Children Time to Accept Your New Partner

My kids just couldn't seem to understand how happy I was to have finally met someone I really loved and cared about.

A divorced father

One of the advantages of divorce may be your escape from living in a dead marriage. A divorced man has gained the opportunity to find the person with whom he wants to share his life. However, divorced fathers often have mixed feelings about new romantic relationships. Social worker Geoffrey Grief of the University of Maryland at Baltimore found in his classic study of single fathers that they were ambivalent about their level of commitment to a new partner and unsure if they wanted a short- or long-term commitment.[1] But, within 3 years, most divorced fathers become open to new relationships. Indeed, divorced fathers who report greater satisfaction in their role as father also report having a satisfactory dating life. Eventually, the vast majority fall in love again and look forward to a new life with their partner. One recently separated father told me:

Leaving was the best thing that ever happened to me. I felt like a leper with my wife. She was just not interested in me emotionally or sexually . . . only my paycheck. I've already met someone new . . . I think I'm going to like this. While the emotional and economic price of divorce is high, it does offer the opportunity to start a new relationship with someone who will kiss you back.

Although most divorced fathers end up focusing on one woman, they may not start out that way. For many, there is a period of dating several women at the same time. Such a pattern is best on your own time so that each new person is not brought into your home and introduced to your children. Should they develop a liking for one of them and she has been replaced by the next weekend the children are with you, your kids may feel personally rejected. As a result, they may view all of your new girlfriends as temporary and have no interest in getting to know any of them—including the one for whom you develop a special fondness. Wait until you are certain that you want a future with a woman before you begin to integrate her into the lives of your children.

WHEN YOU FALL IN LOVE WITH A NEW PARTNER BUT YOUR CHILDREN DON'T

It is important not to expect your children to share your enthusiasm for your new partner. Although she (or, in the case of a gay dad, he) may be the most wonderful experience in your life, your children may view her negatively, at least at first. You should be prepared to understand your children's feelings.

Before your new relationship became serious, your children may have enjoyed being the sole focus of your time and energy. When they were with you, you orchestrated weekends around them and did what they wanted. Suddenly, the presence of a new woman changed your focus and now your children may feel that they have to compete for your time. Most children don't like the competition and wish the woman would go away so that dad could get back to focusing on their needs. One 9-year-old said, "When dad first moved out, every weekend we were together it was just us. I loved that. Then he started bringing this woman with him everywhere we went. I didn't like it and I'm sure I showed it."

Children may also feel like they are betraying their mother if they become friends with dad's new partner, so they keep his new partner at a distance. Indeed, some children hope that if they refuse to accept your new partner, she will leave, thereby eliminating their loyalty conflicts with their mother. Also, having the new partner around on weekends and seeing that she has become a part of dad's life ends the illusion that mom and dad will get back together, and the death of this hope is often painful. These are normal feelings and you should try to understand them—even better, you might talk with your children about these feelings.

Should your children reject your new partner and show no willingness to be friends, be careful how you view their behavior and how you respond. As discussed in Chapter 3, the context in which your children live is an important influence on their perceptions. A mother who bad-mouths your new partner is very likely the source of their feelings. As your children get older and move out of this context, they will develop a relationship with your partner in a new unbiased context. It may take years for this to happen. There may be little you can do about it in the meantime, but be sensitive to the process your children are experiencing.

Part of the problem of introducing a new partner to your children lies in identifying what role she will play in your family. Children rarely like the idea that they are, expected to relate to your new partner as their mother. They already have a mother and various conflicting loyalty issues may arise if there is an attempt to force her into that role—an alternative definition is that of "dad's friend." This puts the primary relationship between you and her and does not obligate your children. In time, the new partner may also become their friend. But such a friendship cannot be forced. Hence, your new friend is your friend, not their mother.

Being the new partner is a very difficult role. Not all women can do it. Chapter 10 is for the new partner—and was written by my partner, who has experienced firsthand what it is like to be involved with a divorced man who has children. For now, those who survive this role do not take the rejection personally and are able to see the rejection by your children as a result of the context in which your children live. With time, the new partner hopes the children may be more willing to accept her. In the meantime, she should expect nothing from them. Rather, she should understand that they are children and she is the adult and that it is her role to know what is going on and to rise above it. Her partner's children, as children, are probably incapable of seeing the biased context in which they live. The new partner has a choice of how she views the situation and she can exercise this choice to her advantage.

The new partner should also continue to be polite and open to opportunities to engage with your children. But no such opportunity may come in the first year or two. Rather than be put off by being shut out, the new partner should focus her attention on issues other than the way your children treat her.

How the father deals with the negative way his children treat his new partner is another issue. He should not tolerate impoliteness to anyone, including his new partner. But the focus should be on politeness to people in general and not be specific to the new partner. One divorced dad said to his children:

> When Jill was here last weekend, she asked you a question about school and you got up and left the room. You completely ignored her. That's impolite and unacceptable. It is important to be polite to any of my friends just as I will be polite to any of yours. You don't have to like her; you do have to be polite to her.

To expect that your partner love your children while they hate and reject her is unrealistic. A more appropriate expectation is that she be kind to them and open to their friendship. What is important is that neither you nor your partner become obsessed with how your children are treating her. Their feelings and behaviors are beyond your control. What you can control is how you respond to their indifference and the energy you invest in this area. View them as children caught in a negative context and give them time to grow out of it. In the meantime, enjoy your relationship with each other.

It is also important to separate the frustrations you are experiencing with your former spouse and your strained relationship with your children from the relationship with your new partner. Although being open with your partner about your frustrations is appropriate, making this a constant theme of your relationship with her is a mistake and will put a strain on your relationship. Such a strain over time may become too much baggage and it may be instrumental in sinking the entire relationship. One divorced father described his experience this way:

> I learned too late to keep separate the anger and depression I was feeling about not seeing my kids from the relationship with a new woman that I had been seeing. Every time we were together, I would end up telling her something that had happened with the ex, and how my kids were rejecting me, and on and on. She got sick of it and stopped going out with me. With the new partner I am seeing, I may tell her that I'm frustrated about something, but I won't dwell on it. It has made a lot of difference.

Again, put your frustrations with your former spouse and your children in perspective and have a life independent of them with your partner.

In the difficult task of getting your kids to accept your new partner, time is your best ally. The older the children, the more likely they are to feel more positively about your new partner. To help ensure that they "grow" into an acceptance, it is important that your new partner do nothing to alienate them. Treating them differently from her own children, talking negatively about their mother, being impolite to them, and criticizing them are guaranteed to keep the distance between the two.

Over time, the children will come to see some positives in dad's new partner. The most obvious of these will be that you are happier than you

---

| SELF-ASSESSMENT |

WILL IT BE POSSIBLE TO BLEND YOUR NEW PARTNER INTO LIFE WITH YOUR CHILDREN?

To gauge the possibility of integrating your new partner into the life you have with your children, read each sentence below and circle the appropriate number. The higher the number circled, the easier the integration will be for you, your children, and your new partner.

1 = Definitely Not   4 = Mostly Yes
2 = Mostly Not   5 = Definitely Yes
3 = Sometimes

	DN	MN	S	MY	DY
1. My former wife and I are still friends.	1	2	3	4	5
2. My former wife is interested in my being happy.	1	2	3	4	5
3. My former wife is accepting of my involvement with a new woman.	1	2	3	4	5
4. My former wife will encourage my children to enjoy my new partner.	1	2	3	4	5
5. My former wife will only say good things about my new partner to my children.	1	2	3	4	5
6. My former wife can see benefits of a stepmother for the lives of her children.	1	2	3	4	5
7. My new partner has a healthy self-concept and can accept rejection by my children.	1	2	3	4	5
8. I can tolerate it if my children reject my new partner.	1	2	3	4	5
9. My children seem to enjoy being around my new partner.	1	2	3	4	5
10. My children have told my new partner that they like her.	1	2	3	4	5

Add the numbers you have circled. The lowest possible score is 10, which means that integration of your new partner into life with your children will be very difficult and challenging. The highest possible score is 50, which means that your children's acceptance of your new partner into your life will be very easy. An intermediate score is 30. The higher your score, the easier it will be to blend your new partner into the life you have with your children.

were when the divorce was still a fresh wound. They will also notice a greater sense of calm in your life, and the new relationship will serve as a better model than the one you had with their mother. When mom and dad were together, fighting was predictable. Dad and his new partner may never fight, but rather discuss and resolve issues. When the adults are happier, the whole home is more relaxed; children notice this and like it.

After feelings of competition, conflicted loyalties, and other negatives are resolved, children can learn to enjoy dad's new friend. She may be bright, engaging, and attentive to the needs of the children and show a genuine interest in their welfare. Children sense this and may see her as their new friend.

Short of trying to ensure that your new partner is polite and respectful toward your children, your expectations of them should be minimal. As you cannot force their feelings, leave them alone. Accept the possibility that they may never like your new partner and resolve to enjoy life with her anyway. Although it would be nice if they did accept her, it is not critical to your happiness with her.

ISSUES TO CONSIDER IN THE MEANTIME

Until there is a legal document that dissolves your marriage, you and your new partner should be very discrete about spending any time together. Knowledge of such relationships can be used against you by your spouse's lawyer in court. Some conservative judges look with disfavor on a father who leaves his wife for a new partner.

Even after the divorce is final, who sleeps where when the children visit is still a difficulty to be worked out. Ideally, the noncustodial father should focus his weekends around his children. As this is the only time he may see them for 2 weeks, it is important to maximize the time with them. In some cases, this means he will not see his new partner the weekends his children are with him. In other cases it means he will see her after the children have gone to bed. In still other cases, he may spend Friday night alone with his children, and on Saturday night invite his new partner to dinner with the kids. There are no strict rules, but the goal is to nurture the father–child relationship and balance this with your new life. Individuals will vary as to how they go about this.

Some children cringe when they see their father being physically affectionate with a new partner. Not only do they view it as a betrayal of their mother, but they may feel that they must disapprove to show loyalty to their mother. From the father's perspective, he is legally separated from the children's mother and has the "right" to be affectionate with another woman. But should he?

The answer is yes, but he should do so *gradually*. Just as it takes about a year for children to give up the idea that their parents will get back together, it may take even longer for them to become accustomed to their dad being affectionate with a new woman. From their perspective, he is an old man, and it may seem disgusting to them for him to act like a lovesick teenager. These feelings are compounded by the fact that the new woman is not their mother. Hence, the new lovers should reserve the "heavy stuff" for the bedroom. Sitting close together and holding hands is certainly appropriate. But go slowly.

Although some weekends alone with the children is essential to ensure a continued relationship with them, there are also occasions where the father, new partner, and children may do something as a group. This might be something special so that the kids will be too distracted by the activity to focus on the fact that dad's new partner is with them. One divorced dad with a new partner told me:

> Divorced fathers who meet a new woman and think that taking her on vacation with his kids will be great are dreaming. It doesn't happen. They may not even speak to her the whole trip. And throwing them all in a station wagon and driving to the beach is asking for trouble. It's been 8 years since my kids first met my partner and things have finally leveled out. But Jesus, it took forever.

The more trips the children take with the new partner, the easier it becomes. But don't expect the comfort level to kick into high gear for a long time.

IT HAPPENS: THE EX SAYS, "THE CHILDREN CAN'T VISIT IF *SHE'S* THERE"

Some women become so angry when their ex-husbands find a new partner that they can't bear for their children to be in the new woman's presence. Out of anger, they inform him that "you can't take my children near that bitch" and whisk the children out of town the weekend they are to be with you and your new partner.

Legally, you have the right to the company of your choice when your children are with you. The fact that your former wife does not like your choice is irrelevant. Similarly, you may not like it that your former spouse is having an affair with your best friend. No matter. She can do as she pleases.

Should your former wife abscond with the children on your weekend, your attorney must file a petition for contempt of court, which will bring your ex into court to hear the judge order her to stop withholding the children from you. She may ignore the judge's order again but eventually she will stop. One judge told a woman that if she disobeyed his order again, he would give her former husband full custody of both children. She stopped.

CONCLUSION

Most divorced men are interested in meeting a new partner. Within a year or two, many focus on one person. Sharing your life with a new partner and maintaining your relationship with your children is challenging. Initially, it may be easier to keep the new person and your children separate. But eventually, they will meet and begin the process of developing their own relationship.

You should have minimal expectations that your children will be jubilant about your new partner. In fact, they may totally reject her. So be cautious and *gradually* increase their exposure so their relationship can develop. Demanding that your children accept and love your new partner will definitely not work. Be patient. Most such relationships take years to develop (some never do). In the meantime, enjoy your relationship with your new partner.

For the New Partner— by the New Partner

(Dads—this chapter is for your partner. You can skip this one but may suggest that she read it.)

Hi! I am married to the author of this book. We began dating when his children were aged 9 and 13, and my own daughter from my first marriage was 5. Now, almost a decade later, my husband, David, and I look back at the difficulties and challenges we faced in blending our families and our lives. Despite the almost unavoidable feelings of rejection, resentment, jealousy, and other complications of stepfamily relationships, we have survived as a stepfamily and flourished as a couple.

In my youth, I never imagined that I would become involved with a divorced man, let alone one who had children. I had the same fantasies as most young heterosexual women—find a single, never-married man, have children with him, and live happily ever after. But, contrary to the fairy tales I learned as a child, each husband had two children and a bitter ex-wife.

The relationship with my first husband lasted 10 years. Despite the anger, hurt, and confusion involved in our divorce, we have been successful in coparenting our daughter and remain, for the most part, cordial. Now I am in my second marriage, to a man who is also divorced with two children. Together, we have endured the emotional, financial, and legal difficulties associated with divorce.

This chapter is divided into three parts. The first part is about what to expect if you are in a relationship with a divorced dad. The second part gives some pointers on how to be supportive of your partner as he tries to be the best father he can be to his children from a previous relationship.

Finally, I suggest ways to avoid or cope with problems common to "step-couples." The stories and real-life examples come from my experience as a marriage and family therapist and divorce mediator, family and friends, and my own involvement in two marriages with two sets of stepchildren. Names and other identifying information have been changed to protect the privacy of the individuals involved. Although this chapter reflects my experience as a heterosexual woman, a gay male partner bonding with a divorced dad will no doubt have similar experiences of relating to a man and his children as a package deal.

KNOW WHAT YOU'RE GETTING INTO

If this is your first relationship with a divorced man with children, you may not be fully aware of what you are getting into. When I fell in love with my first husband, I had many illusions and unrealistic expectations about our future together. When my illusions gave way to reality, my disappointments were as deep as my expectations were high.

Your Relationship with His Children: The Rocky Road Ahead

One of the most common unrealistic expectations of "the new woman in daddy's life" is that his children will like you when they get to know you. Eventually, you think, they will even grow to love you like a mom. Some women's expectations are not that high. Beth, a divorced woman who became involved with Paul, a divorced man with two grown children, said she never expected Paul's children to love her—only to respect her as their father's partner.

Many stepchildren *do* develop good, loving relationships with their stepmothers. However, whereas your partner may have experienced "love at first sight" when he met you, the same will not be true for his children. More likely, his children will probably have a hard time accepting you into their lives. Depending on their ages, maturity level, personality, and mother's influence, they may view you as the woman who stole daddy away from them, or as someone who is more important to daddy than they are.

Common feelings and reactions children have to their divorced fathers' girlfriends and new wives include jealousy, resentment, anger, hatred, and dislike. Later, I'll talk about how to build relationships with stepchildren. For now, just be aware that it is usually a long and difficult process to win even their respect, never mind their affection. And some children never grow to like their father's new partner. One grown woman said of her stepmother 10 years after her father remarried, "I've never liked her, and I never will. I'm polite to her and she's polite to me. But that's all."

Related to the issue of how the children feel about and behave toward you is the issue of how you feel about his children. You may think that because you love your man, you will love his children as well. After all, they are a part of him. In reality, you may or may not grow to love his children. You may not even like them. One woman in counseling described her stepdaughter as a "spoiled brat who is selfish and inconsiderate."

And if you don't like his children, is your relationship doomed? Not necessarily. Cynthia, recently engaged to marry Tom, a divorced man with children, suggested that they go to premarital counseling. Tom didn't see the need to, but agreed to go. In the counseling session, Cynthia revealed that before they got married she needed to confess something to Tom. She revealed that, as much as she had tried to like Tom's 13-year-old son Jake, she just did not like him. To her relief, Tom said that as long as she treated Jake well and related to him positively, it was OK that she didn't like Jake. Tom said that he didn't expect Cynthia to love or even like Jake, but he did expect her to be polite and positive with Jake. Tom went on to say that "Jake gets on my nerves too."

Whether or not his kids like you, or you like them, know that your partner and his kids are a package deal. If you realize from the start that his children may not like or accept you, you may not be as disappointed in the future when you face their rejection, disrespect, or hostility.

The Emotional Fallout of Divorce: His State of Mind

Getting involved with a divorced father also means dealing with the emotions that he is feeling about being separated from his children (if they live with their mother, which they usually do). If he initiated the divorce, he may also be struggling with feelings of guilt about breaking up his family and leaving his children. If his wife initiated the divorce, he may be feeling a range of emotions, including betrayal, hurt, anger, and worthlessness. In either case, divorced men (as well as divorced women) often go through a period of vulnerability, confusion, and perhaps depression. If his ex is keeping their children from seeing him, or if she is interfering with his relationship with his children, his anger and frustration may at times consume him—and you. This emotional roller coaster may last for years.

When I met my first husband, he was going through a tumultuous divorce and was separated from his two young children, whom he loved very much. He was an emotional time bomb that was always ticking, and I never knew when it would go off. When it did go off, it sometimes exploded in anger; at other times it fizzled into a deep depression. Sometimes his anger was directed at me—I was close by and an easy target. I told myself that he just needed a little time to adjust to the divorce and the periods of separation from his children. I did not realize that period of time would last several years.

Your partner's emotional response to being divorced and separated from his children is not a bad thing—it is normal and understandable. If your partner did not experience emotional pain, you might wonder if he is made of stone or if he is emotionally shallow. But you may be concerned about how he expresses his emotions and how his state of mind affects his behavior, self-concept and self-confidence, and interactions with you. Does he have violent outbursts? Does he get verbally caustic and abusive? Does he drink too much or use drugs to try to alleviate his pain? Does he withdraw into a depressive and noncommunicative state? The lesson here is that whatever his emotional reactions and state of mind following a divorce, realize that he may be this way for a long time. And, although he may love you deeply and sincerely, and you may feel the same for him, that love alone may not be enough to resolve his anger and pain, compensate for his guilt, or make him feel good about himself again.

The Economic Fallout of Divorce

Although the media emphasize the economic plights of women and children following divorce, divorced men also suffer a financial burden. Yes, there are "deadbeat dads" who don't pay child support or don't pay it on a regular basis. But, if your partner is reading this book, he is obviously a dedicated father who probably continues to support his children.

In addition to child support, which may be over 50% of his gross income, he may be paying alimony (also called spousal maintenance) to his ex-wife. Half of his assets (or more), including any retirement money he has, may have gone to his ex. But that's not all. Many fathers pay beyond what the court requires in child support and even spousal support. You also need to realize that child support does not necessarily end when the children turn 18. Many fathers contribute to their children's college education. Even beyond college, fathers (and mothers) often provide a financial safety net for their adult children.

Most couples do not talk about money issues early in courtship. But if you are planning a future with a divorced father, you need to know what kind of financial future you are looking at together. What are his financial obligations to his children and ex-wife? How will these financial obligations affect you? By asking these questions early in your relationship, you will know what kind of financial situation you are entering if you continue your relationship with him.

Does He Want Any More Children?

Frank Gifford (before his highly publicized infidelity) once said on a talk show that he had been married before, already had children, and didn't need any more. But, he continued, if Kathy Lee wanted children of their own, it was OK with him—they had two.

So one issue with a divorced dad is whether or not he wants to, or is willing to, have more children with you. If he doesn't, don't count on changing his mind. A friend of mine married a divorced man with kids; she wanted children and he did not. She thought he would change after marriage but, instead, became more adamant and had a vasectomy. They are still together, childless, but she is resentful. If you want children of your own, don't marry a man who makes it clear that he doesn't want to be a dad again.

On the other hand, if you do not want to have children with him, but he wants more children, you need to make your intentions clear. If he wants more children with you, he may assume that you want them too—especially if you do not already have children of your own. Not only do you need to know what his desires are regarding having additional children, he needs to know if you want or don't want to have children with him in the future.

What to Expect if You Already Have Children

Some women already have children from a previous marriage and don't want another. What they do want is a new husband who will accept, engage, enjoy, and, hopefully, love their children.

But what if your new partner does not like your children or love them like you want him to? What if he does not relate to them the way you would like? What if your children do not get along with his children? Because the focus of this book is on divorced fathers maintaining a relationship with their own children, I won't elaborate on issues related to your children. But be aware that these issues exist and just as his children are part of the package deal, you and your children are a package deal too.

One final note concerning his relationship with your children: Be wary of the man who is nice to your child just to win you over. This happened to a woman I saw in therapy who discovered that after their marriage her new husband stopped any semblance of interest in her kids. "It dawned on me it was an act he put on to get me to marry him. My kids now hate him and it has definitely affected my feelings toward him."

BEING A SUPPORTIVE PARTNER

If your partner is reading this book, he values his children and wants to have the best possible relationship with them. What can you do to help him achieve this? Being a supportive partner to a divorced dad involves understanding and accepting how important his children are to him, being supportive of his spending time alone with his children, and respecting and supporting his financial responsibilities to them. But I begin this section by looking at one of the benefits of involvement with a divorced dad.

What Kind of Father Is He?

One of the benefits of being involved with a divorced father is that you have the opportunity to see what kind of father he is before you have kids of your own with this man (if you plan on having any children with him). If you disapprove of his parenting style now, you will probably also be unhappy with his parenting should you have children with him in the future. On the other hand, if you are happy with and respect how he parents his children now, you will probably be on the same parenting wavelength should you have children with him in the future.

One woman confided that she did not like how her partner parented his children from his first marriage—he was inconsistent in his discipline and used severe and hurtful language in punishing them. She excused his parenting flaws, blaming them on his "temporary" emotional state following the divorce. But years later, when they had a child of their own, she observed the same patterns in his parenting behavior. Watch carefully how your partner parents his children. And remember, what you see in terms of his parenting behavior is what you will likely get if you have children with him down the road.

However, some men who have two sets of children do not parent them in the same way. Country singer Kenny Rogers explained that in a previous marriage, he was busy building his career and did not spend much time with his children or participate in their day-to-day care. In a subsequent marriage he had another child and vowed he would do things differently and spend more time with his son.

Understand and Accept How Important His Children Are to Him

If you have children of your own, you know the strength of the bond between a parent and a child. You know that your partner's children are forever an important part of his life, just as your children are an important part of yours.

If you do not have children of your own, it may be more difficult for you to understand and accept the central place your partner's children have in his life. You may feel jealous of the love and affection your partner feels and displays toward his children. You may think that he loves his children more than he does you. But to weigh his love for you against his love for his children is to compare apples and oranges. A parent's love for a child is qualitatively different than an adult's love for an intimate partner.

To understand what I'm getting at, think of a family member you love. This could be your mother or father, sister or brother, or other family member. (Of course, if you have children, you could think of them.) Now, ask yourself this question: Does your love for this family member mean that you have less love for your partner? I hope my point is clear: Love is not a finite quantity—the love you feel for one person does not take away from the love you have left to feel for another person. The love a divorced father feels for his children does not take away from the love he can feel for an intimate partner. Indeed, the more love a father feels for his children, the higher his capacity may be for loving others in general.

Be Supportive of His Spending Time Alone with His Children

Do you ever resent the time that your partner spends with his children? If you do, you are not alone. Women who get involved with divorced dads often feel jealous and resentful of the time their partner spends with his children. But it is important that your partner have this time on a frequent and regular basis. By doing so, the children benefit, your partner benefits, and you benefit.

Spending time alone with his children (without you present) helps to strengthen the relationship between your partner and his children. (This, of course, assumes that your partner provides positive experiences and interacts with his children in a loving and caring way). Children of divorced dads, especially soon after the marital separation or divorce, may feel that "daddy left them" or "daddy doesn't love them anymore." The bond children have with their divorced father is often weakened by infrequent time together and/or a mother who may tell the children negative things about their father and discourage their relationship with him. So from the point of view of his children, spending time alone with their dad on a regular basis helps to reestablish their importance in his life and to provide emotional security in their relationship with him.

There are many reasons why having a close and secure relationship with one's father is good for the development of children and adolescents (see Chapter 13). But even if the well-being of your partner's children is not a priority for you, their dad's well-being probably is. The time divorced fathers spend alone with their children is an investment in their own sense of efficacy and pride in being a good father. If, by spending time alone with his children, your partner develops a strong relationship with them, he will reap more satisfaction and joy in his role as a father.

Being supportive of your partner spending time alone with his children also benefits you. How so? First, his happiness affects yours. If he is unhappy because his relationship with his children is strained and distant, that unhappiness will spill over into his relationship with you. Conversely, if he is content with his relationship with his children, that feeling of contentedness will also benefit you. Although his spending time alone with his children does not guarantee that he will develop or maintain a satisfying relationship with them, it certainly increases the odds.

Being supportive of your partner spending time alone with his children also increases your value as a partner to him. Encouraging your partner to spend time alone with his children reassures him that you feel secure in your relationship with him and that you are considerate of his needs and his children's needs. Being supportive, rather than resentful, of your partner spending time alone with his children may endear you to him even more. Frank related the following about his girlfriend Pamela:

> You know, other women I've dated have made me feel guilty about spending time with my kids. But Pamela, she's great about it. She understands how important it is for me to be with my kids. Sometimes we do things together—I want the kids to get to know her and want her to get to know the kids. But its not a problem when I tell Pamela that I want to take my sons on a weekend fishing trip, without her. I love her even more for her understanding and acceptance.

Third, the more your partner's children feel good about their dad, the more likely they will also develop good feelings about their dad's new girlfriend or wife (that is, you). If his children have a secure relationship with their dad, they are less likely to feel threatened by you. So, by encouraging your partner to spend time alone with his children, you are, indirectly, helping to build a better relationship between you and his children.

One last way in which your partner spending time alone with his children may benefit you: It gives you an opportunity to do things you want to do—without him! If you have children of your own, do something special with them while your partner is with his children. If you don't have children, make the most of your time when your partner is booked up with his children. Visit with friends, finish that novel you started, catch up on your sleep, get lost surfing the Net, do things he would not like to do with you (clothes shopping?).

A final note here: It is easier for you to be supportive of your partner spending time alone with his children if he is also spending time alone with you on a regular basis. My husband's photo album is full of pictures of trips and events he shared with his children over the years of our relationship. But during that same period of time, we also compiled quite a photo album of our own times together. So, while you are supporting his spending time with his children, also make sure that the two of you are spending time together as a couple. But if you are not supportive of his relationship with his children, including the time he spends alone with them, you may not be the kind of person he wants to spend time alone with!

Support and Respect His Financial Obligations to His Children

Unless your partner's children live primarily with him, he is most likely obligated to pay court-ordered child support every month. How can you be supportive of your partner's financial obligations to his children? First, you can verbally reinforce him for meeting his financial responsibilities as a father. Tell him you admire his dedication as a father. Praising him for meeting his financial parenting responsibilities may be especially helpful to the father who is struggling financially, who resents his ex-wife's higher standard of living, who is experiencing rejection or apathy on the part of his children, or who does not have the opportunity to see his children as often as he would like.

A woman I know was in a relationship with a divorced father who occasionally complained about his financial situation and what he viewed as an unfair divorce settlement. He would say things like the following:

> My children and ex-wife are living in a big house in a nice neighborhood. She drives a new car, and kept most of our expensive household furnishings. Meanwhile, I live in a small apartment, don't have a kitchen table to eat on, drive an old junk heap, and struggle to pay child support. She [the ex-wife] probably spends most of the child support I send on herself, not on the kids.

Another divorced father lamented,

> I don't know why I send child support. My ex moved across the country with the kids, and I only get to see them twice a year. When I do, they don't even treat me like a father and act like it is a chore to be with me. When I call them on the telephone, they have nothing to say to me. They never write or call.

If either of the men above sound like your partner, you can help ease the pain he feels when he sends his monthly child support check by saying something like the following:

> You know, there are a lot of divorced dads out there who feel the way you do and who stop paying child support. But you are not a deadbeat dad, and even though your children may not appreciate you now, as they grow older they will understand that you helped to support them financially after the divorce. And just as important, you will be able to hold your head high, knowing that by supporting your children, you have done the right thing.

This kind of verbal reassurance lets a divorced father know that he isn't struggling in a vacuum; others notice and appreciate the sacrifices he makes for his kids.

You can also be supportive of your partner's financial responsibilities to his children by not placing excessive economic demands on him. Does his budget comfortably allow him to buy you expensive presents, take you out to expensive restaurants, or go on exotic vacations? If so, no problem. But if your partner is paying spousal support to his ex-wife, child support to his children, and attorney bills from his divorce, he may be in no position to run up bills on his credit cards. One divorced father ended his relationship with his girlfriend because she had financial expectations he could not meet. He said:

> She made enough money in her job that she could afford the lifestyle she was used to. She could buy expensive clothes, airplane tickets, and jumbo shrimp. The problem was that she expected me to be able to do the same thing. We actually ended our relationship over the brand of coffee I buy. She wanted me to join this gourmet coffee club. When I told her it was too expensive, she called me "cheap" and stormed out of my apartment. I told her not to bother to come back.

On the other hand, if you are sensitive to your partner's financial situation and do not make economic demands on him, he may love you even more for it. One divorced father said of the woman he was about to marry:

> Terri has been great about money. She knows how strapped I am financially, and tells me we don't need to live in a big house and drive fancy cars to be happy . . . that we can have a good life together without all the frills. She told me not to go into debt over a diamond engagement ring—she didn't need or want one. For her wedding band, she picked out a simple silver band—cost $8! I may be poor, but boy did I hit the jackpot with her!

Still another way to help your partner is to educate him about ways in which he can live within his means and stretch his budget (of course, this assumes that you have skills and knowledge in this area!). When I met my husband, dinner with his children meant taking them out to restaurants— he didn't know how to cook. Teach him a few simple dishes he can prepare to save on meal expenses. When he suggests going to the movies, you might suggest renting a movie (or taping one shown on television) to watch at home. Teach him about finding inexpensive things at yard sales and thriftshops and to look for the markdown rack in stores. But don't try to take over your partner's budget or make financial decisions for him. Respect his right to spend his money as he chooses, especially when it comes to spending money on his children.

Beyond paying child support, many divorced fathers spend additional money on their children. Parenting is about nurturing and one expression of nurturing is spending money on someone. Money symbolizes love and importance, and so by spending money on their children, some divorced fathers are demonstrating that they love their children and that their children are important.

If his children live primarily with their mother, he may spend money on them as a way of assuaging his guilt for divorcing their mother or for not being present in their day-to-day lives. Even if his children live with him, a divorced father may try to make up for their growing up in a "broken" home by providing expensive material things.

Have you ever felt that your partner overindulges or "spoils" his children with expensive gifts or vacations? Perhaps he does. In our society, the traditional role of the father is as a provider—a breadwinner for the family. Divorced men with children may feel that their role as a father is threatened—they are not physically present in their children's day-to-day lives, they may feel they have been replaced by their children's stepfather, their ex-wife minimizes their importance in their children's lives, and their children may be emotionally distant from them. To top it off, society stereotypes divorced fathers as "deadbeat dads." Spending money on their children may be the divorced father's way of saying to his children, and to himself, "I am still your father."

Even after a father's legal obligation to support his children is over, he may feel a parental responsibility to help his children financially. Supporting your partner means respecting his right to spend his money on his children as he chooses. A few weeks before his wedding, Carl, a friend of mine, told me that he hoped his stepmother would not show up at his wedding. When I asked him why he felt that way, he related an incident that happened years earlier when he was in graduate school. During a visit with his father and stepmother, Carl asked his father for some financial help—"grocery money"—to help him through his last year of graduate school. Before his father could reply, Carl's stepmother answered for him. "*We* feel that when a child gets to be a certain age, he should be on his own," she said. Carl never forgave her for intervening in a decision that he felt should have been made by his father. Worse, Carl lost respect for his father, who he felt should have not let his new wife answer for him.

There are situations where it is appropriate for you to have input into your partner's financial decisions and spending behavior. If you are married or living together, you may have an understanding about what money is yours to spend as you choose, what money is his to spend as he chooses, and what money is joint money that is to be spent as the two of you agree. If your partner's spending behavior is unrealistic given his budget (or given your joint household budget), your input is warranted. Just be sure your discussions about money reflect respect and consideration for his children and his role in their economic support.

Finally, your input into your partner's spending on his children may be warranted if you are concerned about the appropriateness of what he is spending his money on. When Sam's 13-year-old son John, who had never taken a music lesson in his life, asked his dad to buy him an $800 electric guitar, Sam's new wife expressed her opinion that this was excessive. She suggested that they buy a less expensive guitar and then use the extra money to buy guitar lessons for John. When Robert, another divorced father, wanted to buy BB guns for his 8- and 10-year-old children, his girlfriend Patricia asked him to consider waiting until they were older, for safety concerns.

BUILDING A RELATIONSHIP WITH HIS CHILDREN

Women who are involved with divorced fathers may find their partner's children to be a delight—or a disaster. The relationship between a divorced father's children and his new girlfriend or wife can be rich and rewarding, or it can be frustrating and painful. In this section are some suggestions to consider for building a relationship with his children.

Be Patient and Don't Force Yourself into His Children's Lives

After my husband (David, the author of this book) and I had been dating a few months, we tried to spend some time together with our children. On weekends when his children were with him, we had meals together and engaged in recreational activities together—David, myself, my daughter, his daughter, and his son. It was painfully obvious that this plan wasn't working (you'll see why later in the section "Dealing with the Many Faces of Rejection").

Plan B: David told his children that they did not have to spend time with me (the new woman in dad's life) or with my daughter (the new child in dad's life). Instead, on weekends that his children were with their dad, he would do things alone with them. On longer "visits," such as holidays, school vacations, and summer weeks, David would often take them on trips—just he and his children.

At first, this was hard for me to accept. After all, I was a part of his life, and so was my daughter. His children would just have to get used to the idea. But then again, being together meant that my daughter and I were exposed to rejection. His children felt that their lives had been invaded by aliens who were stealing their father's time, attention, and love away from them, and David was in the middle.

Instead of insisting that we spend time together as a "family" and forcing his children to be around me and my daughter, David and I both recognized that from the children's point of view, I was not a part of their family. From their perspective, "family time" was time with their dad—alone. Instead of resenting the time David spent alone with his children, I admired his dedication to his children and his patience and understanding in giving his children time to get used to their parents' divorce and their dad's new girlfriend (and her daughter). Rather than complain about not being able to be with him on the weekends when his children were with him, I supported his idea to spend time alone with them.

This phase of David spending time with his children—without me or my daughter present—lasted about a year. In the meantime, he would take trips with me and my daughter. At the end of a year, his children wanted to go on trips with us—and they did. From that point, the relationships slowly but steadily improved. This experience taught us firsthand the importance of patience in giving children of divorced parents time and space to grow to accept the new partner in their parent's life.

It is also important to give the children time to adjust to a major change in your relationship status or living arrangements. On a routine visit with her dad, one teenage girl found out that she was going to a wedding that weekend—her dad's. With no preparation or advance notice, Elizabeth was shocked and angry at her dad for not telling her ahead of time that he and his girlfriend were getting married.

Kevin, a sophomore in high school, learned that his dad's girlfriend moved in with him when, on a weekend visit with dad, he walked into the apartment and was told that he no longer had a bedroom there—he was going to have to sleep on the couch. The room that was once his was now occupied by his girlfriend's son. Kevin was hurt and angry at his dad, his dad's girlfriend, and "that little brat that took over my room."

In both of these examples, the fathers did not tell their children ahead of time about the changes that were going to happen in their lives because they were afraid their children would get upset at the news. But if you don't give your children advance notice, then the news drops on them like a bomb—the impact is sudden and intense and the fallout does great damage to the relationships involved. If you and your partner decide to move in together, or decide to get married, it is his responsibility to tell his children. Make sure he doesn't wait until the moving truck has delivered the furniture, or until the night before the wedding, to do so.

Respect and Support His Children's Relationship with Their Mother

In addition to my mediation work with families, I have gone into the public schools to teach mediation and conflict resolution to both teachers and students. When I ask teachers and students for examples of the kinds of conflicts students get into, one of the most common responses is that a student will fight when bad things are said about his or her mother.

You may hear your partner say many negative things about his ex-wife. You may have developed some ill feelings and negative opinions about her yourself. But when you are around his children, follow the old adage: If you have nothing positive to say, don't say anything at all.

If you do say negative things about the children's mother—either to them or in front of them—they may rebel against you to protect their mother's image or to protect their own images. After all, children are a part of their mother, reflections of her, and so by attacking their mother you are indirectly attacking them. If you denigrate or criticize their mother in front of them, they may harbor deep resentment and dislike for you.

It may not be easy for you to respect the mother of your partner's children, especially if she makes life difficult for you and your partner. If your partner's ex is unreasonable, hostile, and hypocritical, the children don't need you (or their father) to tell them that—they will figure it out for themselves as they mature.

Just as not all stepmothers are "wicked," not all ex-wives are hostile and unreasonable—and those who are may change over time. But if she views you as the enemy, don't give her any ammunition. At events where you and she might be present with the children (such as weddings or graduations), ignore her sarcastic or cruel remarks to you. At such events, the children are observing what's going on. Set a good example for them and do not show hostility toward their mother. Even if they reject you now, at some later time they may remember your behavior and respect you for not contributing to a "scene."

Dealing with the Many Faces of Rejection

Probably the most difficult part of your role as a woman involved with a divorced father is the potential rejection you will face from his children. The following examples illustrate the rejection women said they experienced from their partner's children:

His children simply ignored me and wouldn't speak to me. When I would see them on the weekends they were with my partner, I would say "hello," and they would grunt the minimal back.

I would prepare elaborate meals and they would eat nothing but the rolls from the store.

His 9-year-old daughter told me she hated me and wanted to stab me in the heart with a knife. I didn't know what I did to make her hate me so much.

Although you will be hurt each time his children reject you, it is important to remember who is the adult and who are the children, the reason for the children's negative behavior toward you, and how to minimize the rejection. If you lash back at his children in anger, you are moving down to their level and buying into their game of hate. It helps to remind yourself that they are not attacking you personally, but would treat anyone in your role the same way. If you were not in his life, someone else would be, and she would be the target of their hate.

Also consider why they are rejecting you. One reason for their rejection may be that their mother, still angry and hurt over the divorce, has told them what an awful person you are. If you respond to the children's rejection by becoming angry, making sarcastic remarks to them, or calling them names, you become the awful person their mother says you are. Don't confirm their mother's assessment of you. Eventually, if you maintain a positive and supportive demeanor with them, they will evaluate you for who you are, not for who their mother says you are.

The children's mother may even blame you for the divorce and tell the children that you broke up the family or stole their dad away from them. Children are too young to know that marriage is a complex relationship and that both partners are at "fault" when a marriage ends. Children are simply too young to see the big picture. Don't expect them to.

Even if the children's mother is supportive of you (and many women are pleased that their ex-husbands are involved in new relationships), the children may still reject you. After all, their whole world has been altered—the family as they knew it is no more. And the family they knew, whether it was conflictual for the parents or not, was a familiar one. Spending weekends at dad's apartment with a woman they don't know, eating food they are not familiar with, and being away from their friends is not their idea of how life should be. They would rather have dad back with mom in their house.

Resolving Conflict: Focus on Feelings and Getting to the Real Issue

Conflict is inevitable in all close relationships. A major key to the happiness and stability of stepcouples is how successfully they resolve conflict between themselves and their children.

One teenage daughter, Melissa, became upset with her father, Dan, because on his telephone's memory dial function, his new wife Sharon was No. 1 and his daughter was No. 2. Dan felt guilty and changed the memory dial function so that his daughter was No. 1. When he told Sharon about his daughter's reaction, she thought it was ridiculous for Melissa to be upset over such a silly issue. She told Dan that by changing the memory dial function for Melissa, he was reinforcing her unreasonableness. Sharon and Dan argued about what he should do. Should he make his daughter No. 1 on his memory dial or leave it with his wife as No. 1 and his daughter as No. 2? What do you think Dan should do? Take a moment to think about your answer before reading on.

This example illustrates one variation on a common theme. Children of divorced fathers are often jealous and resentful of their father's new partner. They express their jealousy and resentment in countless ways. When they do so, their fathers agonize over what to do about it. The new partner usually has her opinion of what he should do, which is often not the same as what he thinks he should do. Before you know it, the father and his new partner are upset at each other, arguing over what is the best way to handle the child's emotional reaction.

Because the types of issues that children of divorced fathers react to emotionally vary widely, it is helpful for fathers and their partners to use one particular guiding principle in responding to the upset child. What is that principle? Simply put: Focus on the child's feelings. In the above example, the real issue is not "who's on first?" on Dan's telephone memory dial. The real issue is that Melissa, his daughter, feels threatened and displaced by her dad's new partner, Sharon.

Getting to the real issue behind the reactions of children of divorce is half the battle. Rather than focus on their reactions, focus on the feelings behind the reaction. Use their reactions as *information* that conveys their feelings and then address the feelings. If the divorced father and his partner approach a problematic situation involving his child by working together to understand the child's feelings, then that will become the focus rather than arguing about what to do. If both adults have the child's feelings as their foremost concern, then they can work together to find a solution.

Regarding Melissa, Dan did talk with her about her feelings of being No. 2 on the dial function and discovered that she did feel replaced by Sharon. He decided to spend more time alone with his daughter to renew their bond. In time, the question of "who's on first?" faded as an issue.

Learning from Others

Chances are, you have more than one friend, coworker, or relative who has been involved in a stepfamily or who has dated someone with children from a previous relationship. You will learn a great deal by talking to these people about their experiences. What problems did they encounter? What strategies or coping mechanisms worked well for them? What didn't work? What mistakes did they make? What would they have done differently if only they had known better?

In talking with others who have been down the remarriage/stepfamily trail, you can also share your own concerns about your relationship with your partner and his children and ask for feedback or advice. Many of the mistakes I made in my first marriage might have been avoided if I had talked to other women who were married to or involved with divorced men with children. But I was young and had no family or friends who were in that situation. By the time I entered the relationship with my current husband, one of my sisters had already been divorced and remarried to a man with children. I also realized that I was not the only one who had confronted the challenges of a partner with children. Frequent phone calls to my sister helped me through numerous situations with David and his children.

However, you should be selective about what you disclose and whom you seek advice from. One woman confided to mutual friends that they disagreed about how to handle his teenage son's drug use. When the mutual friends brought up the issue with the husband, he became furious with his wife for telling friends about his son's drug use and accused her of deliberately trying to embarrass him by her disclosure. He apparently felt that his son's drug use was a reflection of his inadequacy as a parent and did not want anyone, not even close friends, to know.

In another example, Karen complained to a coworker about her partner Bill's ex-wife's constant requests for money, despite the fact that Bill was already paying over $1000 a month in child support and alimony. At a company party, Karen's co-worker mentioned to Bill that he couldn't believe how much Bill was paying to support his ex-wife and children. Bill later criticized Karen for disclosing what he felt was personal and private information to someone he barely knew. How to avoid a similar faux pas? Before talking to others about any issue concerning your partner or his children, ask your partner what information is OK to disclose to whom. For example, the woman who told friends of her stepson's drug use could have said to her husband, "I am really troubled by John's drug use. I feel it would help me to talk to someone we trust about it. How would you feel if I talked to Mike and Susan?"

Encourage your partner to talk with other divorced fathers. In doing so, he will not feel so alone in his struggles and may learn a thing or two. But caution him against turning discussions with other divorced fathers into ex-wife bashing sessions, which only serve to inflame hostilities.

During the difficult years when David and I experienced rejection and hostility from his children, he frequently phoned two close friends who were also divorced fathers. They assured him that his children's reactions were normal and largely reflected the influence of their mother, and that in time, their relationship with their father would improve. They shared stories with David about their own experiences with rejection from their children, reminding David that his situation was not unique or even unusual, that he was not alone in his plight.

Another option for stepcouples is to learn from others in a support group context. Many communities have stepfamily support groups, where people share their difficulties and learn from others' experiences. Frequently, these support groups invite counselors, therapists, mediators, or other professionals to give presentations at the support group meetings. Parents Without Partners is also a valuable source.

Finally, learning from others can be achieved by doing what you are doing right now—reading. If you are seriously involved with or married to a divorced man with children, I encourage you to delve into the self-help literature on meeting the challenges of stepfamily life and coping with its difficulties. Check out the shelves in your local library or bookstore.

I hope the information, suggestions, and examples provided in this chapter have been useful and relevant to your situation. Following are some of the suggestions and guidelines from this chapter in the form of dos and don'ts.

DOS

1. Know what you are getting into by being involved with a divorced father. Having realistic expectations can help avoid disappointment in the future.
2. Understand how important his children are to him and realize that his love for them does not take away from his capacity to love you.
3. Encourage your partner to spend time alone with his children. Be supportive of his doing so, recognizing that it has benefits for his children, for him, and for you.
4. When your partner is with his children, do things that you find enjoyable. View the time he is away from you as an opportunity to enjoy things he doesn't or that you can most enjoy without him.
5. Be supportive of your partner's financial responsibilities to his children.
6. Be respectful of the mother of your partner's children. Say only positive things about her in front of his children.
7. Be patient with his children. Recognize that their rejection of you (and perhaps of their father) may reflect their mother's influence and/or their feelings of anger, jealousy, and displacement.
8. In dealing with conflict, get to the real issue by focusing on feelings.
9. Learn from others by talking with other women who are pair bonded with divorced dads, joining stepfamily support groups or organizations, and/or reading literature on the topic of stepfamily relations.

DON'TS

1. Don't expect your partner's children to immediately like you.
2. Don't take personally what his children say and do to reject you. They would behave this way toward any new partner in their dad's life.
3. Don't lash back at his children by being sarcastic or calling them names.
4. Don't force yourself into his children's life by making them spend time with you.
5. Don't make the way his children treat you the focus of your relationship with your partner. Enjoy your life together independent of the way his children treat you.

6. Don't make your partner feel guilty for spending time alone with his children and away from you. And don't feel sorry for yourself when he is away from you with his children. Be glad that he has the opportunity to be with them. He will be a happier partner when he is able to enjoy his children.
7. Don't complain about the amount of money your partner spends on his children or ex-wife.
8. Don't tell your partner how he should or should not spend money on his children.
9. Don't say negative things about his children's mother to or in front of his children.
10. Don't go through this alone. Talk with others in your situation and talk with your partner. By sharing experiences with other women involved with divorced dads, you will know that you are not alone.

HOPE AHEAD

One of the things you will learn from other women (who have been involved with divorced dads) is that the relationship you have with his children will usually improve as they grow older, move away from their mother, and establish their own adult lives. It's a long wait, but it gives hope to know that rejection usually does not last forever. But also recognize the possibility that things may never improve and that there may never be a close relationship between you and his children. Although it would be nice if it were otherwise, your happiness and the happiness with your partner are not dependent on their having a close friendship with you.

Gay Dads

> Gay father families help us broaden our thinking about homosexuality, men's roles in parenting, and the diverse sociocultural contexts of parenting.[1]
>
> Jerry J. Bigner

In the film *Birdcage*, Robin Williams played the role of a gay divorced father whose son has just become engaged. The issues surrounding gay fathers were quickly revealed in the film: prejudice and discrimination against gays in general, the need to stay closeted for fear of social disapproval, and the dilemmas of children who have a gay dad. This chapter emphasizes the concerns of gay divorced fathers, who share with heterosexual fathers the desire to stay connected with their children. But there are some special problems, such as coming out to one's wife and kids, trying to get custody/visitation through a homophobic court system, and discussing with one's children their concerns about homosexuality.

WHO ARE GAY FATHERS?

Stereotypes about gay fathers abound. These men are regularly characterized as effeminate, sick child molesters who want their children to be gay too. Professors Robert Barret and Bryan Robinson of the Human Services Department at the University of North Carolina at Charlotte have moved beyond the stereotypes to discover who gay fathers really are:

> Gay fathers are men like other fathers. They are young, old, professionals, blue-collar workers, stable, unstable, financially secure, on welfare, in committed couple relationships, and single. As we talked with gay fathers across the country, it became clear that they have a strong commitment to their children and

169

that the primary focus of their lives is their children's well-being. They struggle as they encounter the homophobia (fear of homosexuals) that prevails in our country, yet they attempt to minimize its negative impact on their children.[2]

Most gay men become fathers after years of living a heterosexual lifestyle. They marry, have children, and live "straight" lives. They may explore homosexual relationships while they are married, or they may abstain from such associations despite the frustration they may feel. Others, aware that they are gay, marry and have children as a way of "protecting" themselves against the disapproval of society. Still others marry and have children because "they truly desire children and value the role children play in their lives."[3]

Although marriage is the path most gay males take to fatherhood, University of Colorado Family Life specialist Jerry Bigner identified several other ways: through adoption of a child, becoming a foster parent, donating sperm for artificial insemination with a heterosexual woman or lesbian friend or couple, or forming a stepfamily with another gay man who is the biological father of children.[4]

Regardless of how they get into the role, gay fathers are out of the mainstream of fathers. Heterosexuals are suspicious of them because they are gay; homosexuals may also be less accepting of gay fathers because the role of father seems contradictory to the sort of personal freedom that is often highly valued in the gay community. Gay fathers solve this dilemma by making friends with heterosexuals who are supportive of gays and homosexuals who are supportive of fatherhood for gays. Dr. Frederic Bozett, professor in the Graduate Program at the University of Oklahoma, referred to this pattern of living outside of the mainstream of both the heterosexual and homosexual mainstreams as "integrative sanctioning."[5]

Psychologist R. M. Scallen compared homosexual and heterosexual fathers on child rearing attitudes and found that gay dads were often more nurturing, less driven by the desire to make money in a career, and more psychologically invested in their role as dad. In addition, gay dads typically had a more positive self-assessment of their performance in the parental role than heterosexual dads.[6]

HOW MANY GAY DADS ARE THERE?

Given prevailing societal attitudes about homosexuality, the exact number of gay dads is impossible to establish with accuracy, but an estimate is possible. Professor Robert T. Michael, dean of the Graduate School of Public Policy at the University of Chicago, and his colleagues found that 3% of a U.S. sample of adult men identified themselves as gay.[7] According to the U.S. Census Bureau there are about 92 million males over the age of 20 in the United States.[8] Three percent of this number translates to 2.6 million gay adult males. Research reported by Professor Bigner estimates that between 20 and 25 percent of self-identified male homosexuals are also dads.[9] So, this leads us to between 520,000 and 650,000 gay dads. Hence, there are well over half a million gay dads with at least that many children involved. With about half of current marriages ending in divorce, the number of gay divorced parents is also significant. The concerns of gay divorced dads are well worth considering.

COMING OUT TO THE WIFE

When a gay man who has married a woman decides that he no longer wishes to hide his real sexual preference from his wife, he does so despite the virtual certainty that she will want to end the marriage. However, evidence indicates that these marriages are often troubled before any formal disclosure occurs. Professor Dorothea Hays of Adelphi University and social worker Aurele Samuels studied 21 heterosexual women about their discovery that their husbands were homosexual or bisexual. The women had been married an average of 16 years when they were told about or learned of their husband's homosexual activities:

> The revelation did not come as a total surprise to most of them. Their suspicions before the actual disclosure had been raised by the decrease in the husband's sexual activity with them and his unwillingness to discuss sexual concerns, by his emotional and physical withdrawal, and by his mood swings directed toward the wives.[10]

About half of the wives reported that their husbands had told them directly. The reasons for disclosure varied, but included the husbands' fear that they may have exposed their wives to HIV or some other sexually transmitted disease. Other gay husbands tell their wives in therapy, after having attempted suicide, or after the wife has had an emotional breakdown. One wife learned of her husband's homosexuality by accident when she became aware he was going to a Gay Fathers' Forum. Still another wife became suspicious of her husband's close relationship with a male friend.

The reactions of the wives to the knowledge that their husbands were gay varied. All except one wife (who felt sorry for her husband) felt anger after the disclosure.

> Others experienced confusion, hurt, jealousy, anger, grief, disgust, and repulsion. Examples are: "I accepted it as part of his personality"; "I was relieved it was not my fault, he loved me and wanted to stay"; "I was not crazy in my suspicion . . . I was concerned about his excessive guilt, pleased at his honesty . . . "; "I reacted with rage that I had spent 30 years struggling, so often alone with children, plumbing, finances, to enable him to spend whatever time he needed on his job, only to find out that he was cruising."[11]

For most wives, the disclosure was a major challenge. "They felt different, stigmatized, and wondered what people would think of them and their marital choice."[12] Professor Bigner, a therapist who has worked with gay dads, noted that divorce is the usual result of finding out that one's spouse is gay.[13]

COMING OUT TO THE CHILDREN

The next set of problems for a gay father is whether, when, and how to tell his children. Gay fathers are motivated to come out to their children for several reasons.[14] Some feel they are living a doubly closeted life and want their children to know them as they are. Others fear that their children will find out from someone else and want their children to hear it directly from them. Still others spend a lot of time with a gay male companion and feel it is important to tell the children what is going on.

Of course, the decision to be openly gay is never easy in our society. Those who do so risk the rejection of spouses, parents, friends, coworkers, and neighbors, but these relationships involve adults who can be expected to grasp the situation and cope with it, even if that means a certain uneasiness or even alienation. On the other hand, coming out to one's children, especially *how* to go about doing so, is one of the most difficult problems gay fathers face. Many worry that being honest with their children on this point will cause the children undue stress, and most men in this situation fear that their children will reject them. Gay fathers struggle with how to break this news so as to avoid such rejection. One gay divorced father I talked with shared what he had said to his son:

> I love you and want to have a close relationship with you but I feel that if I am hiding something from you we can't be close. So I want you to know that I am gay, homosexual. That means that I like to be with men more than women. It

doesn't mean that you are gay or that I want you to be gay. I love you and want you to be who you are.

He said his children didn't take it well. They cried, ran into their room, and shut the door. He summed up his experience with words familiar to all divorced fathers: "It hasn't been easy."

Some gay fathers choose to tell their children in writing. They may prefer a letter to a discussion because they feel that in this way they will have a chance to explain thoroughly and gently, and without embarrassment or confrontation. However, a letter is probably not a good idea because the divorced father has no way of knowing how the children will react or how the letter might be used against him by his ex-partner. Unless you are *certain* that your child will be comfortable receiving the news this way *and* that your ex-spouse will not take advantage of such a written statement, it is advisable to avoid writing to your children about gay issues. A frank discussion, although perhaps somewhat uncomfortable, stands a better chance of resolving your children's concerns.

Still other gay divorced dads choose to let their children figure out the truth for themselves. This might mean taking them to events such as a Gay Pride March and watching from the sidelines. One father began to be gradually more openly affectionate with his male partner in front of his children until finally one of them asked, "Dad, are you gay?" This method of coming out also seems ill-advised, as children may feel uncomfortable bringing up the subject with you directly and so turn to others—peers or straight relatives—for their interpretations of your behavior.

Some gay dads don't decide to come out to their children at all but are outed by their ex-wives, who may feel angry and embittered and seek to hurt their ex-husbands and get the children on their side for an ensuing custody battle. One mother I spoke with said of her gay ex-husband:

> When I found out he was homosexual, all I could feel was rage. . . . I felt stupid for not knowing, betrayed for his infidelity, and disgusted that he was sleeping with men. I wanted to protect my children from this evil and told them that their daddy was a faggot and that he was leaving us to be with his queer friends. It worked. They rejected him and made it clear they wanted nothing to do with him.

Such an outing compounds the stress for the children. Not only do they discover their parents are divorcing but that their father is gay. As a general rule, things will be easier on your relationship with your children if you tell them yourself, face to face.

Dr. Bigner suggested specific guidelines for helping gay fathers tell their children that they are gay.

1. *Come to terms with your own gayness before disclosing to children.* This is crucial. The father who feels negatively about his homosexuality or is ashamed of it is much more likely to have children who also react negatively. The father must create a setting of acceptance by first being accepting of himself. If he tells his children when he is ready and comfortable, it is likely to be a positive experience for everyone.

2. *Children are never too young to be told.* They will absorb only as much as they are capable of understanding. Use words appropriate to the age of the child. Details may be added as they grow older.

3. *Discuss it with children before they know or suspect.* When children discover their father's sexual orientation from someone other than the father, they are often upset that their father did not trust them sufficiently to share the information with them. It is exceedingly difficult for children to initiate the subject, and they will not bring it up even though they may want to.

4. *Disclosure should be planned.* Children should not find out about their father's homosexuality by default or discover it accidentally or during an argument between their parents.

5. *Disclose in a quiet setting where interruptions are unlikely to occur.*

6. *Inform; don't confess.* The disclosure should not be heavy or maudlin but positive and sincere. Informing in a simple, natural, and matter-of-fact manner when the father is ready is more likely to foster acceptance by the child. If possible, discuss or rehearse what will be said to children with another gay or lesbian parent who has been through a similar disclosure.

7. *Inform the children that relationships with them will not change as a result of disclosure.* Disclosure will, however, allow the father to be more honest. Children may need reassurance that their father is the same person he was before. Younger children may need reassurance that he is still their father.

8. *Be prepared for questions.* Here are some questions and possible answers:
   - *Why are you telling me this?* Because my personal life is important, and I want to share it with you. I am accepting of being gay (homosexual), and you don't need to feel ashamed of me.
   - *What does being gay mean?* It means being attracted to other men so much that I might fall in love with a man and express that love physically and sexually.

- *What makes a person gay?* No one knows, although there are lots of theories. (This may be the child's way of asking if he or she will be gay.)
- *Will I be gay, too?* You won't be gay just because I'm gay. It's not contagious, and it doesn't appear to be hereditary. You will be whatever you're going to be.
- *Don't you like women?* (The child might be asking, *Don't you like mom?* or *Do you hate mom?* If this question is asked by a daughter, it also may mean, *Don't you like me?* or *Do you hate me?*) I do like women, but I'm not physically or romantically attracted to them like I am to men.
- *What should I tell my friends about it?* A lot of people just don't understand, so it might be best to keep it between us until you feel safe telling others. You can discuss it with me any time you want. If you want to tell a close friend, go ahead and try it out. The friend might or might not be accepting, and he or she might tell others. You should be prepared for those possibilities. If you do tell somebody, let me know how it turns out. (Couched in these terms, the father's sexual orientation is not framed as a shameful secret but as a matter of personal privacy for children.)[15]

Regardless of how children become aware that their dad is gay, they seem to adjust to the information more easily than their mothers. Dr. Bozett summarized the literature on children's reactions to the fact that their dad is gay. He noted that gay dads "are typically surprised by the positive reactions of their children ... daughters tend to be more accepting than sons, although most children feel their fathers' honesty brings them closer."[16]

In a study by N. L. Wyers, the average age at which children found out that their father was gay was 11. Their reactions ranged from positive with no problems, to mild reactions, to anger and confusion.[17] Researchers Turner, Scadden, and Harris studied 10 gay fathers and their children and concluded that most father–child relationships were positive, there were few long-term problems for the children, and the fact that the father was gay was of little importance in the overall parent–child relationship.[18]

Having a gay dad is a challenging adjustment issue for sons and daughters. But it is not insurmountable and there are some positive aspects of having a gay dad. Indeed, many of the stresses and difficulties children experience are more related to the fact that their parents are divorcing than the fact that their dad is gay. These issues sometimes get confused, as reflected in the statement of a neighbor of a gay divorced dad: "Those kids wouldn't be so messed up if their dad wasn't a queer."

Children differ in their reactions to the knowledge that their father is gay. Children whose parents have reared them from a young age to be aware of and tolerant of diversity should have relatively little trouble with their father being gay. Consider Barry, an 8-year-old whose mother is heterosexual and his father bisexual. As long as Barry can remember, Cliff (dad's friend) has also lived in the house. Cliff has always been like a member of the family, so his presence in the home and his relationship with dad is no big deal. "My friends tell me it's weird but it doesn't feel that way to me," Barry said. "When my mom and my dad divorced, I thought it was natural that he and Cliff live together. My folks have joint custody, so I get to see both my parents as often as I want."

Other children may have entirely different reactions to the knowledge that their fathers are gay. Earlier, I noted the reaction of a wife who discovered her husband's homosexuality and set out to "protect" her children from such "evil." Children who are manipulated in this way may feel anger toward their fathers and avoid close relationships with them. If your ex-spouse reacts this way, there is, unfortunately, very little you can do except wait until your children are mature enough to judge the situation for themselves. As discussed in Chapter 2, a mother's influence, though strong, does not last forever.

In addition to their personal reaction to the knowledge that their father is gay, children must learn how to cope with homophobic agemates. Chip, a 17-year-old high school senior who has known for 5 years that his father is gay, commented on how he copes with his father being gay and his agemates:

> When he invites another guy into the house it's OK. I don't bring friends home then. One of my pals is extremely homophobic and he lets that fact be known. I wouldn't dare risk anything or it would be like "goodbye" to my friend. My other two friends, I don't know how they would react. So I have to be careful about having certain friends over. To me it's blatantly obvious. Having been exposed to so many gay people, I know what to look for and what I'm seeing. Sometimes it's kind of hard because people make fun of gay people. And, if I stick up for their rights, then I get ridiculed. So I just don't say anything at school. It's kind of hard sometimes.[19]

Some children benefit from their father's talking about societal homophobia and the importance in choosing wisely which teachers and which friends are allowed to know what information. Such discussion is often a bonding experience between gay fathers and their children as they cope with a common problem. Being aware of prejudice and discrimination at an early age and learning how to cope with it is a plus for the development of any child. And, in this regard, children of gay fathers may be ahead of the game.

Gay divorced fathers must also be careful not to push homosexuality as a lifestyle and to allow their children to reject it. Children reared in a homophobic society will need time to consider an alternative view and will best do so without pressure. One child interviewed by Professors Barret and Robinson said:

> My dad and I had terrible fights as he put pressure on me to say it was OK. I thought what he was doing was sinful and embarrassing. But over time, I began to realize that he is the same dad he has always been, and now we are closer than ever. My friends have also got used to the idea and like to spend time with him, too.[20]

A more serious problem for children of a gay father is that a male child may wonder if he is gay and become confused about his own sexual identity. It is important to remember that some children whose parents are heterosexual and married may also go through a period of confusion about sexual orientation; this kind of difficulty is in no way confined to the children of homosexual parents. Indeed, such a concern is not uncommon among adolescent males, who may experiment with sex together and define this activity as "what homosexuals do." However, such concerns usually dissipate over time as the boy becomes sensitive to what his body tells him about his own sexual orientation. In the ideal circumstance, the boy will talk about his concerns with his father, who will assure him that it is unlikely that he is gay—only a few males are—but that if he is, they can talk about how to accept and enjoy who he is as well as how to survive in a homophobic society.

CUSTODY AND VISITATION ISSUES FOR GAY DADS

Although gay fathers may serve quite well in their roles as parents, Professors Barret and Robinson have observed that "social service agencies and the legal system are not altogether comfortable with the idea of gay men as parents."[21] That's a nice way of saying what most gay men already know: The courts are homophobic, prejudiced, and biased against gay fathers. Two major cultural fears work against gay fathers who want full or joint custody of their children or a liberal visitation schedule. The first of these fears is that gay fathers will molest their children, and the second is that gay fathers will "recruit" their children into a gay lifestyle.

Concern that a child will not be sexually molested is well placed. Abundant evidence suggests that child sexual abuse has serious, negative, long-term consequences for the child.[22] But the belief that gay men are more likely to molest children is bigoted and false. Although such abuse does occur, it is rare. Indeed, the ratio of heterosexual child molesters to homosexual child molesters is 11 to 1.[23] Evidence also indicates that children living with heterosexual men are at a significantly greater risk of incest than those living with gay fathers.

The fear that children who spend a great deal of time with a gay parent will themselves become gay is also unfounded. The fact that most homosexuals were born and reared in families in which the parents were heterosexual suggests that one's sexual orientation may have more to do with one's biological wiring than one's socialization influences. But there is professional disagreement on this point. Psychologist Scott Hershberger of the University of Kansas studied sexual orientation among 1314 twins. He concluded that "no evidence was found for different genes influencing the sexual orientation of men and women."[24] Dr. Bozett summarized the literature on the issue of children of homosexuals becoming homosexual and concluded that there is "no indication that the children of gay fathers are disproportionately homosexual themselves although, of the children who turned out to be gay, there were more lesbian daughters than gay sons."[25]

Despite these facts, many of the same people in our society who would applaud a heterosexual man's interest in his daughter's well-being quite often become suspicious of a gay man's interest in his son. These attitudes are typical, and gay men who choose to be open about their sexuality do so with the full knowledge of how negatively mainstream society will perceive them. In most cases, such men have already resolved to risk the relationships they had before coming out of the closet. Although the loss of friends and the rejection of relatives are painful, the loss of one's children is always far more distressing. Because the legal system (already biased against fathers in general, as we have seen) is comprised of judges drawn from the mainstream, gay divorced fathers can expect to be confronted with homophobia in court as well, and it is most often there that custody and visitation are decided.

Writing in the *Journal of Homosexuality*, Professor Hitchens noted that judges who are reluctant to give gay divorced fathers custody often express the concern that parenting performed by homosexuals will produce gender-deviant children, such as transsexuals. A transsexual person is one who has the genetic and anatomical makeup of one sex (e.g., a male with XY chromosomes and a penis) but the self-concept of the other sex (e.g., the anatomical male has the self-concept of a woman). The old saying, "I am a woman trapped in a man's body," expresses the dilemma of the transsexual. Transsexuality is not the same as homosexuality. Both heterosexual and homosexual males have the self-concept of being men, and so any modeling influence would be in the appropriate gender direction—the male child would learn from his homosexual father that he is a man. Having a gay or straight father is, once again, unrelated to a child's eventual gender identity.[26]

Some judges feel that a child whose dad is homosexual will be the target of harmful ridicule from his or her peers. Although peers may taunt a classmate because his dad is gay, such intolerance is regularly experienced by other minorities and is certainly no basis on which to restrict a father–child relationship. To the contrary, valuable lessons about handling prejudice and discrimination are available to the child of a gay dad.

The legal mechanisms the courts use to deny gay fathers access to their children include *"per se"* and *"nexus"* standards. The *per se* standard means that, in custodial hearings where one parent is gay, the gay parent should not be the custodial parent because homosexuality in and of itself constitutes unfitness. Listen to the words of a judge presiding over the case of Doris Nadler, a lesbian who lost custody of her 4-year-old daughter when she and her husband divorced:

> Frankly, ma'am, you should take therapy, as the doctor suggested, if you are going to overcome your . . . psychological problem. And the Court—we are dealing with a four-year-old child on the threshold of its development—just cannot take the chance that something untoward should happen to it. . . . I'm sincere in saying that I want this child protected, and if the lady takes therapeutics, and the psychiatrist can assure me, then I will look for unrestrained visitation. It would depend on the factors. Right now, I just can't take the chance.[27]

Although this judge's ruling was eventually overturned, some states still allow *per se* rulings. Other states have a *"nexus"* standard, which means that a clear *nexus* or connection must be made between the parent's homosexuality and harm to the child before custody and/or visitation can be denied.

How gay dads perform as parents is also a big question for judges. But Jerry Bigner and Brooke Jacobsen at Colorado State University compared 33 heterosexual fathers and 33 gay fathers and concluded that:

> gay fathers tend to be more strict and consistently emphasize the importance of setting and enforcing limits on children's behavior significantly more as a group than nongay fathers. Additionally, gay fathers state that they go to greater lengths than nongay fathers in promoting cognitive skills of children by explaining rules and regulations to children. As such, they may place greater emphasis on verbal communications with children as compared with nongay fathers. Gay fathers tend to be more responsive to the perceived needs of children than nongay fathers.[28]

Bigner and Jacobsen explain that the greater strictness on the part of gay fathers results from their feeling under greater scrutiny by judges to be good parents. "They may believe that they are being examined more closely than other fathers due to their sexual preference" and feel that custody/visitation decisions are made on their performance.[29] Indeed, sociologist B. Miller found that gay males who divorce may become even better fathers after the divorce, as fathering seems to be compatible with gayness, which allows for a more nurturing attitude in men. He also noted that although the marriages for the gay fathers had ended, they were very committed to the stability of family relationships and very much wanted to stay connected with their kids.[30]

Despite the fact that no empirical evidence exists that homosexual orientation in a father or other caregiver is detrimental to children's welfare,[31] gay divorced dads are regularly denied custody of their children "simply by virtue of their homosexual orientation."[32] And sometimes the reason is political. One gay divorced dad I know presented a series of witnesses who testified to his loving, nurturing relationship with his child. Not only had he been the primary caretaker for the child as an infant, he had also attended PTA meetings, was the leader for his son's Boy Scout troop, and regularly took him fishing. Nevertheless, the judge denied the father full and joint custody and ruled that he could see his son only on a standard visitation schedule—every other weekend, alternate holidays, a month in the summer, and so on. After hearing the ruling, I asked the lawyer why the judge hadn't at least awarded the dad joint custody. The lawyer told me:

> Judges in this conservative town have one agenda: to get reelected. If the word gets out that this judge "gave a kid to a fag," the judge's days are over. It's not right; it's not fair. But that's what happened.

Even though gay divorced dads are denied custody, they do not go away. Professor Bozett observed, "Gay fathers who do not have physical custody of their children tend to maintain consistent contact with them. . . . Gay fathers try harder to create stable home lives and positive relationships with their children than one would expect from traditional heterosexual parents."[33] Their children seem to benefit not only by their exposure to a more androgynous model but by learning about the insidious nature of homophobic and heterosexist attitudes.[34]

CONCLUSION

In this chapter, we have seen that despite widespread societal attitudes to the contrary, homosexuality on the part of a father need not be a serious barrier to his relationship with his children. Gay men are still people whose rights as parents should not be considered differently from those of heterosexual fathers. Although prejudice and legal barriers remain, gay divorced fathers typically demonstrate strong commitment to their children, even when this may mean risking personal rejection and public humiliation. As attitudes continue to shift toward acceptance of homosexuality, gay fathers can look forward to being judged on their merit as parents rather than being victimized by negative stereotypes. Until then, however, gay divorced fathers will have to struggle with the stigma of their sexuality in addition to the many difficulties that all divorced fathers must face as they try to maintain close, positive relationships with their children.

Remarriage—for You and Your Children's Mother

The myth of instant love and its antithesis of never-ending, unsolvable problems need to be dispelled.

Step Family Association of America

According to the U.S. Bureau of the Census, three-fourths of men remarry at a median age of 37.4.[1] Remarriage moves the relationship with the new partner to a new level. No longer do your children think of her as daddy's "girlfriend," but as daddy's "wife." This chapter is about how remarriage will alter the relationships between you, your partner, and your children. It is also about the potential effects of your ex-wife's remarriage.

WHEN YOU REMARRY

The fact that a man is divorced does not mean that he is sour on marriage. Rather, most enjoy being in love and in a stable marital relationship. The fact that men remarry sooner than women may not only be a function of the availability of interested and marriageable women, but may also indicate that men are ready to renew the marital state sooner. Of course, there are men who are not interested in becoming involved in a new relationship. Instead, they want to focus on caring for their children alone. Such was the scenario of Dustin Hoffman in *Kramer versus Kramer*. These men are sometimes portrayed as fumbling buffoons who can't boil an egg. The reality is that divorced fathers are all types and represent a spectrum of talents and abilities.

Professor E. Mavis Heatherington of the University of Virginia at Charlottesville (and colleagues Martha Cox and Roger Cox) studied divorced

and married fathers and found that divorced fathers were more likely to
see themselves as failures and feel less competent at work, in social situations, and in intimate relationships. These differences were particularly
true the first year following the divorce.[2] However, remarriage seems to
have had a very positive effect in terms of restoring their self-image and
feelings of competence. Indeed, marriage is good for men. On most mea-
sures of mental and physical health (less depression, less suicide, less drug
abuse), married men are much more "healthy" than divorced men. Researcher R. N. Anderson of the National Center for Health Statistics in Hy-
attsville, Maryland, and his colleagues found that married men are more
likely to live longer than all other categories including the divorced, the
widowed, and the never married.[3] The benefits of remarriage for the divorced dad's children are obvious.

The most important thing you can do when you decide to remarry is to
give your children plenty of notice. Some divorced fathers fear that their
children will disapprove of remarriage, so they spring the wedding on
them. One divorced father awakened his children one morning, asked
them to get dressed, and drove them to the courthouse where he married
a woman they had only recently met. The children were shocked and felt
betrayed that they were not allowed to know that their father was serious
about this woman and wanted to marry her. The woman also had a child,
so that by 10 PM these children went to bed in a house that now included a
new stepmother and a new stepsister. The children were not happy about
it. Another reason this divorced father did not tell his children what was
going on was that he feared they would tell their mother and that this information might be used against him in court. Although his rationale is
understandable, the impact of their being kept in the dark about the im-
pending marriage was dramatic. The children were emotionally distant
from their new stepmother and ignored her daughter completely.

Because your new wife is a very significant part of your life, it is important to carefully attend to the relationship between her and your children,
which certainly involves more than a casual knowledge of each other. At
the very least, your partner and children should have known each other for
a year, had meals together, been on vacation together, watched TV together,
and basically "hung out around the house" together. Such exposure will allow your partner and children to get to know each other. If the initial exposure is strained, you may need more time before setting a wedding date.

Of course, you should not let your children control your life in terms of
whom and when you date or marry. But the blending of families is a very

delicate issue and time is often the best antidote for such strain. What's the rush? Is your getting married *now* worth forcing your children to live in a very strained context? Maybe so, maybe not. I waited 9 years after my separation before getting remarried, which allowed considerable time for my children to pass through the rejection to the acceptance stage. If they had not, I would have married the same woman anyway. But their acceptance made our getting married a comfortable event.

BEFORE YOU REMARRY

According to statistician Sally Clarke of the National Center for Health Statistics and her colleague Barbara Wilson, who compared the stability of first and second marriages, remarriages that last over 15 years have a lower chance of divorce than first marriages.[4] But in the early years, remarriages are more likely to break up, perhaps because people who have been married before are less tolerant of unhappy relationships and know they can survive a divorce. Before getting remarried, it is important to pay close attention to certain issues. For instance, it is a mistake to remarry until you are completely healed from your divorce. You should wait until you are no longer depressed and until you can accept your share of responsibility for the divorce. Getting married on the rebound is always a mistake. According to psychologist Jack Turner of Huntsville, Alabama, who works with divorced dads, it takes most people about 18 months to emotionally recover from a divorce. The person who terminated the relationship usually recovers more quickly than the person who was terminated.[5]

Persons getting remarried are more likely to consider a prenuptial agreement that specifies who will get what in the event of divorce or death. Some people feel that a prenuptial agreement destroys the romance of a relationship and that it sets up a couple to divorce, but the reality is that a prenuptial agreement no more causes a divorce than a seatbelt causes a wreck.

If it is important to you that your new partner sign a prenuptial agreement, you should discuss the issue with her as soon as the relationship becomes serious, but at least 6 months before the wedding. If you delay discussing this matter with her, she may feel pressured and resentful. These feelings take time to deal with, and weeks before the wedding is not long enough.

The value of a prenuptial agreement (which is drawn up by an attorney) is in the communication between the partners about their relationship. Sometimes the partners may have different ideas about how things will be handled and a discussion will clarify misunderstandings. Some of the items included in premarital agreements are:

- Names—will the wife keep her maiden name?
- Adoption—will the husband adopt the new partner's children?
- Religion—what religion will the children be reared in?
- Domicile—whose career will determine where the couple lives?
- Money—joint or separate accounts? His economic responsibility for her children? Will the spouses own property as a couple or as individuals? What will the children inherit from whom? Are debts in the marriage considered joint debts or not? Who is responsible for bringing how much income into the unit? How will the money be divided and/or used?
- Financial matters in the event of a divorce.

Having clear answers to such questions may be beneficial to the couple.

I teach a course in Courtship and Marriage at East Carolina University. One of the standard sociological principles of mate selection is called "homogamy," or like marries like. For divorced dads, this means that they are attracted to divorced mothers, as they are likely to feel understood both as divorced people and as parents. The result is that when divorced dads remarry, they are most likely to marry women who have children. Marrying a divorced mother means accepting emotional and financial responsibility for her kids. It is unreasonable for either you or your partner to expect that each of you will feel the same way about your stepchildren as you do about your own biological children. Understandably, you will have different feelings. Although feelings of love may (or may not) come with time, feeling generally positive about your partner's children is crucial.

Their acceptance of you is another issue. If your partner's children are living with their father as the custodial parent and he does not like you as their new stepfather, do not be surprised if your stepchildren are cool toward you. It may be years before they accept you because of the context in which they spend most of their time. Resolve to be kind toward them and do things with them to nurture your relationship with them.

Another consideration is, of course, how the new family situation will impact your new spouse. The stepmother's role is a difficult role. It can be

SELF-ASSESSMENT

WILL IT BE EASY FOR YOUR CHILDREN TO ADJUST TO YOUR REMARRIAGE?

To gauge how your children will adjust to your remarriage, read each sentence below and circle the appropriate number. The higher the number circled, the easier it will be for your children to adjust to your remarriage.

1 = Definitely Not   4 = Mostly Yes
2 = Mostly Not   5 = Definitely Yes
3 = Sometimes

	DN	MN	S	MY	DY
1. My children like the woman I am soon to marry.	1	2	3	4	5
2. My new wife-to-be likes my children.	1	2	3	4	5
3. My children have had time to get to know my new wife-to-be.	1	2	3	4	5
4. My children are old enough to make up their own minds about whom they like and don't like.	1	2	3	4	5
5. My children and my new wife-to-be enjoy playing together.	1	2	3	4	5
6. My children want to be in our wedding.	1	2	3	4	5
7. My former spouse is supportive of the children's relationship with my new wife-to-be.	1	2	3	4	5
8. My wife-to-be, my children, and I have been on vacation together.	1	2	3	4	5
9. My new wife-to-be knows how to get along with children.	1	2	3	4	5
10. My children want me to marry my new partner.	1	2	3	4	5

Add the numbers you have circled. The lowest possible score is 10, which means that your children will have difficulty at this time adjusting to your remarriage. The highest possible score is 50, which means that your children will adjust easily to your remarriage. An intermediate score is 30. The higher your score, the easier it will be for your children to adjust to your remarriage. If you are recently divorced, it is likely that you scored between 10 and 30. If you have been divorced for several years, it is likely that you scored much higher.

particularly difficult if your former wife tries to turn your children against your new wife. Your children may feel that they are being disloyal to their mother if they show signs of "liking" your wife, so they may endeavor to keep her at a distance. Such an arm's length relationship will ensure a strained relationship between your children and new wife.

Expecting your new wife to "love" your children while they are rejecting her is unrealistic. What is important is that both you and your wife view your children's behavior as a result of their living with their mother in a nonsupportive context. As your children grow up and move out of the house, the potential for an improved relationship can begin. In the meantime, both you and your new wife should be realistic about what is possible with your children.

One of the reasons some divorced men wait to remarry is that when they do so, the ex-wife can legally force the new wife to divulge all of her financial records. For example, your ex-wife can ask for more child support as well as ask you to pay for her attorney fees as she drags you back into court. To show that you have the money for such increased child support and attorney fees, she can subpoena not only your financial records but those of your new wife.

Some new wives object to the demand that they divulge their finances. One newly remarried wife told the judge that she was not going to divulge her personal finances to her husband's ex-wife because it was "none of her business" and that she would divorce her husband if necessary so that she would no longer be "the wife" who had to divulge her finances. The judge reconsidered and did not require her to divulge her finances. This is an unusual case. Husbands should be aware that judges can order your new wife to reveal all of her financial records.

CHILDREN'S VIEWS ON REMARRIAGE

Your children's reaction to your remarriage will depend on their age, the amount of time elapsed since your divorce, and how the children's mother has taught them to view your new wife/remarriage. The younger the children, the more dependent they are on the definitions their custodial mother gives them of your divorce and remarriage. Preschool children who are told by their mother that dad is going to marry the woman who "broke up the family" or who "stole your daddy from your mother" will react much more negatively to dad's remarriage than children who are told that daddy's new wife is a wonderful person and that they are lucky to have her as a stepmother.

~Older children who have had time to get to know dad's partner are less vulnerable to the definitions of their mother. Many will completely discount their mother's opinion if it varies from their own perception. "My mom has been bitter since my dad left and wouldn't approve of anybody he remarried," said one daughter I interviewed about her dad's soon-to-be-wife.

Nevertheless, few children are elated about the remarriage of either of their parents. For them, it is the final signal that the marriage has ended and that mom and dad will never get back together. In viewing the reaction of your children to your remarriage, keep in mind that it is your marriage, not theirs, and do not expect them to be as excited as you are. For them to have neutral to positive feelings is a reasonable expectation, but don't require them to have these feelings. Let them experience your wedding in whatever way they can.

If you have not spent sufficient time with your children since the divorce, they may feel that the remarriage is another sign of your abandoning them. They will view this remarriage as your preference to be with someone else rather than them. But, if they have had time to bond with you since the divorce and have spent time with your new wife, their feelings of abandonment will be minimized.

Your children may also fear that they cannot like your new wife without incurring the disapproval of their mother. Their mother may feel territorial and fear replacement by your new wife. Because few stepmothers even try to "replace" the biological mother, this fear is usually unwarranted. But such fear sends a strong message to the children that they should not like this woman too much or mother will be angry.

Discipline becomes an issue in most remarriages. Children often resent dad's new "girlfriend" telling them what to do. "You're not my boss!" said one 9-year-old to his stepmother. Successful stepmothers handle this problem by doing three things: (1) The stepmother should try to become a friend before becoming a disciplinarian. This means spending time with the children and trying to develop an emotional relationship with them. (2) The stepmother should let the father do most of the disciplining of his children. The kids will accept his disciplining more easily and it protects the relationship that is developing between his children and his new wife. (3) The stepmother should let the father make clear to his children that, in his absence, someone has to be responsible for the family and that person is his new wife.

Discipline problems can become major issues in stepfamilies and the new parents should not expect smooth sailing in this area for a long time (years).

Stepfamily living is not only about sharing the time adults have with children but also about sharing living quarters. Teenagers who require a lot of privacy may rebel against having to share a bedroom or bathroom with a stepsibling. It is best to let them deal with this.

Despite the problems associated with stepfamily living, there are some major advantages of stepfamily living for children. Remarried couples typically have more money than single-parent households. According to the Census Bureau, the median income of a married couple family is about $51,000, compared with about $24,000 for a father as a householder living alone with his children.[6] The difference is even greater when compared with the $16,000 for a mother as a householder living alone with her children.[6] Hence, one of the first ways children benefit from a remarriage is through an improved standard of living. This usually translates into moving out of an apartment into a large house and having more income for computers, vacations, and so forth. One of the major problems associated with divorce is a decline in the standard of living (particularly for women). A remarriage simply kicks this standard of living back up, and sometimes even higher, if the new husband has a good income.

When married and divorced people are compared, the former group is more likely to report being happier. They are also healthier because, on average, married people abuse drugs and alcohol less, get more sleep, and eat healthier food. Their partners are also likely to insist that they see a physician if they show unexplained symptoms. Remarried people also have a stable companion with whom to share life. Such companionship translates into being happier, which is an advantage to your kids.

Although children who grow up in single-parent homes and who are loved and disciplined can turn out to be very happy productive members of society, they may be more vulnerable to drop out of school, experience a teen pregnancy, and abuse drugs. Part of this is a result of the custodial parent having to go to work to earn an income, which may mean little supervision of their children. Children reared in two-parent families have a better chance of at least one of the parents attending to their needs. When mom or dad remarries, each gets another person to help with the work of rearing children. Although children may be jealous that someone new has entered their parent's life, the children usually benefit.

Individuals who left their first marriage with the idea of finding bliss in a second marriage are often shocked to discover the challenges of stepfamily living. One divorced dad who remarried a divorced mother with custody said:

> I was very naive. Her kids were no problem as long as I was her boyfriend. But after we married and I moved in, the conflicts and the fighting never stopped. They just never accepted me and when my wife had to choose between her kids and me, I was sacrificed. Now I won't even date a woman with kids.

Stepfamilies are unlike the families created in first marriages in several ways. In stepfamilies, the spouses start off with a child in the house; there is no "child-free" time. This means the remarried parents have little time to nurture their own relationship, as they are constantly distracted by the needs of the children. Also, one of the parents (usually the father) does not have his own children in the house, which means he may be depressed or frustrated at not being able to see or be with his children. His new wife must cope with his frustration and anger.

In stepfamilies, the relationship between the parent and the child has existed longer than that between the two people who have married. This means that a stronger emotional bond already exists between the parent and the child and may interfere with the bonding between the husband and the wife.

Because money in the stepfamily may be going out to a former spouse (e.g., dad pays child support to ex-wife), the new wife may be angry that it cannot be used for her new family. On the other hand, money may be coming into the stepfamily from a former spouse (e.g., new wife receives child support from ex-husband). In this case, the stepfamily may become dependent on an external source of money that can decrease or even stop without notice.

The values of a stepparent may be different from those of the biological parent of the same sex. In this case, the children must adjust to a new set of values when they travel between homes.

Each of these factors is capable of becoming a major problem in your stepfamily. One of the most important choices remarried spouses can make is not to require that their stepfamily living be problem-free. Having realistic expectations is absolutely essential. Some stepchildren may have no interest in ever facilitating a renewed sense of family. These are usually older children who feel detached from their parents anyway. The fact that their mom or dad has remarried may be irrelevant to them.

It takes several years for individuals who have just begun a new stepfamily to feel comfortable with each other. Children must resolve the issues of divided loyalties, sharing territory, and adapting to a new set of values. Time is also needed for the children to develop their own thoughts and ideas if they are living in a nonsupportive context with their mother. For example, preteen children who are living with a mother who tells them that dad's new wife and her children are "not the kind of people we want to associate with" may adopt their mother's view at age 12 but not at age 17.

Stepfamily members who share their own rituals tend to feel more like a "family" sooner. Having certain dinners, going to certain places on vacation, and observing certain holidays are ways in which families experience rituals that provide a bonding context for the family members.

Keeping a balance between nurturing your relationship as a new couple and attending to the needs of your children is a challenge. Couples who do not spend time alone to nurture their relationship may drift apart and be faced with another separation/divorce. Spouses who are too focused on their relationship may neglect the needs of their children. Keep both sets of relationships nurtured.

Nurturing the relationship with children in the stepfamily means each adult spending individual time with each child. It is particularly important for the stepmother and stepfather to spend time alone with their stepchildren. The several years it sometimes takes for a stepfamily to feel like a "real family" can be cut considerably by spending time alone with each child and developing emotional bonds.

The biggest problem of children in stepfamilies is the conflict their biological parents have with each other. Where there is little or no conflict, children adjust quickly to their new stepfamily. The ideal stepfamily is one in which the new mom and dad cooperate with their former spouses with regard to the children. Although this is not always possible, the new stepmother or stepfather should make every effort to create and maintain an amicable relationship with the children's biological mother or father. The parents, former spouses, and children benefit from such a relationship.

THE REMARRIAGE OF YOUR FORMER SPOUSE

No discussion of how remarriage may affect your children's lives would be complete without some attention to the remarriage of your ex-wife to another man. Because most divorced women do remarry within 5 years of the divorce, it is likely to happen, and so you should be prepared for it.

Divorced fathers wonder how the new stepfather will view his role and whether he will attempt to "take over" as the emotional father of their children. Being replaced by a stepfather is a haunting fear of most fathers. Although the fear may be devastating, it is usually unrealistic. As already discussed, fathers who remain active in their children's lives remain "dad" in their children's view. The stepfather may become an important person to your children but this is to their benefit.

Actually, you should set your own ego aside and support the relationship your children have with their stepfather. Most fathers and stepfathers feel awkward about each other. Typically, neither has a high trust level for the other. Nevertheless, you can still be supportive of the relationship your children have with their stepfather. For example, you might say something like, "I hear he is a good man. Try to get along with him and enjoy him" or "It was nice of your stepdad to take you to the beach." The fact that your children can enjoy their stepdad does not diminish their relationship with you.

You should also be supportive of the relationship your children have with their stepsiblings. Although some stepsiblings hate each other, others enjoy each other. Over time, these relationships have the potential to be very valuable to your children and your nurturing them can be in their best interest. Giving the stepchildren Christmas and birthday presents acknowledges their presence and importance in the lives of your children.

Some ex-wives who remarry want to draw a tight circle around their new family (the wife, her husband, and her children) and exclude the biological father. One way they may try to accomplish this is by moving their children to another state to make it difficult for you to remain an active parent in the lives of your children. The best protection you have against this occurring is a court-ordered agreement that allows neither parent to take the child out of the state. But this must be done at the time the original custody order is written.

In the absence of such an agreement, the father must rely on seeing his children when he can during the year and spending a large block of time with them during the summer. The more time the better.

STAGES TOWARD FEELING LIKE A FAMILY AGAIN

One of the difficulties of stepfamily living is not knowing what to expect. In talking with remarried spouses, I have noticed that they typically go through at least four phases before they arrive at feeling like a family again.

"Happy Family" Illusory Phase

Most divorced individuals who think about getting remarried and establishing a new family have a lot of illusions about what it will be like. Because the new partners love each other and are happy together, they assume their children will also find it easy to love their partner and will want to live together as one big happy family. This illusion is usually short-lived.

Reality of Rejection Phase

Rather than acceptance, some children feel abandoned by their dad and resent the intrusion of the new partner and her children into their lives. Sometimes there is overt rejection in that the children will be "cold" to the new partner and have nothing to do with her. Some children model their mother's feelings about the new partner ("She stole your dad") or are impolite in an attempt to run the partner off so that they can have dad to themselves again. This stark reality of rejection is quite different from the earlier illusion created by the new lovers.

"Fighting Back" Phase

After a period of trying to be accepting of the children's feelings, the new parents become frustrated and fight back. They either ignore or let the children know that their behavior is unacceptable. A little of both may help, but stepdads and stepmoms may also be oversensitive and care too much what their children are experiencing. One ploy is to simply back off and ignore whether the children like the situation or not. Another strategy is to hold the children responsible for their own behavior and let them know that being impolite is unacceptable. The parents can also make it clear that it is not expected that they love or have positive feelings toward the new parent. What is important is that they are polite and respectful.

Relax Phase

As noted earlier, stepfamily members report that it takes several years before their family feels "normal" again. Simply letting the clock run while trying to develop emotional ties with each child is very helpful.

CONCLUSION

Most divorced fathers remarry, and those who do report being happier. They are also healthier and live longer, because married men tend to eat healthier food, see their physician more regularly, and go to bed earlier. The divorced father's children may disapprove of their dad's remarriage, viewing his marrying a new woman as rejection of them. They may also feel that if they like dad's new wife, their mother will be mad at them. In addition to conflicted loyalties, they may compete with stepsiblings for affection, space in the house, use of the TV, and so forth. Despite these problems, stepfamily members report that, after several years, most have begun to feel like a "normal" family again. Sharing various rituals and developing emotional bonds with individual family members helps to shorten the time to a smoother family functioning.

The Importance of Staying Connected with Your Children

> Fathers are not insignificant. If you think they are, just ask a child who doesn't have one.[1]
>
> Bob Sammons, M.D., Ph.D.

Along with women being artificially inseminated and rearing children on their own, the cultural belief has emerged that children don't need fathers, as that role can be supplied by a caring single mother, caring grandparents, or other extended kin. The fact that our society makes divorced fathers "visitors" to their children reflects the lack of cultural value assigned to fathers. But fathers are not peripheral. They are crucial to the development of their children. Barbra Streisand in a *20/20* interview said, "Not having a father there left this deep hole that could never be filled."

Although some stepfathers have a profound positive influence on their stepchildren, biological fathers often evidence more commitment to their children across time. Indeed, when spouses in stepfamilies divorce, stepfathers are less likely to maintain a sustained commitment to their stepchildren than divorced biological fathers are to their own children. But whether stepfather or biological father, the impact of one or more fathers on a child's development is crucial.

THE DEVALUATION OF FATHERS

It will be recalled from Chapter 8 that in colonial America, fathers were regarded as the primary and irreplaceable caregivers of their children. Both by law and by custom, fathers bore the ultimate responsibility for the care and well-being of their children—particularly older children. David

Blankenhorn is founder and president of the Institute for American Values, a private, nonpartisan organization devoted to research, publication, and public education on family issues. In his landmark book *Fatherless America*, he points out that "throughout the eighteenth century, child rearing manuals were generally addressed to fathers, not to mothers. Until the early nineteenth century, in almost all cases of divorce, it was established practice to award custody of children to fathers."[2]

The Industrial Revolution refers to the social and economic changes that occurred when machines and factories, rather than human labor, became the primary way goods were produced. Before industrialization, clothes were made at home; after industrialization, in factories. Industrialization occurred in the United States during the early and mid-1800s and represents one of the most profound influences on the family. A major effect was to change the cultural value assigned to fathers in the rearing of their children. As fathers left the home and worked in urban factories, no longer did children have a father around to set a good example. Increasingly, children were cared for by their mothers only—the domestic sphere had become completely femininized. Such feminization became important in cases of divorce, where children were thought to need their mothers during the "tender years"—the idea that fathers would get custody had vanished.

When fathers left the home during the day to work in factories, their importance to children gradually shifted to the money they brought back to the family unit. Even today, the central focus of divorce courts is not how often the father can be with his children, but how much money he can send and how often. A cadre of court clerks, magistrates, and sheriffs await the father who misses a child support payment, but there is no such concern or enforcement effort when the child is taken out of town by the former spouse on the father's weekend. When the man becomes irate that he is denied access to his children, the cultural response is, "What's the big deal? He shouldn't have gotten divorced and left his kids in the first place." The implied belief is that fathers are not really important to their children, that the children and their mother are probably doing just fine as long as the father is still sending money.

That fathers are unnecessary has become a cultural theme. Single mothers are told not to worry—all they really need is a support system to help with child care, and other males in the child's life (e.g., teachers, coaches, uncles) will be substitute enough. Besides, it is commonly thought that fathers don't do much child care, so mothers end up doing all the of work anyway. All she really needs (the cultural belief goes) is the money (and she may have her own career to take care of that). The result of this belief is that our society is gradually being encouraged to accept the notion that fathers are optional. Both sociologist David Popenoe of Rutgers University and David Blankenhorn have made it very clear that fathers are essential to the well-being of children and society. What do fathers have to offer?

HOW HAVING A FATHER IS BENEFICIAL TO CHILDREN

According to the U.S. Bureau of the Census, 16.5 million children under the age of 18 live apart from their dads.[3] What are these children missing?

First, fathers represent strong authority figures and maintain high expectations of disciplined behavior in their children. "If my father found out, he would kill me" is not an unfamiliar phrase of adolescents who have fathers. But for those who don't, the chance of being caught by dad is less likely, so the chance of pushing back the limits of what one tries in adolescence increases.

Can't mothers be good disciplinarians? Of course they can, but in single-parent homes with only the mother as parent, she may feel at a disadvantage. Whereas many teenage boys are bigger and stronger than their mothers, very few mothers can physically overpower grown men. I remember as a 14-year-old being reared in the South where "spare the rod and spoil the child" was the parental guideline for discipline. One day I had done something that my mother thought warranted a "paddling." I recall her approaching me with the paddle to punish me and I took it out of her hand. She was startled, waited till my dad got home, and I got what was coming to me. Such physical strength is the advantage the father brings to the control table. Few adolescents fear their mothers (and can therefore ignore them), but most are afraid to cross their fathers. I am not suggesting that physical punishment is the way to rear children. I am suggesting that having someone in the house whom the adolescent respects as an authority is crucial.

In addition to being strong disciplinarians and authority figures, fathers can provide role models for success outside the home. Modeling is one of the most important ways children learn. Telling the child to stay in school, get a good education, and get a good job are less effective than the child actually seeing parents who have good jobs and who earned the right to get these jobs through advanced education.

One of the developmental tasks of adolescence in male children is to separate from their mothers and become "men." In preliterate societies, when boys are around age 12, the men of the village take them away from their mothers and depart with them on hunting trips, immersing them in the male culture. No similar ritual exists in our society for such separation from one's mother, so adolescent males are often left to their own devices.

One of the ways adolescents try to confirm their masculinity is by being tough and aggressive. Winning a street fight can establish one's masculinity among one's peers. Speeding, stealing, and drinking may also look like avenues to cultural maleness. Such behaviors reflect boys who are searching for a male identity and relying on stereotypical cultural images as their guides. A father in the home who spends time with his son and forges a good relationship with him allows him to see maleness and masculinity up close. The son learns that to be a man need not involve tough aggression but kindness, negotiation, and involvement in one's community. Sons can model their fathers and feel confident in their own masculinity; sons without fathers are at the mercy of an adolescent peer leading the way, and adolescents can't teach what they don't know.

Fathers also teach sons how to relate to women. A father who has a close relationship with his son naturally encourages his son to look to him for an array of "how tos" in the world. One of these is how to interact with women. A son who sees his dad treat women with respect, cooperate in cooking/dishes/housecleaning, and negotiate conflict has a map for his own interaction with the other sex. Sons in single-parent homes dominated by the mother may lack a model that shows them how to relate to women. Although there is no question that mothers love their sons, there are some things they cannot teach them—how to relate to women as a man is one of these things.

Fathers also teach their children about divorced fatherhood. With close to half of marriages ending this way, it is realistic to acknowledge the possibility that your children may someday experience their own divorce. Divorced fathers who continued to be involved in their son's lives have provided a model for their sons. Their sons have felt the importance their dad attached to them, observed his perseverance in being with them, and witnessed his joy in doing things with them. Should his sons need a model for the involved divorced father, they have one.

Finally, fathers are important in the development of a conscience in their children. Psychologist Martin Hoffman studied the moral development of children and focused on seventh-graders. He found that children who grew up in fatherless homes feel less guilty when they do something wrong, are less likely to accept responsibility when they do something wrong, and lack the internal moral compass that tells them *when* they are wrong in the first place.[4] *How* the father is instrumental in instilling a conscience in his children is not clear. But the effect of an involved father in the life of his children is apparent—better citizens result.

Because men typically engage in more criminal behavior than women, the presence of a father is more likely to benefit boys by diverting them from drifting into delinquency and criminal behavior. Similarly, girls benefit from having an active father by being less prone to having children out of wedlock. According to researchers K. D. Peters and colleagues at the Centers for Disease Control and Prevention, about 376,000 unmarried women aged 15–19 give birth to children each year.[5] One of the key background factors found was the absence of a father in the home.

Why? What does a father have to do with his daughter's sexual behavior? First, a caring father is the source of the adolescent female's concept of herself as a woman. If her father is not involved with her or rejects her, she may feel negatively about herself and desperately seek the attention of men to confirm her worth as a woman. The adolescent who is secure in her attractiveness and desirability does not feel this sense of desperation. She is successful in her relationships with men and does not depend on early and frequent sex to maintain them.

Second, it is no secret that single-parent households are stressful. Mom is trying to be two parents in one and working full-time. She is exhausted. There may be little quality time with her daughter, who may want to escape as soon as possible. One ticket out is early pregnancy and marriage. It's a fact that girls from single-parent homes leave to marry earlier than girls who have a father at home. Teenage motherhood has an enormous cost not only to our daughters but also to the children they bear. Teenagers who have children are more likely to live in poverty, which translates into living in substandard housing and having poor nutrition and inadequate medical care. Their children are also more likely to be born prematurely and to have birth defects. The cycle repeats itself. The children reared in teenage single-parent homes are more likely to get pregnant early, to leave home, and to have their own babies as teenagers. An involved father helps to stop this cycle from getting started.

Daughters deprived of a warm relationship with their fathers miss the early feeling of being accepted by a male whose opinion is important to her. Uncles and stepfathers may help, but what dad thinks about her remains important. Single-parent mothers cannot supply the social mirror reflection from a male any more than a father can give his sons information about how women feel about him—his mother must do that.

Affectionate fathers also provide a good model for how they should be treated. One divorced father told me, "I hug my girls every day and tell them that I love them. If they meet some bum who doesn't show them affection and care, maybe they will be more likely to reject him as a potential mate. And I bet they will not tolerate a male who is abusive because they have learned how it feels to have a man's affection."

Children who grow up in homes without a father are also more vulnerable to child abuse. Whether the abuse is physical injury or neglect, statistics show that single mothers are more likely to be abusive to their children. Most single mothers are not abusive, but those who are tend to feel overwhelmed with parenting and sometimes become abusive either out of their own frustration or out of the need to control their children. An involved father may provide a buffer against abuse. Although fathers may also be abusive, whether in one- or two-parent homes, the single-parent home with no father around is the more likely context. Child abuse should be kept in perspective. Sociologist David Popenoe makes the point that our society is very concerned about child abuse but gives little focus to the fact that depriving children of fathers is the most frequent form of child abuse.[6]

As horrible as physical injury and neglect may be, these may seem insignificant when compared with child sexual abuse, which also occurs more frequently when fathers are not there for their kids. A father's presence provides considerable supervision for the child. When he is closely attentive to his children, he acts as a sentinel against those who might contemplate sexual abuse of his children. When he is absent, the daughters may seem like easy prey in the face of a preoccupied single mother caught up in the business of bringing in an income and managing her own social relationships.

Although some biological fathers sexually abuse their daughters, the incidence is low because of the incest taboo and because he is less likely to see his daughter as a sexual stimulus. In contrast, men have lower cultural and personal prohibitions against sexual contact with women they are not related to. Stepfathers, therefore, are more likely to sexually abuse their stepdaughters.

Some men who prey on young girls get emotionally close to the mother so as to have ready access and proximity to their daughters. The mothers enjoy the attention of a new partner so much that they may not be aware of his real agenda of moving in on their daughters. Disaster strikes when the mother is not at home, the forced sex abuse occurs, and the daughter is threatened with her life if she tells. Such a scenario, although not common, is more likely to happen to a girl whose biological father is not involved in her life.

In addition to this loss of physical protection, young women in single-parent homes also become emotionally vulnerable to sexual abuse. Without the affection and love of a father, they may be vulnerable to sex abusers who offer such affection and attention as a way to entice and perpetuate sexual participation. Before the young daughter knows it, she is trapped and abused and scarred for what may take many years of therapy to heal.

The criminal and civil trials of O. J. Simpson focused attention onto the issue of domestic violence. Although some continue to debate whether he is guilty of double murder, his physical abuse of Nicole Brown Simpson is a matter of public record. The statistics on violence of men toward women are alarming, but *who* gets abused is even more enlightening. Statistics show that an unmarried woman is *four times more likely* than a married woman to become the victim of a violent crime. The victim's marital status is an important factor because it tells us about the relationship the woman has to the man who abuses her. Most often, it is the uncommitted boyfriend or the jealous live-in lover. These men are also not committed to the welfare of the woman's children. Men who remain committed to their children have a much lower incidence of violence toward women.[7]

As divorced fathers we have a choice as to whether we remain active parents in our children's lives. Research evidence shows that fathers who are invested in their children's lives are less likely to direct their energy toward abusing women. These same fathers also provide models to their children for responsible fatherhood, which increases the chance that their offspring may also invest in the role of father when they become adults. Although my parents did not have the happiest of marriages, my father loved me and provided the model for a moral compass. He remained involved in my life until his early death at 46. Having such an involved father as a model made it easy for me to be committed to the role of father even in the face of divorce. Whatever the obstacles, I was going to remain a father to my children.

Sociologist David Popenoe notes that the most tangible and immediate outcome of fatherlessness for children is the loss of economic resources.[8] Indeed, the loss of a father can mean a quick trip to poverty. By the most conservative estimates, the income of a household in which a child remains after divorce declines over 20 percent, while expenses go up. Children in single-parent homes are twice as likely to live in poverty, which translates into substandard housing and decreased educational opportunities. Single mothers are thus often forced to live in poorer neighborhoods and their children go to poorer schools, where money for educational field trips and computers is lacking. The result is that children from single-parent homes get lower grades and are less likely to graduate from high school and college than children from two-parent homes.

The consequence of a father dropping out of his young children's lives also has an economic effect into their young adulthood. Unlike children of involved fathers, who can usually expect some help when they need a college education, a car, or a first home, children without fathers grow up in a state of constant economic uncertainty. Blankenhorn offers a frightening prospect when he says that "as fatherlessness spreads, the economic difference between America's haves and have-nots will increasingly revolve around a basic question: Which of us had fathers?"[9]

That children without fathers are associated with a number of negatives is evident. On the positive side, James D. Lambert of the Department of Child and Family Studies at the University of Wisconsin–Madison and his colleagues Marc Cwik and Karen Bogenschneider emphasized some of the characteristics associated with children who have fathers in their lives. Children with active fathers benefit in a number of ways:

- Appropriate male sex role development
- Good grades
- Problem-solving skills
- Higher empathy
- Altruism
- Good health
- Strong marriage as an adult
- Higher life satisfaction
- Higher education level
- Higher income
- Higher job stability
- Close friendships[10]

The fact that you are divorced and no longer live in the home full time with your children does not mean that you cannot have a powerful positive impact on their lives. Some divorced fathers are more involved in their children's lives than fathers still married to their children's mother. Vigilance for your children's well-being and active involvement in their lives are the key.

HOW FATHERING AND MOTHERING DIFFER

Some evidence suggests that fathers relate differently to their children than mothers. Sociologist David Popenoe identified some of the ways in which fathers have different parenting styles than mothers. For example, fathers are more focused on the child's long-term development and their learning how to be independent.[11] Fathers may also be more willing to take risks. For example, scuba diving is a potentially dangerous sport. After my divorce, I sought to find an activity that both of my children would be interested in. A new dive shop had opened in town and offered a "try scuba free" experience, so my kids and I put on full gear and leaped into a local pool with the instructor. We liked it so much that we decided immediately to begin the training, and have had over 100 dives to date. The effects of this experience on my children's lives have not been fleeting. After graduating from college, my daughter moved to another country where from the balcony of her apartment she can see the ocean in which we spent many hours diving together. Had I not remained in her life, there may have been no context to encourage her to "risk" a new experience like scuba diving or to move outside the United States to get a job and live independently.

Fathers and mothers differ in the way each relates to the world. Having both a father and a mother allows the child to develop a more balanced view of their social environment. For example, fathers are typically more concerned with "will it work?" (function) than "how does it look?" (image). In selecting a car, a father may be more likely to focus on the engine , whereas the mother's concern may be more aesthetic. Children reared without involved fathers are likely to miss this balance.

Probably the most significant contribution fathers provide for their children is the male perspective. Children reared by women only (and men only for that matter) may have a biased perspective of the world. Children who grow up exclusively with mothers have little exposure to male interests, attitudes, and views. Sporting events, sports play, hunting/fishing, and the like are all "male" things that women typically have little interest in and, therefore, provide little exposure to. One father of two daughters said that his girls' competing in sporting events was directly tied to his nurturing their love for sports. "Their mother is into shopping and baking, and that's fine. But my daughters need to know how to play soccer," he said. Children benefit from a wider range of knowledge, rather than a narrow range, which might limit their development and future understanding. Mothers and fathers bring different worlds to their children and each is important. Without exposure to both, children do not have the balance that is so beneficial.

Fathers also teach their children a male view of different genders—something mothers cannot do. One father said that he wanted his sons to know that the most important decision in their life was who they married and that the choice of a mate should be made with great caution. "I need them to know," this father said, "that some women are manipulative and to be alert to them. And I need my daughters to know that most adolescent males are sex focused and you can't always trust them. Getting married to the wrong partner can be a fundamental lifetime error."

Fathers also provide more assertive models than do mothers for their children. I was recently in a hotel health club. I had just walked in and selected one of the lifecycles to ride. Before sitting down to peddle, I turned down the blaring volume of the television just above the lifecycle. Immediately, a voice shot from the other side of the room telling me to turn the volume on the TV back up. I was surprised at this request and said, "You're over there, the TV's over here, why should I be subjected to this noise?" He replied, "I always listen to the TV when I exercise." My wife noticed the exchange and quickly motioned for me to select another piece of equipment away from the TV. According to psychologist Jack Turner of Huntsville, Alabama, "women and mothers are more likely to be peacemakers than men and fathers. If women ran the world, there would be more negotiation and fewer wars. If we are lucky, we will elect a woman President."[12] Fathers and mothers provide a balanced view of life for their children. Each view is better than neither. Fathers who do not insist on continuing to be involved in their children's lives send their children into the world with a biased perspective.

Another difference between fathers and mothers concerns communication. For example, young children often find that when they have a problem with their peers, their mothers are available to listen and to talk.

Fathers either appear uninterested or simply dictate solutions such as "don't fight with your friends" or "punch him out if he does it again." In addition, fathers tend to disclose less than mothers to their children about themselves. The lack of such disclosure results in children not having a clue about what their fathers think and feel. Alternatively, because their mothers disclose frequently, children learn early about the psychological complexity of their mothers. Their fathers remain a mystery.

Mothers and fathers also attend to different aspects of their children. Mothers are concerned about how their children look (e.g., clothes, hair) and fathers are more focused on their performance. One father said, "My wife wants to know how our son *looked* at the karate match; I want to know if he won." Mothers want to know if the jacket is clean; fathers want to know if he needs one at all.

Another important reason for fathers to remain involved in their children's lives is the effect that such involvement has on the child's self-esteem. Children who are abandoned by their fathers feel a deep sense of rejection. Although social fathers in the form of stepfathers or males in the extended family may surface to help fill this role, the child is required by his or her culture to answer the question, "Why wasn't I important enough for my daddy to *be* my daddy?"

Barry Manilow, Dennis Rodman, and Barbra Streisand are celebrities who have talked about the absence of a father in their lives. No matter how famous a person may become, such fame is difficult to compensate for the attention and love of a father.

Children also need to know who they are, have models for integrity, and feel competent about their abilities. Mothers are certainly important parental figures, but fathers provide an equal dose of identity, character, and competence. Our society continues to be dominated by men. Legislators, CEOs, and news anchors are predominately men. Their definitions of reality are typically given more cultural authority. Children who grow up with fathers have an added layer of authority and certainty about who they are and what they can do.

Fathers also provide children with a sense of connectedness to their past. Children need to know who their fathers were and who they are in order to forge their own identity. Children who were adopted often long to know their paternal roots. They may even become obsessed with questions like "where did I come from, and what was my father like?" Fathers who continue to be involved in their children's lives provide answers to these questions. Identity questions are important and only fathers can answer the paternal side of these questions.

In *The Sibling Society*, Robert Bly says that children of today have been reared by their peers and are no longer capable of connecting with the past. Such a "vertical gaze" is important for an individual to know his or her historical roots, to connect with the kinship system and community. Bly maintains that having no connection to the past is a result of the talk show replacing the family, the Internet replacing art, and the mall replacing one's community involvement.[13] The active involvement of fathers can help stop this trend.

Fathers who attend the school events of their children provide social support for them: Father–daughter square dances, father–son dinners, and similar events emphasize the unique role of fathers. Children also need support during setbacks. When they fail a test, are rejected at cheerleading/soccer/tennis tryouts, or are denied admission to college, they might profit from a paternal perspective. Although mothers are important in this regard, fathers lend an authority as to how the world works and how adversity should be dealt with. Fathers can recall that Babe Ruth struck out more often than he had a hit, that rejection is a staple of life, and that the only appropriate response to rejection is to dig in and try harder.

Men continue to have higher incomes than women—significantly so. Even when a man and a woman have the same education, he will make a great deal more money. For example, according to the 1999 *Statistical Abstract of the United States,* a man who graduates from college will make an average of $32,611 per year whereas a woman with the same education will make an average of $22,656.[14] Fathers who stay involved in their children's lives share their economic resources with them. Such economic backing translates into a good education, which helps to spin the children into a secure economic future.

Involved fathers continue to provide a layer of protection for their children that is lacking in mother-only homes. As we have seen, when fathers are in the home their children are less often victims of child/sexual abuse. The image of a mother bear protecting her cubs becomes even more profound when we see the father bear at the front of the cave.

Increasingly, fathers are actively involved in the physical care and nurturing of their children. My 25-year-old nephew and his wife just had a son. My nephew is one of the most involved dads I have seen. Alternating with his wife, he is up at night with the demands of feeding and diapering and he takes and picks up his son at day care. On Saturdays, as his wife sleeps in, he departs with his son on their Saturday morning outing. Little does his son know as he sits in the back seat strapped into his car seat that he is growing up in a world where too few children are as privileged as he is. Not only is he benefiting from direct care by his dad, he is learning how to be an involved father for his own children. So in 25 years, he will be in the front seat looking through the rearview mirror at his child. The father, the mother, the child, and society all benefit when fathers are involved with their children.

THE NEED FOR NEW SOCIAL POLICIES

Most social policy directed toward fathers emphasizes getting them to pay child support [child support enforcement (CSE)] or paternity establishment, which is simply a tool for CSE—you can't make a dad pay if he can't be identified as the father. In other words, fathers are viewed as valuable for their money and little else.

In the book *Fatherless America*, David Blankenhorn says that "the most important absence our society must confront is not the absence of fathers but the absence of our belief in fathers."[15] It is imperative that we rethink our ideas about fathers—that fathers are not peripheral but crucial figures in their children's lives. Anthropology teaches us a central lesson, namely, that societal success is largely dependent on parental investment. When fathers are allowed and encouraged to *be* fathers, both their children and the fathers themselves benefit. Children benefit from having a moral rudder, a loving parent, and a disciplinarian, and fathers benefit from staying out of trouble and having happier lives. Society benefits from lower poverty, less crime, and more involved citizens.

This book is about how the noncustodial divorced father can maintain a good relationship with his children. It is not about how our society must change in terms of new social policies to support the father–child relationship. But the absence of cultural support for this relationship is a major obstacle to fathers continuing meaningful relationships with their children. The fact that our society will tolerate the idea of a "visiting" father (recall there are about 5 million in the United States) and relegate one-half of the child's parentage to 2 weekends a month is revealing, and it is devastating to children, their fathers, and our society.

Social changes are imperative. One of these changes is to end the belief that only mothers are important to their children and that, somehow, children will be "just fine" without their fathers. The media can help to emphasize the importance of fathers by developing sitcoms around involved fathers and spotlighting examples of fathers involved in this role. Some of this has already begun. Sylvester Stallone's involvement with his sick baby daughter made headlines, as did the attempts of actor John Heard to remain an active father despite a difficult divorce. Bill Cosby is already on record as an advocate for fatherhood. We should see more such examples.

The news media and television journalism might feature regular stories on how and why fathers are important to family life. NBC Nightly News has a regular feature on "The Fleecing of America," which presents new examples of how taxpayers are getting ripped off. How about giving equal attention to "The Fleecing of Children" by pointing out that over 40 percent wake up each morning in a house without a father?

The government might also take an active role. Just as the Surgeon General is frequently seen emphasizing the dangers of smoking for teenagers, he or she might also be on national television talking about the importance of keeping fathers and children together after divorce. That fathers are kept from their children is as much a national disgrace as letting children go hungry in America. They need fathers as well as food.

A major overhaul of the divorce process is necessary. Before spouses are given a formal separation/divorce decree, they should be required to attend parenting classes that emphasize the active involvement of both parents in their children's lives following divorce. Fathers should insist that their attorneys fight for a custody order ensuring that both mothers and fathers are provided equal access to their children. The term "visitation" should be replaced with "parenting time" to emphasize involvement, not ownership. Regarding visitation, psychologist Richard Warshak has done an extensive study of custody decisions in America and concluded that making children wait 13 days before seeing their father and repeating this ordeal twice a month for the duration of their childhood is "cruel."[16] Custody laws might assume the obvious, which is that children profit most when both parents continue to be involved in their lives and that such involvement includes being with their children on a frequent, regular, and consistent basis.

Judges are very powerful social agents in our society. Were they to keep in mind that children benefit from continued involvement with their fathers, they could reflect this in their custody/visitation orders. Admittedly, attorneys must present the case and judges must rule on the evidence as they apply the custody laws of the state. But there are times that judges have discretionary power, and such power should be used to encourage joint parental involvement. Appendix III is an example of a letter you might send to domestic judges in your area if you are not actively involved in litigation in their court.

Changes in social policy alone will not result in fathers being more actively involved in the lives of their children. The whole perception of fatherhood must change. Men often think of parenthood in reference to their partners. That marriage leads to having children and divorce leads to the father seeing less of his children is a belief bought into by both ex-wives and ex-husbands. Both parents must accept that their responsibilities to their children continue beyond the breakup of their marriage. Mothers should be supportive of their children continuing involved relationships with their fathers. Fathers must continue such involvement with or without the support of their former spouses. Such commitment to fatherhood has begun. Sociologist Michael Schwalbe interviewed men about their relationships with their fathers and found that "nearly all" lamented the emotional and nurturing absence of their fathers and were intent on specific involvement with their own children.[17] Researcher Theodore Cohen interviewed another sample of fathers who had the same goal—to be "better parents," "interact more," and "be more involved" than their own fathers had been. Cohen also found that the social class of the father made no difference on his intent to be involved. Working-class fathers were as likely to be concerned about nurturing their children as middle-class fathers.[18]

14

Some Tips on Fathering

> In describing the good father, the men we interviewed frequently chose words such as "instilling," "advising," "teaching," "setting an example," "preparing."[1]
>
> David Blankenhorn

Men often enter the role of fatherhood relatively unprepared for its demands. Women have an advantage. They gather to socialize each other on how to be mothers and how to care for their infants. There is no male equivalent of a baby shower, the event where mothers tell expectant mothers about mothering and give practical gifts to help care for the baby.

There is an old saying that having a piano does not make one a good piano player. As fathers, we quickly learn that having children does not make us good fathers. This chapter will review who divorced fathers are, how they view fatherhood, some facts about fatherhood, and what children need from their fathers.

A PROFILE OF DIVORCED FATHERS

Sociologist Alfred DeMaris of Bowling Green State University and social worker Geoffrey Grief of the School of Social Work, University of Maryland at Baltimore, studied 1132 divorced fathers who were members of Parents Without Partners (see Appendix V) and developed a profile of the study group. Although these particular fathers had custody of their children, this may be one of the few differences between them and noncustodial fathers. The average age of the fathers was 40 and they had been divorced about 4 years from a marriage that lasted about 11 years. Most had two children, and half were professionals or businessmen and had been to college about 2½ years. Their average income was $33,500. The divorced fathers in this study were more likely to be white; the geographical distribution of the sample was nationwide.[2]

Balancing work and parenting was difficult (women will not be surprised). Only 17 percent said that parenting had not been a problem, but almost three-fourths (72 percent) of the divorced fathers said that they were comfortable in the role of single parent. Support from employers who were flexible in their expectations and understood parenting obligations, having less conflict with their ex-wives, and having been an involved father before the divorce were all factors associated with having a positive fatherhood experience. But the road was tough. Only 20 percent of these fathers rated the quality of the relationship with their children as "good" or "excellent" and defined themselves as having "successful parenting experiences."[3] No one ever said divorced fatherhood was easy. One divorced father I talked with who was the sole parent of his children said:

> It's tough trying to work all day and take care of kids at night. I'm sure the frustrations I feel will come as no surprise to single mothers. But the rewards are also there . . . the bond you feel with your kids . . . watching them develop . . . being proud of their accomplishments . . . I've become a "soccer mom."

As this man's experience indicates, the sacrifices required of fathers as single parents can be trying, but the results are well worth the effort.

David Blankenhorn asked a group of fathers to talk about what it means to be a good family man. I have also asked fathers I know to talk about what fathering means. Several themes emerged. At the top of the list for these fathers is commitment to their children—that nothing be allowed to seriously interfere with their role as father. Even fathers who can't be with their children maintain a commitment to taking care of them. One black divorced father interviewed by Professor Erma Lawson of the University of Kentucky and her colleague Aaron Thompson of the University of Missouri said:

> I suffered so my children could live in the house 'cause I did not want my children to grow up on welfare. I felt the responsibility to bear the brunt financially and to start all over again 'cause my former spouse had custody of my son and daughter. I told my ex-wife to take it all 'cause I looked at it as giving it all to my children. I told my former spouse to take the car, take it all—I walked 4 miles to work each morning 'cause I gave her the car for the children.[4]

Corporate America is hearing for the first time that its CEOs are willing to earn less money in exchange for more time with their families. The value of time with one's children is also being realized at the other end of the economic spectrum. While I was lifting weights recently in a gym, a friend who was also a father and local businessman told me that he had decided to close his business one day a week and to cut back on the hours he was open on the other days. He had been invited by his son to go jet skiing, but initially had declined because he was too busy. The father reconsidered, telling me, "If I make a lot of money but don't use it to enjoy my kids, I'm nuts. So, I closed the store, bought the jet ski, and last Saturday was our first time out . . . I did the right thing." This father's experience echoes that of other fathers who have begun to evaluate and question the cultural mold they find themselves cast in. They are discovering that relationships are more important than things.

But fathers still feel responsible as providers and still try to see that the money is there for the needs of their children. Being a good provider remains a prominent role for most fathers. Their wives earn money, but this does not absolve the fathers from feeling responsible when bills become due.

Being a good provider and a good worker go together. The modeling effect on one's children is important. Xavier McDaniel is a basketball star for the Boston Celtics. A reporter once asked McDaniel where he got his competitive intensity. McDaniel was quick to point out that his father had been the model for this quality:

> My father worked two jobs—one loading and unloading trucks for a food service company, and the other as a janitor at the University of South Carolina—in order to support six kids. Some days our family didn't even see our dad. I saw him in a situation where he didn't give up, so why should I give up?[5]

Blankenhorn also feels very strongly that working to provide economically for their families is a central role that fathers must continue to fill:

> In service to the child and to the social good, fathers do certain things that other people, including mothers, do not do as often, as naturally, or as well. When fathers do not do this work—as is increasingly the case in our society—child and societal well-being decline.[6]

Beyond working hard for their families, fathers say that their role also includes teaching their kids about life, being a moral model, and being a good model for adult relationships. Divorced fathers feel that they have important information to impart about women and relationships. If the father sought the divorce, he may feel it is necessary for his children to know that a good marital relationship *is* important and that divorced people don't lack commitment in their character, but rather may not want to settle for a bad marriage. If the father was left by his former spouse, he can emphasize to his children that life has no guarantees and that to adjust to any hand dealt is a challenge that must be accepted. Either way, the father feels that his "lessons of life" are important for his children. Most parents do. Of course, fathers should not expect their children to be as interested in learning what they have to teach. Many children, in fact, resist parental teaching in favor of learning it on their own.

FOUR FACTS ABOUT FATHERHOOD

Because most of us have been reared to think in terms of our adult roles as employee/worker rather than father, it is little wonder that we have a lot to learn about fatherhood. Bill Cosby has a thought for all of us on this:

> If the new American father feels bewildered and even defeated, let him take comfort from the fact that whatever he does in any fathering situation has a fifty percent chance of being right. Having five children has taught me a truth as cosmic as any that you can find on a mountain in Tibet: There are no absolutes in raising children. In any stressful situation, fathering is always a roll of the dice. The game may be messy, but I have never found one with more rewards and joys.[7]

Cosby's role as a father has recently been the focus of public attention—first as the bereaved father whose son was murdered on a Los Angeles highway, and then as the target of extortion from an alleged daughter, Autumn Jackson. But his words about fatherhood remain true—fathers do the best they can but should recognize that there are no predictable outcomes.

Along with the idea that there are no absolutes in parenthood, there are several other facts to keep in mind about being a father. The first is that *fathers are only one influence in their children's lives.* Although we may want our children to listen to our words of wisdom as we show and tell them about life, they may choose to be neither looking nor listening. They may be attentive to another drummer—their mother, siblings, peers, teachers, musical lyrics, and television. Regarding television, Professor Horst Stipp, director of Social and Developmental Research at the National Broadcasting Company Inc. in New York City, reported that children between the ages of 2 and 17 watch an average of 23 hours a week.[8] These multiple influences make it clear to the father that he is only one voice among many in the lives of his children.

Another fact dads should be familiar with is that *the demands of fatherhood are different for children of different ages*. How and what a father is supposed to do changes as his children grow up and move through various developmental stages. Infants, toddlers, preschoolers, preadolescents (8–11), new adolescents (12–15), middle adolescents (15–18), and young adults (18–22) all show different behaviors and require different emotional, social, and psychological support from their fathers.

Over time, children grow from a state of total dependence to one of total independence. *Knowing how much freedom to give at what age for what events is a challenge for most dads*. During the period of adolescence, for example, the dad's role is like flying a kite—the string must be let out to give the kite height, but if the string is kept too tight, it will snap and the kite will fall. Children must be encouraged to take risks but within limits.

As every father knows, *children differ in their tolerance for stress, in their capacity to learn, in their comfort in social situations, in their interests, and in innumerable other ways*. Fathers of two or more children are often amazed at how children who have the same parents can be so different. Some of these differences are related to the sex of the child (boys are typically more aggressive), and other differences are related to the different ways boys and girls are socialized.

FOUR DIFFERENT PARENTING STYLES

Just as children are different, so are dads in terms of their parenting style. One typical parenting style is *authoritarian*, where dad lays down the law and expects unquestioned obedience from his children. Unless dads temper this style with love and affection, children are likely to resent dads who try to force everything. This style, by the way, is probably the one most of us were reared under. It has both advantages and disadvantages. On the plus side, the authoritarian style generally keeps children within society's parameters and makes for order in the family. On the negative side, children may learn to follow orders and not think for themselves. It is hard for them to grow and learn from their mistakes if they are always told what to do. Children reared in this style can become incapable of making decisions as adults. However, other children model on their fathers and become very decisive themselves.

Another parenting style is *permissive-indulgent,* in which dad allows his children to do about anything they want and he gives them things to make them happy. There is little conflict with the children because they usually get their way. The drawback to this method is that the children don't have any sense of direction and may become aimless as adults. As will be noted later, some limits are necessary for the child's safe development.

A third parenting style is *permissive-neglect,* which is similar to the previous style, but unlike permissive-indulgent fathers, who know where their children are, permissive-neglective fathers don't know where their children are or what they are doing until it's too late. This may be because dad is preoccupied with his own life and too busy to be attentive to his children's lives. Children growing up under these conditions often feel that they aren't important to their fathers. In short, permissive-neglect is not so much a style of parenting as it is a style of *not* parenting.

Permissive-firm dads give their children the freedom to experience their world but put firm limits on their activities and behaviors. Such children experience both the trust of being allowed to explore and the affection of their dad's firmness. This is not a bad style for rearing children.

EIGHT NEEDS OF CHILDREN

Regardless of the father's parenting style, all children have basic needs beyond material necessities.

Love

All fathers know the importance of communicating to their children that they love them, but fathers may talk a better game than they play. They may be good at telling their children that they love them, but not always deliver the behavioral goods. For noncustodial fathers, being late to pick them up for planned visits (or worse, not showing up at all) teaches a child to be suspicious of his or her father's love.

Children need fathers who show up at piano recitals and soccer games. Bo Jackson, who won the Heisman Trophy and played both professional football and baseball, related that in the locker room after a game, many of his teammates would mention seeing their fathers in the stands and hoped they hadn't missed the big plays in which they had been involved. Bo Jackson kept silent. His father was never in the stands and never saw him play in a game. He lamented his father's absence and wondered how it would feel to have a father with whom he could share his trophies.

Time

Because popular culture views men primarily as workers, not as fathers, there is continuous pressure on men to work longer hours instead of spending more time with their children. Men are rewarded for working on projects at night, not for doing homework with their children. Being an economic provider is only one aspect of fathering—some men who concentrate on making money to the exclusion of spending time with their children may be using work as an escape from a role they really do not enjoy.

Indeed, some fathers do not feel comfortable spending time with their children. They feel awkward or unsure. Some also feel that they must play sports or take their children fishing or do traditional "father things" to be a good father. But not all fathers have a fishing boat or enjoy playing catch. One man, who became a father at the age of 43, said of his experience:

> Two-plus years into this fatherhood business, I know at least that what kids require of their fathers is a lot of attention, a lot of love, and I suspect, if mine ever reach the age of understanding, a lot of that, too. They can find other people to throw balls at them.[9]

Praise

Praise is one of the most important things a father can give his children. One young man said that his father never attended any sporting event that he had played in and never complimented him on anything. Children can get attention and praise from peers, teachers, and their mother, but praise from their father is special.

The late Henry Fonda once said that his father was initially against his becoming an actor. But, reluctantly, his father agreed to attend a play in which Henry had the leading role. After the play, the family was back at home discussing Fonda's performance. One of Fonda's siblings asked him, "How'd you do?" His father interrupted and answered in one word, "perfect." In telling this story, Fonda noted that his father's one-word compliment had a profound influence on his commitment to a career in acting.

Praise your children frequently. Tell them you are glad to see them, tell them you are proud of them—say it in words directly to them.

Self-Confidence

"One of the greatest mistakes a parent can make," confided one father, "is to be anxious all the time about your children, because they interpret your anxiety as a lack of confidence you have in them." Rather, this father said that it is best to convey to your child that you know he or she will be OK and that you are not going to worry about it because you have confidence in him or her. "The effect on your child," he said, "is a heightened sense of self-confidence." Another way to conceptualize this parental principle is to think of the self-fulfilling prophecy as a mechanism that can spin your child into having a secure and confident self-concept. When the child realizes that dad has confidence in him or her, the child begins to accept these social definitions as real and becomes more self-confident.

Limits

Children must learn the limits of acceptable social behavior. Those who never internalize these limitations are the most likely to become criminals. A large part of successful parenting is helping your children learn to monitor their behavior to fit within socially prescribed parameters. Those who cannot place limits on their own behavior are doomed to social failure, and children may best learn internal limits by having external limits imposed by parents.

Consequences

Setting limits without providing consequences is a waste of time. We live in a world of consequences, and children profit from being reared in a cause-and-effect world. Divorced fathers are particularly vulnerable to letting their children get away with anything because they have so little time with them. Despite that, to let children be disrespectful to you or others or not be responsible to chores or curfews or whatever is to set them on a path of destruction. Never mind if their mother lets them get away with just about anything; you can draw the line and stick to it when they are with you.

Consequences must be age specific. "Time out," or placing a young child (3–8) in the bathroom or an isolated back bedroom for an appropriate period of time, is usually an effective alternative to using a belt on the bottom. The term "time out" refers to "time out from reinforcement." For example, if your 5- and 7-year-olds are fighting in the back room, rather than scream at or whip both of them, you could separate them by putting them in different rooms. The time-out period should allow the child time to calm down and consider why he or she has been disciplined. One full minute per year of the child's age is a good rule of thumb, so the 5-year-old will be isolated for 5 minutes and the 7-year-old for 7 minutes. Be sure the child understands exactly what unacceptable behavior has caused the time out. This provides a consequence for the inappropriate behavior, in this case fighting.

The type of punishment should be adjusted as the child gets older. Placing a 5-year-old in time out should be replaced by withdrawing privileges from a 9-year-old. Failure to come in from playing outside when called might be met with no TV for that evening. For teens, failure to get off the phone by midnight could be met with a suspension of phone privileges for a day. Failure to put gas in the car or respect a curfew agreement might result in loss of car privileges or spending time with friends.

All of these negative consequences are only effective if the father acknowledges to the child appreciation when the child does what he or she is asked to do. Children who come when called should be told, "Thanks for coming in when I called you." Teenagers who put gas in the car or come in at curfew should be told, "Thanks for putting gas in the car and coming in at a reasonable time last night."

A personal note about curfew for teenagers: I never had a curfew as an adolescent and never imposed one on either my son or daughter when they were growing up. My dad told me, "If I tell you to be home by midnight, you might speed home and get in a wreck just so you can make curfew. Be reasonable about when you come in." I was. So were my children. It was never a problem, and this may work for your teenagers as well if you and they agree on what is "reasonable."

Consistency

Earlier, I emphasized the importance of being consistent with your children about when you will be with them. To make a promise that you will pick up your children for a certain event and not show is devastating for them. One divorced mother told me that her young daughter was so looking forward to her father taking her out to a fancy restaurant for getting good grades on her report card. The father was to arrive at 6 but did not show up till 7:30 and had already eaten. He took his daughter to McDonald's for a hurried "Happy Meal." Children will learn what we teach them. It is important to teach them that they are important to us—important enough so that we arrange our schedules to do what we say we will with them. Just as we are consistent in visitation, we owe it to our children to be consistent in our attitudes and responses to their behavior, whether positive or negative.

Peer Relationships

As children reach their teen years, they gradually drift more toward their peers and prefer to spend time with them. The world of youth seems alive and fresh, while the world of parents may seem dull and tedious. As a father, it is important to acknowledge the value your children's peer group has for their development and to be supportive of your children being with their friends. Not to support these relationships may result in children who have no skills to attract and maintain friends. Be glad that your children have friends and be willing to let them be with their friends some of the time they are scheduled to be with you.

For dads who have full custody and who move with their child(ren) to another state, it will be important to immerse your child in new peer relationships. Although school will provide a place for your child to meet other children, check out the various resources in the new community that provide contexts in which your child can meet new friends. Recreation centers, YWCA, YMCA, Little League, tennis, athletic clubs, dance studios, martial arts studios, and Parents Without Partners are some examples.

GUIDELINES TO IMPROVING YOUR CHILD'S BEHAVIOR

As every father knows, kids can drive you crazy. Disobedience, destructiveness, and outright delinquency (skipping school and stealing) are problems we didn't really count on when we became fathers. We should be careful how we think about our kids when they upset us. Rather than think of them as bad kids, we need to focus on the fact that they are engaging in behavior that makes us upset. Some parents think of their child as a "bad seed," when what they really mean is "my kid does things I don't like." Bickering, bad grades, disrespect, smoking, loud music, drugs, cursing, and not doing chores do not indicate that your son or daughter is "bad." Rather, talking back to you (being disrespectful), not doing the dishes when you ask (disobedience), and bickering with siblings (being unkind) are examples of children engaging in behavior you don't like. This is an important distinction because you can't do anything about a "bad seed," but you *can* do something about your child's *behavior*. So, when you find yourself upset, focus on the *behavior your child is engaging in* that upsets you.

Behavior, the things your children do, is learned. They learn to engage in behavior the same way we do, on the basis of the consequences of the behavior—what happens after the behavior occurs. If good things happen after children do something (if they are rewarded or "reinforced"), they learn to engage in the behavior again. If bad things happen after children do something (if they are punished), they learn to stop engaging in that behavior. These principles of reward and punishment help to explain most of the behavior that people learn to engage in.

Let's consider bickering. How do children learn to raise hell and fight with each other in the house? First, it is rewarding—good things happen when they fight. To begin with, it is energizing. Rather than be bored, children feel better when they are active and being in a squabble makes their adrenaline flow. So, there is an internal, physiological payoff for each sibling—the feeling of being excited and active is enjoyable.

There is also a social payoff for the older or dominant sibling. The sibling who changes the channel his younger brother is watching gets to enjoy watching the program he wants. In addition, he maintains control over his sibling by teaching him that he is "king of the mountain" and not to threaten his authority.

The younger sibling gets less out of the confrontation, but is rewarded by yelling "foul," which he hopes will result in you saying, "Tell your brother to come in here. . . ." Bothering the parent has a payoff for the younger sibling because he or she is able to mobilize your parental power on his or her behalf to get back at the older brother. The point of this scenario is to be aware that your kids bicker and come crying to you because they are getting something out of it. They have *learned* to do what they are doing. The point for us dads is that we can get them to learn behaviors we like (squabble outside, play quietly inside). The principles of learning (reward and punishment) are at work all of the time. It is important to use these principles to our advantage. But before putting these principles in motion, you need to talk about the issues.

When your child does something you do not like, and he or she does so over and over, it is important that you talk about it with your child. If you don't bring the issue up for discussion, the behavior that upsets you will likely get worse and you can become furious before you know it.

There are some reasons dads don't confront their children about unacceptable behavior. Some fathers feel that they don't want to nag the child about something. Others say that it's not worth the time to talk about an issue—that it really isn't that important. And still others are afraid of their child's disapproval. "My kid gets mad at me and won't speak to me for several days when I call him down about something," one man said.

Although being careful only to bring up things that really matter and wanting to avoid harping on something are good reasons for not talking about an issue, fear of your child's disapproval is *not* a good reason. Earlier, I discussed how behavior is learned. If we don't talk to our children about something they do that bothers us because we fear they won't speak to us, they are, in effect, teaching *us* to be quiet. That is a lesson we as parents should not let our children teach us. We are legally responsible for them until they are 18 and talking about things they do that upset us is critical to fulfilling that parental responsibility. Not to talk about a problem is to run the risk that the problem may become larger. It may seem petty to make an issue when an 8-year-old takes a quarter off the dresser without asking. But letting the child become comfortable with such behavior could result in a 13-year-old in trouble for shoplifting or a 17-year-old in prison for holding up a convenience store. I know a parent whose son is in prison for holding up a 7-11.

Every father wants his children to have a set of values. These may be thought of as moral guidelines for behavior. But, as one voice in a crowd of influences, how can dads teach their children to be moral? The best answer is through modeling. By giving money back when you are overchanged, by opening the door for others, and by telling your child that you are sorry for something you did teaches the values of honesty, kindness, and taking responsibility (as well as asking for forgiveness). Of course, your children's mother can be a good model, but they will also look to you for moral choices.

Not modeling values you *don't* want to teach is equally important. Fathers who abuse alcohol, tell secrets, and consistently criticize others will have a hard time teaching their children moderation, confidentiality, and being positive.

WHEN DADS MUST FIND DAY CARE

One of the first discoveries divorced dads make is that, from time to time, they need help. This is something mothers have known all along. Dads who have full custody really need help, and this comes in the form of day care. According to the Census Bureau, about 31 percent of children aged 5 and under are in some type of organized center-based program including day-care centers.[10] The quality of these day-care centers varies. Professor Suzanne Helburn, Principal Investigator of the Cost, Quality, and Child Outcome Study Team, and her colleagues at the University of Colorado at Denver studied 400 day-care centers in California, Colorado, North Carolina, and Connecticut. They rated the various centers and found that only 14 percent earned a rating of "good" or "excellent." In these centers, the children's health and safety needs were met, they received warmth and support from their caretakers, and learning was encouraged. Twelve percent were rated as minimal—the children were ignored, their health and safety were compromised, and no learning was encouraged. The remainder (74 percent) received a rating just above "minimal," suggesting that the health/safety needs, nurturing needs, and educational needs were barely met. Care for infants was particularly lacking. Of 225 infant or toddler rooms observed, 40 percent were rated less than minimal with poor hygiene and marginal safety.[11] Parents should be cautious when choosing day-care facilities for their children.

The time it takes to investigate a quality day-care center before you turn your children over to them may be well spent. *U.S. News and World Report* conducted a survey of day-care deaths in 1996 in all 50 states and the District of Columbia and uncovered 76 deaths.[12] The causes included drowning, falls, being struck by autos, and sudden infant death syndrome—the latter is sometimes a function of putting the infant to sleep on its stomach rather than its back.

It is clear that fathers should be very cautious about putting their young kids in day care. Most fathers prefer and are able to find a suitable arrangement such as having the child's mother, grandparents, friends, or a new partner care for the children. A day-care facility seems like the last resort. However, it need not be, as many are excellent. But be careful, and feel free to show up at the day-care center unexpectedly for a spot inspection if you have any suspicions about the quality of care your kids receive there.

Conclusion

THE CHOICE OF EVERY DAD

I conclude this book with the words of Sandy MacKay, a divorced dad with three children. He writes of the time of desperation experienced shortly after he moved out of the house, leaving his three boys behind:

> I was alone and staying in the house that my father and mother had built in Stonington. (I was lucky to have a place to go to—many men don't.) I had the barest of furnishings as I did not want to take anything out of our house. I felt that it would disturb my kids. It was early February, cold with snow on the ground. I had no one. No friends would call or stop by, I felt totally alone, discarded.
>
> A friend was supposed to stop by and see me this particular evening and was a no-show. This only helped me to sink deeper. By 11 PM I was now a basket case of tears and "woe is me" when the bottom of the fall hit. After the crying, I started having a very simple discussion with myself about what to do. It seemed as though I was at a crossroad of either going down deeper or going up. What a novel idea! I had a choice. So I started writing about my feelings of everything that had transpired that had brought me to this point.
>
> I worked madly and diligently through the night not realizing the passage of time until twilight broke. It was just me, a candle, and no more paper to write on at that point. I crashed in bed and awoke around 10 AM, showered, and revisited the desk and pile of writing I had done earlier. The earlier rumblings were full of self-pity and "why me?" Then the tone went on to a resolve to rise up out of this despair and do something. An awareness that I had me and my children and a responsibility to both hit me. I located more paper and wrote out my synopsis in one shot to kind of form a contract with myself to carry on no matter what.[1]

The road ahead for the divorced father is never easy, but we can resolve to carry on no matter what—that's what dads are for.

Endnotes

INTRODUCTION AND OVERVIEW

1. Kay Pasley and Carmelle Minton, "Generative Fathering After Divorce and Remarriage: Beyond the 'Disappearing Dad,' " *Generative Fathering: Beyond Deficit Perspectives*, ed. Alan J. Hawkins and David C. Dollahite (Thousand Oaks, CA: Sage Publications, 1977) 133. [Kay Pasley is associate professor of Human Development and Family Studies, University of North Carolina at Greensboro, and Carmelle Minton is a doctoral student there.]
2. Douglas MacKay, Stonington, CT, personal interview, 1997.
3. U.S. Bureau of the Census, *Statistical Abstract of the United States, 1999* (Washington: GPO, 1999) Table 83.
4. U.S. Bureau of the Census, This figure is based on the fact that there are 8.3 million divorced men in America (Table 62), 60% of whom had children at the time of their divorces.
5. David Popenoe, *Life Without Father* (New York: Free Press, 1996) 191.
6. Maureen Pirog-Good and Lydia Amerson, "The Long Arm of Justice: The Potential of Seizing the Assets of Child Support Obligors," *Family Relations* 46 (1997): 47–54.
7. Terry Arendell, *Fathers & Divorce* (Thousand Oaks, CA: Sage Publications, 1995) 45–46.
8. Ralph LaRossa, *The Modernization of Fatherhood* (Chicago: University of Chicago Press, 1997) 27.
9. Bernard Goldberg, "All Dads Aren't Deadbeats," *Newsweek* (February 6, 1984): 10, 11.

CHAPTER 1

1. John W. Jacobs, "The Effect of Divorce on Fathers: An Overview of the Literature," *American Journal of Psychiatry* 139 (1982): 1235–1241. [John Jacobs, M.D., is a psychiatrist at Montefiore Hospital and Medical Center, Bronx, NY.]

2. Robert Bly, *Iron John* (Reading, MA: Addison–Wesley, 1990) 25.

3. E. M. Heatherington, M. Cox, and R. Cox, "Divorced Fathers," *Family Coordinator* 25 (1976): 417–428.

4. Heatherington *et al.*

5. Jacobs.

6. H. Wineberg, "Marital Reconciliation in the United States: Which Couples Are Successful?" *Journal of Marriage and the Family* 56 (1994): 80–88.

7. U.S. Bureau of the Census, *Statistical Abstract of the United States, 1997* (Washington: GPO, 1997) 63. Table 75.

8. Bill Walz, Asheville, NC, personal interview, 1997.

9. James Walters, Athens, GA, personal interview, 1997.

CHAPTER 2

1. H. Friedman, "The Challenge of Divorce to Adequate Fathering: The Peripheral Father in Marriage and Divorce," *Psychiatric Clinics of North America* 5 (1982): 565–580. [Henry J. Friedman, M.D., is a psychiatrist at the Harvard University School of Medicine.]

2. U.S. Bureau of the Census, *Statistical Abstract of the United States, 1997* (Washington: GPO, 1997) Table 149.

3. R. Neugebauer, "Divorce, Custody, and Visitation: The Child's Point of View," *Journal of Divorce* 12/13 (1989): 153–168.

4. Neugebauer.

5. Neugebauer.

6. Neugebauer.

7. Frank F. Furstenberg, Christine W. Nord, James L. Peterson, and Nicholas Zill, "The Life Course of Children of Divorce: Marital Disruption and Parental Conflict," *American Sociological Review* 48 (1983): 656–668.

8. Furstenberg *et al.*

9. Rachel Crenshaw, Greenville, NC, 1997. Used by permission.

10. Robert D. Hess and Kathleen A. Camara, "Post-Divorce Family Relationships as Mediating Factors in the Consequences of Divorce for Children," *Journal of Social Issues* 35 (1979): 79–95.

11. Judy Colich, "The Effects of Late-Life Parental Divorce on Adult Women," *Family Systems Research and Therapy* 5 (1996): 161.

12. Nancy E. Lang and Marjorie A. Pett, "Later-Life Parental Divorce: The Adult Child's Experience," *Family Perspective* 26 (1992): 121–146.

13. Jennifer Kwaitkowski, Greenville, NC, 1997. Used by permission.

CHAPTER 3

1. U.S. Bureau of the Census, *Statistical Abstract of the United States, 1997* (Washington: GPO, 1997) 468. Table 719.

2. U.S. Bureau of the Census, 469. Table 728.
3. Alison Clarke-Stewart and B. L. Bailey, "Adjusting to Divorce: Why Do Men Have It Easier?" *Journal of Divorce* 13 (1989): 75–94.
4. U.S. Bureau of the Census, Table 637.
5. H. Friedman, "The Challenge of Divorce to Adequate Fathering: The Peripheral Father in Marriage and Divorce," *Psychiatric Clinics of North America* 5 (1982): 565–580.
6. Marty Zusman, Indiana University Northwest, Gary, IN, personal interview, 1997.
7. Judith S. Wallerstein and Joan B. Kelly, *Surviving the Breakup: How Children and Parents Cope with Divorce* (New York: Basic Books, 1980).

CHAPTER 4

1. Ken Lewis, Glenside, PA, personal interview, 1997. [Ken Lewis is director of Child Custody Evaluation Services of Philadelphia, Inc., Glenside, PA.]
2. David Popenoe, *Life Without Father* (New York: Free Press, 1996) 183.
3. Bonnie L. Barber, "Support and Advice from Married and Divorced Fathers: Linkages to Adolescent Adjustment," *Family Relations* 43 (1994): 433–438.
4. Judith A. Seltzer, "Relationships Between Fathers and Children Who Live Apart: The Father's Role After Separation," *Journal of Marriage and the Family* 53 (1991): 79–101. Copyright © 1991 by the National Council on Family Relations, 3989 Central Ave. NE, Suite 550, Minneapolis, MN 55421. Reprinted by permission.
5. Frank F. Furstenberg, Christine W. Nord, James L. Peterson, and Nicholas Zill, "The Life Course of Children of Divorce: Marital Disruption and Parental Conflict," *American Sociological Review* 48 (1983): 656–668.
6. H. Friedman, "The Challenge of Divorce to Adequate Fathering: The Peripheral Father in Marriage and Divorce," *Psychiatric Clinics of North America* 5 (1982): 565–580.
7. Robert Sammons, Grand Junction, CO, personal interview, 1997.
8. U.S. Bureau of the Census, *Statistical Abstract of the United States, 1999* (Washington: GPO, 1999) Table 378.
9. A. J. Turner, Huntsville, AL, personal interview, 1997.
10. A. J. Cherlin and F. F. Furstenberg, " A Special Case: Grandparents and Divorce," *The New American Grandparent: A Place in the Family, a Life Apart*, ed. A. J. Cherlin and F. F. Furstenberg (New York: Basic Books, 1986) 136–137.
11. Cherlin and Furstenberg.
12. C. Johnson, "Grandparenting Options in Divorcing Families: An Anthropological Perspective," *Grand Parenthood*, ed. V. L. Bengston and J. F. Robertson (Thousand Oaks, CA: Sage Publications, 1985) 81–96.
13. R. A. Thompson, R. B. Tinsley, M. J. Scalora, and R. D. Parke, "Grandparents' Visitation Rights: Legalizing the Ties that Bind," *American Psychologist*, 44 (1989): 1217–1222.

CHAPTER 5

1. Janice Roberts Wilbur and Michael Wilbur, "The Noncustodial Parent: Dilemmas and Interventions," *Journal of Counseling and Development* 66 (1988): 434–437. [Both authors are family therapists in the Boston Overseas Program.]
2. Jack A. Turner, Huntsville, AL, personal interview, 1997.
3. Judith A. Seltzer, "Relationships Between Fathers and Children Who Live Apart: The Father's Role After Separation," *Journal of Marriage and the Family* 53 (1991): 79–101. Copyright © 1991 by the National Council on Family Relations, 3989 Central Ave. NE, Suite 550, Minneapolis, MN 55421. Reprinted by permission.
4. Seltzer.
5. Doug Mace, Greenville, NC, personal interview, 1997.
6. Erma Jean Lawson and Aaron Thompson, "Black Men's Perceptions of Divorce-related Stressors and Strategies for Coping with Divorce: An Exploratory Study," *Journal of Family Issues* 17 (1996): 249–273.

CHAPTER 6

1. Jean Wylder, "Including the Divorced Father in Family Therapy," *Social Work* 27 (1982): 479–482. [Jean Wylder is a Clinical Social Worker at the Comprehensive Community Mental Health Center of Rock Island and Mercer Counties, Rock Island, MD.]
2. Constance R. Ahrons, *The Good Divorce: Keeping Your Family Together When Your Marriage Comes Apart* (New York: HarperCollins Publishers, 1995).
3. Gay C. Kitson, "Attachment to the Spouse in Divorce: A Scale and its Application," *Journal of Marriage and the Family* (May 1982): 379–390.
4. Judith S. Wallerstein and Joan B. Kelly, *Surviving the Breakup: How Children and Parents Cope with Divorce* (New York: Basic Books, 1980).
5. Ahrons.
6. Carol Masheter, "Post-Divorce Relationships Between Ex-Spouses: The Roles of Attachment and Interpersonal Conflict," *Journal of Marriage and the Family* 53 (1991): 103–110.
7. David Finkelhor, Gerald Hotaling, and Andrea Sedlak, "Children Abducted by Family Members: A National Household Survey of Incidence and Episode Characteristics," *Journal of Marriage and the Family* 53 (1991): 805–815.
8. Rebecca L. Hegar and Geoffrey L. Grief, "Parental Abduction of Children from Interracial and Cross-Cultural Marriages," *Journal of Comparative Family Studies* 25 (1994): 135–142.
9. Geoffrey L. Grief and Rebecca L. Hegar, "Parents Who Abduct: A Qualitative Study with Implications for Practice," *Family Relations* 43 (1994): 283–288.
10. Peggy S. Plass, David Finkelhor, and Gerald T. Hotaling, "Police Response to Family Abduction Episodes," *Crime and Delinquency* 41 (1995): 205–218.

11. Sharlene A. Wolchik, A. M. Fenaughty, and S. L. Braver, "Residential and Non-residential Parents: Perspectives on Visitation Problems," *Family Coordinator* 45 (1996): 230–237.
12. Wolchik *et al.*
13. Cheryl Buehler, Phyllis Betz, Catherine M. Ryan, Bobbie H. Legg, and Belinda B. Trotter, "Description and Evaluation of the Orientation for Divorcing Parents: Implications for Post-Divorce Prevention Programs," *Family Relations* 41 (1992): 154–162.

CHAPTER 7

1. D. Neumann, *Divorce Mediation: How to Cut the Cost and Stress of Divorce* (New York: Henry Holt, 1989).
2. Amy Koel, Susan C. Clark, Robert B. Straus, Ruth R. Whitney, and Barbara B. Hauser, "Patterns of Relitigation in the Post-Divorce Family," *Journal of Marriage and the Family* 56 (1994): 265–277.
3. L. Marlow and S. R. Sauber, *The Handbook of Divorce Mediation* (New York: Plenum, 1990).
4. Jessica Pearson and Nancy Thoennes, "Custody After Divorce: Demographic and Attitudinal Patterns," *American Journal of Orthopsychiatry* 60 (1990): 233–247.
5. David Blankenhorn, *Fatherless America: Confronting the Most Urgent Social Problem* (New York: Harper Perennial, 1995) 51.

CHAPTER 8

1. Warren Farrell, *The Future of Fatherhood: The Psychological, Political, and Spiritual Transitions of the 21st Century*, 1996 National Conference for Fathers and Children, Lenexa, KS.
2. Gerald A. Hill, *Divorced Father* (White Hall, VA: Betterway Publications, 1989).
3. Hill, 61.
4. U.S. Bureau of the Census, *Statistical Abstract of the United States, 1999* (Washington: GPO, 1999) Table 76.
5. Marilyn Ihinger-Tallman, K. Pasley, and C. Buehler, "Developing a Middle-Range Theory of Father Involvement Post-Divorce," *Journal of Family Issues* 14 (1993): 551–569.
6. Judith A. Seltzer, "Relationships Between Fathers and Children Who Live Apart: The Father's Role After Separation," *Journal of Marriage and the Family* 53 (1991): 79–101.
7. Robert Sammons, Grand Junction, CO, personal interview, 1997.
8. Bill Walz, Asheville, NC, personal interview, 1997.

9. Dwayne Frutiger, Greenville, NC, personal interview, 1997.
10. Richard A. Warshak, *The Custody Revolution* (New York: Poseidon, 1992) 144.
11. Seltzer.

CHAPTER 9

1. Geoffrey L. Grief, *Single Fathers* (New York: Lexington Free Press, 1985).

CHAPTER 11

1. J. J. Bigner, "Developmental, Postdivorce Parenting, and Therapeutic Issues," *Lesbians and Gays in Couples and Families: A Handbook for Therapists*, ed. Joan Laird and Robert-Jay Green (San Francisco: Jossey–Bass, 1996) 370–403. [Jerry Bigner is professor of Human Development and Family Studies, Colorado State University.]
2. R. L. Barret and B. E. Robinson, "Gay Dads," *Redefining Families: Implications for Children's Development*, ed. Adele E. Gottfried and Allen W. Gottfried (New York: Plenum, 1994) 157–170.
3. Barret and Robinson.
4. Bigner.
5. F. W. Bozett, "Gay Men as Fathers," *Dimensions of Fatherhood*, ed. S. Hansen and F. W. Bozett (Thousand Oaks, CA: Sage Publications, 1985) 327–352.
6. R. M. Scallen, "An Investigation of Parental Attitudes and Behaviors in Homosexual and Heterosexual Fathers," *DAI* 42 (1985): 3809B (California School of Professional Psychology, Los Angeles).
7. R. T. Michael, J. H. Gagnon, E. O. Laumann, and G. Kolata, *Sex in America: A Definitive Survey* (Boston: Little, Brown, 1994) 176.
8. U.S. Bureau of the Census, *Statistical Abstract of the United States, 1999* (Washington: GPO, 1999) Table 21.
9. Bigner.
10. Dorothea Hays and Aurele Samuels, "Heterosexual Women's Perceptions of Their Marriages to Bisexual or Homosexual Men," *Journal of Homosexuality* 18 (1989): 81–100.
11. Hays and Samuels.
12. Hays and Samuels.
13. Bigner.
14. J. J. Bigner and F.W. Bozett, "Parenting by Gay Fathers," *Marriage and Family Review* 14 (1989): 155–175.
15. Bigner & Bozett, copyright © 1989. The Haworth Press, Binghamton, NY, *Marriage and Family Review* "Parenting by Gay Fathers," volume 14. pp. 166–168. Used by permission of Haworth Press.
16. F. W. Bozett, "Gay Fathers: A Review of the Literature," *Journal of Homosexuality* 18 (1989): 137–162.

17. N. L. Wyers, *Lesbian and Gay Spouses and Parents: Homosexuality in the Family* (Portland, OR: School of Social Work, Portland State University, 1984).
18. P. H. Turner, L. Scadden, and M. B. Harris, "Parenting in Gay and Lesbian Families," First Annual Future of Parenting Symposium, Chicago, March 1985.
19. Barret and Robinson.
20. Barret and Robinson.
21. Barret and Robinson.
22. See, for instance, J. M. Chandy, R. W. Blum, and M. D. Resnick, "Female Adolescents with a History of Sexual Abuse," *Journal of Interpersonal Violence* 11 (1996): 503–518. Also, J. M. Chandy *et al.*, "Gender Specific Outcomes for Sexually Abused Adolescents," *Child Abuse and Neglect* 20 (1996): 1219–1231.
23. C. Moser, "Lust, Lack of Desire, and Paraphilias: Some Thoughts and Possible Connections," *Journal of Marital and Sexual Therapy* 18 (1992): 65–69.
24. Scott L. Hershberger, "A Twin Registry Study of Male and Female Sexual Orientation," *The Journal of Sex Research* 34 (1997): 212–222.
25. Bozett, "Gay Fathers: A Review."
26. D. Hitchens, "Social Attitudes, Legal Standards, and Personal Trauma in Child Custody Cases," *Journal of Homosexuality* 5 (1980): 89–95.
27. L. Benkov, *Reinventing the Family* (New York: Crown Publishers, 1994) 42.
28. J. J. Bigner and R. B. Jacobsen, "Parenting Behaviors of Homosexual and Heterosexual Fathers," *Journal of Homosexuality* 18 (1989): 173–186.
29. Bigner and Jacobsen.
30. B. Miller, "Gay Fathers and Their Children," *The Family Coordinator* 28 (1979): 544–552.
31. See, for instance, Judith G. Fowler, "Homosexual Parents: Implications for Custody Cases," *Family and Conciliation Courts Review* 33 (1995): 361–376; A. Samuels, "The Good-Enough Father of Whatever Sex," *Feminism and Psychology* 5 (1995): 511–530; D. H. McIntyre, "Gay Parents and Child Custody: A Struggle Under the Legal System," *Mediation Quarterly* 12 (1994): 135–149; C. J. Patterson, "Children of Lesbian and Gay Parents," *Child Development* 63 (1992): 1025–1042.
32. Bigner.
33. Bozett, "Gay Fathers: A Review."
34. J. J. Bigner, "Raising Our Sons: Gay Men as Gay Fathers" unpublished paper, 1997.

CHAPTER 12

1. U.S. Bureau of the Census, *Statistical Abstract of the United States, 1999* (Washington: GPO, 1999) Table 158.
2. E. M. Heatherington, M. Cox, and R. Cox. "Divorced Fathers," *Family Coordinator* 25 (1976): 417–428.
3. R. N. Anderson, K. D. Kochanek, and S. L. Murphy, "Report of Final Mortality Statistics, 1995," *Monthly Vital Statistics Report* 45, Supplement 2 (April 1997).

4. Sally C. Clarke and Barbara F. Wilson, "The Relative Stability of Marriages: A Cohort Approach Using Vital Statistics," *Family Relations* 43 (1994): 305–310.
5. Jack A. Turner, Huntsville, AL, personal interview, 1997.
6. U.S. Bureau of the Census. Table 730.

CHAPTER 13

1. Robert Sammons, Grand Junction, CO, personal interview, 1997.
2. David Blankenhorn, *Fatherless America: Confronting the Most Urgent Social Problem* (New York: Harper Perennial, 1995) 13.
3. U.S. Bureau of the Census, *Statistical Abstract of the United States, 1999* (Washington: GPO, 1999) Table 83.
4. Martin Hoffman, "Father Absence and Conscience Development," *Developmental Psychology* 4 (1971): 400–406.
5. K. D. Peters, J. A. Martin, S. J. Ventura, and J. D. Maurer, "Births and Deaths: United States, July 1995–June 1996," *Monthly Vital Statistics Report* 45, Supplement 2 (April 1997).
6. David Popenoe, *Life Without Father* (New York: Free Press, 1996).
7. Popenoe.
8. David Popenoe, "A World Without Fathers," *Wilson Quarterly* (Spring 1996): 12–29.
9. Blankenhorn, 45.
10. James D. Lambert, Marc Cwik, and Karen Bogenschneider, "Government's Role in Promoting Positive Father Involvement," Paper, Annual Meeting of the National Council on Family Relations, Portland, OR, November 1995.
11. Popenoe, *Life Without Father*, 144, 145.
12. Jack Turner, Huntsville, AL, personal interview, 1997.
13. Robert Bly, *The Sibling Society* (Reading, MA: Addison–Wesley, 1996).
14. U.S. Bureau of the Census, Table 758.
15. Blankenhorn, 3.
16. Richard A. Warshak, *The Custody Revolution* (New York: Poseidon, 1992).
17. Michael Schwalbe, *Unlocking the Iron Cage: The Men's Movement, Gender Politics, and American Culture* (New York: Oxford University Press, 1996).
18. Theodore Cohen, "What Do Fathers Provide?" *Men, Work, Family,* ed. Jane C. Hood (Thousand Oaks, CA: Sage Publications, 1993) 1–22.

CHAPTER 14

1. David Blankenhorn, *Fatherless America: Confronting the Most Urgent Social Problem* (New York: Harper Perennial, 1995).
2. Alfred DeMaris and Geoffrey L. Grief, "Single Custodial Fathers and Their Children: When Things Go Well," *Generative Fathering: Beyond Deficit Perspec-*

tives, ed. Alan J. Hawkins and David C. Dollahite (Thousand Oaks, CA: Sage Publications, 1997) 134–146.

3. DeMaris and Grief.

4. Erma Jean Lawson and Aaron Thompson, "Black Men's Perceptions of Divorce-Related Stressors and Strategies for Coping with Divorce: An Exploratory Study," *Journal of Family Issues* 17 (1996): 249–273.

5. Steve Fainary, "McDaniel Gives Celtics Some Punch," *Boston Globe* (March 26, 1993): 49.

6. Blankenhorn, 122.

7. Bill Cosby, *Fatherhood* (New York: Berkley Publishing, 1987).

8. Horst Stipp, "New Ways to Reach Children," *American Demographics* (August 1993): 50–56.

9. Alexandra Towle, *Fathers* (New York: Simon & Schuster, 1986).

10. U.S. Bureau of the Census, *Statistical Abstract of the United States, 1999* (Washington: GPO, 1999) Table 639.

11. Suzanne Helburn, Mary L. Culkin, John Morris, Naci Moran, Carollee Howes, Leslie Phillipsen, Donna Bryant, Richard Clifford, Debby Cryer, Ellen Peisner-Feinberg, Margaret Burchinal, Sharon Lynn Kagan, and Jean Rustici, "Cost, Quality, and Child Outcomes in Child Care Centers: Key Findings and Recommendations," *Young Children* 50 (1995): 40–44.

12. Victoria Pope, "Day-Care Dangers: A Special Report," *U.S. News and World Report* (August 4, 1997): 31–37.

CONCLUSION

1. Douglas MacKay, 29 Barnes Rd., Stonington, CT 06378 (860-585-0817), personal interview, 1997. Used by permission.

Legal Terms

Your attorney or mediator may use legal terms that you should be familiar with as you make decisions about your divorce and child custody.

Alimony (Spousal Support)   The money a husband or wife is required to pay his or her former spouse. This may be temporary alimony paid during the separation period, time-defined alimony for a specific number of years, or permanent alimony. Only about 15 percent of divorce cases involve alimony.

Child Support   The money paid by one parent to the other to help pay the costs of feeding, clothing, and housing the child. All states have guidelines for determining the amount.

Community Property   All of the property acquired by the spouses during their marriage. This includes pension plans, but may not include gifts or inheritance money that either spouse has received during the marriage.

Discovery   Before either the pendente lite hearing or the regular hearing, both you and your spouse can obtain (through your lawyers) information from the other to prepare for trial. Discovery is basically a time to find out what case your wife has against you. This is also the time for you to get your lawyer to subpoena all of your wife's income information. The more she has, the less you will have to pay.

Joint Legal Custody   Both parents have equal legal authority and control over the educational, medical, and psychological decisions that affect their children. In effect, joint physical custody refers to where the children live; joint legal custody refers to decision-making power.

Noncustodial Parent   Usually the father, the parent who does not have sole custody of the children and has few, if any, parental rights.

Pendente Lite Hearing (Latin for "pending litigation")   Also called "a temporary hearing"; this is when a judge decides who gets custody, who pays how much child support and the like during the period of separation and before the divorce becomes final. It is usually the only time the father will get a real hearing, so go prepared to ask for what you want.

Petition   Asking the court to hear a case. The person who starts the case is the plaintiff; the person who responds is the defendant.

Sole Custody   Refers to the individual who has legal control of the children and authority to make decisions on their behalf—where the children go to school, medical treatment, and so forth. In some states, the court grants sole custody as a "temporary order" when you and your spouse are about to separate.

Split Custody   One or more children live with one of the parents while one or more children live with the other parent; e.g., an infant daughter might live with mom and the teenage son with dad.

Summons   An official document usually delivered by the sheriff to one's home or office informing the person that a petition has been filed against him or her. Usually there is a specified time limit to answer the complaint. If you receive a summons, get a lawyer immediately.

Visitation   Specific times that the noncustodial parent may visit the children under a sole custody arrangement.

APPENDIX II
Legal Specification of Visitation Rights

Some fathers feel that it is in their children's best interests for their former wives to have primary custody. Traditional fathers who have focused on their careers while their wives took care of the children are more likely to feel this way. But before giving primary custody to your former wife, get specific visitation rights made a part of the court order. A worthless clause in the divorce settlement is "the parents will identify such times that are mutually agreeable." Although your former wife may be very amicable and agreeable to almost anything now, she may not always be. Your involvement with a new woman in a remarriage may alter her feelings about her children visiting you, and you may suddenly discover that there are no longer any "mutually agreeable" times for you to see your kids. Make sure your divorce decree spells out in detail exactly what your visitation rights are as a father.

In addition, traditional visitation rights have been every other weekend, alternate holidays, and a week in the summer. This is too restrictive and does not allow the father to continue active involvement in his children's lives. Kidmate (see Resources in Appendix V) is an excellent computer program that specifies visitation times in detail. In the absence of such a program, a specific visitation schedule that fosters such a continued relationship follows.

Weekends: From 5:30 PM on the first, third, and fifth Friday of each month until 5:30 PM on the following Sunday. Alternatively, this may read "from the time the child's school day ends, if any, on the first, third, and fifth Friday of each month until 5:30 PM on the following Sunday."

Extra Weekends: Six times a year, the father may request an "additional weekend" with the children. The only requirement is that he give his former wife a month's notice in writing.

241

Alternate Weekends: On weekends that the father does not have regular weekend visitation, he may pick up the children on Sunday at 4 PM and return them at 8 PM.

Midweek: Every Wednesday, the father may pick up the children at 5:30 PM and keep them overnight and deliver them to school the next day. Alternatively, this may read that the father will pick up the children after school, keep them overnight, and deliver them to school the next morning.

Christmas Holidays: In even-numbered years, the father will have the children from 5:30 PM on the day they get out of school for Christmas holidays until 2 PM Christmas Day. In odd-numbered years, the father will pick up the children at 2 PM Christmas Day and return them by 6 PM the night before they are to return to school.

Thanksgiving: In even-numbered years the father is to have the children from 5:30 PM the day before Thanksgiving and return them the following Sunday at 5:30 PM.

Easter: In odd-numbered years, the father is to have the children from 5:30 PM Friday until 5:30 PM Easter Sunday.

Spring Break: In even-numbered years, the father is to have the children from 5:30 PM on the Friday the children get out of school until 5:30 PM Wednesday. If spring break and Easter occur at the same time, the children will spend the first half of the break with their father in even-numbered years and the last half with their mom.

Summer: Six weeks in the summer, with the father giving the mother notice of which weeks by April 1. The weeks may be consecutive or alternate weeks when the children are with their mother.

Father's Day: The children will be with their father from 5:30 PM Father's Day until the next morning (8 AM). (The children will be with their mother on Mother's Day.)

Birthdays: If the children are not regularly scheduled to be with their father on the child's birthday, he will pick them up at 5:30 PM and return them at 8:30 PM on their birthday. If they are scheduled to be with the father, the mother may pick them up at 5:30 PM and return them at 8:30 PM.

There are two other items that your attorney should insist be included in the order that the judge issues. One is in reference to phone access, namely, that you are free to call any time to talk to your children but specifically at 8 PM on Tuesdays when the mother is to ensure that they are in the house for the phone call. Second, any relocation by your former spouse outside a limited radius of her current residence will constitute a "change of circumstance" and require a new evaluation of custodial arrangement that is in the best interest of the child. Also, your former spouse agrees to pay transportation costs for your visitation times if she moves more than 10 miles away from her current residence. Don't expect to get all of these items included in your final custody agreement, but ask your attorney to press for as many of them as possible.

APPENDIX III

An Open Letter to Judges

Judges who read this book might read the following as a plea from concerned, divorced fathers.

Judges of Custody Cases

You hold one of the most important positions in society. No other role provides the power to affect the psychological, social, and emotional development of children as does your role. I and other divorced fathers like me implore you to acknowledge the value to children and to society of being given equal access to our children. Limited time with our children in the form of visitation weekends, alternate holidays, and one month every summer only contributes to a weakening of the relationship with our children. Such a schedule means that we are allowed to be with our children only about 25% of the time in any year. Some fathers don't care about and have abandoned their children. We care and want time with our children. No wonder we are called Disneyland dads; we are not permitted the time to be otherwise.

Research is clear on the value of fathers to the lives of their children. Children without fathers have higher incidences of teen pregnancies, running away from home, substance abuse, dropping out of school, and juvenile delinquency. German psychologist Alexander Mitscherlich said, "Where the father is absent from the child's life, a hole forms and demons rush in to fill that hole." Fathers provide a stabilizing influence in the lives of their children.

The next domestic case that comes before you, please recognize the right of the child to have his or her fantasy come true—that both parents remain active in his or her life. And allow nothing to enter the court order that limits such equal access.

Also, please consider the mother's interfering with the father's visitation an abuse equal to that of the father not paying child support. Illinois has an "Unlawful Visitation Interference" statute that provides penalties (including jail time for up to a year) for the mother who interferes with the right of her children to be with their father. As fathers, we seek not to be punitive. We only want access to our children.

Thank you.

APPENDIX IV

National and International Listing of Attorneys, Mediators, and Custody Evaluators

Disclaimer: The listing of the professionals in this section does not imply an endorsement. A = Attorney; CE = Custody Evaluator; M = Mediator.

ALABAMA

Huntsville
Frankie L. Preston, Psy.D. (CE)
120 Holmes Ave., NE, Suite 404
Huntsville, AL 35801
P: (205) 536-9255
F: (205) 536-9288

ALASKA

Anchorage
Ardis J. Cry, R.E. (CE)
Trial Courts 3rd Judicial District
Custody Investigator Office
303 K St., Rm. 275
Anchorage, AK 99501
P: (907) 264-0428
F: (907) 264-0522

Mary Ann Dearborn, B.A. (M)
Dearborn Family Mediation
308 G St., Suite 202
Anchorage, AK 99501
P: (907) 276-6001

Susanne Di Pietro (A)
Alaska Judicial Council
1029 W. Third Ave., Suite 201
Anchorage, AK 99501-1981
P: (907) 279-2526
F: (907) 276-5046

Karla F. Huntington, J.D. (A)
Mendel & Huntington
845 K St.
Anchorage, AK 99501
P: (907) 279-5001
F: (907) 279-5437

Katherine Yeotis, M.S. (CE)
Alaska Court System, Custody
  Investigators
303 K St., Rm. 275
Anchorage, AK 99501
P: (907) 264-0428
F: (907) 264-0522

Fairbanks
Teresa Foster Brimner, J.D. (A, M)
Alaska Mediation Services
3427 Airport Way
Fairbanks, AK 99709
P: (907) 479-7074
F: (907) 474-3814

Thekla Johnson (CE)
Alaska Court System
604 Barnette St., Rm. 209
Fairbanks, AK 99701
P: (907) 452-9360
F: (907) 452-9206

Juneau
Colin C. Scholle, M.A. (CE)
State of Alaska
1st Judicial District
PO Box 114100
Juneau, AK 99811
P: (907) 463-4755
F: (907) 463-4783

David T. Walker, J.D. (A)
417 Harris St.
Juneau, AK 99801
P: (907) 586-3537
F: (907) 586-1350

ARIZONA

Chandler
Nancy Opre Logan (A)
PO Box 471
Chandler, AZ 85244
P: (602) 497-9555
F: (602) 497-8165

William Spence, J.D. (A)
1351 N. Alma School Rd.,
  Suite 265
Chandler, AZ 85244
P: (602) 234-0034
F: (602) 732-9202

Flagstaff
Sidney Buckman, M.A. (CE)
Gestalt Institute for Family
  Therapy
15 E. Cherry, Suite 203
Flagstaff, AZ 86001
P: (602) 773-9722

Kevin G. Fowler (M)
Arizona Attorney General's
  Office
2501 N. 4th St., Suite 8A
Flagstaff, AZ 86004
P: (602) 773-0474
F: (602) 773-1190

Elaine Fridlund-Horne, J.D.
  (A)
PO Box 2811
Flagstaff, AZ 86003-2811
P: (520) 526-6079

Ellen Seaborne, J.D. (A)
324 W. Birch Ave.
Flagstaff, AZ 86001
P: (520) 774-4220
F: (520) 774-9171

Kingman
Bonnie S. Kleiman, J.D. (A, M)
Superior Court of Mohave County
401 E. Spring St.
PO Box 7000
Kingman, AZ 86402
P: (520) 753-0790
F: (520) 753-8908

Mesa
Ruth L. Gourley, M.C. (M)
1703 S. Cholla Ave.
Mesa, AZ 85202
P: (602) 838-8460

Suzanna Anstine Norbeck, J.D.
  (A, M)
1807 E. Hale
Mesa, AZ 85203
P: (602) 649-9970

Kevin Therlot, Ph.D. (CE)
Independent Custody Evaluations
1550 E. University, Suite Q
Mesa, AZ 85203
P: (602) 844-3650
F: (602) 969-5530

Phoenix
Irwin Bernstein, LL.B. (A)
1951 W. Camelback Rd., Suite 210
Phoenix, AZ 85015
P: (602) 249-0117

Bruce R. Cohen, J.D. (A)
Cohen & Fromm, P.C.
2198 E. Camelback Rd.,
  Suite 365
Phoenix, AZ 85064
P: (602) 955-1515
F: (602) 955-0509

Robert Cottor, M.D. (CE)
Cottor Associates, P.C.
727 E. Bethany Home Rd., #118
Phoenix, AZ 85014
P: (602) 274-9872
F: (602) 285-0663

Sharon Cottor, M.S.W. (CE)
Cottor Associates, P.C.
727 E. Bethany Home Rd., #118
Phoenix, AZ 85014
P: (602) 274-9872
F: (602) 285-0663

John R. Fox, J.D. (A, M)
2001 N. 3rd St., Suite 202
Phoenix, AZ 85004
P: (602) 254-4948
F: (602) 257-9542

Marilyn Fox, J.D. (A)
2001 N. 3rd St., Suite 202
Phoenix, AZ 85004
P: (602) 254-4948
F: (602) 257-9542

Bruce Kushner, Ph.D. (CE, M)
8940 N. 19th Ave., Suite 104
Phoenix, AZ 85021
P: (602) 843-0035
F: (602) 843-8963

Ronn Lavitt, Ph.D. (CE)
1130 E. Missouri Ave. #570
Phoenix, AZ 85014
P: (602) 266-5823
F: (602) 266-0521

Donald W. Lindholm, LL.B. (A)
Burch & Cracchiolo, P.A.
702 E. Osborn, Suite 200
Phoenix, AZ 85014
P: (602) 234-9918
F: (602) 240-3823

Margaret Marshall, Ph.D. (CE, M)
777 E. Missouri Ave. #121
Phoenix, AZ 85014-2831
P: (602) 264-5678
F: (602) 277-8291

John Patrick Moore, J.D.
  (A, M)
394 N. 3rd Ave.
Phoenix, AZ 85003
P: (602) 258-3400
F: (602) 258-7557

John W. Nelson, B.A., J.D. (A)
519 E. Thomas Rd.
Phoenix, AZ 85012
P: (602) 264-7433
F: (602) 277-9909

Mark J. Robens (A)
Mariscal, Weeks, Mcintyre &
  Friedlander, P.A.
2901 N. Central Ave.
Phoenix, AZ 85012
P: (602) 285-5049
F: (602) 285-5100

Prescott
Janis Ann Sterling, J.D. (A)
Yavapai County Courthouse
Prescott, AZ 86303
P: (602) 445-1279
F: (602) 771-2228

Scottsdale
Joy B. Borum (A, M)
7520 E. 2nd St.
Scottsdale, AZ 85251
P: (602) 945-8909
F: (602) 941-2650

Sandra Bregman, J.D. (A, M)
Bregman & Bregman
6902 E. 1st St., Suite 2000
Scottsdale, AZ 85251
P: (602) 945-9131

Joel B. Glassman, Ph.D. (CE)
7520 E. 2nd St. #1
Scottsdale, AZ 85251
P: (602) 947-9591
F: (602) 481-0790

Sheryl W. Harrison, Ph.D. (CE, M)
7373 N. Scottsdale Rd., Suite C-127
Scottsdale, AZ 85253
P: (602) 483-9066
F: (602) 483-2375

Kathleen Infeld (CE, M)
Scottsdale Counseling &
  Mediation Associates
10900 N. Scottsdale Rd., Suite 201
Scottsdale, AZ 85254
P: (602) 948-2635
F: (602) 948-8163

Lynne Kenney, Psy.D. (CE, M)
Developmental Pediatric
  Associates
5040 E. Shea Blvd., Suite 166
Scottsdale, AZ 85254
P: (602) 443-0050
F: (602) 443-4018

Anna Scherzer (CE)
Scottsdale Institute for Behavioral
  Science
10900 N. Scottsdale Rd.,
  Suite 504
Scottsdale, AZ 85254
P: (602) 951-3066
F: (602) 951-8453

Tucson
Robert Louis Barrasso, J.D. (A)
15 W. Washington
Tucson, AZ 85701
P: (520) 624-7550
F: (520) 624-9024

Lisa Bibbens (A)
Liberty & O'Neill
70 W. Cushing
Tucson, AZ 85701
P: (520) 792-0006
F: (520) 624-9011

Jimmy Crabb (M)
3010 E. Loretta Dr.
Tucson, AZ 85716-2527
P: (520) 323-1801

H. Eugene Evans, Ph.D. (CE)
6614 E. Carondelet Dr.
Tucson, AZ 85710
P: (520) 296-8572
F: (520) 885-3922

William Andrew Ivy (M)
Our Town Family Center
PO Box 26665
Tucson, AZ 85716
P: (520) 323-1708
F: (520) 323-5900

Andres Kerns, Ph.D. (CE)
1476 W. Stockwell Pl.
Tucson, AZ 85746
P: (520) 881-6875
F: (520) 327-2298

Kathleen McCarthy, J.D. (A)
Solese & McCarthy, P.C.
130 W. Cushing St.
Tucson, AZ 85701
P: (602) 623-0341
F: (602) 628-9495

Barry G. Nelson, J.D. (A)
Oracle at the River
4750 N. Oracle Rd.,
  Suite 115
Tucson, AZ 85705
P: (520) 690-0468
F: (520) 690-0353

James L. Stroud (A)
Stompoly, Stroud, Giddings &
  Glicksman
1820 Northwest Tower
One S. Church Ave.
Tucson, AZ 85702
P: (602) 628-8300
F: (602) 628-9948

ARKANSAS

Ft. Smith
Frances D. Still, M.S.W. (M)
Peacemakers
1622 N. B St.
Ft. Smith, AR 72901
P: (501) 785-3004
F: (501) 785-3004

CALIFORNIA

Alameda
Eileen Preville, J.D. (A)
2223 Santa Clara Ave., Suite B
Alameda, CA 94501
P: (510) 865-2223
F: (510) 865-0375

Alamo
Marlene G. Posner, Ph.D.
  (CE, M)
17 Robbins Pl.
Alamo, CA 94507
P: (510) 820-0778

Brian D. Thiessen, Esq. (A, M)
3201 Danvile Blvd., Suite 295
Alamo, CA 94507
P: (510) 837-3355
F: (510) 837-3352

Apple Valley
Kay Bergman, M.F.C.C. (M)
PO Box 536
Apple Valley, CA 92307
P: (619) 247-6050

Aptos
Melissa Berrenge, Ph.D.
  (CE, M)
Family Mediation Service
6233 Soquel Dr., Suite C
Aptos, CA 95003
P: (408) 688-7904
F: (408) 688-0820

Donald T. Saposnek, Ph.D. (M)
6233 Soquel Dr., Suite E
Aptos, CA 95003
P: (408) 476- 9225
F: (408) 662-9056

Arcata
Bryan W. Gaynor, LL.B. (A)
1731 G St., Suite C
Arcata, CA 95521
P: (707) 826-8540
F: (707) 826-8541

Bakersfield
Family Court Services Unit
  (CE, M)
Kern County Probation
  Department
PO Box 3309
Bakersfield, CA 93385
P: (805) 634-4530
F: (805) 634-4520

Berkeley

Gerard A. Aglioni, Ph.D. (CE, M)
2709 Alcatraz Ave., Suite 1
Berkeley, CA 94705
P: (510) 970-0459
F: (510) 649-9041

Carol Amyx, J.D. (A)
1919 Addison St., Suite 201
Berkeley, CA 94704
P: (510) 644-3360
F: (510) 644-9553

Henry Elson, J.D. (M)
Wells Fargo Bldg., Suite 1011
2140 Shattuck Ave.
Berkeley, CA 94704
P: (510) 843-0880

Gerald Michaels (CE, M)
2140 Shattuck Ave., Suite 707
Berkeley, CA 94704
P: (510) 658-2191
F: (510) 658-2191

Carol Thompson, M.S.W. (M)
1808 4th St., Suite B
Berkeley, CA 94710
P: (415) 845-1412

Beverly Hills

Kathleen A. Memel, M.F.C.C. (M)
Divorce & Child Custody
Mediator, Marriage & Family
  Therapy
420 S. Beverly Dr. #100
Beverly Hills, CA 90212
P: (310) 286-9201
F: (310) 551-1884

Susan C. Rempel, Ph.D. (CE, M)
433 N. Camden Dr., Suite 400
Beverly Hills, CA 90210
P: (310) 858-6820
F: (818) 952-3241

Fern Topas Salka, J.D. (A)
9595 Wilshire Blvd. #900
Beverly Hills, CA 90212
P: (310) 278-9307

Blythe

Gerald L. Hoemann, M.Div.
  (CE, M)
Zion Counseling Center
721 E. Chanslorway
Blythe, CA 92225
P: (619) 922-7321
F: (619) 921-7941

Burlingame

Pamela G. Krell, Ph.D. (CE, M)
1515 Trousdale Dr., Suite 208
Burlingame, CA 94010
P: (415) 759-0730
F: (415) 431-4526

Carmel Valley

Ann M. Flood, Ph.D. (CE, M)
PO Box 1427
Carmel Valley, CA 92924
P: (408) 659-0712
F: (408) 373-1723

Castro Valley

Jo Ellen Hilmo, Ph.D. (CE)
20980 Redwood Rd., Suite 230
Castro Valley, CA 94546
P: (510) 889-0359
F: (510) 727-0877

Claremont
Sandra N. Baldonado, M.A., J.D.
  (A, M)
414 Yale Ave.
Claremont, CA 91711
P: (909) 626-1224
F: (909) 626-5004

Corte Madera
Joan B. Kelly, Ph.D. (M)
Northern California Mediation
  Center
100 Tamal Plaza #175
Corte Madera, CA 94925
P: (415) 927-1422
F: (415) 927-1477

Culver City
Joanne S. Feigin, M.S.W. (M)
PO Box 5063
Culver City, CA 90231
P: (310) 313-4357

Cupertino
Lindy F. Barocchi, Esq. (A, M)
20111 Stevens Creek Blvd.,
  Suite 245
Cupertino, CA 95014
P: (408) 996-9949
F: (408) 996-3977

Danville
Martha C. Anthony, J.D. (A)
375 Diablo Rd., Suite 200
Danville, CA 94526
P: (510) 743-9730
F: (510) 831-0155

Missy Eidman (CE)
2425 Holly Oak Dr.
Danville, CA 94506
P: (510) 838-4408

Stuart I. Goldware, J.D. (A, M)
375 Diablo Rd., Suite 200
Danville, CA 94526
P: (510) 820-8712
F: (510) 831-0155

Marcia Jensen Lassiter, J.D. (A)
Frankel & Goldware
375 Diablo Rd., Suite 200
Danville, CA 94526
P: (510) 820-8712
F: (510) 831-0155

Dublin
Philip Stahl, Ph.D. (CE)
Bay Tree Psychology
  Associates
11740 Dublin Blvd., Suite 206
Dublin, CA 94568
P: (510) 828-7660
F: (510) 828-8238

El Cerrito
Valerie E. Shopher, J.D. (A, M)
PO Box 1254
El Cerrito, CA 94530
P: (510) 620-0122
F: (510) 620-0123

Emeryville
Martina Reaves (M)
4300 Horton St., Suite 15
Emeryville, CA 94608-2956
P: (510) 601-4095
F: (510) 601-4091

Encinitas
William Dess, Ph.D. (CE, M)
Clinical Psychology Counseling
345 Saxony Rd. #201
Encinitas, CA 92024
P: (619) 295-6448
F: (619) 753-6403

Encino
Bernice H. Shanin, M.S.,
  M.F.C.C. (CE)
PO Box 261004
Encino, CA 91426-1004
P: (818) 995-4049

Leslie Ellen Shear, C.F.L.S. (A, M)
Encino Law Center
15915 Ventura Blvd., Suite 201
Encino, CA 91436-2785
P: (818) 501-3691
F: (818) 501-3692

Stefanie Somers (M)
17004 Strawberry Dr.
Encino, CA 91436
P: (213) 974-5524

Eureka
Eric Olson (M)
Family Court Service
Humbolt County Probation
2002 Harrison Ave.
Eureka, CA 95501
P: (707) 445-7401
F: (707) 443-7139

Fairfield
Jerri Curry, Ph.D., M.F.C.C.
  (CE, M)
Center for Family Mediation &
  Counseling
1530 Webster St., Suite D
Fairfield, CA 94533
P: (707) 428-0228

Murray A. Sobel (CE, M)
Center for Family Mediation &
  Counseling
1530 Webster St., Suite D
Fairfield, CA 94533
P: (707) 421-2111
F: (707) 421-2111

Folsom
Alicia A. Santos-Coy, M.F.C.C.
  (M)
1004 River Rock Dr., Suite 235
Folsom, CA 95630
P: (916) 988-1224
F: (916) 622-4465

Fresno
Elizabeth O'Neill, J.D.
  (CE, M)
6300 N. Palm Ave. #126
Fresno, CA 93704

Fullerton
William M. Bush, B.A., J.D. (A)
110 E. Wilshire Ave., Suite 210
Fullerton, CA 92632
P: (714) 992-0800
F: (714) 879-5811

Mary O'Connor Harris, M.A.,
M.F.C.C. (CE)
514 W. Chapman Ave.
Fullerton, CA 92632
P: (714) 879-9616
F: (717) 879-2041

Linda K. Ross (A)
1440 N. Harbor Blvd., Suite
800
Fullerton, CA 92635
P: (714) 449-3352
F: (714) 738-8420

Glendora
Donald S. Eisenberg, J.D. (A)
Stettner, Eisenberg & Morris
1433 E. Alosta Ave.
Glendora, CA 91740-3747
P: (818) 914-2791
F: (818) 914-3946

Pamela Panasiti Stettner, B.A.,
M.A., J.D. (A)
1433 E. Alosta Ave., Suite E
Glendora, CA 91740-3747
P: (818) 914-2791
F: (818) 914-3946

Gold River
Carol F. Delzer (A, CE, M)
11211 Gold Country Blvd.,
#109
Gold River, CA 95670
P: (916) 851-0555
F: (916) 851-0550

Green Brae
S. Margaret Lee, Ph.D. (CE)
481 Via Hidalgo, Suite 200
Green Brae, CA 94904
P: (415) 461-8363
F: (415) 383-1217

Hayward
Ruthanne Allen, M.A. (M)
Alameda County Family Court
Services
224 W. Winton Ave., Suite 208
Hayward, CA 94544
P: (510) 670-6350
F: (510) 670-6457

Paul Z. Goldman, J.D. (A)
1290 B St., #109
Hayward, CA 94541
P: (510) 582-2300
F: (510) 582-2098

Judith Linzer, Ph.D. (CE)
25125 Santa Clara St., Suite 170
Hayward, CA 94544
P: (510) 887-8819

Barbara J. Miller, J.D. (A)
Alameda County Superior Court
24405 Amador St., Dept. 35
Hayward, CA 94544
P: (510) 670-6316
F: (510) 670-6587

Hollister
Barbara Girard, M.A. (M)
San Benito County Superior
Court
440 Fifth St., Rm. 206
Hollister, CA 95023
P: (408) 636-4425
F: (408) 636-5682

Huntington Beach
Michael P. Dennis, M.A. (M)
Parent Pros
PO Box 1458
Huntington Beach, CA 92647-
1458
P: (714) 377-3767

Indio
Vahan Hovsepian, M.A. (M)
46-209 Oasis St., Rm. 3100A
Indio, CA 92201
P: (619) 342-8205

Irvine
Elizabeth Eckhardt, Ph.D. (M)
University Tower
4199 Campus Dr., Suite 870
Irvine, CA 92715-4580
P: (714) 854-4580
F: (714) 673-7125

Zena Polly, Ph.D. (CE)
111 Pacifica, Suite 125
Irvine, CA 92718
P: (714) 450-8270
F: (714) 951-7456

Thea Reinhart, Ph.D. (CE, M)
15435 Jeffery Rd., Suite 132
Irvine, CA 92720
P: (714) 651-1011
F: (714) 651-0276

Jackson
Amador County Family Court
Services (CE, M)
c/o Gary Davis
108 Court St.
Jackson, CA 95642
P: (209) 296-4787

Kensington
Karen Hobbs, Ph.D. (CE)
267 Berkley Park Blvd.
Kensington, CA 94707
P: (510) 526-8122

Lafayette
A. Tom Fingerhut, Ph.D. (M)
3470 Diablo Blvd., Suite A-150
Lafayette, CA 94549
P: (510) 283-4692

Stephen Hobbs, Ph.D. (CE, M)
Lafayette Psychological
Services
3468 Mt. Diablo Blvd.,
Suite B-203
Lafayette, CA 94549
P: (510) 283-2787
F: (510) 283-2787

Marcia Hofer, Ph.D. (CE, M)
938 Dewing Ave., Suite 4
Lafayette, CA 94549
P: (510) 283-8132
F: (510) 283-8132

Joyce Sasse Wood, J.D. (A)
1020 Aileen St.
Lafayette, CA 94599
P: (510) 743-1444
F: (510) 838-9019

Laguna Hills
Carol R. Hughes, Ph.D. (CE)
23441 S. Pointe Dr., Suite 130
Laguna Hills, CA 92653
P: (714) 855-2740

La Jolla

Stephen Doyne, Ph.D. (CE, M)
9834 Genesee Ave., Suite 321
La Jolla, CA 92037
P: (619) 452-5900
F: (619) 452-7610

Noel Phelan, D.Md. (M)
Family Court Services of San Diego
8531 Via Mallora
La Jolla, CA 92037
P: (619) 457-1943

Long Beach

Sam Leonard, B.A., M.Div. (M)
The Leonard Institute
Consulting & Education, Ltd.
Box 440
Long Beach, CA 90801
P: (310) 436-3398
F: (310) 299-5572

Marjorie Cain Mitchell, Ph.D.
(CE, M)
5175 E. Pacific Coast Hwy.,
Suite 304
Long Beach, CA 90804
P: (310) 494-6722
F: (310) 985-1377

Richard B. Rothell, L.C.S.W. (M)
Los Angeles County Superior
Court
415 W. Ocean Blvd., Rm. 503
Long Beach, CA 90802
P: (310) 491-6130

Carole C. Rouin, J.D., M.A.
(A, M)
Center for Divorce Mediation
1 World Trade Center, #2320
Long Beach, CA 90802
P: (310) 437-5409
F: (310) 437-4610

Los Angeles

Elayne Bernstein-Landy, M.S.W.
(M)
Los Angeles County Family
Court System
111 N. Hill St., Rm. 241
Los Angeles, CA 90012
P: (213) 974-5544
F: (213) 680-1043

Tara Fass, M.S. (M)
Conciliation Court-Los Angeles
Superior Court
6330 Maryland Dr.
Los Angeles, CA 90048
P: (213) 936-4209

Dianna J. Gould-Saltman, J.D.
(A, M)
4727 Wilshire Blvd., Suite 500
Los Angeles, CA 90010
P: (213) 939-8400
F: (213) 939-8405

Neal Raymond Hersh, J.D.
(A, M)
1999 Avenue of the Stars,
Suite 1400
Los Angeles, CA 90067
P: (310) 788-4603
F: (310) 788-4622

David Joel Jimenez, Ph.D. (CE)
2001 S. Barrington Ave.,
   Suite 202
Los Angeles, CA 90025
P: (310) 553-3905
F: (310) 553-3905

David Kuroda, L.C.S.W. (M)
Los Angeles County Superior
   Court
111 N. Hill St., Rm. 241
Los Angeles, CA 90012
P: (213) 974-5524
F: (213) 680-1043

Barbara Jean Lang (M)
4101 Don Luis Dr.
Los Angeles, CA 90008
P: (310) 222-1688

Forrest S. Mosten, J.D. (A)
Mosten & Wasserstrom
10990 Wilshire Blvd., Suite 940
Los Angeles, CA 90024
P: (310) 473-7611
F: (310) 473-7422

Patricia Roback, M.S.W. (M)
Los Angeles Family Court
   Services
111 N. Hill St., Rm. 241
Los Angeles, CA 90012
P: (213) 974-8926

Jane Shatz, Ph.D. (CE)
501 S. Beverly Dr., Suite 210
Los Angeles, CA 90212
P: (310) 286-6737

Dan Sniderman (CE, M)
1556 N. Curson Ave.
Los Angeles, CA 90046
P: (213) 876-6429

Beryl J. Turner (M)
338 Bonhill Rd.
Los Angeles, CA 90049
P: (310) 260-3711

Pamela Britton White, J.D.
   (A, M)
850 Colorado Blvd., Suite 102
Los Angeles, CA 90041
P: (818) 796-1093

Madera
Yoshi Asanuma, M.A. (CE, M)
Freson County Family Court
   Services
1256 Rd. 34 3/4
Madera, CA 93638
P: (209) 645-1150
F: (209) 488-3337

Betsy Brandt (CE, M)
Madera Superior Court
209 W. Yosemite Ave.
Madera, CA 93638
P: (209) 675-7810
F: (209) 675-0701

Catherine L. Wieland, M.A.
   (M)
24668 Brook Dr.
Madera, CA 93638
P: (209) 673-2106

Malibu
Ann Forisha Thiel, Ph.D. (M)
29169 Heathercliff Rd.,
Suite 201
Malibu, CA 90265
P: (310) 457-7606
F: (310) 457-7144

Martinez
Ted Jorgensen (CE, M)
Contra Costa County, Court
Services
724 Escobar St.
Martinez, CA 94553
P: (510) 646-2681
F: (510) 646-1409

Menlo Park
Edward Kovachy, Jr., M.D., J.D.,
M.B.A. (M)
1187 University Dr.
Menlo Park, CA 94025
P: (415) 329-0600

Donald A. (Dan) Wilcox,
M.F.C.C. (M)
D.A. Wilcox & Associates
770 Menlo Ave., Suite 203
Menlo Park, CA 94025
P: (415) 324-0711
F: (415) 322-5579

Mill Valley
Steven Rosenberg, J.D. (A, M)
Shelter Point Business Center
591 Redwood Hwy., Suite 2275
Mill Valley, CA 94941
P: (415) 383-5544
F: (415) 381-4301

Modesto
Donald Strangio, Ph.D. (M)
309 N. Santa Rosa Ave.
Modesto, CA 95354
P: (209) 577-1667

Napa
Robin Fielding, M.S. (M)
Napa County Family Court
Services
1710 Soscol Ave., Suite 5
Napa, CA 94559
P: (707) 253-4206
F: (707) 253-4602

Nevada City
Janet A. Minch, J.D. (A)
206 Sacramento St., Suite 101
Nevada City, CA 95959
P: (916) 265-4587
F: (916) 265-3447

Newport Beach
Stephen D. Adam, Ph.D. (CE)
1151 Dove St., Suite 230
Newport Beach, CA 92660
P: (714) 752-5111
F: (714) 833-1523

W. Russell Johnson, Ph.D. (CE)
Orange County, Clinical
Psychologist, Inc.
1101 Dove St., Suite 155
Newport Beach, CA 92660
P: (714) 833-8280
F: (714) 833-9897

Oakland

Mary L. Brutocao, J.D. (A)
171-12th St., Suite 100
Oakland, CA 94607
P: (510) 452-2238
F: (510) 835-0415

Marian Chapman, J.D.
  (A, M)
Mediation Services
1999 Harrison St., Suite 1900
Oakland, CA 94612
P: (510) 444-0599
F: (510) 444-3981

Mary A. Duryee, Ph.D. (M)
319 Lenox Ave.
Oakland, CA 94610
P: (510) 839-7080
F: (510) 832-6620

Jacqueline Karkazis, M.S.W.
  (M)
Mediation Services
1999 Harrison St.
Oakland, CA 94612
P: (510) 452-2034
F: (510) 444-3981

Robert Kaufman, Ph.D. (CE)
5625 College Ave., Suite 209
Oakland, CA 94611
P: (510) 658-0161
F: (510) 658-0161

Judy Law, J.D. (A)
5315 College Ave.
Oakland, CA 94618
P: (510) 655-4250
F: (510) 655-3942

Sharon Lazaneo, B.S. (M)
Mediation Services
1999 Harrison St., Suite 1900
Oakland, CA 94612
P: (510) 452-2034
F: (510) 444-3981

John Allen Lemmon, Ph.D. (M)
5248 Boyd Ave.
Oakland, CA 94618
P: (510) 547-8089

Erica Meyers, Ph.D. (CE, M)
445 Bellevue Ave., Suite 201
Oakland, CA 94610
P: (510) 832-0991
F: (510) 527-4800

Christine D. Pigeon, Ph.D.
  (CE)
5625 College Ave., Suite 209
Oakland, CA 94618
P: (415) 653-5238

Dennis K. Rothhaar, J.D. (A)
436 14th St., Suite 1417
Oakland, CA 94612
P: (510) 763-5611
F: (510) 763-3430

Roberta J. Schear, Ph.D. (CE, M)
5460 Carlton St.
Oakland, CA 94618
P: (510) 655-7240
F: (510) 272-0711

Miriam Steinbock, J.D. (A)
436 14th St., Suite 1417
Oakland, CA 94612
P: (510) 763-5611
F: (510) 763-3430

Rosemary Vasquez, L.C.S.W. (M)
1221 Oak St., Rm. 260
Oakland, CA 94612
P: (510) 272-6030
F: (510) 272-6023

Oceanside
Judith P. Sill, Ph.D. (CE)
2181 El Camino Real, Suite 201
Oceanside, CA 92054
P: (619) 721-1111
F: (619) 728-0028

Orange
Marvin L. Chapman, M.F.C.C. (M)
595 The City Dr., Suite 202
Orange, CA 92668
P: (714) 385-1002

Stephanie Macneille, M.A. (M)
Orange County Mediation &
    Invest. Services
341 The City Dr.
5th Flr., Suite 507
Orange, CA 92668
P: (714) 935-6550
F: (714) 935-6545

Orinda
Rodney Nurse, Ph.D. (CE, M)
PO Box 175
Orinda, CA 94563
P: (510) 254-3606
F: (510) 254-3606

Laro Peggy Thompson, Ph.D.
    (CE, M)
Family Psychological Seminars
PO Box 175
Orinda, CA 94563
P: (510) 254-3606
F: (510) 254-3606

Pacific Palisades
Karen Raiford, M.S.W. (CE)
1120 Fiske St.
Pacific Palisades, CA 90272
P: (310) 454-4288

Palm Desert
Michael C. Leitman, Ph.D.
    (CE, M)
Applied Psychological Services
74333 Hwy. 111, Suite 105
Palm Desert, CA 92260
P: (619) 346-3664
F: (619) 346-7117

Palo Alto
Jessica F. Arner, J.D. (A)
Lakin Spears
PO Box 240
Palo Alto, CA 94302
P: (415) 328-7000
F: (415) 327-2501

Anne P. Mitchell (A)
701 Welch Rd., Suite 323
Palo Alto, CA 94304
P: (408) 244-1204
F: (408) 244-4684

Bonnie Sorensen (A)
2501 Park Blvd.
Palo Alto, CA 94306
P: (415) 328-8254

Palos Verdes
Christine Campisi (M)
Superior Court
1125 Via Zumaya
Palos Verdes, CA 90274
P: (310) 222-8881

Pasadena
Shauna Weeks, J.D. (A)
Vienna & Weeks, APC
1550 Raymond Ave., Suite 204
Pasadena, CA 91105
P: (818) 583-9777
F: (818) 583-9775

Placerville
Vivian Carlson, M.A., M.F.C.C.
(M)
El Dorado County Superior
Court
495 Main St.
Placerville, CA 95667
P: (916) 621-6463
F: (916) 622-9774

Pleasant Hill
Joyce C. Dickey, M.A. (M)
Family & Divorce Mediation
Services
101 Gregory Ln. #49
Pleasant Hill, CA 94523
P: (510) 689-2326
F: (510) 825-4106

Pleasanton
Sara Lapides, M.F.C.C. (M)
5424-10 Sunol Blvd., #115
Pleasanton, CA 94566
P: (510) 346-1466

Dale M. Siperstein, Ph.D. (CE)
4713 First St., #290
Pleasanton, CA 94566
P: (510) 484-5441

Rancho Cucamonga
James H. Papen, Ph.D. (CE)
9121 Haven Ave., Suite 140
Rancho Cucamonga, CA 91730
P: (909) 945-2965
F: (818) 967-9750

Rancho Palos Verdes
Maxine Baker-Jackson, J.D.,
L.C.S.W., R.N. (M)
7405 Via Lorado
Rancho Palos Verdes, CA 90274
P: (213) 526-6671
F: (213) 881-3792

Edward Hummel, Jr., M.S.W.
(M)
6903 Hartcrest Dr.
Rancho Palos Verdes, CA 90274
P: (310) 541-6986

Red Bluff
Heidi Uptegrove (CE, M)
PO Box 810
Red Bluff, CA 96080
P: (916) 527-2170
F: (916) 527-4974

Redding
Victoria Pickering Edelstein,
Ph.D. (CE)
1864 South St.
Redding, CA 96001
P: (916) 241-5077
F: (916) 241-0289

Phil Reedy, M.A. (CE)
Shasta County Family Court
  Services
1558 West St., Suite 1
Redding, CA 96001
P: (916) 225-5707
F: (916) 245-6337

Sacramento
Mary Ann Frank, Ph.D., M.S.W.
  (M)
2717 Cottage Way, Suite 7
Sacramento, CA 95825
P: (916) 481-7431

Shaaron Garey, M.F.C.C. (M)
PO Box 22308
Sacramento, CA 95822
P: (916) 395-0598
F: (916) 395-0598

Penny R. Hancock, M.F.C.C. (M)
2277 Fair Oaks Blvd., Suite 190
Sacramento, CA 95825
P: (916) 923-1763
F: (916) 923-9372

Diane Vodrey Mayo (A, M)
1430 Alhembra Blvd.
Sacramento, CA 95816
P: (916) 452-5500

Debra Warwick-Sabino, M.Div.,
  M.A. (M)
2200 L St.
Sacramento, CA 95816
P: (916) 274-8156
F: (916) 273-7796

Wendy Wulff, R.N., L.C.S.W.,
  M.S.W. (M)
2277 Fair Oaks Blvd., Suite 190
Sacramento, CA 95825
P: (916) 920-7833

San Bernardino
R. L. Moore (M)
Family Court Services
San Bernardino
351 Arrowhead, Rm. 200
San Bernardino, CA 92415
P: (909) 387-3912
F: (909) 387-3055

San Carlos
Barbara Ellis Long, Ph.D. (CE)
1622 San Carlos Ave., Suite D
San Carlos, CA 94070
P: (415) 591-8191
F: (415) 591-1307

San Clemente
Mildred Daley Pageflow, Ph.D.
  (M)
Educational Consulting
  Services
401 Avenida Del Mar A-5
San Clemente, CA 92672
P: (714) 361-9411
F: (714) 366-3653

San Diego
Penny Angel-Levy, M.Ed.,
  M.F.C.C. (CE, M)
5060 Shoreham Place, Suite 200
San Diego, CA 92122
P: (619) 458-5878

Cheryl K. Daily (A, M)
3550 Camino Del Rio N
San Diego, CA 92108
P: (619) 521-5700
F: (619) 521-5703

William A. Eddy, M.S.W., J.D.
  (A, M)
160 Thorn St., Suite 2
San Diego, CA 92103
P: (619) 291-9644
F: (619) 692-4061

Russell S. Gold, Ph.D. (CE)
4060 Fourth Ave., Suite 615
San Diego, CA 92103
P: (619) 574-1694
F: (619) 574-1649

Jeannette Holm (A)
4515 Benhurst Ave.
San Diego, CA 92122
P: (619) 458-1153
F: (619) 452-8912

Bleema Moss (CE, M)
3551 Front St.
San Diego, CA 92103
P: (619) 296-9401

Mark L. Schlissel, M.S.W.,
  L.C.S.W. (M)
3914 Third Ave.
San Diego, CA 92103-3095
P: (619) 291-4808
F: (619) 291-4426

Nancy Stassinopoulos, J.D.
  (A)
591 Camino de la Reina,
  Suite 802
San Diego, CA 92108-3110
P: (619) 688-6505
F: (619) 688-3985

San Francisco
Jeanne Ames (CE, M)
203 Willow St., 5th Flr.
San Francisco, CA 94109
P: (415) 928-2079
F: (415) 928-2595

Marcia Belfer (CE, M)
633 Folsom St., Rm. 302
San Francisco, CA 94107
P: (415) 554-5080
F: (415) 554-5018

Nordin F. Blacker, J.D. (A)
535 Pacific
San Francisco, CA 94133
P: (415) 397-3222
F: (415) 394-0375

Sandra Blair, J.D. (A, M)
Law Offices of Sandra Blair
455 Market St., 19th Flr.
San Francisco, CA 94105
P: (415) 495-2040
F: (415) 882-3232

Suzanne M. Eisenhut, J.D.
  (A)
465 California St., Suite 200
San Francisco, CA 94104
P: (415) 395-9136
F: (415) 395-9137

Christopher F. Emley, J.D.
(A)
530 Bush St., Suite 500
San Francisco, CA 94106
P: (415) 433-6166

David Fink (A, M)
Nachlis & Fink
260 California St., 7th Flr.
San Francisco, CA 94111
P: (415) 399-8380
F: (415) 399-8390

Diana Gould, M.S. (M)
San Francisco Superior Court,
   Juvenile Division
375 Woodside Ave., Superior
   Court Rm. 101
San Francisco, CA 94127
P: (415) 753-7697
F: (415) 753-7888

Dana Iscoff, M.A., M.F.C.C.
(CE, M)
1301-17th Ave.
San Francisco, CA 94132
P: (415) 566-4567
F: (415) 566-4580

Maureen Kammer (M)
Family Court Services
633 Folsom St., Rm. 302
San Francisco, CA 94107
P: (415) 554-5085

Susan B. King (A)
220 Montgomery St., Suite 600
San Francisco, CA 94104
P: (415) 397-1110
F: (415) 397-1577

Lorie S. Nachlis, J.D. (A)
Nachlis & Fink
260 California St., 7th Flr.
San Francisco, CA 94111
P: (415) 399-8380
F: (415) 399-8390

Jessica Notini, J.D. (A, M)
155 Alma St.
San Francisco, CA 94117
P: (415) 753-3125

Michelle Patterson, J.D., Ph.D. (A)
3885 Jackson St.
San Francisco, CA 94118-1610
P: (415) 752-1381
F: (415) 752-1391

Pamela Pierson (A)
685 Market St., Suite 370
San Francisco, CA 94105
P: (415) 495-4499
F: (415) 495-3202

Diana Richmond (A, M)
595 Market St., Suite 2860
San Francisco, CA 94105
P: (415) 543-2990
F: (415) 543-1882

Susan Romer, Ph.D. (A, M)
220 Montgomery St., Suite 1020
San Francisco, CA 94104
P: (415) 392-3678
F: (415) 421-1299

Charles P. Roth, Ph.D. (CE, M)
2538 California St.
San Francisco, CA 94115
P: (415) 929-8701
F: (415) 567-0432

M. Dee Samuels, LL.B. (A)
1388 Sutter St., #1210
San Francisco, CA 94109
P: (415) 567-7000
F: (415) 567-6116

Milton Schaefer, Ph.D. (CE, M)
2491 Washington St.
San Francisco, CA 94115
P: (415) 776-3400
F: (510) 828-8238

Susan A. Scherman, Esq. (A, M)
465 California St., Suite 200
San Francisco, CA 94104
P: (415) 989-8999
F: (415) 989-8947

Joel Shawn, J.D. (A)
1388 Sutter St., Suite 1210
San Francisco, CA 94109
P: (415) 567-7000
F: (415) 567-6116

Bruce S. Silverman, J.D. (A, M)
Laughlin Falbo Lery & Moresy
Two Embarcadero Center #500
San Francisco, CA 94111-3823
P: (415) 781-6676
F: (415) 781-6823

Leslie Abbott Smith, J.D. (A)
Law Offices of James P.
   Preovolds
220 Montgomery St., Suite 600
San Francisco, CA 94104
P: (415) 397-1110
F: (415) 397-1577

Suzie Thorn, J.D. (A)
1242 Market St., 5th Flr.
San Francisco, CA 94104
P: (415) 431-5772
F: (415) 552-3942

Ann Van Balen, J.D. (A)
2832 Diversade Rd.
San Francisco, CA 94123
P: (415) 928-7141
F: (415) 931-4346

San Jose
Steve Baron, M.A. (CE, M)
Santa Clara County Family
   Court Services
170 Park Center Plaza
San Jose, CA 95113
P: (408) 299-3741
F: (408) 287-4109

June Boudreau, Ph.D. (CE)
1777 Hamilton Ave., S204A
San Jose, CA 95125
P: (408) 559-6299

Anne L. Kutilek (M)
Family Court Services
170 Park Center Plaza
San Jose, CA 95113
P: (408) 299-3741
F: (408) 287-4109

Laurie Williams (M)
960 W. Hedding #175
San Jose, CA 95126
P: (408) 247-6646
F: (408) 241-2174

San Luis Obispo
Larry Helm (M)
Family Court Services
778 Osos St.
San Luis Obispo, CA 93408
P: (805) 781-5423
F: (805) 781-1131

San Mateo
Gail W. Berkley, M.F.C.C. (CE, M)
St. Matthews Station
PO Box 731
San Mateo, CA 94401
P: (415) 342-1315

Linda R. Schwarz (M)
636 Caribbean Way
San Mateo, CA 94402
P: (415) 345-1919
F: (415) 345-2927

Dianne Thomas, M.A. (M)
325 Avila Rd.
San Mateo, CA 94402
P: (415) 349-0461
F: (415) 358-9666

San Rafael
Rudeen Monte, M.S. (M)
Rudeen Monte & Associates
PO Box 150092
San Rafael, CA 94915
P: (707) 224-2595

San Ramon
Elizabeth H. Braunstein, Psy.D.
(CE)
2817 Crow Canyon Rd. #202
San Ramon, CA 94583
P: (510) 820-0975
F: (510) 843-0891

Santa Ana
Rita G. Berlin (CE, M)
1801 B. Park Court Pl., Suite 101
Santa Ana, CA 92701
P: (714) 541-5581
F: (714) 541-2409

Gerri M. Olin, Ph.D. (CE, M)
1801 B. Park Court Pl.,
Suite 101
Santa Ana, CA 92701
P: (714) 541-5581
F: (714) 541-2409

Santa Barbara
Brian H. Burke, J.D. (A)
Hill-Carrillo-Adobe
15 E. Carrillo
Santa Barbara, CA 93101
P: (805) 965-2888

Penny Clemmons, Ph.D. (A)
214 E. Victoria St.
Santa Barbara, CA 93101
P: (805) 962-6468
F: (805) 962-6576

Alice Houghton Esbenshade
(CE, M)
226 E. Canon Perdido, Suite 1
Santa Barbara, CA 93101
P: (805) 966-1212

Nancy Madsen (A, M)
800 Gorden St., Suite A
Santa Barbara, CA 93101
P: (805) 564-4481
F: (805) 564-2402

Gail Rappaport, J.D. (A, M)
1231 State St., Suite 206
Santa Barbara, CA 93101
P: (805) 965-4525
F: (805) 962-0242

Santa Cruz
Michael Scott, M.A. (M)
Family Mediation Service
333 Church St., Suite B
Santa Cruz, CA 95060
P: (408) 423-0521

Santa Monica
Constance R. Ahrons, Ph.D. (M)
211 California Ave.
Santa Monica, CA 90403-3617
P: (310) 393-8591
F: (310) 393-0289

Joelle Bailard, Ph.D. (M)
Attn: Dean Mellor
1337-G Ocean Ave., Garden Suite
Santa Monica, CA 90401
P: (310) 312-4523
F: (310) 450-9797

Robin Drapkin, Ph.D. (M)
2110 Main St., Suite 303
Santa Monica, CA 90405
P: (310) 399-6789
F: (310) 399-1185

Dean J. Mellor (M)
1337 Ocean Ave.
Santa Monica, CA 90401
P: (310) 451-1004

Alice Oksman, Ph.D. (CE, M)
1543 7th St., Suite 200
Santa Monica, CA 90401
P: (310) 458-1913
F: (310) 394-8783

Lynette Sim, M.S.W., B.C.D. (M)
1536 6th St., Suite 100
Santa Monica, CA 90401
P: (310) 394-7484
F: (310) 823-1493

Santa Rosa
Margaret Anderson, J.D. (A)
412 Aviation Blvd., Suite A
Santa Rosa, CA 95403-1089
P: (707) 546-4677
F: (707) 576-8182

Lawrence C. Buchanan (A, M)
Divorce Resolution Project
5213 El Mercado Pkwy., Suite G
Santa Rosa, CA 95403
P: (707) 544-6086
F: (707) 528-0977

Sonoma County Family
  Mediation (M)
1450 Guerneville Rd.
Santa Rosa, CA 95403
P: (707) 524-7160

Betty Ann Spencer, J.D., M.S. (A)
Law Offices of Margaret L.
  Anerson
412 Aviation Blvd., Suite A
Santa Rosa, CA 95403
P: (707) 546-4677
F: (707) 576-8182

Sausalito

Sandra J. Bushmaker, J.D. (A)
100 Bridgeway, Suite D
Sausalito, CA 94965
P: (415) 331-1916
F: (415) 331-0654

Edward J. Hyman, Ph.D.
   (CE, M)
39 Seacape Dr.
Sausalito, CA 94965-9740
P: (415) 388-4479
F: (415) 388-5009

Soquel

Michelle C. Samis, M.A. (CE, M)
3065 Porter St., Suite 102
Soquel, CA 95073
P: (408) 475-3661

Peggy Williams, J.D. (A)
Sherman, Williams & Lober
1221 Old San Jose Rd.
Soquel, CA 95073
P: (408) 464-1114
F: (408) 464-0509

Torrance

Saul Leopold, Ph.D., L.C.S.W. (CE)
3250 W. Lomita, Suite 308
Torrance, CA 90505
P: (310) 539-1434
F: (310) 377-4459

Tustin

Richard A. Dinnebier, J.D. (A)
Dinnebier, King & Werts
14131 Yorba #204
Tustin, CA 92670
P: (714) 838-1099
F: (714) 838-5116

Ruth D. Shapin, J.D. (A, M)
161 Fashion Ln., Suite 105
Tustin, CA 92680
P: (714) 544-0155
F: (714) 832-0327

Vacaville

Deanna S. Myhre, C.F.L.S. (A, M)
600 E. Main St., Suite F
Vacaville, CA 95688
P: (707) 447-3028
F: (707) 447-0633

Vallejo

Floyd Schlosser, Ph.D. (CE, M)
723 Amador St.
Vallejo, CA 94590
P: (707) 643-1915
F: (707) 643-0814

Valyermo

Corinne Schroeder, Ph.D. (CE)
20313 Big Pines Hwy.
Valyermo, CA 93563
P: (800) 346-3444
F: (800) 346-3444

Ventura

Patrick C. Barker, Ph.D. (CE, M)
206 Maple Ct., Suite 129
Ventura, CA 93003
P: (805) 654-1018
F: (805) 654-1098

Robert L. Beilin, Ph.D. (M)
1000 S. Hill Rd., Suite 220
Ventura, CA 93003
P: (805) 658-0606
F: (805) 658-0147

Ellen Gay Conroy, B.A., J.D. (A)
Taylor McCord, A Law
 Corporation
721 E. Main St.
Ventura, CA 93001
P: (805) 648-4700
F: (805) 653-6124

Nina Meierding, M.S., J.D. (A, M)
Mediation Center for Family
 Law
857 E. Main St.
Ventura, CA 93001
P: (805) 643-3543
F: (805) 653-6107

Dee Shafer, Ph.D. (CE)
Buena Ventura Center for
 Psychotherapy
15 N. Fir St.
Ventura, CA 93001
P: (805) 648-6963
F: (805) 648-6985

Marsha Leah Wylie, L.C.S.W.
 (M)
Ventura County Superior Court
800 S. Victoria Ave., Rm. 307
Ventura, CA 93006
P: (805) 654-2671
F: (805) 648-9209

Visalia
Patricia Foster (M)
Tulare County Superior Court
Courthouse, Rm. 303
County Civic Center
Visalia, CA 93291
P: (209) 733-6207
F: (209) 737-4290

Vista
Cheryl L. Tomac, J.D. (A, M)
San Diego County Bar Assoc.
400 S. Melrose Dr., Suite 214
Vista, CA 92083
P: (619) 941-9494
F: (619) 945-0941

Walnut Creek
Susannah J. Convery, J.D. (A)
1776 Ygnacio Valley Rd., #209
Walnut Creek, CA 94598
P: (510) 946-1756
F: (510) 946-9095

Marc Elliot Hallert, J.D. (A)
Hallert & Hallert, A Law Corp.
710 S. Broadway #312
Walnut Creek, CA 94596
P: (510) 933-4033
F: (510) 933-1435

John E. Manoogian, J.D. (A)
100 Pringle Ave., Suite 560
Walnut Creek, CA 94596
P: (415) 930-6585

Rosemary Matossian, B.S., J.D. (A)
100 Pringle Ave., Suite 560
Walnut Creek, CA 94596
P: (510) 937-1180
F: (510) 937-5264

Iris F. Mitgang, J.D. (A, M)
1850 Mt. Diablo Blvd. #605
Walnut Creek, CA 94596
P: (510) 935-9350
F: (510) 935-9843

Lawrence J. Norton, J.D. (A, M)
1655 N. Main St., Suite 260
Walnut Creek, CA 94596
P: (510) 930-7707
F: (510) 930-0759

Lee C. Pearce, J.D. (A, M)
1333 N. California Blvd., Suite 525
Walnut Creek, CA 94596
P: (510) 946-0450
F: (510) 746-8799

Barbara Suskind (A, M)
1475 N. Broadway, Suite 440
Walnut Creek, CA 94596
P: (510) 906-1300
F: (510) 906-1305

Westlake Village
Fred Norris, Ph.D. (CE)
2659 Townsgate Rd. #202
Westlake Village, CA 91361
P: (805) 495-4747

Woodland
Yolo Family Service Agency (M)
c/o Sally Snell
445 Elm St.
Woodland, CA 95695
P: (916) 662-2211
F: (916) 662-4315

Woodland Hills
Joan Mandell, M.S.W. (CE)
23241 Ventura Blvd., Suite 209
Woodland Hills, CA 91364
P: (818) 887-4782
F: (818) 346-2102

Yorba Linda
Theresa Reagan-Blood (A)
18200 Yorba Linda Blvd., Suite 100
Yorba Linda, CA 92686
P: (714) 572-8497
F: (714) 572-1454

Yreka
Cathy Lyman (M)
322 W. Center St. #6
Yreka, CA 96097
P: (916) 842-8107
F: (916) 842-8093

COLORADO

Aurora
Nancy Cohen Nowak, M.A.,
    L.P.C. (CE, M)
2600 S. Parker Rd.
Building 7, Suite 270
Aurora, CO 80014
P: (303) 750-6260
F: (303) 337-4109

Boulder
Christine A. Coates, M.Ed., J.D.
    (A, M)
4890 Riverbend Rd.
Boulder, CO 80301
P: (303) 443-8524
F: (303) 545-9901

Edie Israel, Psy.D. (CE)
236 Pearl St.
Boulder, CO 80302
P: (303) 444-3823
F: (303) 449-1883

Bernie Mayer (M)
C.D.R. Associates
100 Arapahoe, #12
Boulder, CO 80302
P: (303) 442-7367
F: (303) 442-7442

Sue Ellen Strother (M)
1343 Alpine Ave.
Boulder, CO 80304
P: (303) 444-8130

Colorado Springs
Rick Lohman (A)
Susemittl, Lohman &
    McDermott, P.C.
660 Southpointe Ct. Suite 210
Colorado Springs, CO 80906
P: (719) 579-6500
F: (719) 579-9339

Linda Sutton, M.A. (M)
611 N. Nevada Ave., Suite 1
Colorado Springs, CO 80903
P: (719) 632-0465

Catherine Woelk-Rudisill, J.D. (A)
Susemittl, Lohman &
    McDermott, P.C.
660 Southpointe Ct., Suite 210
Colorado Springs, CO 80906
P: (719) 579-6500
F: (719) 579-9339

Denver
Irene M. Cohen, L.C.S.W.,
    M.S.J.A. (M)
Divorce Support Services
1692 S. Eudora
Denver, CO 80222
P: (303) 756-6175

Byrnece Gluckstern (CE, M)
1050 S. Monaco #16
Denver, CO 80224
P: (303) 333-4808
F: (303) 333-4808

Robert T. Hinds, Jr., J.D. (A)
600 S. Cherry St.
Denver, CO 80222
P: (303) 320-0300
F: (303) 321-1121

Les Katz (CE)
1191 S. Packer Rd., Suite 100
Denver, CO 80231
P: (303) 752-2878
F: (303) 752-1119

Donna Kearney Hinds (M)
600 S. Cherry St., Suite 1400
Denver, CO 80222
P: (303) 320-0300
F: (303) 321-1121

Michael L. Maudlin, M.A. (M)
Acceptable Terms Mediation
    Service
5353 W. Dartmouth Ave., Suite 401
Denver, CO 80227
P: (303) 988-5191

Claire Purcell, Ph.D. (CE)
2305 S. Jackson
Denver, CO 80210
P: (303) 756-2739

Helen C. Shreves, J.D. (A, M)
Judicial Resolutions
3200 Cherry Creek Dr. S, #200
Denver, CO 80209
P: (303) 722-0066
F: (303) 778-6136

Roberta J. Steinhardt, J.D. (M)
Acceptable Terms Mediation
  Service
5353 W. Dartmouth Ave.,
  Suite 401
Denver, CO 80227
P: (303) 988-5191
F: (303) 989-6610

Sue A. Waters, M.A. (M)
Parenting After Divorce
3300 E. 1st Ave., Suite 350
Denver, CO 80206
P: (303) 329-9942
F: (303) 355-7328

Englewood
  Martin D. Meltzer, M.A., L.P.C. (M)
  6979 S. Holly Circle, Suite 190
  Englewood, CO 80112
  P: (303) 721-9779
  F: (303) 721-7350

Fort Collins
  Kathleen Luker Brunson, M.A. (M)
  Mediation, Communication &
    Training
  701 Westshore Ct.
  Fort Collins, CO 80525
  P: (970) 225-9473
  F: (970) 223-8096

Mary Robertson, M.S. (CE, M)
1045 Robertson St.
Fort Collins, CO 80524
P: (970) 484-4087
F: (970) 484-6866

Frisco
  Dixie N. Agnew (CE, M)
  Mediation West
  PO Box 60
  Frisco, CO 80443
  P: (970) 668-3001
  F: (970) 668-3108

Grand Junction
  Steven Landman, L.S.W.
    (CE, M)
  2600 N. 12th St.
  Grand Junction, CO 81501
  P: (303) 245-6624
  F: (970) 241-2832

Dave L. Olson (M)
PO Box 4157
Grand Junction, CO 81502
P: (970) 257-7341

Raymond J. Taylor (CE, M)
Mediation & Counseling Services
2004 N. 12th St., Suite 4
Grand Junction, CO 81501
P: (303) 242-6061
F: (303) 243-8515

Gunnison
  David Baumgarten, J.D., M.Ed.
    (A)
  Gunnison County
  200 E. Virginia
  Gunnison, CO 81230
  P: (970) 641-5300
  F: (970) 641-3061

Lakewood
Marcia Hughes, J.D., M.A. (A, M)
Collaborative Growth, Inc.
390 Union Blvd. #415
Lakewood, CO 80228-1556
P: (303) 980-8893
F: (303) 980-9551

Littleton
Randall J. Sims, L.P.C. (M)
2305 E. Arapahoe Rd., Suite 140
Littleton, CO 80123
P: (303) 794-8055

CONNECTICUT

Branford
Elaine S. Haut (CE, M)
New Haven Family Relations
58 Quarry Dock Rd.
Branford, CT 06405
P: (203) 789-7903

Danbury
Dr. Mary Frances Sink (CE)
Assessment & Consulting
   Associates
57 North St., Suite 410
Danbury, CT 06810
P: (203) 778-6440
F: (203) 790-6193

Glastonbury
Lloyd Frauenglass, J.D. (A)
206 New London Turnpike
Glastonbury, CT 06033
P: (203) 633-0300

Sharon M. Friel, J.D. (A)
206 New London Turnpike
Glastonbury, CT 06033
P: (203) 633-0300
F: (203) 657-4096

Greenwich
Alan Rubenstein, M.S., J.D. (A)
Ivey, Bernum & O'Morg
170 Mason St., Box 1689
Greenwich, CT 06836
P: (203) 661-6000
F: (203) 661-9462

Hartford
Barbara Aaron, J.D. (A, M)
Whitehead & Aaron
241 Main St.
Hartford, CT 06106
P: (203) 241-7797
F: (203) 241-7744

New London
Miriam Gardner-Frum, J.D.,
   M.S.W. (A, M)
PO Box 1591
New London, CT 06320
P: (203) 535-2159

Linda L. Mariani, J.D. (A, M)
83 Broad St.
New London, CT 06320
P: (203) 443-5023
F: (203) 443-8897

Mark R. Patterson, B.A.
   (CE)
70 Huntington St.
PO Box 430
New London, CT 06320
P: (203) 443-2826

Barbara Quinn, Esq. (A, M)
377 Broad St.
PO Box 751
New London, CT 06320
P: (203) 444-2101
F: (203) 440-2615

Niantic
Susan M. Connolly, J.D. (A)
Stevens, Harris, Guernsey &
   Connolly, P.C.
351 Main St., PO Drawer 660
Niantic, CT 06357
P: (203) 739-6906
F: (203) 739-2997

Norwich
Kathleen R. Gravalec-Pannone,
   J.D. (A, M)
106 Williams St.
Norwich, CT 06360
P: (203) 885-1275

Barbara J. Masters, J.D. (A, M)
199 W. Town St.
Norwich, CT 06360
P: (203) 886-1986
F: (203) 889-9639

Ridgefield
Resa Fremed, M.A., Ed.D. (M)
New England Counseling &
   Mediation
898 Ethan Allen Hwy., Suite 7
Ridgefield, CT 06877
P: (203) 431-4957
F: (203) 431-7984

Sandy Hook
Wendy H. Davenson, M.F.T.
   (M)
88 Church Hill Rd.
Sandy Hook, CT 06482
P: (203) 426-1997
F: (203) 426-1997

Stamford
Elizabeth Bergen, Ph.D.
   (CE, M)
Superior Court—Family Services
   Unit
123 Hoyt St.
Stamford, CT 06905
P: (203) 965-5282

Waterbury
William Rosa (M)
PO Box 1893
Waterbury, CT 06722
P: (203) 596-4018
F: (203) 596-4032

Wethersfield
Anthony Salius (CE, M)
Family Division
   Administration
225 Spring St., 4th Flr.
Wethersfield, CT 06109
P: (203) 529-9655
F: (203) 529-9828

Willimantic
Judy Hyde (A)
The Children's Law Center
Box 13, 893 Main St.
Willimantic, CT 06226
P: (203) 423-0885
F: (203) 423-0885

Woodbridge
Flora C. White (CE)
7 Evergreen Dr.
Woodbridge, CT 06525
P: (203) 393-2375

DELAWARE

Dover
Susan J. Durham, M.S.W. (M)
907 Schoolhouse Ln.
Dover, DE 19904
P: (302) 736-0193
F: (302) 737-7430

Wilmington
Joel D. Tenenbaum, J.D. (A)
Woloshin, Tenenbaum & Natalie,
P.A.
3200 Concord Pike
Wilmington, DE 19803
P: (302) 477-3200
F: (302) 477-3210

DISTRICT OF COLUMBIA

Judith M. Filner (A)
NIDR
1726 M St., NW, Suite 500
Washington, DC 20036-4502
P: (202) 466-4764
F: (202) 466-4769

Linda K. Girdner, Ph.D. (M)
ABA Center on Children and
the Law
740 15th St., NW, 9th Flr.
Washington, DC 20005-1009
P: (202) 662-1722
F: (202) 662-1755

Deborah Hastings-Black,
B.A. (M)
3312 35th St., NW
Washington, DC 20016
P: (202) 966-6638

Peter R. Maida, Ph.D. (M)
N.W. 6242-29th St.
Washington, DC 20015
P: (202) 362-2515
F: (202) 362-2515

Ellen Sudow, J.D. (A, M)
N.W. 3308 Woodley Rd.
Washington, DC 20008
P: (202) 244-2601
F: (202) 965-7127

FLORIDA

Boynton Beach
Catherine W. Adams, M.Ed. (M)
Adams Mediation Service Inc.
2240 Woolbright Rd., Suite 301
Boynton Beach, FL 33426
P: (407) 737-3337
F: (407) 369-8850

Carol City
Nicholas G. Sileo, Ph.D. (M)
19001 NW 28th Pl.
Carol City, FL 33056
P: (305) 625-0592

Coral Gables
Melvin A. Rubin, J.D. (A)
111 Majorca Ave.
Coral Gables, FL 33134
P: (305) 446-4630
F: (305) 446-4978

Fort Lauderdale
   Sharon Boesl, M.A. (M)
   Nova University, Family Therapy
   3100 SW 9 Ave.
   Fort Lauderdale, FL 33315
   P: (305) 423-1200
   F: (305) 423-1279

   Ailene Hubert, ACSW, L.C.S.W.
      (M)
   Broward County Courthouse
   201 S.E. 6th St., Rm. 211
   Fort Lauderdale, FL 33301
   P: (305) 831-6066

   John Lande, LL.B. (A, M)
   Nova Southeastern University
   3301 College Ave.
   Fort Lauderdale, FL 33314
   P: (305) 424-5711

Fort Myers
   Mary Teresa Linden, Ph.D. (CE, M)
   Center for Behavioral & Family
      Change
   813 Lake McGregor Dr.
   Fort Myers, FL 33919
   P: (813) 433-6474
   F: (813) 433-0841

Gainesville
   Glenna D. Auxier (M)
   Positive Divorce Resolution
   PO Box 12906
   Gainesville, FL 32604
   P: (904) 375-4399
   F: (904) 373-4406

   Rachel E. Dolan, J.D. (A, M)
   University of Florida
   2274 NW 15th Ave.
   Gainesville, FL 32605
   P: (904) 371-1890
   F: (904) 371-1906

   Robin Kuttner Davis, Esq. (A, M)
   8th Judicial Circuit of Florida
   201 E. University Ave.
   Gainesville, FL 32601
   P: (904) 491-4417
   F: (904) 374-5238

Hollywood
   Molly Leban (CE)
   Family Consultants of
      Broward
   PO Box 7165
   Hollywood, FL 33081-1165
   P: (954) 981-0382
   F: (954) 983-6811

Jacksonville
   Francis D. McCloskey, Jr.,
      M.S.W. (M)
   Fourth Judicial Circuit
   Duval County Courthouse
   330 E. Bay St., Rm. 356
   Jacksonville, FL 32202
   P: (904) 630-4700
   F: (904) 630-2979

   Richard Sandler, J.D. (M)
   Fourth Judicial Circuit Court
   Duval County Courthouse,
      Rm. 356
   Jacksonville, FL 32202
   P: (904) 630-4700
   F: (904) 630-2979

Jacksonville Beach
Paul E. Davidson, M.B.A. (M)
Davidson Consulting, Inc.
PO Box 49285
Jacksonville Beach, FL 32240
P: (904) 241-4244
F: (904) 241-4244

Longwood
Carmine M. Bravo, J.D. (A, M)
2957 W. Hwy. 434, Suite 400
Longwood, FL 32779
P: (407) 774-1686
F: (407) 774-7130

Maitland
Nancy S. Palmer, P.A. (M)
213 Flame Ave.
Maitland, FL 32751
P: (407) 260-9786
F: (407) 740-0902

Marco Island
Ann R. Jackson, M.H.Ed. (CE, M)
PO Box 146
Marco Island, FL 33969-0146
P: (941) 394-0278
F: (941) 394-4747

Miami
Linda B. Fieldstone, B.S.W.,
   M.Ed. (M)
10305 S.W. 68 Ct.
Miami, FL 33156
P: (305) 665-5412

Rusela V. Orr, B.S. (M)
Dade County Administration
   Office
73 W. Flagler, Rm. 2201
Miami, FL 33130
P: (305) 375-1650
F: (305) 375-1653

North Miami Beach
Wilhelmina Koedam, Ph.D.
   (CE, M)
1021 Ives Dairy Rd.
Bldg. #3, Suite 212
North Miami Beach, FL 33179
P: (305) 653-0098
F: (305) 654-4412

Pensacola
Susan Harrell, J.D. (A, M)
University of West Florida
Bldg. 50-11000 University
   Pkwy.
Pensacola, FL 32514-5751
P: (904) 474-2344
F: (904) 474-3130

Plantation
Geraldine Lee Waxman, J.D. (M)
9780 N.W. 16th St.
Plantation, FL 33322
P: (305) 472-7458
F: (305) 476-5677

Tallahassee
Jeff Liang, Ph.D. (CE)
1334 Timberlane Rd., Suite 11
Tallahassee, FL 32312
P: (904) 893-7667
F: (904) 894-1070

Patty A. Stuart, M.S. (CE, M)
730 E. Park Ave.
Tallahassee, FL 32301
P: (904) 224-8046

Tampa
Gregory Firestone, Ph.D. (CE, M)
University of South Florida,
    Mediation Institute
2901 W. Busch Blvd., Suite 707
Tampa, FL 33618
P: (813) 975-4816
F: (813) 975-4816

Nancy Porter-Thal, M.S., C.D.M.
    (M)
Counseling & Mediation Services
1315 S. Howard Ave.
Tampa, FL 33606
P: (813) 254-0029

West Palm Beach
Barbara M. Pope (CE)
County Courthouse,
    Rm. 3.1100
PO Box 1989
West Palm Beach, FL 33402
P: (407) 355-2157
F: (407) 355-3175

Winter Park
Deborah O. Day, Psy.D.
    (CE, M)
Psychological Affiliates, Inc.
2737 W. Fairbanks Ave.
Winter Park, FL 32789
P: (407) 740-6838
F: (407) 740-0902

GEORGIA

Albany
Nick Carden, Ph.D. (CE, M)
Renaissance Center
533 Third Ave.
Albany, GA 31703
P: (912) 889-7200
F: (912) 889-7393

Athens
Kay A. Giese, J.D. (A, M)
1090 S. Milledge Ave.
PO Box 1626
Athens, GA 30603
P: (706) 549-0500
F: (706) 543-8453

Atlanta
Bruce Callner, LL.B. (A)
245 Peachtree Center Ave., 4th Flr.
Atlanta, GA 30303
P: (404) 688-8800
F: (404) 420-7191

Karen S. Chandler (M)
Chandler Consulting
23 Matawan Circle, Suite A
Atlanta, GA 30080-8045
P: (770) 436-4617
F: (770) 438-8486

Ann Noel Dettmering (A)
1000 Parkwood Circle, Suite 410
Atlanta, GA 30339
P: (770) 988-9398
F: (770) 988-9497

Tamar Oberman Faulhaber, Esq.
  (A)
Fulton County Superior Court
185 Central Ave., SW, Suite T7955
Atlanta, GA 30303
P: (404) 302-8528
F: (404) 730-4565

Decatur
  Elizabeth Manley, M.Ed., J.D. (M)
  Atlanta Divorce Mediators, Inc.
  150 E. Ponce de Leon Ave.,
    Suite 460
  Decatur, GA 30030
  P: (404) 378-3238
  F: (404) 577-6505

Zebulan
  Marcia J. Callaway-Ingram
    (A, M)
  PO Box 1176
  Zebulan, GA 30295
  P: (770) 227-3737
  F: (770) 227-3982

HAWAII

Hilo
  Andrew Iwashita (A)
  Iwashita & Gleed
  77 Mohouli St.
  Hilo, HI 96720
  P: (808) 935-6011
  F: (808) 935-7030

Honolulu
  Marvin W. Acklin, Ph.D.
    (CE, M)
  850 W. Hind Dr., Suite 209
  Honolulu, HI 96821
  P: (808) 373-3880
  F: (808) 373-1158

Martha Barham, R.N., Ph.D.
  (M)
615 Piikoi St., Suite 2002
Honolulu, HI 96814
P: (808) 591-6296
F: (808) 591-6297

Durell Douthit, LL.B., L.L.M.
  (A, M)
Davies Pacific Center, Suite 680
Honolulu, HI 96813
P: (808) 537-2776
F: (808) 537-9492

James Tom Greene, Ph.D. (CE, M)
1188 Bishop St., Suite 1306
Honolulu, HI 96813
P: (808) 526-1411
F: (808) 534-1015

Sara R. Harvey, Esq. (A)
Stirling & Kleintop
20th Flr., 1100 Alakea St.
Honolulu, HI 96813
P: (808) 524-5183
F: (808) 528-0261

Jacqueline Y. M. Kong, J.D. (A, M)
Takushi Funaki Wong & Stone
733 Bishop St., Suite 1400
Honolulu, HI 96813
P: (808) 543-9800
F: (808) 599-1960

Sue A. Lehrke (CE, M)
735 Bishop St., Suite 218
Honolulu, HI 96813
P: (808) 523-1755
F: (808) 523-1158

Marguerite B. Simson, LL.B. (A)
1065 Kapiolani Blvd. #204
Honolulu, HI 96814-3503
P: (808) 591-0599
F: (808) 591-0680

T. Lynne Wasson, J.D. (A)
735 Bishop St., Suite 430
Honolulu, HI 96813
P: (808) 545-2681

Keaau
Sheila A. Murphy (A)
PO Box 489
Keaau, HI 96749
P: (808) 966-7471
F: (808) 966-7472

Lahaina
Robert P. Smith (A)
PO Box 845
Lahaina, HI 96767
P: (808) 242-7379

IDAHO

Boise
Debra Alsaker-Burke, J.D. (A, M)
967 E. Park Center Blvd. #413
Boise, ID 83706-6700
P: (208) 344-5993

Kristie Browning, B.A. (M)
1690 Trent Point Way
Boise, ID 83712
P: (208) 331-4511

Marie A. Meyer, Ed.D.
   (CE, M)
1454 Shenandoah Dr.
Boise, ID 83712
P: (208) 362-2420
F: (208) 336-7278

Sue A. Stadler (CE, M)
8425 Spring Creek Way
Boise, ID 83703
P: (208) 939-7160

Coeur d'Alene
Sue S. Flammia, J.D. (A, M)
Flammia & Solomon, Attorneys
PO Box 1117
Coeur d'Alene, ID 83816-1117
P: (208) 667-3561
F: (208) 667-3207

Jonelle Sullivan Timlin, Ph.D. (CE)
A Center for Human Development
1802 N. 15th St.
Coeur d'Alene, ID 83814
P: (208) 664-3020
F: (208) 765-9595

ILLINOIS

Arlington Heights
Margaret S. Powers, M.S.W., M.A. (M)
415 W. Golf Rd., Suite 22
Arlington Heights, IL 60005
P: (312) 943-2155
F: (708) 670-0036

Bloomington
Bart L. Pillen, Ph.D. (CE)
McLean County Center for Human Services
108 W. Market St.
Bloomington, IL 61701
P: (309) 827-5351
F: (309) 829-6808

Chicago
Forrest S. Bayard, J.D. (A)
150 N. Wacker Dr., Suite 2570
Chicago, IL 60606
P: (312) 236-3828
F: (312) 704-6746

Kathleen Borland (M)
Circuit Court of Cook County
505 N. Lakeshore Dr. #2708
Chicago, IL 60611
P: (312) 345-8822
F: (312) 345-8801

Frona C. Daskal (A, M)
155 N. Michigan Ave., Suite 700
Chicago, IL 60601
P: (312) 565-6565

Lindsay B. Hahn (M)
649 W. Bittersweet Pl., Suite 2
Chicago, IL 60613
P: (312) 281-7869

Lisa I. January, M.A. (M)
407 S. Dearborn St., Suite 455
Chicago, IL 60605
P: (312) 635-6077
F: (312) 635-6077

Joan Raisner, M.S., M.A. (M)
Circuit Court of Cook County
28 N. Clark St., Suite 600
Chicago, IL 60602
P: (312) 345-8821
F: (312) 345-8801

David Royko, Psy.D. (M)
28 N. Clark St., Suite 600
Chicago, IL 60602
P: (312) 345-8800
F: (312) 609-8760

Brigitte Schmidt Bell, J.D. (A, M)
53 W. Jackson Blvd., Suite 702
Chicago, IL 60604
P: (312) 360-1124
F: (312) 360-1126

Hon. Bernard B. Wolfe (M)
3180 N. Lakeshore Dr. #7G
Chicago, IL 60657-4835
P: (312) 935-9171
F: (312) 348-7975

Sharon K. Zingery (M)
6157 N. Sheridan, Apt. 25E
Chicago, IL 60660-2827
P: (312) 345-8800
F: (312) 345-8801

Dekalb
David C. Bruer, M.A. (M)
PO Box 1043
151 N. 4th St., Suite 1
Dekalb, IL 60115
P: (815) 748-3237
F: (815) 748-5437

Des Plaines
Scott C. Colky, J.D. (A)
Berks & Colky Ltd.
701 Lee St.
Des Plaines, IL 60016
P: (708) 296-0460
F: (708) 296-3382

Edwardsville
Linda L. Cassens, M.A. (M)
Inneraction
610a St. Louis St.
Edwardsville, IL 62025
P: (618) 656-2402

Evanston
Lynn C. Jacob, L.C.S.W. (M)
2234 Asbury Ave.
Evanston, IL 60201
P: (708) 866-6231
F: (708) 866-6718

Geneva
Judy L. Hogan, B.S.W., J.D.
(A)
115 Campbell St., Suite 200A
Geneva, IL 60134
P: (708) 232-1886
F: (708) 232-1890

Eleanor D. Pierce (M)
Resource Alliance, Inc.
115 Campbell St.
Geneva, IL 60134
P: (708) 208-9982
F: (312) 483-5065

Glen Ellyn
Sara Bonkowski, Ph.D.
(CE, M)
Myrtle Burks Center for Clinical
Social Work
450 Duane St.
Glen Ellyn, IL 60137
P: (708) 469-2000
F: (708) 469-0452

Godfrey
Christopher B. Hunter, J.D. (A)
Farrel Law Firm, P.C.
1310 d'Adrian Professional Park
Godfrey, IL 62035
P: (618) 466-9080
F: (618) 466-9105

Highland Park
Mark L. Goldstein, Ph.D. (CE, M)
Adjustment Center P.C.
1893 Sheridan Rd., Suite 215
Highland Park, IL 60035
P: (708) 926-0390

Jerald A. Kessler, J.D. (A, M)
1950 Sheridan Rd., Suite 101
Highland Park, IL 60035
P: (708) 433-2323
F: (708) 433-2349

Itasca
  Richard De Lorto (CE)
  Chicago Divorce Association
  300 Park Blvd., Suite 325
  Itasca, IL 60143
  P: (708) 860-2100
  F: (708) 250-8753

Jerseyville
  Bruce P. Mindrup, M.A. (M)
  106 Goodrich
  Jerseyville, IL 62052
  P: (618) 498-4911
  F: (618) 498-4921

Lake Forest
  Stephen H. Katz, J.D. (A)
  Schiller, Ducanto & Fleck
  207 E. Westminister Ave., Suite 201
  Lake Forest, IL 60045
  P: (708) 615-8300
  F: (708) 615-8284

Libertyville
  Patricia Alberding, M.S.W. (CE, M)
  1590 S. Milwaukee Ave., Suite 303
  Libertyville, IL 60048-3786
  P: (708) 295-6393
  F: (708) 295-6432

Naperville
  Daniel J. Hynan, Ph.D. (CE, M)
  200 S. Main St.
  Naperville, IL 60540
  P: (708) 293-0982
  F: (708) 310-0008

Northfield
  Barbara Behrendt (M)
  Griswald Mediation Associates,
    Inc.
  530 Woodland Ln.
  Northfield, IL 60093
  P: (708) 446-0525

Oak Park
  Robert K. Downs (A)
  Downs & Downs, P.C.
  1010 Lake St., Suite 620
  Oak Park, IL 60301
  P: (708) 848-0700
  F: (708) 848-0029

Park Forest
  Ruth Arkiss, M.A. (M)
  76 Winslow
  Park Forest, IL 60466
  P: (708) 748-5113

Park Ridge
  Barbara J. Beeson, M.S.W. (M)
  1580 N. Northwest Hwy., Suite 224
  Park Ridge, IL 60068-1468
  P: (708) 827-9095
  F: (708) 827-9096

Princeton
  Covenant Counseling Services (M)
  Dr. Phillip J. Ladd
  502 Elm Pl., PO Box 518
  Princeton, IL 61356
  P: (815) 875-1129
  F: (815) 875-1206

Rockford
  Elise Cadigan (CE, M)
  Glenwood Evaluation &
    Treatment Center
  2823 Glenwood Ave.
  Rockford, IL 61101
  P: (815) 968-5342
  F: (815) 968-4656

  D. Stephen Kiley, L.C.S.W. (CE, M)
  2823 Glenwood Ave.
  Rockford, IL 61101
  P: (815) 968-5342
  F: (815) 968-4656

  Steven L. Nordquist (A)
  4249 E. State St., Suite 307
  Rockford, IL 61108
  P: (815) 229-3331
  F: (815) 229- 2900

  Troy Anthony Smith, J.D. (M)
  The Mediation Corporation
  PO Box 6161
  Rockford, IL 61125
  P: (815) 399-8407
  F: (815) 399-2033

  Barbara Giorgi Vella, J.D. (A, M)
  Vella, Sparkman & Altamore
  401 W. State St. #800
  Rockford, IL 61101
  P: (815) 965-7979

Saint Charles
  Susan M. Lonergan, B.S., J.D. (A, M)
  Kane County Judicial Center
  37W777 Rt. 38, Suite 100
  Saint Charles, IL 60175-7530
  P: (708) 232-5856
  F: (708) 406-7177

Sparta
  Jerry K. Thomas, J.D. (A)
  Attorney at Law
  305 Prairie Ln.
  Sparta, IL 62286
  P: (618) 443-2166
  F: (618) 443-3093

Springfield
  Genny Distasio, M.S.W.,
    L.C.S.W. (M)
  Individual & Family Counseling
    Service
  716 S. Second St.
  Springfield, IL 62704
  P: (217) 544-1710

Vernon Hills
  Mary Lee Meyers (M)
  245 East Court of Shorewood
  Vernon Hills, IL 60061
  P: (708) 367-8528

Waukegan
  William Y. Franks, J.D. (A, M)
  311 Washington
  Waukegan, IL 60085
  P: (708) 336-8077
  F: (708) 336-4559

Wheaton
  Lyle B. Haskin, J.D. (A)
  219 E. Wesley St.
  Wheaton, IL 60187
  P: (708) 665-0800

INDIANA

Anderson

D. Eric Hall, J.D. (A, M)
Busby, Austin, Cooper & Farr
407 Anderson Bank Bldg.
PO Box 151568
Anderson, IN 46015
P: (317) 644-2891
F: (317) 644-2894

Ginger K. Shanks, M.A., M.S. (M)
Conflict Management
    Alternatives, Inc.
338 Historic W. 8th St.
Anderson, IN 46016
P: (317) 649-2486
F: (317) 643-3361

Bloomington

Riette Smith (M)
PO Box 1965
Bloomington, IN 47402
P: (812) 332-2558
F: (812) 332-2557

Elkhart

Fay Schwartz, Esq. (A)
421 S. 2nd St., Suite 410
Elkhart, IN 46516
P: (219) 293-9311

Fort Wayne

Stephen G. Ross, Psy.D. (CE)
Citadel Psychiatric Clinic
2001 Reed Rd.
Fort Wayne, IN 46815
P: (219) 422-9077
F: (219) 422-3414

Goshen

Phyllis Stutzman, M.S.W. (M)
2406 S. Main St.
Goshen, IN 46526
P: (219) 533-7917
F: (219) 535-7234

Greencastle

Ann Kelly Newton, A.C.S.W.
    (CE, M)
501 N. Arlington St.
Greencastle, IN 46135
P: (317) 653-3856
F: (317) 653-3856

Greensburg

C. Renee Rust, M.A., D.Min.
    (M)
Renee Rust Family Mediations
420 E. Walnut St.
Greensburg, IN 47240-1759
P: (812) 663-2113

Indianapolis

John C. Ehrmann, Jr., Psy.D. (CE)
Ehrmann & Associates
1815 N. Capitol Ave., Suite 214
Indianapolis, IN 46202
P: (317) 924-2467
F: (317) 925-3326

Thomas Fara, J.D. (A, M)
Phelps & Fara
230 E. Ohio St., 6th Flr.
Indianapolis, IN 46204
P: (317) 637-7575
F: (317) 685-1106

Caryl Forsythe Dill, J.D. (A)
PO Box 47214
Indianapolis, IN 46247-0214
P: (317) 885-9842

Jamia Jasper Jacobsen, Ph.D.
(CE, M)
The Family Counseling Center
9302 N. Meridan St. #355
Indianapolis, IN 46260
P: (317) 843-2300
F: (317) 843-2775

Randall Krupsaw, Ph.D. (CE, M)
Ehrmann & Associates
1815 N. Capitol Ave., Suite 214
Indianapolis, IN 46202
P: (317) 924-2467
F: (317) 925-3326

Randolph W. Lievertz, M.D. (M)
PO Box 21107
Indianapolis, IN 46221-0107
P: (317) 273-6363
F: (317) 273-6359

Barbara Mesalam, M.S. (M)
Castlepoint
7202 N. Shadeland
Indianapolis, IN 46250
P: (317) 849-9646

Catharine H. Stewart, J.D. (A, M)
900 Circle Tower Bldg.
Indianapolis, IN 46204
P: (317) 635-7700
F: (317) 636-2408

Judith N. Stimson, M.S., J.D. (A, M)
Bank One Center Twr.
111 Monument Cir., Suite 3300
Indianapolis, IN 46202-5133
P: (317) 638-0800
F: (317) 638-0300

Lawrenceburg
Sandra Bubenhofer, A.C.S.W. (M)
Community Mental Health
Center, Inc.
285 Bielby Rd.
Lawrenceburg, IN 47025
P: (812) 537-7375
F: (812) 537-5271

Logansport
Janet L. Ward, B.A. (CE, M)
Child Placement Consultant
300 E. Broadway, Logan Square,
Suite 407
Logansport, IN 46947
P: (219) 722-9633
F: (219) 722-1207

Munster
Marguerite P. Rebesco, Ph.D.
(CE, M)
1415 Wellington Terr.
Munster, IN 46321
P: (219) 924-9040
F: (219) 924-9040

South Bend
Beth Kerns, M.A. (CE)
Domestic Relations
County-City Bldg., Rm. 820
South Bend, IN 46601
P: (219) 235-9662
F: (219) 235-5029

Deborah M. Tuttle, B.A., J.D.
(A, M)
300 N. Michigan #219
South Bend, IN 46601
P: (219) 288-5100
F: (219) 282-4344

Valparaiso
Judith A. Hain (M)
213 Wheatridge Ct.
Valparaiso, IN 46383
P: (219) 462-4305
F: (219) 464-7122

IOWA

Dubuque
Paula M. Stenlund, J.D. (A, M)
909 Main St.
PO Box 239
Dubuque, IA 52001-0239
P: (319) 556-8000
F: (319) 556-8009

Iowa City
Betty Buelow King, M.A.,
M.S.W. (M)
University of Iowa, School of
Social Work
359 N. Hall
Iowa City, IA 52242-1223
P: (319) 335-1264
F: (319) 335-1711

Sioux City
Carol Chase, J.D. (A, M)
Children First
PO Box 5414
Sioux City, IA 51102
P: (712) 274-8990

Debra Lulf (A, CE)
505 6th St., #520
Sioux City, IA 51101
P: (712) 258-2903
F: (712) 258-5867

West Branch
Helen M. Kudos, M.S.W. (CE)
325 N. Fourth St.
West Branch, IA 52358
P: (319) 643-5469
F: (319) 643-2779

KANSAS

Dodge City
Denise D. Parker (CE, M)
State of Kansas, 16th Judicial
District
1805 Barham
Dodge City, KS 67801
P: (316) 227-4615

El Dorado
Miles Erpelding, M.S. (M)
13th Judicial District Court
121 S. Gordy
El Dorado, KS 67042
P: (316) 321-5390
F: (316) 321-9486

Neal B. Harrison, Jr., Ed.S.
(M)
13th Judicial District Court
121 S. Gordy
El Dorado, KS 67042
P: (316) 321-2420
F: (316) 321-0357

Kim Kadel, M.S. (M)
1801 Chelsea Dr.
El Dorado, KS 67042
P: (316) 321-7120

Garden City
Di Ann Bunnell, L.B.S.W. (M)
Western Plains Mediation
  Service
2315 Zipper
Garden City, KS 67846
P: (316) 272-3560
F: (316) 275-1529

Hays
Micki Armstrong, B.S. (M)
Western Plains Mediation
  Service
PO Box 882
Hays, KS 67601
P: (913) 628-9419

Wayne L. Lofton, Ed.S. (M)
High Plains Mental Health
  Center
208 E. 7th
Hays, KS 67601
P: (913) 628-2871
F: (913) 625-1438

Hoxie
Ken Eland, J.D. (A, M)
Sloan & Eland
PO Box 645
Hoxie, KS 67740
P: (913) 675-3217
F: (913) 675-3983

Jetmore
Jeannie Schriner (M)
Southwest Mediation
PO Box 424
Jetmore, KS 67854
P: (316) 357-8569
F: (316) 275-2639

Kansas City
Mickey James, M.A.J. (CE, M)
29th Judicial District Court
County Courthouse 1st Flr.
Kansas City, KS 66101
P: (913) 573-2833
F: (913) 573-4136

Donald L. Zemites, B.A. J.D.
  (A, M)
Zemites & Associates
750 Ann Ave.
Kansas City, KS 66101
P: (913) 342-9300
F: (913) 621-4402

Lawrence
Robert W. Fairchild, J.D. (M)
PO Box B
Lawrence, KS 66044
P: (913) 841-4700
F: (913) 843-0161

Nancy J. Hughes, M.S.W., Ph.D.
  (M)
University of Kansas
315 Fraser Hall
Lawrence, KS 66045
P: (913) 864-4121

Bonita J. Yoder, J.D., M.P.A. (A, M)
608 Kentucky
Lawrence, KS 66044
P: (913) 342-2288
F: (913) 342-2298

Leawood
William J. Paprota, B.A., M.A.,
  J.D. (A)
5101 College Blvd., Suite 206
Leawood, KS 66209
P: (913) 491-0922
F: (913) 491-0981

Liberal
Janice L. Kimball, B.S. (CE, M)
State of Kansas
415 N. Washington
Seward County Courthouse
Liberal, KS 67901
P: (316) 626-3243
F: (316) 626-3302

Neodesha
Dennis D. Depew, J.D. (A, M)
620 Main St.
PO Box 313
Neodesha, KS 66757-0313
P: (316) 325-2626
F: (316) 325-2636

Ness City
Sue Fehrenbach, B.A. (M)
24th Judicial District, Court
  Services
105 S. Pennsylvania Ave.
Ness City, KS 67560
P: (913) 798-3695
F: (913) 798-3839

Olathe
Micheline Z. Burger, J.D. (A, M)
302 E. Park
Olathe, KS 66061
P: (913) 829-9118
F: (913) 829-9185

Terri Clinton Dichiser, J.D. (A, M)
12468 S. Greenwood
Olathe, KS 66062
P: (913) 829-4972

Gary Kretchmer (CE, M)
Domestic Court Services
905 W. Spruce
Olathe, KS 66061
P: (913) 782-7252
F: (913) 782-3297

Donna M. Manning, J.D. (A)
200 E. Santa Fe
Olathe, KS 66061
P: (913) 829-2255
F: (913) 829-2270

John J. Phillips (A, M)
PO Box 2294
Olathe, KS 66051
P: (913) 473-0247
F: (913) 768-3472

Hon. Herbert Walton (A, M)
15722 W. Locust St.
Olathe, KS 66062
P: (913) 764-2885
F: (913) 764-2997

Overland Park
  G. Peter Bunn III, J.D. (A)
  9300 Metcalf, Suite 300
  Overland Park, KS 66212
  P: (913) 381-8180
  F: (913) 381-8836

  Christine Hillila, Ph.D. (M)
  4601 W. 109th St., Suite 110
  Overland Park, KS 66211
  P: (913) 469-6150

  John H. Johntz, Jr., J.D. (A)
  Payne & Jones
  11000 King
  Overland Park, KS 66210
  P: (913) 469-4100
  F: (913) 469-8182

  Naomi A. Kauffman, J.D. (A, M)
  4650 College Blvd., Suite 300
  Overland Park, KS 66211
  P: (913) 491-5500
  F: (913) 491-3341

Prairie Village
  Dana L. Parks, J.D. (A)
  Holman, McCollum & Hansen, P.C.
  9400 Mission Rd., 2nd Flr.
  Prairie Village, KS 66200
  P: (913) 648-7272
  F: (913) 383-9596

  David P. Woodbury, J.D. (A, M)
  4121 W. 83rd St.
  Executive Bldg., Suite 125
  Prairie Village, KS 66208
  P: (913) 642-1144
  F: (913) 642-1175

Shawnee Mission
  Maril M. Crabtree, J.D. (A, M)
  6950 Squibb Rd., Suite 400
  Shawnee Mission, KS 66202
  P: (316) 561-1087
  F: (316) 561-1091

Stockton
  Leo C. Bird (M)
  PO Box 181
  Stockton, KS 67669
  P: (913) 425-6043

Topeka
  Bill Ebert (A, M)
  Hein, Ebert, & Weir
  5845 S.W. 29th
  Topeka, KS 66614
  P: (913) 273-8847
  F: (913) 273-9243

Wichita
  Gary L. Ayers, J.D. (A)
  Foulston & Siefkin
  700 Fourth Financial Center
  Wichita, KS 67202
  P: (316) 267-6371
  F: (316) 267-6345

  Jeanne L. Erikson, Ph.D. (CE, M)
  334 N. Topeka
  Wichita, KS 67042
  P: (316) 269-2322

  Sheila J. Floodman (A)
  218 N. Mosley
  Wichita, KS 67202
  P: (316) 269-1100
  F: (316) 269-1443

Lessie Harris, M.S. (A)
Mediation Services
301 W. Central
Wichita, KS 67202
P: (316) 683-4700

Paula Kidd Casey (A)
218 N. Mosley
Wichita, KS 67202
P: (316) 269-1100
F: (316) 269-1443

Donald E. Lambdin, J.D. (A, M)
830 N. Main
PO Box 797
Wichita, KS 67201-0797
P: (316) 265-3285
F: (316) 265-1303

Ronald A. Lyon, J.D. (A)
901 N. Broadway
Wichita, KS 67214
P: (316) 262-4753·
F: (316) 262-5105

Margaret P. Mathewson, J.D. (A)
Fletcher & Mathewson, P.A.
449 N.W. McLean Blvd.
Wichita, KS 67203
P: (316) 263-7770
F: (316) 263-0433

Trip Shawver (A, M)
634 N. Broadway
Wichita, KS 67214
P: (316) 262-6466
F: (316) 262-6012

KENTUCKY

Lexington
Eleanor H. Leonard, J.D. (A)
Fayette Circuit Court, #407
125 W. Main St.
Lexington, KY 40507
P: (606) 255-0136
F: (606) 253-1346

Paducah
Edward A. Jones, Ed.D. (CE)
3035 Clay St.
Paducah, KY 42001
P: (502) 898-7965
F: (502) 898-7965

LOUISIANA

Baton Rouge
Margaret Drake, C.S.W. (CE)
PO Box 16069
Baton Rouge, LA 70893
P: (504) 928-1052

Anita R. White, J.D. (A, M)
11814 Coursey Blvd.,
    Suite 115
Baton Rouge, LA 70816
P: (504) 295-5603
F: (504) 296-0904

Covington
Helen Sims Miller, M.S.W.,
    B.C.S.W., B.C.D. (M)
PO Box 2644
Covington, LA 70434
P: (504) 626-9550

Rebecca Stulb Kennedy (A, M)
22nd Judicial District Court
428 E. Boston St., Rm. 207
Covington, LA 70433
P: (504) 898-2710
F: (504) 898-2387

Harvey
Felicia H. Higgins (M)
PO Box 1900
Harvey, LA 70059
P: (504) 367-3500

Jefferson
Nell I. Lipscomb, M.S.W., J.D.
(A, M)
317 Jefferson Heights Ave.
Jefferson, LA 70121
P: (504) 838-9003
F: (504) 839-7030

Jennings
Andre J. Buisson, B.S., J.D.
(A, M)
PO Box 1111
Jennings, LA 70546
P: (318) 824-8300
F: (318) 824-1254

Lafayette
Blanche B. Fontenot, M.S.W. (M)
Mediation Associates
1819 Pinhook Rd., Suite 207
Lafayette, LA 70503
P: (318) 837-6237

Alice J. Voorhies, M.Ed. (M)
Divorce & Family Recovery
  Center
1819 W. Pinhook Rd., Suite 207
Lafayette, LA 70503
P: (318) 269-1329

Lake Charles
Alvin B. King, J.D. (A)
301 Kirby St.
Lake Charles, LA 70601
P: (318) 433-0840
F: (318) 433-0743

New Orleans
Betsey Backe, M.S.W. (M)
The Divorce Center
620 North Carrollton Ave.
New Orleans, LA 70119
P: (504) 488-9924
F: (504) 488-1092

Eugenia Patru, M.S.W. (CE)
PO Box 750272
New Orleans, LA 70175-0272
P: (504) 899-0925
F: (504) 861-7811

MAINE

Bangor
Bill Donahue, M.S.W. (CE, M)
420 Essex St.
Bangor, ME 04401-3536
P: (207) 941-0879
F: (207) 942-8946

Portland
Cushman D. Anthony, J.D. (A, M)
Anthony, Howison, Landis & Arn
PO Box 585
Portland, ME 04112
P: (207) 775-6371
F: (207) 871-1019

Joan M. Kidman (A)
25 Deblois St.
Portland, ME 04103
P: (207) 772-6274

MARYLAND

Annapolis

Trudy Beth Bond, J.D. (A)
100 Cathedral St., Suite 7
Annapolis, MD 21401
P: (410) 263-4082
F: (410) 263-4082

Maureen C. Vernon, Ph.D.
  (CE, M)
116 Defense Hwy., Suite 210
Annapolis, MD 21401
P: (410) 266-0019
F: (410) 266-5537

Baltimore

Barbara B. Barker, M.Ed., J.D.
  (A)
The Sexual Assault/Domestic
  Violence Center
6229 N. Charles St.
Baltimore, MD 21212
P: (410) 377-8111
F: (410) 377-6806

Laurie Coltri, J.D., Ph.D. (M)
213 Roundtree Ct.
Baltimore, MD 21230
P: (410) 659-0455

Alice Dvoskin (CE, M)
Village Square LI, Suite 217
Baltimore, MD 21210
P: (410) 433-7774
F: (410) 433-7779

Robin Kaplan, B.S., J.D. (A, M)
Y Branchwood Ct.
Baltimore, MD 21208
P: (410) 484-8318

Louise Phipps Senft, J.D. (A, M)
Baltimore Mediation Center
3524 Keswick Rd.
Baltimore, MD 21211
P: (410) 235-9656
F: (410) 235-5487

Bel Air

John C. Love (A)
30 N. Main St.
Bel Air, MD 21014
P: (410) 838-7100
F: (410) 893-3254

Bethesda

Susan Sulami, J.D. (M)
Lifebridge Family Mediation
7104 Exfair Rd.
Bethesda, MD 20014
P: (301) 215-7933
F: (202) 966-9104

Carolyn Talcott (M)
8602 Irvington Ave.
Bethesda, MD 20817
P: (301) 493-6199

Bowie

Rebecca L. Dieter, J.D. (A, M)
14300 Gallant Fox Ln., Suite 223
Bowie, MD 20715
P: (301) 464-3800
F: (301) 464-0502

Catonsville

Sylvia L. Hackett, B.A., J.D.
  (A, CE, M)
1705 Edmondson Ave., Suite 202
Catonsville, MD 21228-4346
P: (410) 747-6840
F: (410) 788-1278

Chevy Chase
Carol L. Ehlenberger, J.D. (A)
4820 Bradley Blvd.
Chevy Chase, MD 20815
P: (301) 656-4914
F: (301) 656-4914

College Park
E. Anne Riley, L.C.S.W.
(CE, M)
9106 48th Pl.
College Park, MD 20740
P: (301) 441-1311
F: (301) 345-7474

Columbia
Neil Edward Axel, J.D. (A)
10320 Little Patuxent Pkwy.,
Suite 311
Columbia, MD 21044
P: (410) 964-9300
F: (410) 964-4458

Hugh J. Forton, Esq. (A)
5360 Graywing Ct.
Columbia, MD 21045
P: (410) 715-0364
F: (410) 997-9571

Stanley Rodbell (M)
10541 Catterskill Ct.
Columbia, MD 21044
P: (410) 730-2211

Elkton
Rebecca L. Benson, M.S.N., R.N.
(CE, M)
Psychotherapy & Counseling
Center
PO Box 2321, 115 Landing Ln.
Elkton, MD 21922-2321
P: (410) 392-6693

Ellicott City
Robert N. Keehner, J.D. (A)
O'Connor, Keehner, Hogg &
McCrone
3525 Ellicott Mills Dr., Suite J
Ellicott City, MD 21043
P: (410) 750-2401
F: (410) 465-6214

Laurel
Melissa M. Henderson, Ph.D.
(M)
1114 11th St.
Laurel, MD 20707
P: (301) 604-5870

Owings Mills
Lisa Lynn Mervis, J.D. (A)
Benter & Mervis, Suite 3 N
9505 Reisterstown Rd.
Greenspring Valley Office Center
Owings Mills, MD 21117
P: (410) 581-9000
F: (410) 581-9006

Rockville
David S. Goldberg, B.S., J.D.
(A, M)
255 N. Washington St., Suite 200
Rockville, MD 20850
P: (301) 279-7500
F: (301) 279-7521

Alan Meiselman, J.D. (A)
Family Law Arbitration Service
600 Jefferson Plaza, Suite 308
Rockville, MD 20852-1150
P: (301) 424-2920
F: (301) 217-9297

St. Joseph
  Beth M. Elder, A.S. (M)
  Buchanan County
  411 Jules St.
  St. Joseph, MD 65602
  P: (410) 271-1480
  F: (410) 271-1521

Towson
  Patricia A. Ferraris, J.D. (A, M)
  305 Allegheny Ave.
  Towson, MD 21204
  P: (410) 828-6830
  F: (410) 337-0460

  Leonard Jacobson (M)
  Baltimore County Circuit Court
  401 Bosley Ave.
  Towson, MD 21204
  P: (410) 583-1182
  F: (410) 828-7012

  Kathryn Rogers (CE, M)
  Baltimore County Circuit Court
  401 Bosley Ave.
  Towson, MD 21204
  P: (410) 887-6576
  F: (410) 887-4806

Upper Marlboro
  Prince George's County Court (A)
  Ramona Buck Courthouse,
    Rm. 08D
  14735 Main St.
  Upper Marlboro, MD 20772
  P: (301) 952-3708
  F: (301) 952-3101

Annie T. Reid, M. A. (M)
Community Mediation Board
1001 Trebing Ln.
Upper Marlboro, MD 20772
P: (301) 350-8320

MASSACHUSETTS

Acton
  Jane Appell, Ph.D. (CE, M)
  518 Great Rd.
  Acton, MA 01720
  P: (508) 263-4878
  F: (508) 635-0386

  Claude Marchessault, M.A. (M)
  Human Services Associates
  42 Davis Rd.
  Acton, MA 01720
  P: (508) 263-6788
  F: (508) 263-6666

Amherst
  Oran Kaufman (A)
  Burres Fidnick & Booth
  190 University Dr.
  Amherst, MA 01002
  P: (413) 253-3900
  F: (413) 256-1207

Arlington
  Carol Evans, M.S.W. (CE)
  821 Massachusetts Ave.
  Arlington, MA 02174
  P: (617) 641-3664
  F: (617) 641-3665

  Susan Kass (CE)
  846 Massachusetts Ave., Apt. 3B
  Arlington, MA 02174
  P: (617) 641-3664
  F: (617) 641-3665

Auburn
Laurie S. Raphaelson (A)
21 Goddard Dr.
Auburn, MA 01501

Barnstable
Kathleen A. Snow, J.D. (A)
Children & Parents, Inc.
Rte. 6A, PO Box 1085
Barnstable, MA 02630-2085
P: (508) 362-4900

Boston
Ruth R. Budd, LL.B. (A)
Hemenway & Barnes
60 State St., 8th Flr.
Boston, MA 02109
P: (617) 227-7940
F: (617) 227-0781

Mary M. Ferriter, J.D. (A)
Probate & Family Court
    Administration Office
3 Center Plaza, 9th Flr.
Boston, MA 02108
P: (617) 742- 9743
F: (617) 720-4122

Edwin Hanada, Esq. (A)
88 Broad St., 4th Flr.
Boston, MA 02110
P: (617) 542-5200
F: (617) 542-5303

Michael L. Leshin, J.D. (A, M)
Hemenway & Barnes
60 State St.
Boston, MA 02109
P: (617) 227-7940
F: (617) 227-0781

Brookline
Rita S. Pollak, J.D. (A, CE, M)
7 Harvard St., Suite 220
Brookline, MA 02146
P: (617) 566-2300
F: (617) 566-9350

Chestnut Hill
Laurence Madfis (A)
220 Boylston St.
Chestnut Hill, MA 02167
P: (617) 964-4100
F: (617) 965-5138

Concord
Jeanne S. Kangas, Esq., J.D. (A)
Arnold & Kangas, P.C.
9 Pond Lane #5D
Concord, MA 01742-2842
P: (508) 369-0001
F: (508) 371-2378

Framingham
Tonia K. Cullen, J.D. (A)
1290 Worcester Rd.
Framingham, MA 01701
P: (508) 370-0384
F: (508) 370-0385

Carol Lynn May, J.D. (A)
Bowditch & Dewey
161 Worcester Rd.
Framingham, MA 01701
P: (508) 879-5700
F: (508) 872-1492

Robert A. Zibbell, Ph.D. (CE, M)
Psychological Assoc. of
 Framingham
One Franklin Common
Framingham, MA 02532
P: (508) 872-6610
F: (508) 872-6722

Greenfield
Mark I. Berson (A)
Levy Winer P.C.
87 Franklin St.
Greenfield, MA 01302
P: (413) 774-3741
F: (413) 774-5187

Littleton
Thelma J. Allem, Ed.D. (CE)
Allem Psychological Services
510 King St., PO Box 306
Littleton, MA 01460
P: (508) 486-8832
F: (508) 486-3996

Lowell
Karen Levitt, J.D. (A, M)
134 Middle St.
Lowell, MA 01852
P: (508) 458-5550
F: (508) 458-5562

Marblehead
Frances N. Goldfield (A)
H36 Atlantic Ave.
Marblehead, MA 01945
P: (617) 631-6161
F: (617) 631-6829

Natick
Thomas F. Carr, L.M.F.T. (CE)
9 Kinsman Pl.
Natick, MA 01760
P: (508) 650-1811
F: (508) 650-3621

Needham
Sheila Schwartz, M.S.W.,
 J.D. (M)
362 Country Way
Needham, MA 02192
P: (617) 444-0891
F: (617) 444-4626

New Bedford
Bonita G. Cade, Ph.D., J.D. (A)
63 Ash St.
New Bedford, MA 02740
P: (508) 990-1077
F: (508) 990-1077

Newton Centre
Barbara N. White, M.A. (M)
Mediation Alternatives
1280 Centre St., Suite 240
Newton Centre, MA 02159
P: (617) 244-0007
F: (617) 244-0007

Newtonville
Jerome H. Weinstein, M.S.
 (M)
Divorce Resource & Mediation
 Center
161 Walnut St.
Newtonville, MA 02160
P: (617) 965-2315

Northampton
Gail L. Perlman, M.S.S., J.D.
(A, CE, M)
Dispute Mediation, Inc.
237 Main St., 3rd Flr.
Northampton, MA 01060
P: (413) 585-0977
F: (413) 585-0999

Northborough
Jane A. Fraier (A)
Law Office of R & D Gabriel
37 South St., Box 761
Northborough, MA 01532
P: (508) 393-5129
F: (508) 393-2516

Salem
Kenneth E. Lindauer, J.D. (A)
14 Lynde St.
Salem, MA 01970
P: (508) 744-5861
F: (508) 744-1319

Jill Aubin Updegraph, J.D. (A)
70 Washington St., Suite 405
Salem, MA 01970
P: (508) 745-7248
F: (508) 744-3782

Sandwich
Linda Werner, Ph.D. (M)
The Borealis Group
99 Main St.
Sandwich, MA 02563
P: (508) 888-6665
F: (508) 888-6690

S. Easton
Carla A. Goodwin, Ph.D.
(CE, M)
855 Washington St.
S. Easton, MA 02375
P: (508) 238-3722
F: (508) 230-7275

Topsfield
Steven Nisenbaum, Ph.D., J.D. (A)
166 Perkins Row
Topsfield, MA 01983
P: (508) 887-6606
F: (508) 887-6606

Wellesley Hills
Lynne C. Halem, Ph.D. (M)
Centre for Mediation & Dispute
   Resolution
37 Walnut St., Suite 220
Wellesley Hills, MA 02181-2107
P: (617) 239-1600
F: (617) 239-0404

Anita Kremgold-Myer, Ed.D.
(CE)
25 Walnut St., Suite 200
Wellesley Hills, MA 02181
P: (617) 235-1521
F: (617) 235-5456

West Bridgewater
Carolyn D. Ross, J.D. (A, M)
New England Family Mediation
353 W. Center St., PO Box 517
West Bridgewater, MA 02379
P: (508) 559-0223
F: (508) 588-2067

W. Newton
Ruth S. Zachary, M.Ed. (M)
257 Prince St.
W. Newton, MA 02165
P: (617) 527-3168
F: (617) 244-5806

Westwood
Barbara N. Mason, J.D. (A, M)
Creative Divorce Options
63 Woodridge Rd.
Westwood, MA 02090
P: (617) 255-9800
F: (617) 255-9858

Woburn
Dorothy D. Driscoll, J.D. (A)
10 Cedar St., Suite 32
Woburn, MA 01801-6306
P: (617) 938-5859
F: (617) 938-5911

Worcester
Barbara A. Cunningham (A)
Schwartz & Cunningham
44 Front St., Suite 330
Worcester, MA 01608
P: (508) 752-0112
F: (508) 752-9844

Lyn A. De Amicis, Ph.D., J.D.
   (A)
126 Francis St.
Worcester, MA 01606
P: (508) 797-4334
F: (508) 797-4745

Shirley A. Doyle (A)
45 Linden St.
Worcester, MA 01609-2658
P: (508) 757-0117
F: (508) 757-8439

Paige Dunmire Firment, J.D. (A)
Arnold & Fiment
7 State St.
Worcester, MA 01608
P: (508) 754-9242
F: (508) 754-3639

Laura Fitzsimmons (A)
Schwartz & Cunningham
44 Front St., Suite 330
Worcester, MA 01608
P: (508) 752-0112
F: (508) 752-9844

Robert G. Lian (A)
Lian, Zarrow, Eynon, & Shea
34 Mechanic St.
Worcester, MA 01608
P: (508) 799-4461
F: (508) 799-6522

Laurie S. Raphaelson, M.A., J.D.
   (A, CE)
Raphaelson & Raphaelson
340 Main St., Suite 565
Worcester, MA 01608
P: (508) 799-0366
F: (508) 753-4433

Zelda J. Schwartz, L.C.S.W. (M)
Jewish Family Service
646 Salisbury St.
Worcester, MA 01609
P: (508) 755-3101
F: (508) 755-7460

Marcia E. Tannenbaum, J.D.
(A, M)
721 Pleasant St.
Worcester, MA 01602-1999
P: (508) 798-4090
F: (508) 798-4782

William Tattan (A)
23 Institute Rd.
Worcester, MA 01608
P: (508) 754-3269

MICHIGAN

Ann Arbor
Joanne Barron, J.D. (A, M)
Ann Arbor Mediation Center
330 E. Liberty, Suite 3A
Ann Arbor, MI 48104
P: (313) 663-1155
F: (313) 663-0524

Mary F. Whiteside, Ph.D. (M)
1248 Bending
Ann Arbor, MI 48103
P: (313) 995-5181
F: (313) 995-9011

Zena Zumeta (A, M)
Ann Arbor Mediation
Center
330 E. Liberty, Suite 3A
Ann Arbor, MI 48104
P: (313) 663-1155
F: (313) 663-0524

Battle Creek
Timothy R. Strang, Ph.D. (CE)
453 Morningside Dr.
Battle Creek, MI 49015
P: (616) 963-7135

Detroit
Beverly Clark, J.D. (A, M)
440 Congress
Detroit, MI 48226-2917
P: (313) 961-4440
F: (313) 961-5830

David Manville, M.S.W. (CE)
Family Counseling and
Mediation Department
710 City County Bldg.
Detroit, MI 48826
P: (313) 224-5266
F: (313) 224-6070

Grand Blanc
Kathleen Desgranges, M.S.W. (CE)
Desgranges Psychiatric Center
G8145 S. Saginaw St.
Grand Blanc, MI 48439
P: (810) 694-2730

Grand Rapids
Julie K. Haveman (M)
Friend of the Court Office
50 Monroe, NW, Suite 260
Grand Rapids, MI 49503-0351
P: (616) 336-2808

Howell
Mary Randles (CE)
4566 Crooked Lake Rd.
Howell, MI 48843
P: (517) 546-0230

Monroe
Charles W. Karm, Jr. (M)
106 E. 1st St.
PO Box 120
Monroe, MI 48161
P: (313) 243-7060
F: (313) 243-7107

Plymouth
Sally R. McCracken, Ph.D. (M)
East Michigan University
1655 Lexington
Plymouth, MI 48170
P: (313) 487-3030

West Bloomfield
Marilyn E. Fessler (M)
7045 Cedarbank Dr., Suite 100
West Bloomfield, MI 48234
P: (810) 363-8716

MINNESOTA

Burnsville
Roger C. Sweet, Ph.D. (CE)
301 W. Burnsville Pkwy. #214
Burnsville, MN 55337
P: (612) 890-2577
F: (612) 890-0529

Cottage Grove
Patricia A. O'Gorman, P.A. (A)
8750-90th St. S
Cottage Grove, MN 55016
P: (612) 458-9114

Edina
Lorraine S. Clugg, J.D. (A)
Kisson & Clugg
3205 W. 76th St.
Edina, MN 55435-5244
P: (612) 896-1099
F: (612) 896-1132

Minneapolis
Doneldon Dennis (CE, M)
Hennepin County Family Court
Services
A-503 Government Center
Minneapolis, MN 55487
P: (612) 348-3614
F: (612) 348-6332

Jeanette A. Frederickson, J.D.
(A, M)
Chestnut & Brooks, P.A.
3700 Piper Jaffray Twr.
Minneapolis, MN 55407
P: (612) 339-7300
F: (612) 336-2940

Christine M. Leick, Esq. (A, M)
Dispute Resolution Services
120 S. 6th St., Suite 2500
Minneapolis, MN 55402
P: (612) 349-5252
F: (612) 349-9242

Phyllis Owens, M.A. (M)
6520 Brooklyn Blvd.
Minneapolis, MN 55429
P: (612) 561-6520

Mary C. Sherman, J.D. (A)
1422 W. Lake St., Suite 320
Minneapolis, MN 55408
P: (612) 827-2641
F: (612) 827-1323

St. Cloud
Karen D. Becker, M.S.W.,
   L.C.S.W. (CE, M)
Caritas Family Services
N. 305-7th Ave.
St. Cloud, MN 56303
P: (612) 252-4121

St. Paul
Donna Cairncross, M.A.
   (CE)
Hamline Park Plaza
570 Asbury St., 101
St. Paul, MN 55104
P: (612) 641-0337
F: (612) 647-0646

Wayne Hensley, Ph.D. (M)
N. 2759 Helena Ave.
St. Paul, MN 55128
P: (612) 770-1374
F: (612) 638-6001

Karen Irvin, Ph.D. (CE, M)
570 Asbury St., #101
St. Paul, MN 55104
P: (612) 649-3600
F: (612) 647-0646

Mary Catherine Lauhead (A)
3985 Clover Ave.
St. Paul, MN 55127-7015
P: (612) 426-0870

Stillwater
Washington County
   Family Court Services
   (CE, M)
c/o Maureen Walton
14900 61st St. N
Government Center
Stillwater, MN 55082
P: (612) 430-6990
F: (612) 430-6947

MISSISSIPPI

Jackson
Mark A. Chinn, J.D. (A)
Chinn & Associates
PO Box 13483
Jackson, MS 39236
P: (601) 366-4410
F: (601) 366-4010

MISSOURI

Chesterfield
David B. Clark, Ph.D. (CE)
14377 Woodlake Dr.,
   Suite 212
Chesterfield, MO 63017-5735
P: (314) 576-2816
F: (314) 576-7484

Clayton
Susan L. Amato, J.D. (A, M)
130 S. Bemiston, Suite 302
Clayton, MO 63105
P: (314) 862-0330
F: (314) 727-5464

Festus
Edward A. (Ted) Jackson, M.S.W.
  (M)
The Counseling Clinic
206-B Main St.
Festus, MO 63028
P: (314) 933-3545
F: (314) 933-0349

Independence
Michael J. Albano, LL.B. (A)
311 W. Kansas
Independence, MO 64050
P: (816) 836-8000
F: (816) 836-8953

Jefferson City
Charlotte M. Balcer, M.D. (CE, M)
Wellness Consultants
PO Box 104415
Jefferson City, MO 65110-4415
P: (314) 634-7632
F: (314) 634-7692

Kansas City
Leslie Guillot, M.A. (M)
One Ward Pkwy., Suite 107
Kansas City, MO 64112
P: (816) 756-1722
F: (816) 756-1533

Mary Anne Kiser, M.A. (M)
Kiser Counseling Services
411 Nichols Road, Suite 217
Kansas City, MO 64112
P: (816) 931-9912
F: (816) 561-5352

Michael B. Lubbers, Ph.D. (M)
8301 State Line, Suite 200
Kansas City, MO 64114-2019
P: (816) 363-5600
F: (816) 363-5159

Debra L. Snoke, M.A., J.D. (A)
204 W. Linwood Blvd.
Kansas City, MO 64111
P: (816) 561-3755
F: (816) 561-9355

Richard C. Sweetland, Ph.D. (CE)
4700 Belleview, Suite 405
Kansas City, MO 64112
P: (816) 756-1227
F: (816) 756-1438

Julienne Thomas, D.Min. (M)
411 Nichols Rd., Suite 235
Kansas City, MO 64112
P: (816) 931-3974

St. Louis
Robert Benjamin, M.S.W., J.D. (A)
8000 Bonhomme, Suite 201
St. Louis, MO 63105
P: (314) 721-4333

Alan E. Freed, J.D. (A, M)
165 N. Meramec, 6th Flr.
St. Louis, MO 63105
P: (314) 727-2266
F: (314) 727-2101

John R. Tripi, M.S.W. (CE, M)
St. Louis City Family Court
920 N. Vandeventer
St. Louis, MO 63108
P: (314) 531-3600
F: (314) 531-1248

NEBRASKA

Omaha
Joseph L. Rizzo, Ph.D. (CE, M)
Rizzo & Associates
8552 Cass St.
Omaha, NE 68114
P: (402) 397-0330
F: (402) 397-8082

NEVADA

Henderson
Dorothy A. Howard, D.S.W.,
    A.C.S.W. (CE, M)
408 Ackerman Ln.
Henderson, NV 89014
P: (702) 731-8134
F: (702) 731-5209

Robert W. Richards, B.A., B.D.
    (M)
549 British Ct.
Henderson, NV 89014
P: (702) 451-6262

Las Vegas
Patricia Coyne, M.A., L.S.W.
    (M)
Bank of America Plaza, Suite 611
300 S. 4th St.
Las Vegas, NV 89101
P: (702) 384-1700
F: (702) 384-8150

Family Mediation & Assessment
    Center (M)
c/o Ladeana Gamble
3464 E. Bonanza Rd.
Las Vegas, NV 89101
P: (702) 455-4186
F: (702) 455-2158

Shari Hendrickson, M.S.W.,
    C.R.C. (M)
Generaux Business Consultants
1700 E. Desert Inn, Suite 304
Las Vegas, NV 89109
P: (702) 796-1913
F: (702) 796-1706

Charlotte S. Kiffer, M.S. (M)
Alternative Solutions
333 N. Rancho Dr.,
    Suite 138
Las Vegas, NV 89106
P: (702) 646-2645

Israel Kunin, J.D. (A)
612 S. 10th St.
Las Vegas, NV 89101
P: (702) 384-8489
F: (702) 384-8464

Gary D. Lang, J.D. (A)
729 S. 7th St.
Las Vegas, NV 89101
P: (702) 386-0444
F: (702) 386-7978

Maria A. Montenegro, Psy.D.
    (CE, M)
428 Vandalia St.
Las Vegas, NV 89106
P: (702) 386-0977

Elizabeth C. Richitt, Ph.D.
(CE)
4055 S. Spencer, Suite 217
Las Vegas, NV 89119-5251
P: (702) 733-0408
F: (702) 733-7787

Ted Shoemaker (CE, M)
Family Court & Services
Building
3464 E. Bonanza Rd.
Las Vegas, NV 89155
P: (702) 455-2031
F: (702) 455-2158

Reno
W. Kathleen Baker, J.D. (A, CE, M)
PO Box 70772
Reno, NV 89570
P: (702) 825-8788

Phil Buschard, D.P.A. (CE, M)
Family Mediation Program
75 Court St., Rm. 100
Reno, NV 89501
P: (702) 328-3556
F: (702) 328-8548

Bill Marinelli, M.S.W. (M)
Family Alliance of Reno
5039 Cassandra Way
Reno, NV 89523
P: (702) 746-1635
F: (702) 746-1635

Jerry Nims, J.D., Ph.D. (CE, M)
3066 Markridge Dr.
Reno, NV 89509
P: (702) 329-3030
F: (702) 324-6467

NEW HAMPSHIRE

Concord
Rose M. Hill, M.A. (M)
84 Ironworks Rd.
Concord, NH 03301
P: (603) 224-8043

Keene
Olivia A. Ruel, Ph.D. (M)
Alternative & Training
A Center for Mediation
4 Felt Rd.
Keene, NH 03431
P: (603) 355-8066
F: (603) 358-1081

Nashua
Candace Dochstader (M)
Nashua Mediation Program
18 Mullberry St.
Nashua, NH 03060
P: (603) 594-3330
F: (603) 594-3452

Newport
Esther Tardy, J.D. (M)
35 John Stark Hwy.
Newport, NH 03773
P: (603) 863-1905

NEW JERSEY

Freehold
Amy Althenhaus, Ph.D. (CE, M)
80 E. Main St.
Freehold, NJ 07728-2223
P: (732) 780-6644
F: (732) 845-1184

Hackensack
Cynthia M. Johnson, M.S.W. (M)
PO Box 174
Hackensack, NJ 07601
P: (973) 646-9023

Montclair
Victoria Britt, M.S.W. (M)
Foundation for Families
37 Franklin Place
Montclair, NJ 07042
P: (201) 746-5959

Newark
James B. Boskey (M)
Seton Hall Law School
1 Newark Center
Newark, NJ 07102
P: (973) 642-8811
F: (973) 642-8194

Paramus
Judith D. Meringold, M.S.W.,
   L.C.S.W. (M)
254 W. Midland Ave.
Paramus, NJ 70652
P: (201) 447-0754

Short Hills
Concetta Castellan, M.A., M.S.
   (CE)
Brown, Greenfield & Physician
   Consultants
The Short Hills Plaza
636 Morris Tpk. (2c)
Short Hills, NJ 07078
P: (973) 467-3343
F: (973) 467-5521

Thorofare
Dr. Alan S. Kagel (CE)
Sherwood Professional Bldg.
800 Jessup Rd., Suite 809
Thorofare, NJ 08086
P: (609) 845-7800
F: (609) 845-3861

Trenton
Jacqui Sine-Coughlin, M.A. (M)
Mercer County Youth Detention
   Center
1430 Parkside Ave.
Trenton, NJ 08638
P: (609) 538-4458

Watchung
Marcy A. Pasternak, Ph.D. (CE, M)
96 Joan Dr.
Watchung, NJ 07060
P: (908) 769-7949
F: (908) 753-4930

NEW MEXICO

Albuquerque
Elizabeth L. Kodituwakku, Ph.D.
   (CE, M)
Family Court Clinic
PO Box 488
Albuquerque, NM 87103
P: (505) 841-7409
F: (505) 841-7446

Sandra Morgan Little, J.D. (A)
Little & Gilman, P.A.
PO Box 26717
Albuquerque, NM 87125
P: (505) 246-0500
F: (505) 246-9953

Charlene McIver, Ph.D. (CE, M)
4600-A Montgomery NE, Suite 102
Albuquerque, NM 87109
P: (505) 883-0100

Clovis

Diane Manwill, M.A., L.P.C.
(CE, M)
9th District, Family & Children
Court Services
PO Box 1032
Clovis, NM 88102-1032
P: (505) 769-2656
F: (505) 769-2644

Las Cruces

Marc A. Caplan, Ph.D. (CE, M)
Medico-Psychological Services
715 E. Idaho Bldg., Suite C,
Bldg. 1
Las Cruces, NM 88001
P: (505) 523-0482
F: (505) 523-0834

John F. Corso, Ph.D. (M)
PO Box 1420
Las Cruces, NM 88004
P: (505) 525-1027
F: (505) 526-9787

Mary W. Rosner, J.D. (A)
PO Box 1239
Las Cruces, NM 88004-1239
P: (505) 524-4399
F: (505) 524-2550

Santa Fe

Michael J. Golden, J.D. (A)
Moore & Golden, P.A.
PO Box 2401
Santa Fe, NM 87504-2401
P: (505) 982-4313
F: (505) 983-2734

Susan C. Shepard, M.A. (M)
Miraumonte Mediation
116 Balboa Rd.
Santa Fe, NM 87501
P: (505) 988-4205

NEW YORK

Barrytown

Jill Lundquist, C.S.W. (M)
PO Box 23
Barrytown, NY 12507
P: (914) 471-7167

Bayside

Mary N. Miller (M)
The Divorce Resource Center
43-31 223rd St.
Bayside, NY 11361
P: (718) 631-0156
F: (718) 631-0154

Sydell S. Sloan, M.A. (M)
17-26 215th St.
Bayside, NY 11360
P: (718) 631-1600
F: (718) 423-0325

Brooklyn
Elliott Schuman, Ph.D. (CE, M)
116 Prospect Park W
Brooklyn, NY 11215
P: (718) 768-6664
F: (718) 768-6664

Carolyn R. Wah, J.D. (A)
25 Columbia Heights
Brooklyn, NY 11201-2483
P: (718) 596-4993
F: (718) 797-3032

Chittenango
Ann F. Spector, J.D., M.S.W.,
    C.S.W. (A, M)
1559 Route 173
Chittenango, NY 13037
P: (315) 687-6516
F: (315) 687-5427

Clifton Park
Patricia A. Connelly, M.A., J.D.
    (A, M)
Mediation Center
1741 Rt. #9
Clifton Park, NY 12065
P: (518) 371-6830

Garden City
Barbara Badolato, B.S.W (M)
666 Old Country Rd., Suite 705
Garden City, NY 11530
P: (516) 222-0101
F: (516) 745-5745

Goshen
Rosalyn Magidson (M)
Orange County Mediation
    Project
180 Main St.
Goshen, NY 10924
P: (914) 294-8082
F: (914) 294-7428

Huntington
Steven Greenspan (A)
Children's Rights Council
PO Box 1395
Huntington, NY 11743
P: (516) 427-6060
F: (516) 427-6063

Larchmont
Marion Gindes (CE)
16 N. Chatsworth Ave.
Larchmont, NY 10538
P: (914) 833-1944
F: (914) 833-1602

Andrew Schepard, J.D. (A)
43 Magnolia Ave.
Larchmont, NY 10538
P: (516) 463-5890
F: (516) 560-7676

Mineola
Samuel J. Ferrara, B.A., M.A.,
    J.D. (A)
Meltzer, Lippe, Goldstein, Wolf,
    Schlissel & Sazer, P.C.
190 Willis Ave.
Mineola, NY 11501
P: (516) 747-0300
F: (516) 294-3188

Stephen W. Schlissel, J.D. (A)
Meltzer, Lippe, Goldstein, Wolf,
   Schlissel & Sazer, P.C.
190 Willis Ave.
Mineola, NY 11501
P: (516) 747-0300
F: (516) 294-3188

Monsey
   Howard Yahm, C.S.W. (M)
   Center for Family & Divorce
      Mediation
   146 Willow Tree Rd.
   Monsey, NY 10952
   P: (914) 354-3158

New City
   Steven L. Abel, J.D. (A, M)
   Center for Family & Divorce
      Mediation
   2 New Hempstead Rd.
   New City, NY 10956
   P: (914) 638-4666
   F: (914) 634-1675

New York
   Leonard G. Florescue (A)
   Tenzer, Greenblatt, Fallon &
      Kaplan
   405 Lexington Ave.
   New York, NY 10174
   P: (212) 573-4396
   F: (212) 573-4313

   Kenneth D. Kemper, J.D., Ph.D.
      (A)
   Sharp, Kemper
   276 Fifth Ave., Suite 306
   New York, NY 10001-4509
   P: (212) 889-9800
   F: (212) 889-9699

Eileen Montrose, C.S.W.,
   L.C.S.W. (CE)
654 Madison Ave.
New York, NY 10021
P: (212) 980-9660
F: (212) 980-9769

Ildaura Murillo-Rohde, Ph.D. (M)
300 W. 108th St. #12A
New York, NY 10025
P: (212) 865-9795

Kenneth Neumann, M.S. (M)
Center for Family & Divorce
   Mediation
111 W. 90th St., Townhouse B
New York, NY 10024-1285
P: (212) 799-4302
F: (212) 721-1012

Anne Reiniger, J.D., C.S.W. (A)
NY Society for the Prevention of
   Cruelty to Children
161 William St.
New York, NY 10038-2607
P: (212) 233-5500
F: (212) 791-5227

Pearl River
   Ellan A. Heit, J.D. (A)
   Box 734
   Pearl River, NY 10965
   P: (914) 735-0059
   F: (914) 735-9225

Port Jefferson
   David A. Martindale, Ph.D. (CE)
   Child Custody Consultants
   46 Old Homestead Rd.
   Port Jefferson, NY 11777-1155
   P: (516) 473-8254
   F: (516) 473-6447

Rochester
  Dennis Boike, Ph.D. (CE)
  120 Linden Oaks
  Rochester, NY 14625
  P: (716) 385-1950
  F: (716) 385-9315

  Laura Taylor, M.S., J.D. (A, M)
  250 Mill St.
  Rochester, NY 14614
  P: (716) 647-6620

Scarsdale
  Naomi S. Eckhaus, M.S. (M)
  56 Hutchinson Blvd.
  Scarsdale, NY 10583
  P: (914) 725-1244

Staten Island
  Dennis Guttsman (CE, M)
  11 Pearl St.
  Staten Island, NY 10304
  P: (718) 442-2078
  F: (718) 442-2078

Stony Brook
  Lawrence C. Gulino (M)
  4 Freshman Ln.
  Stony Brook, NY 11790
  P: (516) 751-3813

NORTH CAROLINA

Asheville
  Bill Walz, Ed.S. (M)
  The Mediation Center
  189 College St.
  Asheville, NC 28801
  P: (704) 251-6089

Boone
  Cathryn Fishman Alschuler,
    M.S., Ed.D. (M)
  Rt. 7 Box 132
  Boone, NC 28607
  P: (704) 464-6744
  F: (704) 465-8448

Cary
  Claudia Kelsey, M.S. (M)
  Kelsey Mediation Practice
  1150 SE Maynard Rd.,
    Suite 140
  Cary, NC 27511
  P: (919) 859-4344

Chapel Hill
  Barbara Anderson, J.D. (A)
  Lewis & Anderson, P.C.
  PO Box 2851
  Chapel Hill, NC 27515
  P: (919) 489-3327

  Charles T. L. Anderson, J.D. (A)
  Northern, Blue, Rooks, Thibant,
    Anderson & Woods
  PO Box 2208
  Chapel Hill, NC 27515-2208
  P: (919) 968-4441
  F: (919) 942-6603

  Annette Kahn, M.S.W. (M)
  25 B Mount Bolus Rd.
  Chapel Hill, NC 27514
  P: (919) 967-1291
  F: (919) 967-3336

  Susan Lewis, LL.B. (A)
  800 Eastowne Dr., #208
  PO Box 2851
  Chapel Hill, NC 27514
  P: (919) 967-8989

Charlotte
Elaine K. Cigler, Ph.D. (M)
Mecklenburg County-26th
   Judicial District
1224 Wareham Ct.
Charlotte, NC 28207
P: (704) 344-1441

Durham
Jean R. Livermore, A.C.S.W.
   (M)
18 W. Colony Pl., Suite 250
Durham, NC 27705
P: (919) 493-2674

Goldsboro
Deborah L. Nowachek (A)
202 S. William St.
Goldsboro, NC 27530
P: (919) 736-9981
F: (919) 736-9973

Greensboro
Susan Green, M.S.W. (M)
1210-B Westridge Rd.
Greensboro, NC 27410
P: (910) 288-7131
F: (910) 288-2102

Raleigh
Jan Hood (M)
Administrative Office of the
   Courts
PO Box 2448
Raleigh, NC 27602
P: (919) 733-7107
F: (919) 715-5779

Lee S. Rosen, J.D. (A)
Theo Rosen Law Firm
4101 Lake Boone Trail, Suite 305
Raleigh, NC 27607
P: (919) 737-6668
F: (919) 787-6361

NORTH DAKOTA

Bismark
Patricia Garrity (A)
Zuger, Kirmis & Smith
PO Box 1695
Bismark, ND 58502-1695
P: (701) 223-2711
F: (701) 223-7387

Grand Forks
Doug Knowlton, Ph.D. (CE)
Family Institute
2100 S. Columbia
Grand Forks, ND 58201
P: (701) 777-3189
F: (701) 777-4393

Glenn W. Olsen, Ph.D. (M)
The Mediation Center
421 Demers Ave.
Grand Forks, ND 58201
P: (701) 777-3145
F: (701) 777-4393

OHIO

Akron
Gerald J. Glinsek, J.D. (A)
Glinsek, Higham & Kristoff
88 S. Portage Path, Suite 301
Akron, OH 44303
P: (216) 867-6600
F: (216) 867-9864

Athens
  Jack Arbuthnot, Ph.D. (M)
  Center for Divorce Education
  PO Box 5900
  Athens, OH 45701
  P: (614) 593-1065

Batavia
  Michelle Applegate (CE)
  Clermont County
  Domestic Relations Court
  66 Riverside Dr.
  Batavia, OH 45103
  P: (513) 732-7327

  Carol C. Hake, J.D. (A, M)
  Barbeau & Hake
  410 W. Main St.
  Batavia, OH 45103
  P: (513) 732-1072
  F: (513) 732-1076

Beachwood
  Phyllis D. Hulewat, M.S.W. (M)
  Cleveland Jewish Family Service
    Association
  24074 Commerce Park Rd.
  Beachwood, OH 44122
  P: (216) 292-3999
  F: (216) 292-6313

  Nancy J. Huntsman, Ph.D. (M)
  Center for Effective Living, Inc.
  25101 Chagrin Blvd., Suite 310
  Beachwood, OH 44122
  P: (216) 464-7555
  F: (216) 464-8733

  Michael B. Leach, Ph.D. (CE, M)
  Center for Effective Living, Inc.
  25101 Chagrin Blvd., Suite #310
  Beachwood, OH 44122-5619
  P: (216) 464-7555
  F: (216) 464-8733

Canton
  Frederick W. Scoville, M.Ed.
    (M)
  4593 South Blvd. NW, Apt. 2
  Canton, OH 44718-2024
  P: (216) 492-1755

Cincinnati
  Barbara Thompson Doll, M.S.W.
    (M)
  30 E. Central Pkwy.
  Cincinnati, OH 45202
  P: (513) 651-1010
  F: (513) 421-3455

  Dona T. Lansky, Ph.D. (M)
  The Center for Mediation of
    Disputes
  8 W. 9th St.
  Cincinnati, OH 45202
  P: (513) 751-0392

Cleveland
  Mary Ann Theby (CE, M)
  Family Conciliation Service
  1 Lakeside Ave.
  Cleveland, OH 44113
  P: (216) 443-8805
  F: (216) 443-4943

Columbus
Susan T. Blalock, M.S.W. (M)
1555 Bethel Rd.
Columbus, OH 43220
P: (614) 442-0664
F: (614) 442-0620

Geraldine T. Clausen, Ph.D. (M)
4355 N. High St., Suite 214
Columbus, OH 43214
P: (614) 261-1828
F: (614) 262-7200

Franklin County Court of
   Domestic Relations (A, M)
373 S. High St., 3rd Flr.
Columbus, OH 43215-4595
P: (614) 462-6640
F: (614) 462-5363

James Rundle, L.I.S.W. (M)
Family Counseling, Crittention
1414 E. Broad St.
Columbus, OH 43205
P: (614) 251-0103
F: (614) 251-1177

Paula J. Trout, Esq. (A)
338 S. High St.
Columbus, OH 43215
P: (614) 222-0531
F: (614) 228-6364

Cortland
Paula A. Smigrocky, M.S.W.
   (M)
3303 Fowler St.
Cortland, OH 44410
P: (216) 638-6514

Cuyahoga Falls
Norma Hudson Blank, J.D.,
   M.S.S.A. (A, M)
2365 Grant Ave.
Cuyahoga Falls, OH 44223
P: (216) 438-0456
F: (216) 438-0837

Dayton
Eugene Cherry, Ph.D. (M)
5335 Far Hills Ave.
Dayton, OH 45429
P: (513) 433-0726
F: (513) 433-2336

Theodore Fields (CE, M)
Montgomery County, Family
   Services
301 W. Third St.
Dayton, OH 45422-4248
P: (513) 225-4098
F: (513) 496-7443

Findlay
Elizabeth Candler, J.D. (A, M)
330 S. Main St.
Findlay, OH 45840
P: (419) 422-8446

Napoleon
Denise Herman McColley
   (A,M)
105 W. Main St.
Napoleon, OH 43545
P: (419) 592-0010
F: (419) 592-2873

Painesville
  Pamela G. Baker (CE, M)
  Lake County Domestic Relations
    Court
  784 Liberty St.
  Painesville, OH 44077
  P: (216) 639-9068

Tipp City
  William E. Brown, Ph.D. (CE, M)
  1440 W. Main St.
  PO Box 28
  Tipp City, OH 45371
  P: (513) 667-4612
  F: (513) 667-6479

Toledo
  Elizabeth C. Guerra, B.A., J.D. (A)
  University of Toledo, College of
    Law Dispute Resolution
  2801 W. Bancroft St.
  Toledo, OH 43606-3390
  P: (419) 530-6108
  F: (419) 530-2605

  Michele MacFarlane (CE, M)
  Lucas County Domestic
    Relations Court
  429 Michigan St.
  Toledo, OH 43624
  P: (419) 249-6800

  Ron L. Rimelspach, J.D. (A, M)
  414 N. Erie St., Suite 200
  Toledo, OH 43624
  P: (419) 241-2153
  F: (419) 241-6858

Warren
  Ralph Tecca (M)
  New Genesis Academy, Inc.
  5000 E. Market St., Suite 27
  Warren, OH 44484
  P: (216) 856-4820
  F: (216) 544-5690

Washington Court House
  Sandy Fackler (M)
  Fayette County Mediation
  110 E. Court St.
  Washington Court House,
    OH 43160
  P: (614) 333-3501
  F: (614) 333-3530

Westerville
  Allan J. MacDonald, Ph.D. (M)
  218 Spring Hollow Ln.
  Westerville, OH 43081-1156
  P: (614) 890-6529
  F: (513) 382-3809

  Virginia Petersen, M.S.W. (M)
  Children's Hospital
    Guidance Center,
    Divorce Services
  595 Copeland Mill Rd.
  Westerville, OH 43081
  P: (614) 794-2145
  F: (614) 794-0579

Xenia
  Beth Leger (M)
  Greene County Domestic
    Relations Court
  45 N. Detroit St.
  Xenia, OH 45385
  P: (513) 376-5180
  F: (513) 376-5139

Rebecca L. Rubin (CE)
Greene County Courthouse
45 N. Detroit St.
Xenia, OH 45385
P: (513) 376-5180
F: (513) 376-5139

Wayne Wisniewski, B.A. (CE, M)
Greene County Domestic
   Relations Court
45 N. Detroit St.
Xenia, OH 45385
P: (513) 376-5180
F: (513) 376- 5139

Yellow Springs
Michael D. Lang, LL.B. (M)
Antioch University
800 Livermore St.
Yellow Springs, OH 45387
P: (513) 767-6321
F: (513) 767-6461

Youngstown
John Polanski, M.Ed. (M)
Mahoning County Domestic
   Relations Court
120 Market St.
Youngstown, OH 44503
P: (216) 740-2009
F: (216) 740-2503

OKLAHOMA

Oklahoma City
Arlene B. Schaefer, Ph.D. (CE,
   M)
3330 NW 56th St., Suite 600
Oklahoma City, OK 73112-4474
P: (405) 947-0975
F: (405) 947-0984

David E. Sears (M)
New Beginnings Mediation &
   Therapy Center
1500 S.W. 86
Oklahoma City, OK 73159
P: (405) 682-4881
F: (405) 682-4881

OREGON

Albany
Michael F. McClain, J.D. (A)
34295 Oakville Dr.
Albany, OR 97321-9471
P: (503) 752-3885

Ajax Moody, M.S.W. (M)
6128 Piedmont Pl.
Albany, OR 97321
P: (503) 928-8599

Bend
Dave Hakanson (M)
Deschutes County Human
   Services-Mediation
1010 NW14th St.
Bend, OR 97701
P: (503) 385-1719
F: (503) 385-8033

Corvallis
Alan Hansen (M)
PO Box 10
Corvallis, OR 97339
P: (503) 928-4137

Eugene
Kathleen O'Connell Corcoran,
    M.S., N.C.C. (CE, M)
The Mediation Center
440 E. Broadway, Suite 340
Eugene, OR 97401
P: (503) 484-9710
F: (503) 345-4024

R. N. Lowe, Ph.D. (M)
University of Oregon
86362 Bailey Hill Rd.
Eugene, OR 97405
P: (503) 342-8522

Dick Takei, A.C.S.W., R.C.S.W. (M)
315 W. 10th St.
Eugene, OR 97401
P: (503) 683-2469

Grants Pass
Michael Belsky, Ed.D. (M)
Juvenile Department
Courthouse
Grants Pass, OR 97526
P: (503) 488-5676
F: (503) 474-5105

Manzanita
S. Chris Mcisaac, M.S.W. (M)
716 Cherry St.
PO Box 307
Manzanita, OR 97130
P: (503) 368-7942
F: (503) 368-7942

McMinnville
Kathleen Horgan (M)
Lutheran Family Service
819 N. Hwy. 99W, Suite B
McMinnville, OR 97128
P: (503) 472-4020
F: (503) 472-8630

Robert McNamee, L.C.S.W. (M)
602 N. Davis
McMinnville, OR 97128
P: (503) 472-5715
F: (503) 434-6471

Jane Parisi-Mosher (M)
Yamhill County Mediation
    Program
435 N. Evans
McMinnville, OR 97132
P: (503) 472-0210

Medford
Peter Silverman (M)
Jackson County Health &
    Human Services
1005 E. Main St.
Medford, OR 97504
P: (503) 776-7063

Newberg
W. A. Willett (M)
Pragmatic Peacemaking
PO Box 744
Newberg, OR 97132-0744
P: (503) 538-4476

Oregon City
  Clackamas County Family Court
    Services (M)
  c/o Alison Taylor, M.S.
  704 Main St., Suite 200
  Oregon City, OR 97045
  P: (503) 655-8415

Portland
  Susana Alba (A)
  900 S.W. 5th Ave., Suite 2100
  Portland, OR 97204
  P: (503) 224-0644
  F: (503) 228-7112

  Greg Austin (A)
  522 S.W. 5th Ave. #905
  Portland, OR 97204
  P: (503) 222-6102
  F: (503) 222-9781

  Harvey N. Black, Jr., J.D. (A, M)
  Mediation Services
  2715 N.W. Thurman St.
  Portland, OR 97210-2204
  P: (503) 294-0280
  F: (503) 294-0286

  Patricia Cox, M.S.W. (CE, M)
  9221 S.W. Barbur Blvd., Suite 307
  Portland, OR 97219
  P: (503) 768-9127
  F: (503) 768-4851

  Lois Gold, A.C.S.W. (M)
  1020 S.W. Taylor #650
  Portland, OR 97205
  P: (503) 248-9740
  F: (503) 295-0814

Sharon Johnson (M)
6824 S.W. Capitol Hwy.
Portland, OR 97219
P: (503) 452-7959

James W. McClurg, J.D. (A, M)
106 Sylvan Office Bldg.
1834 S.W. 58th Ave.
Portland, OR 97221
P: (503) 292-6673
F: (503) 292-0670

Hugh McIsaac (M)
Multnomah County Family
  Services
1021 S.W. 4th Ave., Suite 350
Portland, OR 97204-1184
P: (503) 248-3189
F: (503) 248-3232

Barbara Mealey (CE)
American Counseling
6536 N.E. Wygant
Portland, OR 97218
P: (503) 287-5511
F: (503) 280-6016

Albert A. Menashe, LL.B. (A)
1515 S.W. 5th Ave., Suite 808
Portland, OR 97201
P: (503) 227-1515
F: (503) 243-2038

Multnomah County Family
  Services (CE, M)
1021 S.W. 4th Ave., Suite 350
Portland, OR 97204-1184
P: (503) 248-3189
F: (503) 248-3232

Jeremy Sayers, L.C.S.W. (M)
Cascade Trainings
2171 NE Weidler
Portland, OR 97212
P: (503) 288-1708

Roseburg
Douglas County Mental Health
   (CE, M)
621 W. Madrone
Roseburg, OR 97470
P: (503) 440-3532
F: (800) 866-9780

Salem
Lynda M. Bridges (CE, M)
Family Transition Services
2040 Commercial St. SE
Salem, OR 97302
P: (503) 364-2016
F: (503) 364-2585

Ben Coleman (M)
1698 Liberty St. S
Salem, OR 97302
P: (503) 363-5487
F: (503) 363-5487

Patricia Dixon, M.S. (M)
2695 12th Pl. SE
Salem, OR 97302
P: (503) 363-8075
F: (503) 391-5348

Tigard
Stephen Peirce, Ph.D. (M)
12525 S.W. 68th St.
Tigard, OR 97223
P: (503) 639-9523
F: (503) 620-4673

Robert M. Smith, J.D., M.Div. (M)
PO Box 230076
Tigard, OR 97281-0076
P: (503) 524-4810
F: (503) 524-4810

PENNSYLVANIA

Allentown
Don S. Klein, Esq. (A, CE, M)
1436 Hampton Rd.
Allentown, PA 18104
P: (610) 395-1010
F: (610) 395-6995

Nancy A. Longenbach, Esq.
   (A)
Lehigh County, Court of
   Common Pleas, Custody
   Office
523 Hamilton St., 2nd Flr.
Allentown, PA 18101
P: (610) 820-3390
F: (610) 820-2075

Samuel Young, D.Min. (M)
2415 Tremont St.
Allentown, PA 18104
P: (215) 435-4486

Beaver
Robert R. Rose (M)
Court of Common Pleas, Beaver
   County
Western Ave.
Beaver, PA 15009
P: (412) 774-8870
F: (412) 728-6444

Bryn Mawr
Stanley Clawar, Ph.D. (CE, M)
Walden Counseling & Therapy
950 County Line Rd.
Bryn Mawr, PA 19010
P: (215) 525-5725
F: (215) 525-6861

Camp Hill
Stanley E. Schneider, Ed.D.
(CE, M)
412 Erford Rd.
Camp Hill, PA 17011
P: (717) 732-2917
F: (717) 732-5375

Carlisle
Henry Weeks, Ph.D. (CE)
211 Echo Rd.
Carlisle, PA 17013-9510
P: (717) 249-5512
F: (717) 258-4940

Harrisburg
Arnold Shienvold, Ph.D.
(CE, M)
Rieger, Shienvold & Associates
2151 Linglestown Rd., Suite 200
Harrisburg, PA 17112
P: (717) 540-9005
F: (717) 540-1416

Hatfield
Winfred Backlund, M.Ed. (M)
2331 Merel Dr.
Hatfield, PA 19440
P: (215) 721-1813
F: (215) 723-1211

Johnstown
Robert J. Yaskanich, Ph.D. (CE)
Metcomm, Inc.
406 Main St., Wallace Bldg.
Johnstown, PA 15901
P: (814) 539-5985
F: (814) 539-5985

Media
Steven B. Moss, J.D. (A, M)
755 N. Monroe St.
PO Box 1908
Media, PA 19063
P: (610) 565-6688
F: (610) 891-1645

Philadelphia
Edward Blumstein, LL.B. (A, M)
1518 Walnut St., 4th Flr.
Philadelphia, PA 19102
P: (215) 790-9666
F: (215) 790-1988

Nancy Cohen, J.S., M.Ed.
(A, M)
2043 Naudain St.
Philadelphia, PA 19146
P: (215) 575-9140
F: (215) 386-1743

Faye Kahn, M.A. (M)
716 S. 23rd St.
Philadelphia, PA 19146
P: (215) 732-2010

Felicity Lavell, Esq. (A, M)
The Mediation Center
6322 Argyle St.
Philadelphia, PA 19111
P: (215) 725-8310
F: (215) 725-9235

Pittsburgh
Ann Lee Begler, LL.B. (A, M)
3220 Grant Bldg.
310 Grant St.
Pittsburgh, PA 15219-2301
P: (412) 391-4000
F: (412) 391-8518

Hon. Lawrence W. Kaplan (M)
414 Grant St.
626 City-County Bldg.
Pittsburgh, PA 15219-2479
P: (412) 355-7127
F: (412) 350-5599

Paul D. Lyons, M.S. (M)
1102 S. Braddock Ave.
Pittsburgh, PA 15218-1238
P: (412) 241-4000
F: (412) 241-3950

Thomas M. Mulroy, J.D. (A)
Pillar & Munroe, P.C.
312 Boulevard of the Allies
Pittsburgh, PA 15222
P: (412) 471-3300
F: (412) 471-6068

Gary S. Schermer, M.Ed., J.D. (A)
ADR Mediation Services
Gatehouse At Station Square
2 Station Sq., Suite 300
Pittsburgh, PA 15219
P: (412) 367-1681

M. Farley Schlass, Esq. (A)
1121 Boyce Rd. #1500
Pittsburgh, PA 15241-3918
P: (412) 942-3770

Hans Siegel, J.D. (A)
Davis & Abramovitz
1034 Fifth Ave., Suite 400
Pittsburgh, PA 15219
P: (412) 391-4305
F: (412) 391-1789

Gary Stout, Esq. (A)
Family Court Administrator
633 City-County Bldg.
Pittsburgh, PA 15219
P: (412) 355-7127

Villanova
Brynne V. Rivlin (CE)
2204 N. Stone Ridge Ln.
Villanova, PA 19085
P: (215) 527-3071

Warminster
Kathryn M. McHugh, M.A., J.D.
(A, M)
550-C West Street Rd.
Warminster, PA 18974
P: (215) 674-8181
F: (215) 675-0244

West Chester
Melanie McAteer (A)
Chester County Courts
2 N. High St., Suite 310
West Chester, PA 19380-3030
P: (610) 344-6405
F: (610) 344-6127

West Reading
Edward P. Hanna, D.S.W. (M)
661 Reading Ave.
West Reading, PA 19611
P: (610) 373-5005

Wexford
   James D. Adelman, Ph.D. (CE, M)
   Tri-County Counseling
      Association
   PO Box 221
   Wexford, PA 15015
   P: (412) 935-5130

Yardley
   Dr. Charles Kaska (CE)
   55 Lookover Ln.
   Yardley, PA 19067
   P: (215) 493-6757

SOUTH CAROLINA

Charleston
   Susan K. Dunn, J.D. (A)
   171 Church St., Suite 160
   Charleston, SC 29401
   P: (803) 722-6337
   F: (803) 577-0460

Columbia
   Donna W. Upchurch, Ph.D.
      (M)
   1403½ Calhoun St.
   Columbia, SC 29201
   P: (803) 252-1866

   Nancy M. Young, J.D. (A, M)
   Young & Sanders, P.A.
   950 Taylor St., Suite 450
   Columbia, SC 29202
   P: (803) 799-7666

Sumter
   Karen Zimmerman, M.S.W. (CE)
   7 East Calhoun St.
   PO Box 2667
   Sumter, SC 29151
   P: (803) 773-3434
   F: (803) 775-7181

SOUTH DAKOTA

Aberdeen
   Charles Pelton, M.D., J.D. (A)
   1811 N. Jay
   Aberdeen, SD 57401-1360
   P: (605) 229-5590

Rapid City
   Thomas L. Collins (CE)
   Department of Social Services
   PO Box 2440
   Rapid City, SD 57709
   P: (605) 394-2224
   F: (605) 394-2568

TENNESSEE

Chattanooga
   Carol Berz, J.D., Ph.D., L.C.S.W.
      (M)
   312 Bass Rd.
   Chattanooga, TN 37402
   P: (615) 894-7050
   F: (615) 894-2777

   Don Moore (A, M)
   5700 Brainerd Road
   6100 Building, Suite 3701
   Chattanooga, TN 37411
   P: (615) 499-3007
   F: (615) 499-3004

Memphis
Jocelyn Dan Wurzburg, J.D.
(A, M)
5118 Park Ave., Suite 232
Memphis, TN 38117-5708
P: (901) 684-1332
F: (901) 684-6693

Oak Ridge
Margaret Burns, Ed.D., R.N.
(M)
1345 Oak Ridge Tpk.
M350
Oak Ridge, TN 37830
P: (615) 481-3555

TEXAS

Austin
Robert W. Moats, Ph.D., J.D.
(M)
1001-A West Ave.
Austin, TX 78701
P: (512) 476-0606

P. Caren Phelan, Ph.D. (CE)
Stillhouse Office Park, Bldg. 1,
Suite 1140
4807 Spicewood Springs Rd.
Austin, TX 78759
P: (512) 346-6038
F: (512) 346-0916

Dianne Pingree, Ph.D. (M)
2015 Mistywood Dr.
Austin, TX 78746
P: (512) 306-0964
F: (512) 306-0964

Diane W. Slaikeu, J.D.
(A, M)
1301 W. 25th St., Suite 540
Austin, TX 78705
P: (512) 476-2388
F: (512) 476-4026

Karl A. Slaikeu, Ph.D. (M)
Chorda Conflict Management
1717 W. 6th St., Suite 215B
Austin, TX 78703
P: (512) 482-0356
F: (512) 474-4645

Wade Wilson (A)
609 W. 9th
Austin, TX 78701
P: (512) 473-8373
F: (512) 472-1808

Brenham
Janet L. Wilson, M.A., L.P.C.
(M)
222 E. Main St.
Brenham, TX 77833
P: (409) 830-0673
F: (713) 467-0151

Dallas
Susanne C. Adams, M.A. (M)
The Mediation Group, Inc.
2401 Turtle Creek Blvd.
Dallas, TX 75219-4760
P: (214) 238-5050
F: (214) 238-1499

Herbert V. Cooke, Jr., B.B.A.,
 M.Ed. (M)
3400 Carlisle, Suite 240 LB-9
Dallas, TX 75204-1261
P: (214) 754-0022
F: (214) 754-0378

Gay G. Cox, J.D. (A, M)
714 Jackson, Suite 200
Dallas, TX 75202
P: (214) 747-2608
F: (214) 749-4911

Martha Ann Garber, M.Ed. (M)
2650 Valley View LB7
Dallas, TX 75234
P: (214) 247-4902
F: (214) 690-2969

Linda Hahn (CE, M)
600 Commerce, Suite 7-134
Dallas, TX 75202
P: (214) 653-6034
F: (214) 653-6613

Cynthia Pladziewicz, J.D. (A)
UT Southwestern Medical
 Center
6612 Santa Anita
Dallas, TX 75214
P: (214) 987-3428
F: (214) 768-3910

Rena Silverberg, M.S.S.W. (M)
13355 Noel Rd., Suite 500-
 One Galleria Twr.
Dallas, TX 75240
P: (214) 702-7200
F: (214) 369-2288

Kelly Simpson, M.A. (M)
4424 Fairfax
Dallas, TX 75205
P: (214) 993-6499

Denton
Rhonda L. Herd, M.A., M.L.S.
 (CE)
407 N. Ruddell
Denton, TX 76201
P: (817) 381-1020

El Paso
Janna Magee, Ph.D. (CE)
El Paso Psychological
 Consultants
4050 Rio Bravo, Suite 220
El Paso, TX 79902
P: (915) 532-2976
F: (915) 532-2976

Fort Worth
Sandra Fultz (CE, M)
Tarrant County Family Court
 Services
100 Houston
Fort Worth, TX 76196
P: (817) 884-1616
F: (817) 884-2591

Beth Krugler, M.S., J.D. (A, M)
3901 W. Vickery Blvd., Suite 4
Fort Worth, TX 76107
P: (817) 377-8081
F: (817) 377-8082

Grapevine
Anthony Picchioni, Ph.D.
(M)
1218 Chelsa
Grapevine, TX 76051
P: (214) 269-2606

Houston
Joan S. Anderson, Ph.D. (CE)
4550 Post Oak Pl., Suite 320
Houston, TX 77027
P: (713) 622-5430
F: (713) 622-7381

Yoli Ecrette, B.A. (M)
Dispute Resolution Professionals
11041 Westheimer Box 225
Houston, TX 77242-2850
P: (713) 556-9654
F: (713) 556-1681

Lynn K. Roney (CE)
16340 Park Ten Pl. #203
Houston, TX 77084
P: (713) 840-7556
F: (713) 840-8312

Eva S. Stubits, Ph.D. (CE)
24 Greenway Plaza, Suite 806
Houston, TX 77046
P: (713) 629-0220
F: (713) 629-0760

E. Wendy Trachte, J.D. (M)
A.A. White Dispute Resolution
Institute
University of Houston
325 Melcher Hall
Houston, TX 77204-6283
P: (713) 743-4933
(F: (713) 743-4934

Charla Trader, B.A., S.O.C. (M)
57 Legend Ln.
Houston, TX 77024
P: (713) 461-6126

Nancy Westerfeld, J.D. (A)
Harris County Domestic
Relations Office
1310 Prairie, Suite 700
Houston, TX 77002
P: (713) 755-6771
F: (713) 755-8856

Lubbock
Gene Valentini, M.A. (M)
PO Box 3730
Lubbock, TX 79452
P: (806) 762-8721

Rockwall
Lynelle C. Yingling, Ph.D. (M)
570 E. Quail Rund Rd.
Rockwall, TX 75087
P: (214) 771-9985
F: (214) 772-3669

San Antonio
Frank C. Paredes, Jr., Ph.D.
(CE)
717 W. Ashby Pl.
San Antonio, TX 78212
P: (210) 733-7373
F: (210) 733-7398

John K. Reid (CE, M)
717 W. Ashby Pl.
San Antonio, TX 78212
P: (210) 733-7373
F: (210) 733-7398

F. John Sherwood, M.A. (M)
2020 Babcock Rd., Suite 29
San Antonio, TX 78216
P: (210) 615-8412
F: (210) 615-3724

Sugar Land
Jay P. Bevan, Ph.D. (CE)
101 Southwestern Blvd., Suite 109
Sugar Land, TX 77478
P: (713) 586-6419

UTAH

Salt Lake City
Elizabeth L. Hickey, M.S.W.
(CE, M)
575 E. 4500 South, Suite
B-250
Salt Lake City, UT 84107
P: (801) 268-2800
F: (801) 261-2529

Amy A. Jackson, J.D. (A, M)
1317 E. Murphy's Ln.
Salt Lake City, UT 84106
P: (801) 486-8677
F: (801) 486-8677

Marcella L. Keck, J.D. (A, M)
Accord Mediation
6914 S. 3000 East
Salt Lake City, UT 84121
P: (801) 944-5400
F: (801) 944-8761

VERMONT

Fairfax
Susan Feldman-Fay (M)
A Mediation Partnership
PO Box 321
Fairfax, VT 05454
P: (800) 564-6859
F: (802) 849-6975

Johnson
Joe Fortin (M)
Conflict Management Services
RR#2, Box 985
Johnson, VT 05656
P: (802) 635-2200
F: (802) 888-5392

South Burlington
Pamela Langelier (CE, M)
PO Box 9238
South Burlington, VT 05401
P: (802) 862-0020

VIRGINIA

Alexandria
Jacqueline Urow-Hamell (M)
1512 Stonewall Rd.
Alexandria, VA 22302
P: (703) 998-5606
F: (703) 739-8842

Arlington
Emily M. Brown (M)
Key Bridge Therapy &
  Mediation Center
1925 N. Lynn St., Suite 700
Arlington, VA 22209
P: (703) 528-3900
F: (703) 524-5666

Diane Gilbert, M.A. (M)
1509 N. Greenbrier St.
Arlington, VA 22205
P: (703) 532-5380
F: (703) 360-1006

Karen K. Keyes (A, M)
Bean, Kenney & Korman, P.C.
2000 N. 14th St., Suite 100
Arlington, VA 22201
P: (703) 525-4000

Ashland
Carol C. Hughes, Ed.D. (M)
303 Caroline St.
Ashland, VA 23005
P: (804) 752-7376

Chester
Jerome Bagnell, M.Ed., M.S.W.
(M)
Divorce Mediation Service
6104 Holly Arbor Ct.
Chester, VA 23831-7760
P: (804) 768-1000
F: (804) 768-1010

Falls Church
Suzanne Borgo, Ph.D. (M)
207 Park Ave., Suite 101
Falls Church, VA 22046
P: (703) 536-7347
F: (703) 761-3168

Anne E. Wilson (M)
Falls Church Court Service
Unit
301 N. Washington St., Suite 200
Falls Church, VA 22046-3432
P: (703) 241-7649
F: (703) 241-7613

Fredericksburg
Susan D. Rosebro, Ph.D. (M)
417 Chatham Square Office Park
Fredericksburg, VA 22405
P: (540) 372-7099
F: (540) 372-4317

Barbara C. Willis, B.A. (M)
Rappahannock Mediation
Center
8 Old Ridge Rd.
Fredericksburg, VA 22407
P: (703) 786-4503

Oakton
Ilene N. Kesselman (M)
10174 Oakton Terrace Rd.
Oakton, VA 22124
P: (703) 255-7263

Reston
Mary Ellen Craig, B.S., M.A., J.D.
(A)
Craig & Hirsch P.C.
12110 Sunset Hills Rd., Suite 120
Reston, VA 22090
P: (703) 481-6063
F: (703) 481-6066

WASHINGTON

Bellevue
Susan Dearborn, Ph.D. (M)
Pacific Family Mediation Inst.
12505 Bel-Red Rd. #211
Bellevue, WA 98005
P: (425) 451-7940

Bellingham

Barbara Z. Rofkar, R.N., M.A. (M)
Family Mediation Services
1155 N. State St. #524
Bellingham, WA 98225
P: (360) 671-6416

Whatcom Dispute Resolution
  Center (M)
c/o Ron d'Aloisio, Director
1911 C St., Rm. 201
Bellingham, WA 98225
P: (360) 676-0122
F: (360) 738-1407

Bremerton

Laurie F. Jones (A, CE, M)
3849 N.E. Roosevelt St.
Bremerton, WA 98311
P: (360) 377-3730
F: (360) 377-2056

Cathryn R. Richardson Johns,
  A.R.N.P. (CE)
6005 Kestrel Pl.
Bremerton, WA 98312
P: (360) 373-8821

Colfax

Jack W. Lien, A.A., B.S., M.A.
  (CE, M)
Whitman County Juvenile Court
  Services
PO Box 598, N. 400 Main St.
Colfax, WA 99111
P: (509) 397-6246

Everett

Linda Moon, M.S.W. (CE)
Snohomish County Family
  Court
2918 Colby, Suite 205
Everett, WA 98201
P: (425) 388-6350

Kirkland

Christopher J. Fox, LL.B. (A)
50-16th Ave.
Kirkland, WA 98033
P: (206) 827-8757

Mukilteo

Sue Taninecz, M.S.W. (C E)
8490 Mukilteo Speedway,
  Suite 202
Mukilteo, WA 98275
P: (206) 356-6519
F: (206) 356-6515

Port Orchard

Tadina Crouch (CE)
Kitsap County Juvenile
  Court
1338 S.W. Old Clifton Rd.
Port Orchard, WA 93366
P: (360) 895-4919
F: (360) 895-5798

Susan Daniel, J.D. (A, M)
104 Tremont St., Suite 230
Port Orchard, WA 98366
P: (206) 876-4800
F: (206) 895-1445

Seattle

David L. Hodges (CE, M)
King County Family Court
   Services
300-810 Third Ave.
Seattle, WA 98104
F: (206) 296-9420

Andrew D. Kidde, J.D.
   (A, M)
119 First Ave. S. #400
Seattle, WA 98104
P: (206) 625-1865
F: (206) 587-0568

King County Family Court
   Services (CE, M)
Central Bldg., Suite 300
810 Third Ave.
Seattle, WA 98104
P: (206) 296-9400
F: (206) 296-9420

John Kydd, M.S.W., J.D. (A, M)
1616 Bank of California Center
900 4th Ave.
Seattle, WA 98164-1001
P: (206) 623-5221
F: (206) 623-5214

Spokane

Joan Chase, M.N., R.N., C.S.
   (CE)
Spokane Counseling Group
908 N. Howard, Suite 202
Spokane, WA 99201
P: (509) 328-4243
F: (509) 328-4256

Madeline F. Kardong (M)
The Mediation Center
628½ N. Monroe, Suite 304
Spokane, WA 99201
P: (509) 324-9052
F: (509) 326-8316

Rita Zorrozua, D.C.S.W.,
   A.C.S.W. (CE)
Spokane Counseling Group
908 N. Howard, Suite 202
Spokane, WA 99201
P: (509) 328-4243
F: (509) 328-4256

Vancouver

Marshall M. Goldsmith, M.S.
   (M)
7524 S.E. Evergreen Highway
Vancouver, WA 98664
P: (360) 695-5420
F: (360) 695-0150

Mary J. Hatzenbeler, M.S.W. (M)
316 E. 4th Plain Blvd.
Vancouver, WA 98663
P: (360) 695-6188
F: (360) 737-7686

Woodinville

Joanne M. Horn, J.D. (M)
PO Box 2136
Woodinville, WA 98072
P: (206) 633-4283
F: (206) 487-6526

WISCONSIN

Beaver Dam
Lisa L. Derr (A, M)
200 E. Front St., Suite 2E
Beaver Dam, WI 53916
P: (414) 885-5549
F: (414) 885-5804

Cambridge
Kenneth H. Waldron, Ph.D. (M)
2765 Evergreen Dr.
Cambridge, WI 53523
P: (608) 256-5176
F: (608) 256-0349

Hartland
Leonard R. Narus, Jr., Ph.D.
  (CE, M)
Waukesha Arrowhead Family
  Counseling
N53 W30465 Arrowhead Dr.
Hartland, WI 53029
P: (414) 367-6488

Janesville
Rita Costrini-Norgal (M)
Rock County Marriage & Family
  Court Services
51 S. Main St.
Janesville, WI 53545
P: (608) 757-5549
F: (608) 757-5725

Kenosha
Frank J. O'Hara (CE, M)
5407-8th Ave.
Kenosha, WI 53140
P: (414) 657-7188
F: (414) 657-0760

La Crosse
Bonnie Sacia, M.S. (CE, M)
La Crosse County Courthouse
400 N. 4th St.
La Crosse, WI 54601
P: (608) 785-6162

Madison
Kathleen Jeffords, A.C.S.W.
  (CE, M)
108 City-County Bldg.
210 Martin L. King Jr. Blvd.
Madison, WI 53709
P: (608) 266-4607
F: (608) 266-6588

James E. Marker, M.A. (CE, M)
c/o Family Mediation Services
430-D Cantwell Ct.
Madison, WI 53703
P: (608) 283-7887
F: (608) 251-5161

Marygold S. Melli, J.D. (A)
University of Wisconsin, Law
  School
611 Law Bldg.
Madison, WI 53706
P: (608) 262-1610
F: (608) 262-1231

Ann Milne, A.C.S.W. (M)
329 W. Wilson St.
Madison, WI 53703
P: (608) 251-0604
F: (608) 251-2231

Linda Roberson, J.D. (A, M)
Balisle & Roberson, S.C.
PO Box 870
Madison, WI 53701-0870
P: (608) 259-8702
F: (608) 259-0807

Peter Salem, M.A. (M)
Association of Family &
   Conciliation Courts
329 W. Wilson St.
Madison, WI 53703
P: (608) 251-4001
F: (608) 251-2231

Manitowoc
Diane M. Berry, M.S.W. (M)
1607 New York Ave.
Manitowoc, WI 54220
P: (414) 683-1840

Medford
Max D. Harris, J.D. (A)
125 Doyle Pl.
Medford, WI 54451
P: (715) 748-4774

Jean Nuernberger, B.S. (CE, M)
Taylor County Circuit Court
224 S. Second St.
Medford, WI 54451
P: (715) 748-1435
F: (715) 748-2465

Menasha
Donald B. Derozier, Ph.D. (M)
Psychology Associates, Ltd.
1486 Kenwood Dr.
Menasha, WI 54952
P: (414) 727-1820

Milwaukee
Lynn Ellen Hackbarth, J.D.
   (A, CE, M)
212 W. Wisconsin Ave., Suite
   1004
Milwaukee, WI 53203
P: (414) 273-2522
F: (414) 273-7584

Marcia E. Huber, M.S.W. (M)
Perez-Pena, Ltd.
126 S. 2nd St., Lindsay Bldg.
Milwaukee, WI 53204-1407
P: (414) 273-1262
F: (414) 273-1165

James J. Podell, J.D. (A)
Podell & Podell
250 W. Coventry Court,
   Suite 204
Milwaukee, WI 53217
P: (414) 228-5800
F: (414) 228-5815

Peggy L. Podell, J.D. (A)
Podell & Podell
250 W. Coventry Ct., Suite 204
Milwaukee, WI 53217
P: (414) 228-5800
F: (414) 228-5815

Richard J. Podell, J.D. (A, M)
100 E. Wisconsin Ave.,
   Suite 2800
Milwaukee, WI 53202
P: (414) 224-6060
F: (414) 224-6067

Linda Swagger Maris, J.D.
(A, M)
Richard J. Podell & Associates
100 E. Wisconsin Ave., Suite 2800
Milwaukee, WI 53202
P: (414) 224-6060
F: (414) 224-6067

N. Prairie
Theresa R. Kelly, B.S.W. (M)
Collaborative Solutions, Inc.
513 Chad Ct.
N. Prairie, WI 53153
P: (414) 289-1031

Oshkosh
Tom Werner, M.A. (CE, M)
Winnebago County Family
Court Services
415 Jackson, PO Box 2808
Oshkosh, WI 54903-2808
P: (414) 236-4793
F: (414) 236-4799

Portage
Marsha L. Varvil-Weld, M.S.
(CE)
Pauquette Center for Mental
Health
304 Cook St.
Portage, WI 53901
P: (608) 742-5518

Racine
Carrie R. Michelson, J.D. (A)
PO Box 67
617 6th St.
Racine, WI 53401-0067
P: (414) 638-8400
F: (414) 638-1818

Ripon
Nancy L. Buck-Hynson, M.S. (M)
960 Thomas St.
Ripon, WI 54971
P: (414) 748-7696

Superior
Ann Richtman, J.D. (A, M)
Attorney & Mediation
Services
1022 Clough Ave.
Superior, WI 54880
P: (715) 394-4029

Wausau
Gail J. Gumness (M)
Lutheran Social Services
725 Gilbert
Wausau, WI 54403
P: (715) 842-5577
F: (715) 842-4976

Whitehall
Don A. Powis, C.S.W. (CE, M)
Country Counseling Center
Rt.#2, Box 149B
Whitehall, WI 54773
P: (715) 538-4016

AUSTRALIA

New South Wales
Tom Altobelli, LL.M. (A, M)
1st Flr., 184 Forest Rd.
Hurtsville, NSW 2220
P: (612) 570-9866
F: (612) 579-5221

Carole Brown, Ph.D. (CE, M)
Family Court of Australia
GPO Box 9991
Sydney, NSW 2001
P: (612) 212-4675
F: (612) 212-4731

Terence Markham O'Donohue,
    B.A. (M)
Family Court of Australia
61 Bolton St., PO Box 9991
Newcastle, NSW 2300
P: (049) 26-4299
F: (049) 26-4804

Queensland
Susan Purdon, LL.B. (A, M)
Kinsey Bennett & Gill
Level 8-Comalco Pl.,
    12 Creek St.
Brisbane, Queensland 4000
P: (07) 3229-2961
F: (07) 3220-0210

CANADA

Alberta
Eileen A. Baril, M.Ed. (CE, M)
#1290 Manulife Pl., 10180-101st.
Edmonton, ALB T5J 3S4
P: (403) 424-1560
F: (403) 424-3752

Dr. Mark Dimirsky (CE, M)
Systemics Behavioral Services
508, 4808 Ross St.
Redd Deer, ALB T4N 1X5
P: (403) 347-1500
F: (403) 342-1150

Dr. A. E. Mason (CE)
12227-42A Ave.
Edmonton, ALB T6J 0X5
P: (403) 424-1555
F: (403) 424-0338

Joanne McKay, B.S.W. (M)
McKay Mediation Services
RR #3
Red Deer, ALB T4N 5E3
P: (403) 347-7661
F: (403) 346-9030

Ellen Muller, Ph.D. (CE, M)
E. Joy Muller & Associates Ltd.
8617-104 St.
Edmonton, ALB T6E 4G6
P: (403) 433-2225
F: (403) 431-1704

Robert Pollick, J.D. (A)
#200-10006 101 Ave.
Grande Prairie, ALB T8V 0Y1
P: (403) 538-8290
F: (403) 538-4515

Peter Portlock (M)
University of Alberta
110 Law Center
Edmonton, ALB T6G 2H5
P: (403) 433-4881
F: (403) 433-9024

British Columbia
J. Gary Cohen (A, M)
#211-7313-120th St.
Delta, BC V4C 6P5
P: (604) 599-1982
F: (604) 599-1975

Paul Daltrop, J.D. (A)
Maxwell, Schuman & Co.
900 Helmcken St.
Vancouver, BC V6Z 1B3
P: (604) 669-4912
F: (604) 662-3975

Lawrence A. Kahn, LL.B. (A, M)
#270-10711 Cambie Rd.
Richmond, BC V5X 3C9
P: (604) 270-9571
F: (604) 270-8282

Angela S. Kerslake (A)
36 Begbie St.
New Westminster, BC V3M 3L9
P: (604) 520-6275
F: (604) 520-5765

Gerald Lecovin, LL.B. (A)
1404-808 Nelson St.
Box 12180
Vancouver, BC V6Z 2H2
P: (604) 687-1721
F: (604) 488-0124

Lynda Lougheed, B.S.W., M.S.W.
 (M)
Simon Fraser University
E.A.A. Rm. 2019
Psychology Department
Burnaby, BC V5A 1S6
P: (604) 291-3548
F: (604) 291-5846

M. Jerry McHale (A, M)
Ministry of Attorney General
609 Broughton St.
Victoria, BC V8W 1C8
P: (604) 356-8436
F: (604) 356-9284

Donald S. Moir, LL.B. (A)
Box 12150-808 Nelson St.
Suite 1107, Nelson Square
Vancouver, BC V6Z 2H2
P: (604) 685-7996
F: (604) 682-7466

William R. Storey (A)
3683 W. Fourth Ave.
Vancouver, BC V6R 1P2
P: (604) 731-5676
F: (604) 731-7637

Pamela Temple, R.S.W. (CE, M)
10000 Sussex Dr.
R.R. #1
Rosedale, BC V0X 1X0
P: (604) 794-3225
F: (604) 794-3558

Manitoba
Fay-Lynn Katz (A, M)
Family Mediation
PO Box 2369, Manitoba Ave.
Winnipeg, MAN R3C 4A6
P: (204) 945-8215
F: (204) 948-2142

Orysia Z. Kostiuk, B.A., B.S.W.
  (CE, M)
Family Conciliation
14th Fl., Woodsworth Bldg.
405 Broadway
Winnipeg, MAN R3C 3L6
P: (204) 945-8215
F: (204) 948-2142

Manitoba Family Services
  (CE, M)
Family Conciliation
14th Fl., Woodsworth Bldg.
405 Broadway
Winnipeg, MAN R3C 3L6
P: (204) 945-7236
F: (204) 948-2142

Jim Stoffman (A)
47 Ambassador Row
Winnipeg, MAN R2V 3M2
P: (204) 949-1312
F: (204) 957-0945

New Brunswick
  G.B. Ljungstrom, B.A., LL.B. (A)
  Gorman Nason Ljungstrom,
    Barristers & Solicitors
  PO Box 7286, Station A
  Saint John, NB E2L 4S6
  P: (506) 634-8600
  F: (506) 634-8685

  Anne D. Wooder, B.A., LL.B.
    (A, M)
  Hanson, Hashey
  P.O. Box 310
  Suite 400 Phoenix Sq., 371
  Queen St.

Fredericton, NB E3B 4Y9
P: (506) 453-7771
F: (506) 453-9600

Nova Scotia
  Marie-Claire Declerck, Ph.D.
    (CE)
  PO Box 993
  Antigonish, NS B2G 2S1
  P: (902) 863-2501
  F: (902) 863-3708

  John A. Manning, M.Psyc, M.Ed.
    (CE, M)
  Individual Development &
    Counseling Services
  35 Beckfoot Dr.
  Dartmouth, NS B2Y 4H9
  P: (902) 465-2223
  F: (902) 461-2365

  V. Francine McIntyre (A, CE, M)
  Cruikshank, McIntyre, Hastey
  2585 Beech St.
  Halifax, NS B3L 2X9
  P: (902) 420-9010
  F: (902) 422-2140

  Andrew Pavey, LL.B. (A, M)
  Pavey Gavras Associates
  5162 Duke St., 6th Flr.
  Halifax, NS B3J 1N7
  P: (902) 423-5711
  F: (902) 423-1565

  Annette Strug, M.S.W. (M)
  PO Box 3474, South
  Halifax, NS B3J 3J1
  P: (902) 422-3681
  F: (902) 422-5519

Ontario

Catherine Aitken, LL.B. (A, M)
Nelligan, Power, Barristers
1900-66 Slater St.
Ottawa, ONT K1P 5H1
P: (613) 238-8080

Gary Austin, Ph.D. (M)
c/o London Family Court
 Clinic
254 Pall Mall St., Suite 200
London, ONT N6A 5P6
P: (519) 679-7250
F: (519) 675-7772

Sandra Birnbaum, LL.B. (A, M)
Ontario Legal Aid Plan
5415 Dundas St., West
Etobicoke, ONT M9B 1B5
P: (416) 237-1216
F: (416) 783-4097

Barbara A. Chisholm, M.S.W.,
 C.S.W. (CE, M)
Chisholm, Gafni & Block
2 Bloor St. W, Suite 700
Toronto, ONT M4W 3R1
P: (416) 926-1416
F: (416) 923-2071

Linda Chodos, M.S.W.
 (CE, M)
40 Sheppard Ave. W
Suite 610
North York, ONT M2N 6K9
P: (416) 250-8398
F: (416) 229-9735

Cettina G. Cornish, B.A., M.A.,
 LL.B. (A, M)
Snelius Associates
3410 S. Service Rd.
Burlington, ONT L7N 3T2
P: (905) 681-8399
F: (905) 681-6019

Carole Curtis, LL.B. (A)
288 Jarvis St.
Toronto, ONT M5B 2C5
P: (416) 340-1850

Rodica David (A)
David, Demson & Hynes
47 Gloucester St.
Toronto, ONT M4Y 1L8
P: (416) 923-7407

Resa S. Eisen, M.S.W. (M)
200 St. Clair Ave. W
Suite 300
Toronto, ONT M4V 1R1
P: (416) 924-2404
F: (416) 960-0193

Rolf B. Frick, LL.B. (M)
8 Valley View Ct.
PO Box 587
Fonthill, ONT L0S 1E0
P: (905) 892-3402
F: (905) 892-3402

Carisse M. Gafni, M.S.W.
 (CE, M)
29-90 Chapman Ct.
London, ONT N6G 4X5
P: (519) 474-0559
F: (519) 646-5820

Lorne Glass, LL.B. (A, M)
Glass, Friedland
2 Bloor St. W, Suite 2108
Toronto, ONT M4W 3E2
P: (416) 968-3995
F: (416) 968-6899

Stephen M. Grant (A, M)
Gowling, Strathy & Henderson
Suite 4900
Commerce Ct. W
Toronto, ONT M5L 1J3
P: (416) 862-4290
F: (416) 862-7661

R. John Harper, J.D. (A)
Suite 1215
25 Main St. W
Hamilton, ONT L8P 1H1
P: (905) 522-3517
F: (905) 533-3555

Jacqueline Hoffman-Fitz (M)
390 Wellesley St. E
Suite 21
Toronto, ONT M4X 1H6
P: (416) 922-0928

Stanley P. Jaskot, LL.B. (A)
PO Box 2069, Station A
4th Flr., 1 James St. S
Hamilton, ONT L8N 3G6
P: (416) 527-6877

Lena K. Jones, M.A. (CE, M)
Center for Counseling
  & Mediation
110-261 Cooper St.
Ottawa, ONT K2P 0G3
P: (613) 237-7444
F: (613) 841-6038

Barbara Landau, Ph.D. (A, CE, M)
137 Sheppard Ave. E
Willowdale, ONT M2N 3A6
P: (416) 223-5111
F: (416) 223-5359

Andrea Litvack, M.S.W. (CE, M)
40 Sheppard Ave. W
North York, ONT L3T 7E2
P: (416) 250-8398
F: (416) 229-9735

H. Christina MacNaughton,
  B.A., LL.B. (A, M)
Lancaster, Mix & Welch
55 King St., Suite 800
PO Box 790
St. Catharines, ONT L2R 6Z1
P: (905) 641-1551
F: (905) 641-1830

Lorraine Martin, B.A., M.S.W.
  (CE, M)
Ministry of the Attorney General
393 University Ave., 14th Flr.
Toronto, ONT M5G 1W9
P: (416) 314-8066
F: (416) 314-8050

Robert McWhinney, M.A.,
  M.S.W. (M)
180 Bloor St. W
Suite 1200
Toronto, ONT M5S 2V6
P: (416) 968-3262
F: (416) 968-6430

Virginia Mendes Da Costa (A)
15 Bold St.
Hamilton, ONT L8P 1T3
P: (416) 529-3476

Kathleen Metcalfe (CE, M)
180 Bloor St. W
Suite 1200
Toronto, ONT M5S 2V6
P: (416) 968-3262
F: (416) 968-6430

Gordon Morton (A)
One King St. W
Suite 700
Hamilton, ONT L8O 1A4
P: (416) 522-8147
F: (416) 527-6286

Clifford S. Nelson (A)
Ricketts, Harris
Suite 806, 181 University Ave.
Toronto, ONT M5H 2X7
P: (416) 364-6211
F: (416) 364-1697

Janet E.H. Pond, B.N., LL.B.
   (A, M)
32 Monarchwood Crescent
Don Mills, ONT M3A 1H4
P: (905) 884-9242
F: (905) 884-5445

Judith Ryan, M.S.W., LL.B.
   (A)
12 Birch Ave.
Suite 207
Toronto, ONT M4V 1CB
P: (416) 928-1154

Mary T. Satterfield, M.S.W.,
   LL.B. (A, M)
#301-2490 Bloor St. W
Toronto, ONT M6S 1R4
P: (416) 763-5251
F: (416) 763-6876

Mary E. Shamley, B.A., M.Div.
   (M)
747 Hyde Park Rd., Suite 206
London, ONT N6H 3S3
P: (519) 473-7055
F: (519) 473-7053

John G. Starzynski, LL.B. (M)
R.R. #2
Guelph, ONT N1H 6H8
P: (519) 837-9459

Carey Stevens, Ph.D. (CE, M)
2301 Carling Ave.
Suite 200
Ottawa, ONT K2B 7G3
P: (613) 721-0081
F: (613) 721-8576

Christine A. Torry (A)
35 Queen St. S
Mississauga, ONT L5M 1K2
P: (905) 819-8377
F: (905) 819-8379

Rollie Willis (A)
35 Queen St. S
Mississauga, ONT L5M 1K2
P: (905) 819-8377
F: (905) 819-8379

Paul Zarnke, M.S.W. (M)
22 Wellesley St. E
Toronto, ONT M4Y 1G3
P: (416) 922-3144

Quebec

Linda L. Greenberg, M.A. (CE)
Jewish General Hospital
4333 Cote Ste Catherine Rd.,
   Rm. 148
Montreal, QUE H3T 1E4
P: (514) 340-8226
F: (514) 932-7331

Claire Jodoin (CE)
2720 Machabee
St. Laurent, QUE H4K 1K1
P: (514) 335-0637
F: (514) 956-0850

Richard J. McConomy (A)
McConomy, Tremblay,
   McIninch & MacDougall
1253 McGill College,
   Suite 955
Montreal, QUE H3B 2Y5
P: (514) 875-5311
F: (514) 875-8381

Patrick B. McLaughlin (M)
Place Cavendish
2525 Cavendish, #745
Montreal, QUE H4B 2Y6
P: (514) 483-1083

Kathy L. Whittaker (M)
32 Canvin St.
Kirkland, QUE H9H 4S4
P: (514) 630-9985

Abe Worenklein, Ph.D. (CE)
806 Antonine Maillet
Outrement, QUE H2V 2Y7
P: (514) 345-9465
F: (514) 345-9465

Saskatchewan

K. W. Action (M)
Mediation Services
Department of Justice
2151 Scarth St.
Regina, SASK S4P 3V7
P: (306) 787-5747
F: (306) 787-0088

Anne Edwards (CE)
#103-1640 11th Ave.
Regina, SASK S4P 0H4
P: (306) 352-2799
F: (306) 352-2799

Daniel L. Hamoline, B.A.,
   M.S.W., LL.B (M)
Fifth Ave. Mediation &
   Counseling
215-728 Spadina Crescent E
Saskatoon, SASK S7K 4H7
P: (306) 653-2599
F: (306) 653-2523

CHILE

Arturo Roizblatt, M.D. (M)
Universidad de Chile
Malaga 950, Apt. 52 Las Condes
Santiago
P: (56) 2-206-5802
F: (56) 2-231-0825

ENGLAND

Thelma Fisher (M)
National Family Mediation
9 Tavistock Pl.
London WC1H 9SN
P: (0171) 383-5993
F: (0171) 383-5994

Tony Wells (M)
University of Bristol
Socio-Legal Department
Priory Rd.
Bristol, Avon BS8 1TX
P: (7) 928-8136
F: (7) 974-1299

GERMANY

Elisabeth Nader (M)
Hirtenue 50
69118 Heidelberg
P: (06) 221-802791

Roland Proksch, J.D. (M)
Labenwolf Strasse 15
90409 Nuernber
P: (49) 91-155-8200

ISRAEL

Orna Cohen, Ph.D. (M)
Tel Aviv University
School of Social Work
Ramat Aviv, PO Box 39040
Tel Aviv 69978
P: (972) 36407-155
F: (972) 35459-182

Susan Zaidel, Ph.D. (M)
10 Koyfman St.
Haifa 34780
P: (972) 4825-6123

NEW ZEALAND

Roger Chapman (A, M)
PO Box 1213
Wellington
P: (64) 4-472-0940
F: (64) 4-473-4673

Michael Dodds, LL.B. (A)
McBrearty, Dodds
3 Dickerson St.,
    PO Box 633
Kaikohe
P: (64) 9-401-1650

Ann Gardner, LL.B. (A)
PO Box 952
20 John St.
Whangarei, Northland
P: (64) 9-438-9022
F: (64) 9-438-5302

Robert G. Metcalf, LL.D. (A)
PO Box 85
Wellington
P: (64) 4-720-071

PUERTO RICO

San Juan
Luis E. Palacios, M.A. (A)
Interamerican University of
    Puerto Rico
School of Law
Galapagos 873, Country
    Club
San Juan, PR 00924
P: (809) 769-3703

SPAIN

Trinidad Bernal, Ph.D. (M)
Ibiza, 72-5 B
Madrid 28009
P: (07) 341409782

APPENDIX V

Resources and Websites

ABUSE ACCUSATIONS

Abuse Excuse
Dean Tong, Forensic Consultant
9213 Roundtree Ct.
Tampa, FL 33615
(813) 885-6173

ATTORNEYS

American Bar Association
750 N. Lake Shore Drive
Chicago, IL 60611
(312) 988-5000

Association of Family and
  Conciliation Courts
329 W. Wilson Street
Madison, WI 53703-3612
(608) 251-4001

DadsDivorce
10425 Old Olive Street Road
Suite 7
Creve Coeur, MO 63141
(314) 983-0001

Split-Up.Com, Inc
831 Beacon Street Suite #2900
Newton Centre, MA 02459

CUSTODY

Alliance for Non Custodial Parents
  Rights
Lowell Jaks, Director
P.O. Box 788
Inyokern, CA 93527-0788
(202) 478-1736

Child Custody Evaluation Services
  of Philadelphia, Inc.
Dr. Ken Lewis, P.O. Box 202
Glenside, PA 19038
(215) 576-0177

FACE: Fathers' and Children's
 Equality
P.O. Box 117
Drexel Hills, PA 19026

Kidmate: A Joint Custody Program
 for Family Law Specialists
Lapin Agile Software
1484 Durango Ave
Los Angeles, CA 90035
(310) 842-9990

Single and Custodial Father's
 Network, Inc.
One Parks Bend
Suite 213, Box 31
Vandergrift, PA 15690
(724) 845-9767
Pennsylvania Hotline
(724) 388-DADS

FATHER'S RIGHTS

American Coalition for Fathers
 and Children
1718 M Street, NW
Suite 187
Washington, DC 20036
(800) 978-DADS

Fatherhood Initiative
One Bank Street, Ste. 160
Gaithersburg, MD 20878
(301) 948-0599

Fatherhood Project
James A. Levine, Director
Families and Work Institute
330 Seventh Ave, 14th Floor
New York, NY 10001
(212) 337-0934, ext 210

DIVORCE MEDIATION

Academy of Family Mediators
4 Militia Drive
Lexington, MA 02173
(800) 292-4236

Coast to Coast Mediation
P.O. Box 230637
Encinitas, CA 92023
(800) 748-6462
(760) 436-8414

DIVORCE SUPPORT

Parents without Partners
1650 South Dixie Hwy., Ste. 510
Boca Raton, FL 33432
(561) 391-8833

Smart Divorce
24 Sunbeam Ct.
St Peters, MO 63376
(636) 278-2202

Divorce Helpline
2425 Porter St, Ste. 18
Soquel, CA 95073
(813) 426-0195

DIVORCE PUBLICATIONS

Divorce Magazine
145 Front Street East, Ste. 301
Toronto, Canada M5A-1E3
(416) 368-8853

The Down to Earth Dad
   (newsletter)
Patrick Mitchell, Founding Editor
P.O. Box 1907
CDA, ID 83816-1907

Solo: A Guide for the Single Parent
   Hall/Sloane Publishing
10840 Camarillo St. #10
Toluca Lake, CA 91602-1395
(800) 477-5877

REMARRIAGE

Second Wives Crusade
Dianna Thompson
22365 El Toro Rd, #115
Lake Forest, CA 92630
(800) 978-3237

Websites

Abuse Excuse
   www.abuse-excuse.com

American Coalition for Fathers and Children
   www.acfc.org

Child Custody Evaluation
   www.expage.com/page/childcustody

Choices of the Heart
   www.heartchoice.com

Coast to Coast Mediation
www.ctcmediation.com

Dads Divorce
www.dadsdivorce.com

Divorce Father
www.divorcedfather.com

Divorce Helpline
www.divorcehelp.com

Divorce Magazine
www.divorcemagazine.com

Divorce Room
www.heartchoice.com

Divorce Transitions
www.divorcetransitions.com

Down to Earth Dad
www.downtoearthdad.com

Fatherhood Initiative
www.fatherhood.org

Fatherhood Project
www.fatherhoodproject.org

Fathers' and Children's Equality
www.facenj.org/

Fathers for Equal Rights
www.fathers4kids.org/fer/

Fathers' Rights to Custody
www.deltabravo.net/
custody/index.htm

Kidmate
www.kidmate.com
www.kidshare.com

Making and Breaking Families
ourworld.compuserve.com/
homepages/j_curtis2/

Parents without Partners in the
United States
www.parentswithoutpartners.org

Parents without Partners in
Australia
www.freeyellow.com/
members5/pwp-act/INDEX.html

Single and Custodial Fathers'
Network
www.scfn.org

Second Wives
www.secondwives.org

Smart Divorce
www.smartdivorce.com

Split-Up
www.split-up.com

Index